Teshuvot for the Nineties

Reform Judaism's Answers
to Today's Dilemmas

Edited by
W. Gunther Plaut
and
Mark Washofsky

CENTRAL CONFERENCE OF AMERICAN RABBIS
355 LEXINGTON AVENUE
NEW YORK, NY 10017

D1417089

Library of Congress information available upon request.
ISBN: 0-88123-071-5

Teshuvot for the Nineties

Reform Judaism's Answers
to Today's Dilemmas

TABLE OF CONTENTS

Orach Chayim — The Realm of Prayer and Synagogue

Yoreh De'ah — Reform Jewish Practice

Even Ha-Ezer — The Jewish Family

Choshen Mishpat — Social Issues

PREFACE

This new volume of Reform responsa is part of a tradition that has turned the letter of the law into a living and livable experience. The writings of the first Reformers, in the early part of the 19th century, buttressed their innovations by responding to the basic question: Is this particular proposal compatible with Jewish law? They tried to show that the new developments in religious life were actually grounded in sacred tradition; they answered questions about liturgy and practice, about family relations and social issues. The volumes of the path breaking rabbinical conferences of the 1840s testify to the vitality of Reform responses to the issues of the day.

The Central Conference of American Rabbis (CCAR), founded in 1889, pursued this tradition. Its learned spokesmen published their responsa in the Yearbooks of the Conference. They were the individual expressions of these rabbis, just as throughout Jewish history it was the stature of the respondent that determined the acceptance of his responsa. Thus, rabbis like Gotthard Deutsch, Kaufmann Kohler, Jacob Zvi Lauterbach and Israel Bettan became interpreters of Reform ideology. Beginning with the late 1940s their mantle was assumed by Rabbi Solomon B. Freehof, whose seven volumes of responsa became guide posts of our movement. Upon his retirement, Rabbi Walter Jacob became the chair of the CCAR's Responsa Committee, and he began to give meaning to the term "committee." While the two volumes of his responsa represent primarily his own opinions, he included a fair number of decisions that had been commented upon by members of the committee.

As his successor, I decided to take this development a step further and make all members of the committee equally responsible for our responsa, and some of them participated actively in the writing process itself. However, the great majority of the responsa published in this volume came to be researched and written by the Chair and Vice-Chair of the Committee (the editors of this volume). Drafts were distributed and discussed and eventually voted upon, and the questioner was advised whether or not the decision of the committee was unanimous. Occasionally, when particularly contentious material was at

ix

issue, these dissents were transmitted along with the majority opinion. This process resulted in lively debate and greater participation, but it also lengthened the time between question and answer.

Our procedure was marked by two considerations. First we asked: "How might Tradition answer this question?" Then, after exploring this aspect, we asked: "Are there reasons why, as Reform Jews, we cannot agree? If so, can our disagreement be grounded in identifiable Reform policy?" In this way we placed Reform responsa into the continuum of halakhic literature.

Some of *teshuvot* published in this volume are of unusual legnth and are accompanied by many notes. They testify to the importance we ascribed to the topics. Examples are "Gentile Participation in Synagogue Ritual" and "Treatment of the Terminally Ill." Also, our extensive "Indroduction" speaks to the nature and function of Reform responsa.

During my tenure, the following colleagues served as members of the Committee: Rabbis Judith Z. Abrams, Richard A. Block, A. Stanley Dreyfus, Joan S. Friedman, Peter S. Knobel, David Lilienthal, Jerome Malino, Dow Marmur, Bernard Mehlman, Richard S. Rheins. Daniel L. Schiff, Richard Rosenthal, Louis J. Sigel, and Faedra L. Weiss. Elyse M. Goldstein, Walter Jacob and Moshe Zemer served as ex-officio members; and the presidents and chief executives of the CCAR received our ongoing internal correspondence.

Special thanks are extended to Rabbi Elliot L. Stevens and his associates on the publication, Sarah B. Morgan and Judith Redlener and the copy editor, Rabbi Steven Chatinover.

Recently, some of the Committee's work has been carried on via the Internet, and this has infused the participatory process with undreamed of vigor. In previous years, occasional face-to-face meetings were called, while the new process allows constant interaction. Future dissemination of our responsa will no doubt also benefit, for any member of the Conference could, theoretically, be involved in shaping Reform responsa.

It is my great pleasure to acknowledge the invaluable assistance and guidance provided by Rabbi Mark Washofsky, professor of Talmud at Hebrew Union College-Jewish Institute of Religion, without whose knowledge and friendship I could not have carried on, and I am delighted that he has been chosen to guide the Committee into the next century.

W. Gunther Plaut

INTRODUCTION

RESPONSA AND THE REFORM RABBINATE

The rabbinate is a literary calling. For two millennia, rabbis have pursued their vocation, the study of Torah and sacred text, largely through the medium of the written word. In so doing they have produced a literature that embraces many genres: Bible commentary, legal codes and novellae, works of *aggadah* (homiletical exposition), liturgy, religious poetry, philosophy, ethics, and mysticism, and more; a vast body of writing that explores and gives voice to the rabbinic conception of God's will for the Jewish people.

Mostly, though, rabbis have written responsa, answers to questions on individual issues of observance, practice, or belief. From Talmudic times Jews have submitted their questions (*she'elot*) to noted rabbinic scholars, whose responsa (*teshuvot*) conveyed learned opinions as to the correct interpretation of Jewish law (*halakhah*) and tradition on the issues at hand. Since the days of the Babylonian Geonim (6th-11th centuries C.E.), the responsa have been collected in separate volumes and have comprised a distinct and--to put it mildly--huge literary corpus. Indeed, we know of approximately 300,000 *teshuvot*, and we can assume that many more were published and never reached us. From this statistic we may draw the following conclusion: in its size and scope the responsa literature exceeds all other types of rabbinic writing. And this fact teaches us a great deal about the nature of rabbinic Judaism: the very size of this literature tells us that the religion of the rabbis has been predominantly one of "questions and answers," and that, to a great extent, the rabbis constructed their religious universe by writing responsa. If we wish to understand the mind and religious experience of the rabbis, then, we have no choice but to study this most typically "rabbinic" form of literature. We must, that is, become acquainted with the *she'elot uteshuvot*.

Reform rabbis, too, write responsa. They always have done so. In early-nineteenth century Europe, progressive rabbis published *teshuvot* defending on grounds of Jewish law and tradition the innovations that the reformers had introduced into Jewish ritual practice. In America, the Responsa Committee of the Central Conference of American Rabbis was founded in 1906. Chaired over the years by such outstanding figures as Kaufmann Kohler, Jacob Lauterbach, Jacob Mann, Israel Bettan, Solomon B. Freehof, and Walter Jacob, the Committee has issued more than 400 opinions on a wide array of questions submitted by rabbis and laypersons. In addition, many hundreds of *teshuvot* have been composed by individual Reform rabbis, notably Solomon B. Freehof and Walter Jacob in the United States and Moshe Zemer in Israel. There exists, in other words, a considerable and steadily growing body of Reform literary discourse on issues and problems of Jewish observance. These essays, like the responsa of other rabbis, have become texts in their own right, discussed and debated by a community of committed Jews who look to them as sources of information and guidance concerning religious practice.

It is of no little significance that a rabbinate which describes itself as "modern" nonetheless produces so many responsa which, by their nature, are based upon ancient and medieval sources. Clearly, for all its modernity, our rabbinate understands itself as a "rabbinate" in the traditional sense of that term: as a body of scholars who exist to study and teach the sacred texts, whose task it is to probe those texts for answers to the questions their people ask. That Reform rabbis continue to write and read responsa testifies to the enduring importance of halakhah, of traditional Jewish law, as a resource with which we compose, explain, and express our religious lives as Reform Jews.

Yet despite the pivotal role of responsa in rabbinic literary history and despite our own attachment to this kind of writing, not all of our people are altogether happy that Reform rabbis write responsa. The very existence of such a literature implies that halakhah has something important and relevant to say to us, a notion which makes some Reform Jews exceedingly uncomfortable. It is for this reason that one frequently hears the criticism that there is something "wrong" with the Reform responsa process, that responsa are somehow antithetical to the nature of Reform Judaism as a modern religious movement. Precisely, that is, because ours is a movement committed to a liberal and modern understanding of Judaism, its rabbis ought to prefer some other, more "progressive" means of expression. This criticism is based upon three fundamental assertions.

1. Reform Judaism proclaims personal religious autonomy as its central religious principle. We hold that Reform Jews have the right to legislate their own religious norms, to make their own religious choices. Our movement recognizes no religious authority, rabbinic or otherwise, which has the power to determine correct belief or practice or to restrict the right of individual Jews to define their own Judaism. To set limits, to draw lines that distinguish "right" answers from "wrong" ones, is to transgress upon the individual's freedom of choice. Yet rabbinic responsa offer rulings or opinions in favor of one, "correct" answer over others that Jews might otherwise adopt. It is inappropriate for Reform rabbis to produce a literature whose whole point is to restrict the autonomy of the individual.

2. The rulings in responsa are grounded in the interpretation of traditional sources. Yet these ancient and medieval texts hardly reflect the values and sensibilities of our time and place. Reform Judaism exists because the founders of our movement declared their independence from tradition, from the slavish reliance upon the past. While we honor our ancestors, the literature they wrote does not speak to our situation and to the choices we face. To base our religious decisions upon the texts of old is to grant to generations past, whose ideas and culture we have respectfully but firmly put behind us,

a decisive influence over our Jewish lives. And this, if we wish to be true to ourselves, we must not do.

3. Even if we want to consider "tradition" as a factor in our religious decisions, that tradition ought not to include the halakhah. The texts of Jewish law--the Talmud, the codes, the legal commentaries and the responsa--speak the language of authority and obligation. The thrust of law is to deny choice, to determine "correct" answers as defined by those empowered to enforce them; yet choice, pluralism, and personal freedom are the hallmarks of Reform belief. In addition, the halakhic literature seems to expend the lion's share of its energy and attention upon the minutiae of ritual observance. Reform, by contrast, thinks of itself as "prophetic Judaism," an approach to Jewish faith whose primary concern is to preach ethics, morality, and social justice. Since the halakhic world is not our world, we should not waste our time writing halakhic literature. And since responsa are a species of that literature, they are incompatible with Reform Judaism as we know and teach it.

Those of us who write and study Reform responsa do so in spite of these objections, though we recognize their power and cogency. We acknowledge that the criticism of the Reform responsa process cannot be totally refuted. Indeed, since it springs from the soil of the never-ending debate over the definition of Reform Judaism itself, the dispute over the role of responsa in our movement belongs to that class of discussion known as "arguments for the sake of Heaven" (*machlokot leshem shamayim*), whose importance to Jewish thought lies precisely in the fact that they are eternal and can never be resolved once and for all. Nonetheless, since we have from time to time been accused of producing an "un-Reform" or even "anti-Reform" kind of literature, it is important for us to explain why we do what we do, in terms that hopefully resonate with a liberal Jewish audience. For, contrary to the criticisms, we believe that the writing of responsa is a proper and desirable activity for liberal Jews, one that is absolutely consistent with the worldview of Reform Judaism.

Our position, like that of our critics, is based upon three fundamental assertions.

1. <u>The Insufficiency of Autonomy.</u> It is true that North American Reform Judaism asserts the principle of personal and communal autonomy in religious decision-making. This has been the case, at any rate, since the Second World War. Prior to that time, Reform thinkers spoke little of autonomy and certainly did not exalt it to the status of theological doctrine. But even during the postwar period, mainstream Reform Jewish thought has never regarded autonomy as the sole principle for determining action. Autonomy, that is to say, is by itself an insufficient explanation for Reform Jewish thought and behavior, because our commitment to freedom of choice has always coexisted with other principles. An example of this coexistence can be found in the words of the Centenary Perspective, the most recent "official" statement of Reform religious doctrine, adopted by the Central Conference of American Rabbis in 1976. That document, on the one hand, makes a ringing endorsement of "the Reform principle of the autonomy of the individual"; at the same time, it declares that this freedom must not blur our affirmation of God, the people of Israel, and Torah. Moreover, the Perspective speaks openly of the "obligations" owed by Reform Jews toward the survival of the Jewish people, toward the state of Israel and the Diaspora Jewish community, and toward the necessity of religious observance. We believe in freedom, that is to say, but we also believe in responsibility. The autonomy of the individual Jew must be exercised within acceptable Jewish limits.

It is not a simple matter for Reform Jews to speak of limits. The very definition of "autonomy" as the power to legislate one's own norms suggests that there can be no restrictions upon the freedom to choose. To assert that one's autonomy must be balanced against other principles, however exalted or benign, is to raise the specter of the kind of religious authority that Reform Judaism says it rejects. In fact, however, limits upon our autonomy do exist. Limits exist because we live in the real world, and in the real world there is no such thing as absolute freedom of religious or moral choice. Unlimited religious autonomy is an oxymoron, since "religion" is at its core an exercise in the setting of limits and the drawing of boundaries.

If we enjoy autonomy, this means that we are empowered to choose between available alternatives: yes or no, permitted or forbidden. It does not mean, however, that all possible answers are equally "right" or that we as a community are neutral or indifferent as to the individual's choice. Indeed, the way we approach our religious decision-making indicates that we are anything but neutral. Our religious discourse is replete with the language of value, with such terms as "good and evil" and "right and wrong." This means we believe that, though the choice may rest in our hands, some choices are better than others and some are just plain bad. The doctrine of autonomy gives us the political power of choice, but it does not liberate us from the moral necessity of judgment, of carefully measuring the alternatives we face against some standard of evaluation. And this judgment implies limits upon our freedom of choice, because when we adopt a standard of moral evaluation we intentionally renounce the right to choose bad alternatives.

More than that: we reach our judgments as members of a community rather than as isolated, autonomous individuals. When we say that we are Jews, or Reform Jews, we identify ourselves as part of a religious collective whose members share common standards of evaluation. We are a community, in other words, not because we agree on all the answers, but to the extent that we agree on the terms of argument, on the standards by which answers are to be judged "right" or "wrong." It is because we hold these standards in common that we are able to converse intelligently with each other on matters of religion and to argue among ourselves in the hope of persuading each other than a particular decision is the best one and ought to be adopted. As members of the community we accept its standards of evaluation, whether explicitly or implicitly. And to accept those standards means that we accept clear limits upon our freedom of religious choice.

Do we Reform Jews recognize such limits upon our autonomy? Consider, for a moment, the following scenario. Suppose that we are members of the Board of Trustees of the Union of American Hebrew Congregations, the governing body of our synagogue movement. And suppose we are asked to consider an application for membership in the Union by a congregation of "Jews for Jesus." Our first thought might be to reject the application, on the grounds that "Jews for Jesus" is a denomination of Christianity rather than Judaism. But such an objective determination does not work, because the "Jews for Jesus" contend that they are not Christians but Jews, whether by birth or by choice. True, they define their "Judaism" in a way that differs from ours, but this, they feel, should not matter to us, since the Reform movement recognizes the absolute and unlimited right of Jews to define their religious belief and practice. To deny them membership in the Union on religious grounds, they argue, is to set limits upon their freedom of religious choice, and we Reform Jews, as committed proponents of religious autonomy, are not entitled to set such limits. How shall we rule on their application?

Chances are we would reject it. We would reject it, not because we do not believe in religious autonomy but because we believe that autonomy must be exercised within a Jewish context that we accept, that we understand, and that we as a community determine in advance. We, as a community, define our common religious identity as "Reform Judaism." We may not all agree on what this definition includes; we do agree, though, that it excludes adherence to Christian belief, even when dressed in Judaic garb. We as a community are entitled to make this decision, because to say that we are a community is to say that we are capable of defining those beliefs and affirmations which bring us together. We are able to determine who and what we are and--just as important--who and what we are not. To make this determination requires, unavoidably and inevitably, that we set limits, draw lines, rule some options in and others out. True, we do not like to draw lines; we liberals are uncomfortable setting religious limits that exclude others from our community. The fact remains, though, that we are a community and that few of us would be interested in belonging to a Reform Judaism that renounces the right to define its religion and to make the most basic judgments about the nature of its Judaism. The question, then, is not whether limits and standards exist in the Reform Jewish community; they do, for we could hardly be a community without them. The real question is how we liberals go about setting the limits that we must set, especially when we recognize no institutional authority with the power to set them for us.

We do so through argument, the attempt to convince the other members of our community that a particular answer to a Jewish question is the best one available to us and that other, competing answers may in fact be "wrong." This very kind of argument is central to Jewish religious discussion and is the essence of the responsa. With few exceptions in the history of the literature, authors of responsa are not content to reply to an inquiry with a simple "yes" or "no." They accompany their answers, rather, with arguments, offering proof from the sources to the effect that this answer is the correct one, or at least more correct than others. They resort to argument at least in part because, according to rabbinic doctrine, the ruling conveyed in a responsum is not necessarily binding upon its recipient. The rabbi cannot simply demand that the reader "accept my opinion," but must rather persuade the reader, with arguments the latter will likely find convincing, that "my opinion is correct, because it represents the best available interpretation of the sources that both you and I look to for Jewish religious guidance." If any such thing as "rabbinic authority" exists, its basis lies not in the power of the rabbinate as an institution but in the ability of the rabbis to justify their rulings in the eyes of their fellow Jews.

Each responsum is therefore an exercise in argumentation, an essay which seeks to elicit the agreement of a particular Jewish audience that shares the religious values of its author. As such, no responsum can possibly represent the "last word" on a given issue. We only argue over "interesting" questions, that is, over questions to which the "one right answer" is not immediately obvious. Indeed, we lack the means to prove that one answer is right and the others are wrong. Absolute proof is the province of mathematics, not of Torah; in matters of religion, proponents of competing interpretations will always find persuasive arguments in favor of their own viewpoint. The "right" answer is much more often the provisional outcome of a process of argument that has reached the point of persuasion, when a consensus has formed in favor of one answer over the alternative(s).

If such is the case with traditional responsa, it is certainly true of our own. Reform responsa are best understood as individual building-blocks in a structure of ongoing argument. Our answers therefore claim no finality. We argue our positions, and we realize that others can respond with arguments of their own. The provisional nature of our work, however, in no way diminishes from the importance we attribute to it. As Jews, we cannot live without community; as a community, we cannot survive without making religious judgments. Responsa are therefore extraordinarily useful to us, for as carefully reasoned arguments on individual issues of religious life, they are the means by which we Jews have always made those judgments and determined the necessary and inevitable limits upon our freedom of choice.

2. The Indispensability of Tradition. We affirm, further, that the judgments we must make ought to be informed by a careful and prayerful

consideration of the Jewish tradition. We say this not out of mere ethnic loyalty and nostalgia but out of the conviction that, as Jews, our choices are valid to the extent that they are "Jewish." And the most persuasive index of the "Jewishness" of any particular choice or decision lies in the religious tradition of the Jewish people.

Again, we know that some Reform Jews will disagree. It is their belief that a progressive religious movement is defined chiefly by its attachment to modernity, which involves the abandonment of "tradition" as a positive criterion of evaluation. Through much of its history, in fact, Reform Judaism has measured its choices against other standards: reason, decorum, the "spirit of the times." A well-known expression of this approach is the Pittsburgh Platform, drafted in 1885 and serving for several generations as the preeminent doctrinal statement of Reform Judaism in America. The document declares that "we recognize in Judaism a progressive religion, ever striving to be in accord with the postulates of reason" and that "we accept as binding only the moral laws [of the Torah], and maintain only such ceremonies as elevate and sanctify our lives, but reject all such as are not adapted to the views and habits of modern civilization." The Platform, we should note, does not endorse autonomy. On the contrary: it sets positive standards of judgment by which Reform Jews measure the appropriateness of their religious choices. The point is that these standards deny any significant positive value to tradition as such. That is to say, whether a particular practice or observance is "traditional," the inheritance of the Jewish past, is irrelevant to the question of whether we should retain or follow it today.

The Pittsburgh Platform, of course, is no longer the guiding statement of Reform Jewish religious principle. It has been superseded by the Columbus Platform of 1937 and the Centenary Perspective of 1976, both of which assign a greater weight to historical religious tradition as a standard for our own decision-making. It is also out of step with the important movement taking place in today's Reform, in particular the much-noted (if imperfectly understood) "return to tradition" in the religious practice of the developments during the past several decades. Some critics allege that this reappropriation of once-discarded traditional ritual constitutes an abandonment not only of the Pittsburgh Platform but of Reform Judaism's commitment to progressive values and its striving toward a form of religion more in keeping with the spirit of modernity. We, on the other hand, view these trends as the natural expression of a community which, however "modern," understands itself to be "Jewish" as well.

This is not to suggest that tradition is the only acceptable definition of Jewishness or that a practice or observance is authentically Jewish only because it is old. Reform Jews, after all, insist upon the freedom to reject old observances and to create new ones which better express the mind and heart of a contemporary Jewish culture. But to describe our religion as "creative Judaism" is no better, for in fact we do not and never have practiced and understood our Jewish selves in this way. To affirm "tradition" as a value is simply to acknowledge its powerful influence upon our thinking, that even we "modern" Reform Jews turn readily to the religious heritage of the Jewish people for guidance in our practice.

Consider but a few examples. The form of our liturgy is modeled upon the structure of traditional Jewish prayer as outlined in the siddur. Our observance of Shabbat and the festivals is characterized by numerous traditional practices, from kiddush and Shabbat candles to the Passover seder, the sukkah, the lulav and etrog, the shofar, *megilat* Esther, the Chanukah menorah and more. The rituals by which we mark moments of great transition in the cycles of our lives are likewise drawn from and based upon tradition: circumcision, naming and "covenant" ceremonies, being called to the Torah upon reaching the age of mitzvot, the chuppah and the breaking of a glass at the wedding, the customs of funeral practice and mourning. These observances are the stuff of which our religious life is constructed--and they are all "traditional." We are free, in other words, to abandon tradition, but at the same time we belong to a Jewish community which builds its Jewishness to a great extent upon the forms and precedents of the Jewish past.

It is not difficult to imagine why this is so. For all our modernity, we Reform Jews see ourselves not as a radically separate, new religious creation but rather as part of a continuity that links us to all the generations of our Jewish forbears. We are free to sever that connection, to discard tradition in favor of a religious practice that is entirely a product of our own modern, "enlightened" minds. And we are free to call that creation "Jewish." But these freedoms exist primarily in the abstract, as philosophical constructs. We do not exercise them, because we are a community that understands "Jewishness" primarily as a heritage we share with all other Jews. Our religious thinking proceeds from that understanding, that commonality. To such a community as ours, however "modern," tradition will always play a vital and even decisive role on issues of religious choice.

It is in this spirit that we write Reform responsa. As modern people, we reserve the right to look critically at tradition and to reject its conclusions when persuasive necessity requires us to do so. But we are also Jews, whose religious selves take shape in a process of continual conversation with the past. We therefore assume neither a hostile nor a coldly objective attitude toward the religious heritage of our people. On the contrary: we approach it with love, because the contours of the Jewishness to which we aspire have always been defined by the sacred texts and the historical experience of rabbinic Judaism. For this reason, our responsa accord a significant presumptive weight to the tradition. We seek to adopt and to adapt Jewish tradition into our own practice when possible, to affirm traditional approaches unless there is significant and convincing reason for Reform Jews to reject them. Though we may dispense with particular answers which emanate from it, Jewish tradition remains the indispensable starting-point for our reasoning and our religious discussion.

3. <u>The Centrality of Halakhah.</u> Once we affirm the importance of tradition as a factor in the making of our Jewish religious decisions, we accept as well the essential importance of halakhah, traditional Jewish law, as source material for our thinking.

It will not do to argue that we can link ourselves to Jewish tradition without the halakhah, that we can substitute other, "friendlier" texts in place of the legal literature. The problem is that Judaism, according to the old saw, is "a religion of deed more than creed," whose dominant expression is not the search for correct belief but rather a standard of practice that sanctifies us to God's service. And that branch of traditional Jewish literature which most directly concerns practice is the halakhah. It is here, in the legal sources, in the Talmudic commentaries, the codes, and the responsa, that our tradition works out its thinking on matters of ritual and ethical behavior, applying its doctrines and values so as to determine just how we ought to conduct ourselves in the concrete world of the here and now. If we wish to know how this tradition of sacred deed demands that we act, we have no recourse but to turn to the halakhic literature. There is, in other words, no "tradition" of Jewish practice without halakhah. If we desire a genuine connection to the Jewish heritage, then we cannot overlook the historical fact that this heritage is overwhelmingly a tradition of law. If we are serious in claiming "Jewish tradition" for ourselves, we must also assert our stake in the halakhah.

These statements seem strange, at first glance, in a Reform context. Our movement, after all, consciously adopted the title "prophetic Judaism" to emphasize its revolt against the halakhah. We have put matters of spiritual enlightenment and social conscience, rather than the technicalities of the law, at the center of our concern. But as our teacher, the late Rabbi Solomon B. Freehof, points out, that revolt was never as drastic as it may have seemed.

Reform Judaism may indeed have rejected the "rule of law," the requirement that all questions be submitted to authoritative and final rabbinic decision, but it retained much of the substance of the Jewish legal tradition. To put it differently, if the theology of Reform Judaism is "the faith of the Prophets," its practice remains largely the religion of the rabbis. This can be seen in the fact that, as noted above, much of our religious practice--liturgy, Shabbat and festival observance, life-cycle ceremonies and the like--follows traditional models which are themselves defined in the literature of the rabbinic halakhah. Our continuing attachment to halakhah is evident, too, in the published works that over the years have described the state of Reform Jewish religious practice, sought to derive standards for determining that practice, or traced the connection between our observance and its halakhic origins. These include: A *Guide for Reform Jews*, by Frederick A. Doppelt and David Polish; Solomon B. Freehof's monumental *Reform Jewish Practice* and *its Rabbinic Background*; and the guides published recently under the auspices of the Committee on Reform Jewish Practice of the Central Conference of American Rabbis (*Gates of Mitzvah; Gates of the Seasons; Gates of Shabbat*), which are suffused with halakhic information and insight. Our movement now boasts an academic association, the Freehof Institute for Progressive Halakhah, which devotes itself to the clarification of Jewish legal issues in the spirit of liberal Judaism. Finally, and most significant to our present context, Reform's interest in halakhah is expressed through our responsa process and literature.

We might add that, if we truly claim our share of the "tradition," then simple justice and self-respect demand that we extend that claim of ownership to our tradition's dominant mode of literary expression. It would be a tragedy for us, as rightful heirs to centuries of Jewish religious creativity, to abandon the greater part of that heritage to the exclusive control of Jews whose values and commitments differ so widely from our own. If the past can in any way speak to the present, it is because those who live today take seriously the responsibility to interpret that past in light of contemporary concerns. If we, out of a mistaken assumption that halakhah has nothing to say to us, cede to others an undeserved monopoly over its interpretation, then we guarantee that the voice of Jewish law and tradition will be a voice that is scornful of the values to which we are so deeply committed. If we are forbidden as Reform Jews to do anything, we are forbidden to do that. If, however, we accept the challenge of halakhic study, then we shall do our part to insure the development of a Jewish law that is much more in keeping with the liberal and progressive ideals for which we stand. The choice, quite clearly, is ours.

A Reform Approach to Halakhah. For all these reasons, then, Reform responsa are emphatically halakhic documents; they speak the language of Jewish law and draw their source material from the texts of the Jewish legal tradition. To this extent, they are much like all the other responsa that have been produced over the course of fifteen centuries and more. Yet there are significant differences. These emerge from our particular experience as a modern expression of Judaism and from a conception of halakhah that is very much our own.

A great deal has been written on the general subject of "Reform Judaism and the halakhah," and the present setting is too limited to allow us to consider the issue in a systematic way. We think it is essential, though, to point here to certain features of our responsa that testify to the existence of a distinct Reform Jewish approach to Jewish law and that influence our understanding of and relationship to the halakhic tradition.

1. Reform responsa do not partake of anything resembling an authoritative halakhic process. Our answers are in no way binding upon those who ask the questions, let alone upon anyone else. Our *teshuvot* are advisory opin-

ions; they are intended to serve as arguments in favor of a particular approach to a particular issue of observance. Their "authority," whatever we mean by that word, lies in their power to persuade.

2. We wish to know what halakhah has to say, but we do not identify the "halakhah" with the consensus opinion among today's Orthodox authorities. The "right" halakhic opinion is rather the one which best expresses the underlying purposes and values of Jewish religious observance as we conceive them to be. Thus, a minority ruling, or an interpretation abandoned long ago by most rabbis, may offer a superior understanding of the tradition than does the view adopted by the majority. In saying this, we follow the lead of Maimonides and other great theorists of Jewish law who hold that the correct halakhic ruling is not determined by the weight of precedent but by the scholar's honest and independent interpretation of the sources. We, too, assert the right of independence in halakhic judgment, our right to adopt the minority opinion when that position appears to us to be the correct one.

3. Our decisions are based upon the sources of Jewish tradition. For us, those sources include the tradition of Reform Jewish thought as expressed in our previous responsa, resolutions and publications of the Central Conference of American Rabbis, trends and tendencies in Reform Jewish observance and the like. This reflects our understanding of Reform as a continuation of Jewish tradition and not, as is sometimes asserted, a radical departure from it.

4. As an expression of our identification with the Jewish heritage, we seek to uphold traditional halakhic approaches whenever fitting. But we reserve for ourselves the right to judge the degree of "fit." We will modify standards of halakhic observance to bring them into accord with the religious, moral, and cultural ideals to which we Reform Jews aspire and which, as we see it, characterize Jewish tradition at its best. And we will depart from

the tradition altogether in those cases where even the most liberal interpretation of its sources yield conclusions which are unacceptable to us on religious or moral grounds.

Ultimately, the essays contained in this book are called "Reform responsa" because their authors understand them as arguments, drawn from halakhic sources, interpreted through the eyes of Reform rabbis and directed toward a Reform Jewish readership. Together with all previous Reform responsa, and indeed with the responsa literature as a whole, they are an element in the age-old argument over religious practice that stands at the center of Jewish religious discourse. The primary goal of argument is to persuade, and we certainly hope that those who read our teshuvot will find them convincing. But even if they fall short of that goal, Reform responsa can still serve as arguments, inviting their intended audience to think about the standards with which they define their Judaism and to consider just how we Reform Jews of the 1990s ought to express, explain, and justify the choices we make in the construction of our religious lives. We hope that the arguments collected in this volume succeed, in some small measure, in realizing that purpose.

Mark Washofsky

ABBREVIATIONS

ARR	American Reform Responsa
BT	Babylonian Talmud
CARR	Contemporary American Reform Responsa
CCAR	Central Conference of American Rabbis
CM	Choshen Mishpat
CRR	Current Reform Responsa
EH	Even Ha-Ezer
HUC-JIR	Hebrew Union College-Jewish Institute of Religion
JTS	Jewish Theological Seminary
M	Mishnah
MRR	Modern Reform Responsa
NARR	New American Reform Responsa
	(Questions and Reform Jewish Answers)
NRR	New Reform Responsa
OC	Orach Chayim
R.	Rabbi
RR	Reform Responsa
RRT	Reform Responsa for Our Time
Sh.A.	Shulchan Arukh
TRR	Today's Reform Responsa
UAHC	Union of American Hebrew Congregatons
YD	Yoreh De'ah
YT	Jerusalem Talmud

Orach Chayim
The Realm of Prayer and Synagogue

Congregation Choosing To Remain Small
5752.12

She'elah

A congregation, located in the suburb of a metropolitan area in the American Midwest, is inquiring whether limiting its membership and choosing to remain small would find support in Jewish tradition.

"It is important to know (writes the rabbi) that most of our families are young and do not have enough financial resources to finance the building of a new structure. We could, perhaps, build an addition for religious school classrooms, but that still doesn't answer our major objective--to create a family of friends."

The rabbi adds a document which sets forth how such a close-knit community is envisaged. The congregation is about ten years old and grew from small beginnings into its present size of more than 350 members, with 320 children in the religious school. The present building is not large enough to hold all classes at once, and different sessions have been introduced. There are other Reform congregations in the general metropolitan area, each with more than 1,000 members.

The rabbi of the inquiring congregation writes: "While we are not anxious to put a 'cap' on our membership, we are concerned that if we do not, we will turn into a congregation too large to continue to promote the ideals and values for which we were founded." (Rabbi Norman M. Cohen, Hopkins, MN)

Teshuvah

Historical and Halachic Precedents.
The Responsa Committee of the CCAR has previously dealt with membership limitation,[1] but it addressed only matters of geographical and demographic import. The issue before us is different and, in fact, we have not found any material which speaks directly to it.

At best there are general analogies. They show that communities welcomed large numbers of worshippers, a prime example being the synagogue of ancient Alexandria.[2] The centrality of the crowded Temple/synagogue remained a major feature of Judaism, and this sentiment raised public worship to a higher level than private prayer.[3]

The large community was considered the ambiance in which God was best approached. One traditional source emphasizes--and this speaks to the question before us--that even if one can pray with a minyan at home it is preferable to go to the synagogue, because "the glory of the King [i.e. God] is found in the multitude of people."[4]

Another authority concludes that in a choice between a large and a small synagogue one should choose the former, unless its noise and confusion make such a choice undesirable.[5]

Contemporary Perspectives.

It may be argued that the traditional preference for worshipping in community, and if possible in a large community, was based on the need for "security in numbers" in an unfriendly non-Jewish environment, a consideration fortunately not applicable to a North American congregation.

Nowadays, it may be said, the pressure of society, with its depersonalizing impact, engenders in us a need to be recognized as individuals and to make interpersonal connections, an objective easier to realize in a small group than in a large congregation, which is often considered "cold." These are worthy objectives, and the Committee is sympathetic to them.

Still, there are other and, in our opinion, weightier considerations that we would bring to the attention of the rabbi and his congregation.

There is, first of all, the principle of *mar'it ayin*, the avoidance of giving false impressions. A congregation with a "cap" on its membership, will be considered by others as elitist, for organizations that aver to strive for intimacy all too frequently use this claim as a cover word for exclusivity. The very idea of a *numerus clausus*[6] is odious to Jews, and while our Committee does not in any way assign unworthy motives to the congregation, we would have its members realize what the public impact of membership limitation might be.

A congregation should not be considered like a country club which has considerable social prestige, is admittedly elitist, has a waiting list, and selects its members. A congregation should be open to all Jews who wish to worship and educate their children there.

Also, waiting lists in congregations have in our experience led to notable inequities. Well-to-do applicants waiting in line are likely to be advanced over the others, for they can better help to alleviate a congregation's financial problems.

Further, a family who has moved into the neighborhood would wish to have its children associate in religious school with the same friends they have come to know in public school. Sending such children to another part of the city would make their attendance at religious school a less than pleasant and possibly counter-productive experience.

The Committee is not unmindful of the congregation's financial strictures. There are limits to building new accommodations for sanctuary and school. But every effort should be made to find acceptable alternatives: double worship sessions on holy days; school sessions on Shabbat and Sunday; use of portables and, if needed, external facilities. All these have at one time or another served other congregations to good advantage.

At the same time, the congregation's desire for an environment that creates closer interpersonal relationships can be satisfied by the expansion of havurot in its own midst.

If nonetheless circumstances require it, let the congregation help to establish another synagogue in the area, either a satellite or a sister congregation, one that will serve the Reform Jewish community to best advantage.

Conclusion.

The congregation's identity is well known to some of the Committee members. They are impressed with the religious spirit that prevails in its midst and with the rabbi's and the members' earnest desire to advance not only congregational goals but the welfare of the Jewish people.

We therefore conclude that our tradition clearly favors the openness of the congregation to all Jews and that openness should be maintained. Neither in personal nor organizational life can we have all our desires fulfilled, and in our view this is one of such conundrums. Let there not be in your community a tension between those who already belong and those who wish to join but cannot and have no good alternative.

One member of the Committee, who dissents from the majority and would allow limitation of membership, insists however that indigent applicants or others with special needs must not be refused.

NOTES

1 *ARR*, ed. Walter Jacob (1983), no. 9, pp. 44-45.

2 R. Yehudah averred that anyone who had not seen that synagogue had not seen the glory of Israel. It was so large that flags were raised to let the congregation know that they should respond with an "Amen." See BT Sukkah 5b; *Tosefta* Sukkah 4:3.

3 *Sh. A.*, OC 90:9; see also BT Berkhot 7b-8a.

4 Prov. 14:28. *Magen Avraham* on *Sh. A.*, OC 90, no. 15.

5 *Mishnah Berurah* on *Sh.A.*, *loc.cit.*, 90 no. 28. There is a controversy involving the desire of a rich man to retain access to his seat without encumbrance and therefore objects to having the empty spaces surrounding him sold to other people; one side upholding his rights (*Resp. Rivash*, no. 253) and the other, denying them (R. Binyamin Slonik, *Resp. Mash'at Binyamin*, no. 4).

6 Literally, "closed number," the usually unofficial limit of certain ethnic or religious groups by the regnant powers in an institution (often a university). The *numerus clausus* was frequently used against Jews.

Naming a Synagogue after a Donor
5751.1

She'elah

What Jewish precedents are there regarding the naming of a synagogue after an individual, and especially when the name is bestowed not because of the person's piety or contribution to the Jewish community but because of a monetary gift. (Name withheld, to prevent identification of donor.)

Teshuvah

Enclosed herewith please find a responsum by the late Dr. Solomon B. Freehof,[1] which deals with your question and, in effect, warns against naming a synagogue after a donor.

We would add the following: While it is quite customary to name parts of synagogue buildings (like the library or youth wing or social activities hall) after an individual, it is done sometimes because of the service the person has rendered to the congregation, and sometimes in consequence of significant donations. *But we would find it inappropriate to name the whole synagogue complex after someone in exchange for a monetary gift, and would strongly discourage such practice.*

The fact that this was occasionally done in the past should not be a determining factor, for circumstances may not be the same today as they were then. A synagogue is a place for prayer, devotion, piety and learning--and if it should ever bear the name of an individual, it should be to exalt his or her spiritual qualities and be a sign of gratitude for them.

We cannot judge the legal status of your congregation's decision. That is a matter which you will have to determine on the local level.

NOTES
1 *NRR,* (1980), no.1, pp. 7-10

Humanistic Congregation
5751.4

She'elah

A secular humanistic congregation is interested in joining the Union of American Hebrew Congregations (hereafter referred to as "the Union") whose constitution provides in Article III (1) that "any Jewish congregation"...may become a member; and in Article II (d) that it is among the objects of the Union "to foster the development of Liberal Judaism." Does this humanistic congregation comply with these objectives? Its rabbi is a graduate of Hebrew Union College-Jewish Institute of Religion (hereafter called "HUC-JIR") and a member of the Central Conference of American Rabbis (hereafter called "CCAR").

(The inquiry comes from Rabbis Alexander Schindler, James Simon and Allen Kaplan of the Union.)

Teshuvah

The question before us is twofold:

1. Can the Congregation for Humanistic Judaism (hereafter referred to as "the Congregation") be considered a "Jewish congregation" in the meaning of Article III (1) of the Union's constitution?

2. Can it be said to "foster the development of Liberal Judaism" in the meaning of Article II (d)?

1. The Congregation sees itself as a legitimate member of the Jewish community. It is not syncretistic like the Hebrew-Christians. It is, quite simply, a Jewish group that has banded together for the celebration of festivals, life cycle events, etc., but without the traditional theistic framework.

In its statement of belief (adopted December 1989) the Congregation avows:

> Judaism is a way of life from which a rich tradition has
> evolved. Interpreting and preserving the history and tradition
> for posterity is the responsibility of Jews in every generation.

9

The publications of Congregation leave no doubt about its being a Jewish congregation in the meaning of the Union's constitution.

2. The Congregation proclaims itself as a Reform congregation. Seeing that it acclaims the human being and not a supernatural power as the ultimate reference point, may it indeed be said to "foster Liberal Judaism"?

Reform Judaism has been an open-ended and variegated movement. It is historically flexible, but how far does its flexibility go? Can it accommodate the philosophy and liturgy of this particular Congregation?

The Congregation's liturgy deletes any and all mention of God, either in Hebrew (of which there is almost none) or in English. One of its publications, entitled *A Concept of God,* explains the congregation's position in this regard as follows.

> The concept of God has undergone constant modification in Judaism...There has always been and continues to be great diversity in the Jewish understanding of God.

There can certainly be no disagreement with the statement that Reform Jews (like other Jews) have different conceptions of God. Our *Gates of Prayer*, in the sixth Shabbat eve service, while leaving the traditional *Hebrew* God-language undisturbed, does not use the word "God" in the *English* text. Instead it speaks of "The Power that makes for freedom" and says: "We worship the power that unites all the universe into one great harmony" (p.210). It is clear that the sixth service remains a *prayer service*, which leaves it to the worshippers to fill the word "Power" with their interpretation of the supernatural. The language is purposefully ambiguous only within these limits.

That kind of ambiguity does not, however, exist in the Congregation's liturgy. To be sure, the above-mentioned statement says:

> Many falsely assume that humanism is atheistic...The definition of Humanistic Judaism does not preclude one's having a concept of God.

This affirmation of people's right to interpret the God-concept in their own way is, however, not borne out by the liturgy which *precludes the exercise of this right by omitting any and all references to a supernatural power in whatever language*. In fact, the congregation's *Statement on Liturgy* goes on to say unequivocally:

The use of prayer in services would be incompatible with such
a theological system.

The Congregation's liturgy therefore, and quite logically in its view,
does not include either *Kiddush* or *Kaddish*. The rabbi of the Congregation
states expressly (in his publication *Resources and Reflections*) that on principle
he will not say *Kaddish*, though he would allow someone else to say it if so
desired by a congregant.

Needless to add that such key liturgical portions as *Barekhu, Shema,
Ve'ahavta, Amidah* or *Aleinu* are also absent, as are selections from Psalms, or
the familiar songs *Yigdal, Adon Olam,* and *Ein keloheinu.*

The congregation's *Haggadah* is equally instructive. In the song "Who
knows one?" (*Echad mi yode'a?"*) the traditional response, "One is our God
who is present everywhere," is replaced by "One is all the universe." And in
the second verse (where the number two stands traditionally for the two Tables
of the Covenant), the two we are to remember are the "two people in the
Garden of Eden."

The latter change is especially noteworthy: Because of its elision of
God, the Congregation's philosophy *does not admit of Covenant or commandments*.
Hence, the *shenei luchot ha-brit* (the two Tables of the Covenant) have been
replaced by two human beings.

While the Congregation's liturgy contains a number of sensitive and
poetic meditations, may we consider the Congregation's agenda as a recogniz-
able form or development of Reform Judaism? Can Reform Judaism accommodate this kind of philosophy? It is well, therefore, to turn to the three basic
Reform statements, the Pittsburgh and Columbus platforms and the CCAR's
Centenary Perspective, which attempt to define the nature of Reform Judaism.

<u>Pittsburgh (1885).</u>

We recognize in every religion an attempt to grasp the Infinite
One, and in every mode source or book of revelation held
sacred in any religious system the consciousness of the
indwelling of God in man...We hold that Judaism presents the
highest conception of the God-idea as taught in our holy
Scriptures...*We maintain that Judaism preserved and defended...this
God-idea as the central religious truth for the human race.*

Columbus (1935).

The heart of Judaism and its chief contribution to religion is the doctrine of the One, living God, who rules the world through law and love. In Him all existence has its creative source, and mankind its ideal of conduct ...

Judaism affirms that man is created in the Divine image...He is an active co-worker with God ...

The Torah, both written and oral, enshrines Israel's ever-growing consciousness of God and the moral law.

Centenary Perspective (1976).

The affirmation of God has always been essential to our people's will to survive. In our struggle to preserve our faith we have experienced and conceived of God in many ways. The trials of our own time and the challenges of modern culture have made steady belief and clear understanding difficult for some. Nevertheless, *we ground our lives, personally and communally, on God's reality* and remain open to new experiences and conceptions of the Divine. Amid the mystery we call life, we affirm that human beings, created in God's image, share in God's eternality despite the mystery we call death ....

Torah results from the relationship between God and the Jewish people
..

The Congregation has cut itself loose from the three platforms that define Reform Judaism for their times. Instead, it declares itself to be a group that makes the human being the measure of all things. This concept, with its roots in Greek philosophy, has been opposed by Judaism, which has always staunchly affirmed its belief in a supernatural God and Creator who sustains the world. Reform has never wavered in its adherence to this faith and has never abandoned the central role of prayer from its belief structure. Persons of various shadings of belief or unbelief, practice or non-practice, may belong to UAHC congregations *as individuals*, and we respect their rights. *But it is different when they come as a congregation whose declared principles are at fundamental variance with the historic God-orientation of Reform Judaism.*

In view of these statements we find Congregation's system of beliefs to be outside the realm of historical Reform Judaism.

But should we not open the gates wide enough to admit even such concepts into our fold? Are not diversity and inclusiveness a hallmark of Reform? To this we would reply: *yesh gevul*, there are limits. *Reform Judaism cannot be everything, or it will be nothing.* The argument that we ourselves are excluded by the Orthodox and therefore should not keep others out who wish to join us, has an attractive sound to it. Taken to its inevitable conclusion, however, we would end up with a Reform Judaism in which "Reform" determines what "Judaism" is and not the other way around.

The argument has been made that our doors should always be open to *ba'alei teshuvah*, that is, those who repent and turn back. Our reading of the texts the congregation has published does not bear out the intent that, by joining the Union, it is prepared to turn back to the principles of historic Reform. Rather we find in its literature a declared purpose to redefine the essence of Reform Judaism. The Congregation is of course free to pursue this goal and may wish to attract other groups to its philosophy. It must do this, however, outside and not inside the Union.

In sum, we hold that the Congregation, as presently constituted, breaks the mold of Reform Judaism and does not have a place among the Union's congregations.

Postscript: The above opinion was not unanimous; three members of the Committee disagreed. Prof. Eugene Mihaly of HUC-JIR, whose opinion was also solicited by Rabbi Schindler, published a vigorous critique of our teshuvah, which in turn was rejected by Prof. Michael Meyer of HUC-JIR. The controversy reached the press and was, inter alia, debated before the Board of Governors of the College. The Responsa Committee did not at first involve itself in the public discussion, but in view of the Mihaly responsum (which appeared in printed form) the Committee's teshuvah was printed (along with the dissents) and the following addenda by the Chair:[1]

The above represents the first publication of the responsum (to which the three dissenting opinions are appended). It was sent — as is the custom of the Committee — to the questioners. Not long thereafter, Prof. Eugene Mihaly issued a 14-page counter-responsum which was at once widely disseminated and reprinted in full in a national Jewish newspaper. His major points may be summarized to be:

1. Admission to the Union is a legal question which is not meant for the Responsa Committee.
2. The Union's constitution gives full religious autonomy to its members.
3. The rabbi has been ordained by HUC-JIR.
4. The congregation includes men and women who have achieved prominent positions.
5. Reform Judaism is more authentic when it includes rather than excludes, and inclusion represents sage rabbinic advice.
6. While there is a limit to what may be considered to fit the term "Reform", the exclusion of God from the liturgy and philosophy of the congregation does not go beyond the limit.

Prof. Mihaly was answered in a number of unpublished communications, amongst which was a point-by-point refutation by Prof. Michael Meyer. The refutations of the above-listed points stressed the following:

1. If a legal question were at issue, why ask the Responsa Committee in the first place, and why ask the professor of Midrash for another opinion?
2. Article VI of the Union's constitution affirms the religious autonomy of its constituent congregations, and not of those who apply for membership. Similarly, an American citizen is free to declare the Constitution a worthless document, while applicants for citizenship are in a different class regarding their affirmations. Their admissibility is judged on the basis of that very Constitution.
3. Not relevant; the congregation, not the rabbi, is the applicant.

4. Is prominence of individual persons a ticket for approval?

5. Classical Reform was very particular in marking boundaries between itself and such movements as Ethical Culture, though the latter's founder was a rabbi who considered himself to be the true heir of Reform ideals.

6. If the presence or absence of God does not qualify as a limit, then faith in God or its absence would be irrelevant to Reform Judaism.

It is worth adding that it is not the task of the Responsa Committee to legislate new goals for the movement. That is the task of its constituent national bodies. Our Committee arrives at its decisions on the basis of what Jewish, and in particular, Reform Jewish history and tradition say to us up to this point.

Eventually the controversy reached the Board of Trustees of the Union, whose members overwhelmingly refused to admit the Congregation.[2]

NOTES

1 *CCAR Journal*, Fall 1991, pp 55-63.

2 The vote was 115:13 (with four abstentions); see *Reform Judaism*, Winter 1994, pp. 25-27.

Transfer of Memorial Plaque to another Synagogue
5751.10

She'elah

A newly formed congregation contains a number of persons who formerly were members in Temple Emanuel, the city's older, established synagogue. Some of them are retired and, in the past, had purchased memorial plaques in Temple Emanuel. They naturally feel a great attachment to these plaques and would like to have them moved to the new Temple with which they are now affiliated.

Should they make this request which, the rabbi of the new congregation fears, will contribute to already existing tensions between the two synagogues? On the other hand, if the donors of the plaques have a right to the removal, the rabbi might have to pursue their request. Have they this right?

Teshuvah

The status of gifts made to the community--especially of Torah scrolls-- has been repeatedly considered by our tradition. R. Moses Isserles said that in communities where it was customary to give scrolls to the synagogue, the ownership was not transferred.[1] The reason seems to be that a *Sefer Torah* has a unique status in that the owner may be seen to have placed the scroll in the safekeeping of the synagogue for the purpose of having it read at public services, and not with the intention of transferring ownership.[2] However, the application of this rule has varied in particular circumstances and different localities, especially when local practice has provided differently, in which case even a *Sefer Torah* is presumed to belong to the synagogue where it has been placed.[3]

R. Solomon B. Freehof treated this issue in a responsum, where he gives the sources and concluded that the Sefer Torah now belongs to the synagogue where it has been used.[4] His conclusion is based on the principle that, in this respect, the synagogue is comparable to the Temple of old, so that donated items partake of its holiness.[5] As such they become *k'lei kodesh* in the

literal sense and remain the property of the synagogue, absent specific stipulations or local custom.

We agree with this reasoning and hold that nowadays, with the exceptions noted, all *k'lei kodesh* are to be considered property of the synagogue in
which they were placed. Memorial plaques acquire this status. Usually they are
part of a contract between the donor and the congregation: the donor gives a
sum of money, and the congregation installs the plaque and promises to have
the name of the deceased read in perpetuity at *yahrtzeit* time. This contract
remains in force as long as the congregation is active and performs this service;
should it fail to do so (it might, for instance, cease to exist) the contract would
have been breached and the plaque would then revert to the donor. No one has
claimed that this is the case with regard to Temple Emanuel.

There are two additional considerations.

One, when plaques are affixed to the synagogue's walls they are seen as
permanent parts of the synagogue's ambiance of holiness. Two, while tradition
generally upholds the right of members of the community to establish a new
synagogue, it also warns against such action becoming the source of tension
and intra-communal problems.[6]

We therefore strongly urge not to make the plaques, much as they
mean to the donors, a source of further friction, especially since break-aways
often take place in an atmosphere of tension. The donors, even though they are
no longer members of Temple Emanuel, can certainly return there to say *kaddish* if they so desire.

NOTES

1 *Sh.A,* YD 259:2.

2 See R. Joseph Katz (16th cent.), *Resp. She'erit Yosef*, no. 51: "Thus, the fact that the owner
deposits it in the synagogue does not [in itself] prove that he has donated it to the congregation."

3 The local minhag may set aside the Halachah: *minhag mevattel halachah*, see YT Baba Metsi'a
7:1, and Maharik (R. Joseph Kolon, 15th cent.). *Resp. Maharik*, shoresh 161.

4 ARR, ed. R. Walter Jacob, no. 40, pp. 106-110, citing many authorities.

5 Thus, for instance, BT Megillah 29a.

6 See Rivash (R. Yitzhak ben Sheshet, 14 th cent.), *Responsa* no.. 253, though the position has
not enjoyed unanimous endorsement. Thus R. Eliyahu Mizrachi (16th cent.) disagrees and says that if
the older synagogue is large enough to hold all worshippers, a break-away is forbidden (*Responsa* I, no.
53).

Ark Located on Synagogue's North Wall
5752.4

She'elah

Our synagogue, which was constructed in 1881, is oriented so that the Ark is permanently fixed into the northern wall. During the prayers, when one would normally face east, towards Jerusalem, should we face the Ark?

Teshuvah

The question regarding the orientation of the synagogue has been answered fully in *American Reform Responsa*, no.18, pp. 61-63, where the sources of the tradition are set forth and its maintenance is strongly urged.

The well entrenched tradition of facing east has always known exceptions. Thus, in Brooklyn, among the synagogues which are still in use and others which have been abandoned, there are three (one Reform, two Orthodox) where the Ark is placed on the north wall; two (one Reform, one Conservative) where it is on the south wall; and one on the west wall. The last one is a fairly new congregation, established as an outreach operation of the Lubavitch Movement, in a formerly centrist Orthodox synagogue built in 1925. The Orthodox group uses the basement sanctuary and faces west, because on that level the eastern end of the structure is occupied by lavatories, and it would be considered unseemly to turn in that direction for prayer.

In Toronto, two large congregations are built near each other and both have their front entrances on the west side of the street. One faces west in prayer because of it, while the other, more traditional one, manages to have worshippers enter by as circuitous route, so that the Ark could be placed on the eastern wall.

We do not advise that you contemplate a restructuring of your synagogue. To do so, more than a hundred years after it was built, would seem to cast aspersions upon the Jewish commitment of those who erected, paid for, and maintained the structure. Most likely this matter was considered by the pioneers, who acted in good faith. Let their decision be respected so long as their successors enjoy the bounty of the founders.

Since the Ark with its scrolls is the synagogue's focus of sanctity, the congregation should turn toward it during the service.

Amazing Grace
5752.11

She'elah

A Jewish woman would like to have the song "Amazing Grace" sung at her funeral. She also wonders whether it would be appropriate in general Jewish worship, or whether it is so christological that it should not be used in a Jewish ritual setting.

Further, is the word "grace" so distinctly Christian that it in itself disqualifies the song? The author of the hymn in question was a certain John Newton, a slave trader who had a "born again" experience, repented of his evil, and found in religion a new way of life.

Teshuvah

Let us turn first of all to the meaning of "grace." In Christian theology, it represents the freely offered, and often undeserving, gift of God to an individual or to a people. Two Hebrew terms are the models for this concept: *chen* and *chesed*. In the Septuagint, *chen* is rendered as *charis* (whence "charity", this is the word most commonly translated as grace); and *chesed* as *eleos* ("mercy"). The idea that God does not forget the undeserving is usually expressed by the divine quality of *chesed*; for instance, in II Sam. 7:15 (God's mercy will not depart from David's offspring even if they commit iniquity) and in other places like Isaiah 54:8. Since Christianity adopted the Pauline emphasis on grace and considered Jesus Christ its main vehicle, the English term grace has been avoided by Jewish writers, even though its antecedents in the Hebrew Bible are firm and formidable.

Thus the English word itself has assumed a christological coloring and its liturgical use would lead us into a consideration of the biblical warning not to walk on the custom of other nations, *chukkat ha-goyim*.[1]

The avoidance of *chukkat ha-goyim* in all expressions of living, from ritual practices to daily dress, was enunciated by Maimonides,[2] as well as the *Shulchan Aruch*.[3] These texts have been interpreted more stringently at some times and more leniently at others. However, there can be no question that whenever a custom reminded one of other religions and tempted to lessen the

21

distinctiveness of the Jewish heritage, it was considered to fall under the prohibition of *chukkat ha-goyim*.[4]

Thus the so called "Lord's Prayer" which contain traditional Jewish teachings has become firmly connected with Christian worship and therefore, though its individual components are unobjectionable, would not be acceptable in any Jewish setting.

A similar situation obtains for "Amazing Grace." None of the individual words or concepts of the song "Amazing Grace" in and of itself contradicts Jewish teachings. But its author, John Newton, had been converted under the influence of George Whitefield and John Wesley, became an Anglican priest and a pillar of the emerging Methodist movement. His hymn is a textbook description of a conversion experience in the evangelical Protestant tradition and therefore unsuitable for us.

There are some who believe that a song like "Amazing Grace" has become an expression of contemporary folklore, and therefore the melody at least could be deemed acceptable. We disagree. By analogy, some Christmas and Easter customs have become highly secularized and denuded of specific Christian content, yet they too also fall under the prohibition of *chukkat ha-goyim*.

Surely there are worthy Jewish melodies fit to sanctify a funeral service, and as for the words one might recall the observation of Solomon Schechter: "A people that has produced the Psalmist, a Rabbi Judah Halevi, and other hymnologists and liturgists counted by hundreds, has no need to pass around the hat to all possible denominations begging for a prayer or a hymn."[5]

NOTES

1 Lev.20:23 and 18:3, Ezek. 5:7 and 11:12.

2 *Yad*, Hilchot Akkum 11:1-3; 12:1.

3 *Sh. A.*, YD 178 and commentaries thereto.

4 See also our responsa on "Blessing the Fleet" and "Flags on the Bimah" in this volume.

5 *Studies in Judaism* (New York, 1938), p.136f. One member of the Committee dissented, holding that on the whole, Reform Judaism has attempted to accommodate such poetry and music, and that its strength has been its ability to incorporate secular material into its liturgy in a way that is consistent with tradition. "At a funeral, I take it, this song would express the woman's faith that God's presence had influenced her life and aided her in time of trouble. If the Rabbi is uncomfortable with the words "Amazing Grace", s/he might have the tune played on a musical instrument and incorporate other more traditional Jewish texts expressing these things, thereby satisfying the woman's intent."

Need for a *Minyan*
5752.17

She'elah

A New Zealand congregation inquires about the Reform perspective on the need for a *minyan*, and about what should or should not be done during a service when fewer than ten are present. The rabbi writes that he "would appreciate it if you guide our ritual committee towards setting a policy."

Teshuvah

Leaders of the CCAR have on three occasions addressed aspects of the questions asked.

R. Jacob Mann, in 1936, issued a brief responsum on the need for a *minyan* at Friday night services and, basing himself on an old Palestinian custom, allowed the practice of holding services without a *minyan*. "While every attempt should be made to have a full *minyan*, the importance of regular services in the Temple is such as to conduct them even when there are fewer than ten people present."[1]

R. Solomon B. Freehof, in 1963, ruled on whether a person who could not attend synagogue services could say Kaddish at home, with no one else to join in the prayers. The responsum was quite detailed, permitting the practice under certain circumstances and making alternative suggestions.[2]

R. Walter Jacob, in 1989, responded to the question: "May we conduct a service at home with less than a *minyan*?" This responsum, like R. Mann's, was also quite brief and allowed a *minyan*-less service, urging congregations meanwhile to expend extra efforts to have people come together in the synagogue.[3]

All three were thus permissive, though R. Freehof hedged his ruling with particular cautions.

We have agreed to review the entire matter, not only in order to summarize previous and highly respected opinions, but also because we feel that the developments of Jewish life, and especially in our own movement, call for additional considerations.

Halachic Perspectives.

The need for a *minyan* on certain ritual occasions is not biblical in origin, though the Rabbis tried valiantly to ground the practice in Torah precedent.[4] The fact that rule of *minyan* is *de-rabbanan,* has occasioned repeated attempts at slackening of the reins of the "rule of ten."[5]

R. Jacob[6] cites discussions on whether a child carrying a chumash could be considered as completing the quorum, or what other means of making up the deficiency could be devised. However, as an over-riding rule the requirement of a *minyan* for liturgical portions cited in Footnote 4 was, and in traditional circles is, carefully observed, testifying to the strong sense that public prayer has a place of special importance. Where ten men could not be easily assembled a community would engage available persons as "*minyan* men," who would insure that the ritual requirements of public prayer could be fulfilled.

In sum, traditional Judaism has on the whole steadfastly resisted attempts to be lenient in this matter, except in extraordinary circumstances.

Reform Considerations.

It cannot be denied that the rule of ten is frequently disregarded in Reform congregations, especially in small communities, but not there alone. With lessening worship attendance in general, even in places where adequate numbers of worshippers can be found, attention to the time-honored practice of requiring a quorum is rarely an issue.[7]

Yet there are good reasons why this practice deserves our continued attention and respect, with the proviso, of course, that any Reform *minyan* would count women as equal partners.[8]

As a general rule we are and have been lenient in most ritual matters, and the opinions of Rabbis Mann, Freehof and Jacob reflect this trend. They are in tune with the sentiment of *Pirkei Avot*: "When two sit together and discuss words of Torah the Shekhinah is present with them"[9] --which may be taken to mean that it does not matter how few Jews gather together for services, their sacred intent entitles them to full liturgical expression. Why should they be denied the hearing of Torah and *Kedusha*[10] because others may not feel prompted to come to the synagogue? Why should Jews be dependent on others when they need to say Kaddish, whether at home, at a *shiv'ah*, or when observing *yahrtzeit*?

Having stated these questions we must, however, also ask: *If the needs of the individual can be satisfied without others, what then is the difference between public and private worship?*

Whether six, seven or ten constitute the required forum is not the heart of the issue; rather it is the question whether there is an abiding value in the obligation of Jews to join others in worship. The synagogue functions as the *mikdash me'at* (literally, the small sanctuary) which invokes the image of the Sanctuary of old. Moses and Ezra expounded Torah in the presence of the people, and the reading of Torah on Shabbat and other occasions is a recurring enactment of those hallowed moments. The rabbi, as teacher of the community, expounds sacred texts and traditions, and does so before the *tzibbur*, the representatives of the Jewish people who have come to participate in common rites of prayer and learning. The *tzibbur* is indeed the proper context of certain liturgical rubrics, and by tradition these include, in addition those mentioned, the reading of Torah from a scroll, and the mourner's Kaddish.

It seems to us that the idea of a *minyan* deserves renewed attention. Reform Judaism has broken much new ground by giving individuals a measure of religious scope they did not previously have. Withal, we may not overlook the needs of the community which, when properly met, benefit all its members. Public worship belongs to these categories of Jewish life, and withholding certain individual prerogatives for the benefit of all has always been the context of Jewish prayer.

Thus, the obligation of Kaddish is traditionally fulfilled in community, and therefore the congregation at prayer is the proper locus for it. However, should there be no quorum or should the individual be unable to go to the synagogue, the need for community does not simply fall away.

We can look to tradition and see how such situations have been dealt with in a constructive fashion. The comprehensive prayer anthology of Yitzhak Baer contains a series of prayers for individuals who have missed the opportunity of reciting portions of the liturgy which need a quorum. These substitutes resemble the original but differ sufficiently to remind the person that the community of worshippers possesses the aura of completeness.[11]

Since the substitutes proposed by Baer (for which he cites no authority) are not applicable to our congregations, we as Reform Jews ought therefore to create further innovative, supplementary prayers for those who cannot worship in community, or for whom a *minyan* cannot be assembled. For instance, where there are fewer than ten present, Torah might be read from the printed book rather than from the scroll, and for both Torah and Haftarah the blessings would be omitted. Instead of reciting the Kaddish in its original version, the mourner might read it in English or substitute the *el male rachamim* ("God, full of compassion...").

Or, noting that in many if not most Reform congregations all those present say the Kaddish together, the custom might be introduced--when fewer than a *minyan* are assembled--to have the mourner rise and say the Kaddish alone. In other words, the presence or absence of a *minyan* should not be overlooked.

We would therefore urge the Reform Practices Committee of the CCAR, together with the Liturgy Committee, to take up the need for devising alternate expressions for those who cannot worship in community, be it because of personal circumstances or because a *minyan* has not or cannot be brought together.

The maintenance of the requirement of a *minyan* has also a strong educational force: it reminds all those who are or might be affected by the rule of the importance of public worship. R. Freehof reminds us of the injunction of the *Shulchan Aruch*[12] that it is the duty of the members of the community to exert pressure upon each other so that there should always be a *minyan* in the synagogue. "The feeling of piety at the time of yahrzeit is one of the justifiable motives which urges people to come to public worship."[13] And R. Jacob adds that we should make "a more vigorous effort and assemble a necessary *minyan*, if it is at all possible, for a service whether public or private."[14]

We heartily endorse these sentiments which reflect the abiding value of a *minyan* in our liturgical structure, and we urge the inquiring congregation to devise ways and means to maintain and enhance this ancient Jewish institution.

Dissent: Three members differed somewhat from these conclusions. They felt that Kaddish deserves an exemption from the rule, and that perhaps in special circumstances the rule of three ought to be invoked (as at the *birkat ha-mazon.* One believes that the few should also not be deprived of reading (or hearing) the words of Torah from the scroll, and would have the leader of the service emphasize that the fewer-than-ten who are assembled do not constitute a proper congregation but rather a chug, a small group who have come together for study and edification.

NOTES

1 ARR, ed. Walter Jacob (1983), no.3, p.5

2 Freehof, RRR (1963), no. 1, pp. 14-18.

3 Jacob, NARR (1992), no. 4, pp. 5-6. The *teshuvah* was published while our answer was being prepared.

4 The reasons given are varied and the derivations frequently forced, but that did not matter much because when they were enunciated the requirement of a *minyan* was already an established. The following sources may serve as a survey of the talmudic and post-talmudic statements on the subject.

M Megillah 4:3 and BT. Meg. 23b list the required occasions for a *minyan*: the *sheva berachot* at a wedding; the *chazarat ha-shatz* of the Amidah; the reading of Torah from the scroll and of Haftarah; the *kedusha* (derived from Lev. 22:32, *ve-nikdashti betoch benei yisra'el*, matching the word *toch* with Num. 16:21, *mitoch ha-edah*, where the context makes it clear that sanctification requires a public. The number 10 is derived from Num. 14:27, where the ten spies opposing the invasion were called an *edah ra'ah*. There were also other derivations, one of them being the "ten righteous people" that were lacking in Sodom.

Soferim 10:7 adds Kaddish and *barechu* to the rubrics requiring a *minyan*, though here, the plain text would suggest that the *minyan* could be seven (or even six) worshippers, after the number of words in Judges 5:2. But later interpretation favored the reading of this prescription as signifying that the numbers six or seven refer to persons who, within a regular *minyan* of ten men, have not heard the Kaddish or *barechu*. If we read the Soferim passage plainly it appears that the author(s), writing in Palestine, meant to deal with situations when it was difficult to gather a *minyan*. The Talmud (*YT Meg.* 4:4 and Ber. 7:3) provides that if a *minyan* was present to start with, but some people had left afterwards, the service could conclude as if they were still present, provided that the majority remain (so Rambam, *Yad*, Tefillah 8:8, *Sh. A.* OC, 55:4; and the Hafetz Chayim, *Mishnah Berurah*, no. 24).

R. Freehof's reading of *Magen Avraham*, OC 69, no.4, and Greenwald's *She'eloth u-teshuvot zichron yehudah*, vol 1, no. 4, guides him as a precedent for his lenient answer. While it seems to us that the context of these sources suggests that ten men were present for services but that not all had participated in the study, there were some, like the Taz (*Magen David*, OC 55, no. 3) who would agree with R. Freehof's more lenient reading.

5 According to R. Ovadiah Yosef, *She'elot u-teshuvot yabiah omer*, vol. 4, no. 9:1, the entire prayer service is a rabbinic ordinance. As M Berachot 7:3 makes clear, the Rabbis considered various levels of participation: 3, 10, 100, 1000, 10,000, though in the end only three (for the *birkat ha-mazon*) and ten for *minyan* remained significant. See BT Ber. 49b-50a).

6 *L.c.*, p.6.

7 One member of our Responsa Committee, suggests that the *minyan* "was basically a device to counteract heresy, in the assumption that when a critical mass of Jews assembles for some religious enterprise, there will always be found among them at least several who dare to refute heterodox opinions

and to guide the errant faithful back to the correct path." This was true especially before there was an established liturgy, but today, he writes, that reason can no longer be compelling. He does, however, hold that there are other reasons for requiring a *minyan* in our congregations, but would exempt the Kaddish and allow it at all times (see below).

8 As to children, we could take our lead from BT. Berachot 48a, which allows minors who understand to Whom our prayers are addressed, to be counted in the required quorum of three when saying the *birkat ha-mazon*, and count them in like manner for the quorum of ten.

9 M Avot 3:2.

10 The prayer which features the words of Isaiah, *kadosh, kadosh, kadosh*, holy, holy, holy...(Isaiah 6:3)

11 *Seder Avodat Yisra'el,* p. 120. While Baer cites no authorities there are other texts which list surrogate prayers. See, e.g., the *siddur* of Y. Ganzfried (Vienna, 1859),. Wolf Heidenheim's *Safah Berurah* (Roedelheim, 1821), and Jacob Emden's *Siddur Amudei shamayim* (Altona, 1744-1747). The latter attributes this minhag to the *Sefer HaRoke'ach* (12th-13th century, from the school of the Hasidei Ashkenaz. *HaRoke'ach*, ch. 362, specifically discusses the practice of reciting surrogate texts when the worshipper has missed essential prayers (*devarim she-bikedushah*.) A fairly recent edition of *Siddur HaGra* (Jerusalem 1977) also lists substitute prayers, though on the whole it may be said that regnant Ashkenazic tradition has not favored this practice. See also Freehof, RRR p. 16.

12 *Sh.A.* OC 55:22.

13 Freehof, *loc. cit.*, p. 17.

14 *Loc. cit.,* p. 6.

Flags on the Bimah
5753.8

She'elah

It is customary in many synagogues to place flags on the bimah, both the national flag and that of the state of Israel. Is it appropriate for Reform synagogues to exalt national symbols to the same rank as the symbols of Jewish worship? Specifically, does this practice border upon idolatry (*avodah zarah*)? (Rabbi Philip Bentley, Huntington Station, NY)

Teshuvah

<u>General Considerations.</u> Our sources regard the synagogue as a sacred place. The rules concerning its proper use,[1] discussed in the third chapter of the *Mishnah's* tractate Megillah,[2] are linked to Ezekiel 11:16: "I have become for them a small sanctuary (*mikdash me'at*)." This midrash, of course, is not to be taken literally. Clearly, many of the rules which apply to the Sanctuary in Jerusalem (for example, those dealing with priestly status and access, ritual purity and defilement) do not apply to the synagogue. Yet in many significant respects it is patterned after the Temple. The synagogue *bimah* is customarily adorned with the *ner tamid*, the *aron hakodesh*, and the *menorah*, symbols which evoke the original Sanctuary. None of the appurtenances of the Sanctuary, however, were connected with what we would view as the cult of nationhood. The only symbolism permitted there was that devoted to the worship of the God of Israel.

The point is obvious: God is to be exalted above all rulers and nations. Israel, to be sure, is a nation, but it exists only to serve God; that is the essence, perhaps the entirety of its national identity. To have included purely national symbols within the Sanctuary would have invited the suspicion that we were equating devotion to the nation with the service of God. This, in turn, would have been seen as idolatry, for God alone is worthy of worship.[3]

We might well draw the same conclusion with regard to our "small Sanctuary" and forbid the placement of national flags on the *bimah* as an improper invasion of the secular into the realm of the sacred.

Jewish tradition, however, does *not* draw that conclusion. The *Talmud*[4] reports that four sages prayed in a synagogue in Babylonia which contained a statue of the king. From this we might infer that the presence of a national symbol, even a graven image which might otherwise create the suspicion of idolatry, is not necessarily prohibited in a synagogue on the grounds of *avodah zarah*, idolatry.

Halachic Perspectives. Our specific question, that of national flags, has been the subject of several contemporary responsa.

R. Moshe Feinstein sees them as purely secular symbols (*chulin*) which, unlike those associated with idolatry, are not forbidden in the sanctuary. He writes: "these flags are not set up in the synagogue because they are regarded as sacred symbols but rather as indications that the congregation's leaders love this country and the state of Israel and wanted to display their affection in a public place."[5]

This Committee has explicitly supported the custom to place national flags on the *bimah*. Writing in 1954, R. Israel Bettan[6] argued that the presence of the national flag is the symbolic equivalent of the prayers which we have long recited for the welfare of the government and its leaders.[7] A separate opinion, from 1977, finds "no religious objection" to placing a national flag on the pulpit.[8] Given such precedents, and given the fact that it has become a widespread *minhag* (customary observance) among Reform congregations to place flags in their sanctuaries, we would certainly not urge their removal.

At the same time, we see nothing wrong with a congregation's desire to reconsider this practice. The mere fact that the presence of flags on the *bimah* violates no ritual prohibition does not mean that they *ought* to be there, that to place national flags in the sanctuary is a positive good which achieves some high religious purpose.[9] Indeed, the opinions we have cited differ widely over this issue. R. Feinstein, for example, declares that it is "improper" (*lo min ha-ra'ui*) to put secular symbols in a sacred space, especially next to the Ark. It would be best to remove these objects of "nonsense" (*hevel ve-shtut*) from the synagogue. In his opinion, this is particularly true of the flag of Israel, a nation founded by nonobservant Jews (*resha`im*) who have rejected the Torah. Still, since there is no actual prohibition against them, the flags should not be removed if doing so would lead to community strife and dissension.

R. Bettan, by contrast, believes that the display of the national flag performs a vital religious function, that "it may well serve to strengthen in us the spirit of worship." He declares that the flag symbolizes our loyalty to our country and our "zealous support of its rights and interests." The flag "speaks to us with the voice of religion and partakes, therefore, of the sanctity of our religious symbols." The 1977 responsum strikes a different chord and does not make this comparison. It simply reminds us that gratitude for one's land, hope for its welfare, and concern for the Jews of the land of Israel are valid Jewish religious sentiments which can be symbolized through the placement of flags in the sanctuary. Some congregations, however, choose to express these sentiments by placing flags in the social hall rather than on the pulpit; still others do not place flags in their buildings at all. "In any case, both the loyalty of our communities to (our country) and our common concern for Israel are clear with or without the placement or possession of flags."

This Committee reaffirms the ruling and the attitude expressed in the 1977 responsum. As Reform Jews we believe that our acceptance of the responsibilities and privileges of citizenship, our devotion toward the prophetic ideals of social justice, and our love for the state of Israel imply a more positive disposition toward national flags than that assumed by R. Feinstein. We care deeply, about the welfare of our societies; their symbolic representations must not be dismissed as "nonsense."

At the same time, the Committee believes that the language employed by R. Bettan no longer reflects the precise relationship of many, and perhaps most, Reform Jews to their national state. We are properly suspicious of rhetoric equating "God and King" or "God and Country." While it may have been proper at one time to speak of the flag as a religious symbol, and while such language may not be, strictly speaking, a case of idolatry, it connotes for many of us today some of the most disturbing historical tendencies of our time: chauvinism, racism, and ethnic intolerance. If it is true that God alone is worthy of our religious worship, we ought to avoid language which, rightly or wrongly, suggests otherwise.

We would therefore say rather that, for us, the flag serves as an expression of a religiously legitimate devotion, a devotion which *may* be expressed, should the congregation so choose, by the placement of national flags in the sanctuary or in some other location within the synagogue building.

NOTES

1 See *Sh.A.*, OC 151.

2 The same arrangement is preserved in the *Talmud Yerushalmi.* In the *Babylonian Talmud*, however, this material—*perek "Beney Ha`ir"*—comprises chapter four, pp. 25b ff. The midrash discussed here is located in BT Meg. 29a.

3 *Cf. Gates of Prayer,* p. 75: "We are Israel: our Torah forbids the worship of race or nation, possessions or power."

4 BT Rosh Ha-shanah 24b.

5 *Resp. Igrot Moshe,* OC I, no. 46. The opinion was written in 1957.

6 ARR, no. 21.

7 Both in the Diaspora and in Israel, elements of the "civil religion" have assumed a prominent place in Jewish ritual practice. See our responsum 5751.3, "Blessing of the Fleet." In Israel, these issues are exemplified by the debates over the observance of Israel Independence Day in synagogues. While the subject is controversial, many observant Jews do recognize this national festival as a religious holiday. See N. Rakover, ed., *Yom Ha-Atsma'ut ve-Yom Yerushalayim: Berurey Halachah* (Jerusalem: Ministry of Religions, 1973).

8 ARR, no. 22, pp. 66-68. This *teshuvah* extends the approval to the placing of the Israeli flag in the sanctuary, a practice which Rabbi Bettan regarded as inappropriate in a Diaspora synagogue except on special occasions.

9 Indeed, while the four sages prayed in the presence of the king's image (see note 4, above), that passage does not in any way suggest that such statuary *should* be placed in synagogues.

See-through Fabric for an Ark Curtain
5754.20

She'elah

A group of people in our congregation are working on a plan to replace the current needle-point Torah curtain with one made out of light fabric, which would enable Torah scrolls to be seen at all times. The new curtain is to be opened when the Torah is to be taken out and read. At present some members of the congregation stand whenever the Ark is opened and the scrolls are visible. Would people be obligated to stand or be otherwise discomforted if this change were to occur in the fabric of the *parochet*? (Rabbi Arnold S. Task, Alexandria, LA)

Teshuvah

The origins of the Ark curtain go back to the curtain in the wilderness Tent[1] and later the Jerusalem Temple. When the Romans came and entered its holy precincts, so the story goes, their general pierced the curtain with his weapon, firmly believing that he would thus kill off the secret being within.

The *parochet* may be seen as a parallel to the incense which, according to most biblical scholars, was meant to hide the Divine Presence. Halachically, the *parochet* partakes of the sanctity of the Ark and may not be disposed of when it can no longer be used.[2]

While standing up when the Ark is opened is not, according to the Halachah, a requirement,[3] many Jews are so accustomed to it that indeed they feel discomfited when they find themselves in the presence of the scrolls without rising in their honor. For them, standing up when the scrolls of the Torah come into view becomes their acknowledgment that they are in the presence of holy objects. Many would therefore consider a see-through curtain something of an oxymoron.

Much is to be said for this point of view. For it would tend to further demystify the *kelei kodesh*, at a time when we should promote respect for the holy, the basic meaning of which is "something set apart." In contrast, what is always on view is, in the end, not seen at all.[4]

We would therefore discourage anything that further enfeebles this apperception, Perhaps the fabric can be thickened sufficiently so that the shape of the scrolls may be seen in vague outline only. But barring this possibility, we would counsel against using the proposed materials.

Even if there are but few of your members who would feel uncomfortable with the proposed *parochet*, their sensibilities ought to be respected.

NOTES

1 Exodus 26:33.

2 *ShA*, OC 154:3.

3 BT Sotah 39a; ShA, OC 146:4. *Turei Zahar ad loc.*

4 It is noteworthy that the Rama (R. Moses Isserles) refers to the Ashkenazic custom of removing the *parochet* from the Ark altogether during TiSh.A. b'Av. *ShA*, OC 559:2.

Mezuzah on a Synagogue
5753.14

She'elah

When we built our present synagogue we did not put a mezuzah on the building. We are now expanding and want to revisit the issue. What is your advice and judgment? Should we affix a mezuzah now? (R. Norman D. Hirsh, Seattle, WA)

Teshuvah

The command to affix a mezuzah derives from Deuteronomy 6:9 which says that it should be done to "your house and gates." The term "house" has traditionally been interpreted as a dwelling place, and the *Shulchan Aruch* expressly states that synagogues do not need a mezuzah unless they contain an apartment.[1]

However, *minhag* has gone beyond the minimum requirements of the Halachah. In Israel, all public buildings and synagogues have *mezuzot*, and this custom is also found in the Diaspora. Similarly, in Toronto all synagogues have *mezuzot*, and it is our feeling that the custom will sooner or later spread to most places.

Is there any reason why Reform temples should have a special policy that disagrees with this development? We see no reason for it. On the contrary, the affixing of a mezuzah to the entrance(s) of the building will give you the opportunity to stress the importance of this symbol for every Jew.

For the command to affix mezuzot to our private homes and apartments is being increasingly neglected, and it must be made clear that in this respect as in any other, the synagogue serves as a model but not as a surrogate for our obligations. It will also give you a chance to discuss this with your building and worship committees and thus make the she'elah an instrument for *talmud torah.*

NOTES

1 *Sh. A.*, YD 286:3; see also *Resp. Levi ibn Habib* no.101, and the rhetorical question in Devarim Rabba 7:2.

Applause in the Sanctuary
5751.2

She'elah

During Friday night services in the Sanctuary we have had an Israeli dance performance or a jazz pianist who played contemporary interpretations of traditional Jewish melodies. Congregants were unsure whether applause on such occasions was appropriate. What about a guest speaker? Is it allowable to applaud at the conclusion of the address?

Teshuvah

The Sanctuary--that is, the place where communal worship usually takes place and where the Torah scrolls are kept in an Ark--has served a variety of purposes at different times. At one time wayfarers would spend the night there, and today large communal meetings are often held in the Sanctuary. Some congregations, when they accommodate events that appear to be "secular" in nature, shield the Ark with a screen and thereby signal that the "holy space" has now been converted to ordinary usage. But others do not engage in this practice.

The matter of applause generally arises only at events that are clearly *performances* of one kind or another (which should, of course, be suitable to a synagogue), and applause would be the normal reaction of the audience. In fact, the rule of thumb that might be applied is to ask whether the people assembled are a *congregation* or an *audience*. In the latter instance, applause would be expected and unobjectionable.

But what if the applause takes place during a Shabbat service? Rabbi Solomon B. Freehof permitted it in the case of a couple who were blessed on their Golden Wedding anniversary. He considered the applause as a warm and friendly gesture on the part of the congregation, and deemed it halachicly permissible.[1]

You inquire about applauding a dance group or pianist or guest speaker during the service. While the Halachah is permissive on the subject, we feel it imperative to ask whether such reaction enhances the worship service. Quite evidently your congregation feels somewhat uncomfortable about applauding guest artists or speakers, and we are sure they would consider it totally inappropriate to applaud the rabbi or cantor for their contributions to the service.[2]

The current discomfort of your congregation in this matter suggests that they have a sense that applause is predominantly an every-day expression which somehow runs counter to the sense of apartness ascribed to the religious service, the Shabbat atmosphere and the Sanctuary. That sense ought to be fostered and reinforced. While applauding the golden jubilars might express a sense of family among the congregants, we would counsel against extending such a custom to other occasions. It would be better to discourage all applause for guest artists and speakers *during the worship service itself*, for once we open the door to it there will be a constant problem of distinguishing between the appropriate and the inappropriate.

We would therefore advise that any event which is likely to elicit applause be held *after the conclusion of the prayers*; and then the congregation--having now become an audience--may express itself in the usual manner.[3] A religious service, wherever held, should be an occasion apart, and how much more so a service held in the synagogue.

NOTES

1 His responsum on this matter, which he published not long before his death, set forth the way in which Jewish tradition dealt with the specific halachah regarding the clapping of hands on the Sabbath; see "Applause in the Sabbath Service," TRR (1990), no. 13, pp. 31-34, where rabbinic sources are given. Since tradition forbade music making on the Sabbath, the question arose whether clapping one's hands was a form of rhythmic music; if it was not, it was allowed.

2 During the 1930s the writer of this responsum was present at an Orthodox Rosh Hashanah service in Chicago, during which the congregation repeatedly applauded the chazan.

3 As, for instance, applauding a couple and wishing them mazal tov *after the conclusion of the wedding service.*

New Year's Eve Party on Shabbat in the Synagogue
5753.15

She'elah

This year December 31 falls on Friday, and thus New Year's eve coincides with Shabbat. Many Jews will be tempted to celebrate the secular new year and thereby forsake Shabbat services and observances. What is the religious propriety of hosting a New Year's eve party on Shabbat in the synagogue? (Rabbi Seymour Prystowsky, Lafayette Hill, PA)

Teshuvah

The *she'elah* incorporates two issues. Is it appropriate for a synagogue or a Jewish organization to celebrate the secular New Year? If it is appropriate, what should be done when New Year's eve falls on Shabbat?

1. Celebrating the secular New Year. It is well known that some Orthodox authorities are opposed to any celebration of the secular New Year. In Jerusalem, for example, major hotels have been threatened with a revocation of their *kashrut* license if they hold a New Year's eve party. The opposition to celebrating a non-Jewish festival is based on the Toraitic injunction, "you shall not follow their customs."[1] Talmudic commentators saw in this prohibitions two types of foreign customs: one, any custom that is related to idolatry, and two, any foreign custom that is foolish or superstitious.[2]

Some halachic authorities expanded the rule in order to ensure the separation of Jews from Gentile society.[3] Thus, Maimonides taught:

> Jews should not follow the practices of the Gentiles, nor imitate their dress or their hair styles. . . .The Jew should be distinguished from them and recognizable by the way he dresses and in his other activities, just as he is distinguished from them in his knowledge and his understanding. As it is said, "And I have set you apart from the peoples."[4]

But over the centuries this rigorous judgment has been followed by a minority only, and the definition of what constitutes *chukkat ha-goy* has been reinterpreted.[5]

Some who opposed the celebration of the secular New Year did not want Jews to give the impression that they were observing the Catholic feast of Saint Sylvester,[6] which was celebrated on December 31, and was followed by the Feast of the Circumcision on January 1. (In 1961, the Catholic Church reduced the "Feast of St. Sylvester" to a day of mere commemoration, while the "Feast of the Circumcision" was eliminated altogether.)[7]

It is worth noting that the feasts for December 31 and January 1 were originally created by the Catholic Church as an attempt to overcome the Roman pagan celebrations of those days.[8] Today, when people have festivities on the secular New Year's eve, they are not doing so with any intent to observe a Christian or pagan festival.[9]

Therefore, since Reform, Conservative and modern Orthodox Jews reject the notion that they should be separated and segregated from general society, they need not hesitate to celebrate the civic new year.

2. Celebrating the civic New Year on Shabbat. Inasmuch as our synagogues are not only Houses of Prayer but also Houses of Assembly, and seeing that it is customary to hold social events in the synagogue's social hall, there should be few objections to making it the locus of a New Year's eve party, provided it meets the required standards of moderation and good taste. But may such a party in the synagogue be held on Shabbat?

R. Solomon B. Freehof held that the worshipful mood of Shabbat contrasts too sharply with the hilarity of New Year's eve and said: "Let the joyous New Year party this year be moved to another hall [i.e., outside the temple premises] ... Let the synagogue stand alone and unique as a place of worship."[10]

While this caution needs emphasis, the Responsa Committee believes that the civic new year can be observed on Shabbat, as long as the sacred day's spirit prevails. Indeed, we urge the congregation to explore creative ways to attract Jews to celebrate Shabbat when it falls on December 31. For example, the congregation might consider hosting a more elaborate *Oneg Shabbat;* those attending could listen to Jewish music; or a movie could be shown that is compatible with Shabbat. But the latter, and not New Year's eve should be the dominant focus of the evening.

A further bonus of a Shabbat celebration on New Year's eve would be the presence of a sober, sane and safe environment. While many may choose to forsake the joy of Shabbat for the bacchanalian irreverence of the secular observance, let our Reform congregations offer a sacred alternative.

NOTES

1 Leviticus 18:3.

2 *Tosafot* on BT Avodah Zarah 11a, and see BT Sanhedrin 52b.

3 See *"Chukat Ha'Akum*: Jews in a Gentile Society," *The Journal of Halacha*, vol. I, no. 2, pp. 64-85; *Sefer HaHinnuch: The Book of {Mitzvah} Education* (trsl. C. Wengrow, Jerusalem, 1991), mitzvah 2.

4 Leviticus 20:26; *Yad*, Hilchot Avodah Zarah v'Chukot HaGoyim, 11:1.

5 For details, see our responsum 5751.3, "Blessing the Fleet."

6 He was Pope from 314-335.

7 "Christmas and Its Cycle", *New Catholic Encyclopedia* (New York, 1967), vol. III, 1967, pp. 657-659.

8 The Council of Tours (546 C.E.) declared in its 17th canon that the Church Fathers, "to stamp out the custom of the pagans, imposed a private celebration of litanies of the first of January..." (Alban Butler, *The Lives of the Saints*, Westminster, MD, 1967), vol. I, p.2.

9 R. Moshe Feinstein who was strict about holding a Jewish affair, such as a Bar Mitzvah party, on the day of a Christian festival (lest one should convey even the appearance of apostasy), was, nevertheless, relatively lenient about the secular New Year's celebration; *Igrot Moshe*, EH part 2, no. 13.

10 New Year's Eve Party in the Synagogue,"TRR (1990), p. 25-27.

Memorial Plaques and the Kaddish List:
May a Congregation Cease Reading the Names?
5753.18

She'elah

It is the custom in our congregation at Shabbat services to read aloud prior to the recitation of *kaddish* the names of those whose *yahrtzeit* occurs during that week and whose names are inscribed on the memorial plaques in our sanctuary. The families of the deceased have paid to have these plaques installed and in return have expected that *kaddish* will be recited. Similarly, we read aloud the names of all the deceased members of our congregational family at *yizkor* service on Yom Kippur. We print a memorial book for the occasion; our members contribute to have the names of their loved ones inscribed therein and recited at the service. For how long are we obligated to read the names, particularly if there are no longer mourners for that individual in the congregation? (Rabbi Robert H. Loewy, New Orleans, LA)

Teshuvah

We assume that there is no written contract which specifies the amounts donated by the families and the reciprocal obligations of the congregation. If such a contract existed, it would be obvious that the synagogue would be bound to honor its terms. Yet the fact that no contract exists does not imply that the synagogue is free to cease reading the names inscribed on the memorial plaques. As you describe the case, there is a long-standing custom (*minhag*) in your congregation according to which, in return for the purchase of memorial plaques, families expect that the names of their deceased loved ones will be read in perpetuity at *kaddish* and *yizkor*. The families, in other words, contributed their money *al da`at haminhag*, with the understanding that the custom would be observed and that names would continue to be read. The congregation now wishes to depart from this *minhag*, ostensibly because the reading of long lists of names, especially the names of those whose families no longer belong to the synagogue, has become a tiresome burden to those attending services.

Our response will proceed along two broad lines of inquiry. First, is a synagogue or community entitled according to Jewish law to alter the terms of a gift, whether those terms be defined by contract or by custom, without the consent of the donor? Second, if the synagogue enjoys this power, is it permitted to use that power in this case? Is it the "right" thing to do, or are there ethical and/or policy objections to the congregation's taking that step?

1. May the Synagogue Alter the Terms of a Gift? Jewish tradition grants to the community a broad power to change the terms of a gift, diverting the funds it has received to a purpose other than that specified by the donor, provided that the new purpose is a "higher" one than the old. This is the conclusion reached by R. Asher b. Yechiel, the Rosh (13th-14th century Germany and Spain), who is asked whether funds donated to a synagogue or cemetery may be used instead to support the study of Torah.[1] He answers in the affirmative, citing the tradition which permits the sale of public property or ritual objects, including the synagogue itself, when the proceeds will be used for a higher degree of sanctity.[2] Inasmuch as Torah study is the most sacred of all religious objectives, then surely any existing synagogue monies, including those previously donated toward other ends, may likewise be directed to that purpose.[3] The Rosh is aware that such a decision will not be accepted with equanimity by donors and their relatives, who will complain that the terms of the gift have been altered without their consent. He rules, however, that we may disregard their objections. The Talmud declares that if a Jew donates a ritual object to the synagogue, that object may be sold and its proceeds used for a legitimate religious purpose (*davar mitzvah*). This is true even when the donor's name has not yet been "forgotten."[4] R. Asher's ruling is codified in the *Shulchan Aruch.*[5]

The principle established thereby is that the needs of the community, as determined by the community, take precedence over the desires or stipulations of its individual members. We presume that the members also regard the public good as the highest goal, that they would not object when the community alters the purpose of a gift because it determines that the proceeds can be put to better use than that which was originally intended, and that the minority who do object may be overruled.

According to this theory, we could easily argue that your congregation is entitled to discontinue the reading the *kaddish* list on Shabbat and the *yizkor* list on Yom Kippur. Your congregants may well regard the recitation of these long lists as an unreasonable burden, a *tirchah detzibura,* particularly since many of those memorialized have no relatives or descendants in the synagogue. By ceasing the recitation, you would make the services more aesthetically pleasing, and this would certainly count as a *davar mitzvah,* a legitimate religious purpose, and indeed an *ilu`i kedushah,* the achievement of a "higher" level of sanctity.

In our Reform tradition, aesthetics has long been cited as a justification for many far-reaching liturgical changes. The established *minhag* in our congregations is to permit the community to abandon or to transform ritual practices in the name of improving the worship experience. This is precisely the goal of your congregation when it seeks to discontinue the reading of the *kaddish* and *yizkor* lists. Since these donations were made to a Reform synagogue, it is plausible to maintain that they were given *al da`at haminhag,* with the implicit acceptance of the congregation's right to alter the terms of the gifts for the sake of necessary and desirable improvements in the worship service.[6]

2. Should the Synagogue Discontinue the Recitation of the *Kaddish* and *Yizkor* Lists? On the other hand, even though the congregation is empowered under Jewish law to alter the terms of a gift, some cogent arguments can be made against the use of that power in this case.

First, as R. Asher indicates, the Talmud permits a synagogue community to alter the terms of a gift only if the gift was made by a Jew. If the donor was a Gentile the gift may not be altered, since the resulting dispute would be considered a *chilul hashem,* an embarrassment of the Jewish community in the eyes of its neighbors. This fear does not apply to a donation by a Jew, says the Rosh, because the Jew is likely to accept the rabbinic ruling which permits the alteration of the gift.

Let us now consider this reasoning in light of present-day circumstances. It is not at all obvious that, in our communities, members will be mollified by halachic argumentation allowing a change in the terms of a gift in the absence of the donor's consent. It is more likely that, especially with regard to a gift made in memory of the dead, our people would object rather vociferously to any attempt to alter its terms. The prospect of an embarrassing dispute is quite real, and it is quite possible that the reasoning behind R. Asher's decision is not applicable to our millieu.

Second, a policy that favors public over individual needs, while apparently noble, can be self-defeating. It has long been the practice in Jewish communities to allow individuals to inscribe their names upon ritual objects which they donate to the synagogue. This practice, endorsed by leading authorities,[7] is justified in part on the grounds that it is a good thing to publicize "the deeds of the righteous" as a means of encouraging them and other potential donors to contribute to the community.[8] Were we to deny them the right to inscribe their name upon the donated object, they might very well not donate it at all. In our case, too, it may be argued that if potential donors realize that the terms of their gift might someday be altered without their consent, they will be less likely to contribute. In other words, by favoring the "needs of the community" over the "rights of the individual" we might do injury to both.

Third, it is not necessarily the case that to discontinue the reading of the *kaddish* and *yizkor* lists is a "legitimate religious purpose," let alone the achievement of a "higher level of sanctity." Many of our congregants would perceive this decision as an act of ingratitude toward the memory of the dead, to whom we owe respect, and toward congregational benefactors, to whom we owe the duty to keep our word. To cease reading the names altogether, or to drastically shorten the lists, meets one of these definitions: it is either a *davar mitzvah* or the betrayal of promises made to past generations of our members. The question is: *which* one?

As to the aesthetic arguments you cite in favor of changing your practice, we might respond that not all those in attendance find the reading of lists of names, even lengthy ones, a major interruption in the mood of the service.

The simple piety that is conveyed by the recital of a name can add in a sub-liminal way to the sanctity of the moment. What strikes some as an insuffer-able *tirchah detzibura* may impress others as a solemn act of devotion to the ties that link generation to generation, an acknowledgment of the power of mem-ory which cements our bonds to our predecessors and implants within us a sense of confidence that, as we face the future, we are stronger for the lessons they have taught us.

Conclusion. In sum, a synagogue is permitted to abolish the reading of the *kaddish* or *yizkor* lists altogether, but whether it chooses to do so will depend upon how much weight it assigns to the considerations which argue against this course. If you decide to alter your long-standing custom, we encourage you to replace it with an observance that in some way responds to those considerations. Thus, you might wish to read only the names of those who died during the past month, thereby emphasizing the period of *sheloshim*, and listing on the service card which many congregations prepare for Shabbat the names inscribed on the memorial boards. This may be supplemented by the custom, observed in a number of congregations, of allowing those in attendance to call out the names of those whom they wish to remember. The options are many, and once your congregation decides in principle on this way of solving the impasse, you may arrive at a solution that satisfies almost every-one, or at least the great majority.

NOTES

1 *Resp. HaRosh* 13:14.

2 M Megillah 3:1; BT Megillah 25b-26a.

3 While Torah study (*talmud torah*) is not one of the items listed explicitly M Megilah 3:1, Rosh points to several passages which indicate that *talmud torah* takes precedence over other sacred objects. There is, for example, the Talmud's conclusion that a synagogue can be turned into a school of Torah study (*beit midrash*) while a *beit midrash* may not be turned into a synagogue. (BT Meg. 26b-27a). Moreover, even though the *sefer torah* is listed as the "highest" degree of sanctity in M Meg. 3:1, other passages suggest that the study of Torah is a holier thing than the scroll itself (BT Makkot 22b and Meg. 27a). Rosh concludes that any ritual implement may be sold to support Torah study, "for why does one purchase books and Torah scrolls if not to study them?"

4 That is, everyone knows that "so-and-so donated this candle or lamp to the synagogue"; see BT. Arachin 6b and *Yad*, Hilchot Matanot Aniyim 8:6.

5 YD 259:2-3.

6 See Isserles, YD 259:2: whoever donates to a synagogue does so in accordance with the customary practices of that congregation (*kol demakdish ada`ata deminhag hu makdish*).

7 R. Shelomo b. Adret (Spain, 13th-cent.), *Resp. Rashba*, v. 1, no. 581; Isserles, YD 249:13.

8 Rashba notes that even Scripture engages in this practice. See Genesis 37:21, which recounts Reuben's efforts to save Joseph from death at the hands of his brothers. The Torah, as it were, inscribes the names of the righteous upon their deeds, as a way of encouraging others to follow their example.

Gentile Names on *Yahrtzeit* List
5755.7

She'elah

May the names of deceased parents of a gentile who is married to a Jewish member of the congregation be included in the Temple's yahrtzeit list? If not, may such names which already are included on the list be removed? (Rabbi Douglas Kohn, Hoffman Estates, Illinois)

Teshuvah

The question has been discussed by R. Solomon B. Freehof.[1] In his responsum, he dealt with the question whether gentile visitors to a service should rise for the *kaddish*, and whether there was anything in Jewish tradition contrary to their doing so.

He answered : While the mitzvah to honor father and mother is not one of the seven Noahide commandments, excluding anyone from this act of reverence would needlessly raise inimical feelings on the part of the family. We would therefore caution you to avoid such a likelihood *mipnei darchei shalom* for the sake of peace.

To be sure, R. Freehof's responsum dealt with a passing phase, in that the gentiles participating were only visitors to the synagogue, and the only question that might be asked is whether by including the names of the gentile partner's parents we give further sanction to mixed marriage.

We do not believe that including the names of the gentile spouse's parents will constitute an act of such approval. The couple are de facto members of your congregation, and if the gentile partner wishes to worship in your synagogue s/he is obviously invited and even encouraged to do so. Part of such worship is paying reverence to deceased relatives, and since the *kaddish* contains no proprietary formulation and can be said by anyone without assuming Jewish identity, calling names for whom *kaddish* will be said appears as a proper act of filial piety. *Al achat kama v'chama,* the name(s) should not be removed from the list.

NOTES

1 MRR (1971), p.p. 62 and following.

Christian Jew in the Temple
5753.19

She'elah

One of my congregants, whom I shall call Dave, professes dual religious loyalties. He was born of a Jewish mother, who rejected Judaism and raised him in the Greek Orthodox Church. He is presently a member both of our local Foursquare Church (which he serves as a deacon) and of our Temple (which he serves as a director and chair of the Building and Grounds Committee, and he participates actively in social action work and in the Bible study sessions). He is circumcised, wears *kippa* and *tzitit*, as well as a beard, and dons *tefillin* for his morning devotions.

He considers himself an authentic Jew, and I--as his Rabbi--am satisfied that there is no contradiction in his religious life and therefore find his activities at Temple acceptable and welcome.

However, this satisfaction is not shared by either his pastor (with whom I am otherwise good friends) or by a number of members in my Temple, one of whom has also written to your Committee. My friend, the pastor, "deeply appreciates and admires Dave's dedication and enthusiasm" [in the church] but feels "some discomfort" about it, as do "dissenting voices in his congregation."

My convictions in the matter can be stated as follows:

1) we do not feel that we have the right to "deligitimize" anyone else's Jewishness if his/her expression of Jewishness is rational and sincere;

2) we consider it a credit to our own generation that, for the first time in 1,900 years, it is possible for a person to be a "Christian Jew" without suffering total rejection or even life-threatening violence for practicing such a faith.

The position I have taken has created considerable controversy in my congregation, which has, on occasion, become passionate. While we serve a congregation affiliated with the UAHC, I have an Orthodox ordination. (Rabbi Abraham I. Raich, Santa Maria, CA)

Teshuvah

We will address your two above-noted points in order, for they do indeed touch on the main points at issue.

1. Under traditional halachah, a claim can be made that Dave was born of a Jewish mother, regardless of whether she converted to Greek Orthodoxy before or after he was born. But he would have to acknowledge his Jewishness by his exclusive return to Judaism in order to be accepted in the community. If he was born a Jew but raised as a Christian he would not be considered an apostate; rather he would be like a *tinok*, a babe growing up among Gentiles[1]-a category that was applied to the Karaites.[2] Such a person returns to the community through an affirmation ceremony.

The approach is different under the patrilineal doctrine of the Reform movement, Dave would have to establish his Jewish identity even if his mother had never accepted another faith, for as one born into a mixed marriage he is only presumptively Jewish.[3] Reform would require renunciation of the convert's former faith.[4]

2. There is no question that Dave has rediscovered his roots and has made an effort to live as a Jew in one segment of his existence and has adopted important practices of Judaism. By joining and actively participating in your congregational activities and services he now identifies himself as a Jew. However, though he so identifies himself, we are not constrained to follow suit.

The Jewish people have established rules which categorize one person as Jewish and another as not Jewish. As you yourself state, Dave belongs to that new phenomenon of bi-religious persons who call themselves "Christian Jews." He confesses belief in Judaism and at the same time he is convinced of the authenticity of Christian scriptures.

Like the great majority of our people, Reform Jews have vigorously opposed the claim of "Christian Jews" or "Messianic Jews" to continued Jewish identity, and several of our responsa have spoken to this matter. Thus, in 1981 the Committee said:

Could we...consider a "Messianic Jew" as still a Jew? He may define himself in this manner, but do we? A "Messianic Jew" is one who has designated himself as Jewish, but believes that Jesus of Nazareth is the Messiah and has come to fulfill the messianic promises. By making these assertions that individual has clearly identified himself as a Christian...Unless the young man renounces his belief in Jesus of Nazareth and becomes a Jew rather than a "Messianic Jew," we must consider him a Christian...[5]

We do not question Dave's sincerity and will assume for the moment that he has no intention of inviting members of your congregation to share his dual beliefs. But their worry that he will do so is apparently, and understandably, very real, and it behooves us to respect their desire to safeguard their precious religion. Judaism was, and in today's Diaspora is, an embattled minority that struggles to maintain its pristine identity. Jewish congregations exist to safeguard and enhance and not to dilute it. This is the reason why a number of your members are so disturbed about his presence and activities. We appreciate their concern.

The issue is exacerbated by the fact that Dave has been elected a director and in that capacity becomes a guiding force in your Temple. Furthermore, he participates in your Bible classes and possibly brings to them more learning than many of your congregants. This in turn enhances his status as a "Christian Jew" and legitimizes his syncretistic position.

You say that Dave is concerned about all of this and has offered to resign from the congregation. You do not say, however (nor has his pastor said) that he has offered to resign from the church. In a choice between the two he evidently considers Christianity the more important and, to use the language of "Christian Jews," the more fulfilling.

There is a final point and not the least important. His presence has divided your congregation and threatens it seriously. That in itself should give you and Dave every reason to make the decision which seems to me to be the only one that can be taken: he should voluntarily remove himself from either the congregation or the church. The choice is his, which means that you are

not asked to "deligitimize" him, but you are asked to save the spiritual whole-
ness of your Temple.

<u>NOTES</u>

1 BT Shabbat 68b.

2 *Resp, Radbaz,* II, 796; *Resp. Mabit,* III, 22. In the 19th and twentieth centuries certain
halachic authorities applied this category also to non-Orthodox Jews; see R. Ya'akov Ettlinger, *Resp.
Binyan Tziyon Hachadashot,* no. 23.

3 See the discussion and sources cited in our responsum 5754.13, "Conversion of a Matrilineal
Jew."

4 In the *Rabbi's Manual* (1988), p. 201, the second question asked of the prospective convert
is: "Do you accept Judaism to the exclusion of all other religious faiths and practices?"

5 ARR, p. 473; see also R. Solomon B. Freehof, MRR, no. 30, pp. 169-175.

Gentile Participation in Synagogue Ritual
5754.5

She'elah

What are the traditional and Reform positions on the participation of non-Jews in synagogue services? We are especially interested in the area of ritual and prayer leadership. (Question submitted by the CCAR Committee on Reform Jewish Practice)

Teshuvah

Part of this responsum was based on a study paper prepared by Rabbi Joan Friedman, then of Bloomington, IN. While she was not at the time a member of our Committee, she graciously made her research available to us, but was not responsible for any formulations or conclusions at which this Committee arrived.

INTRODUCTION

During the last quarter of the twentieth century profound changes have taken place in the demography of North American Judaism. The rate of mixed marriage has increased dramatically, with one marriage partner remaining outside the Jewish faith community. When such couples, often with their children, wish to find a synagogue where they can worship and enroll their offspring for a Jewish education, they will most likely turn to Reform congregations, which are sure to welcome and accommodate them.

Since in most congregations the family is the unit of membership, the status of the non-Jewish partners remains frequently undefined, especially when congregational constitutions do not specifically state that members must be of the Jewish religion.[1] But even where the constitution is unequivocal in this respect (as it probably is in the majority of temples), the fact is that emotionally, physically, and financially such families have a stake in the synagogue. They support it; they attend its services; and their children are enrolled in the religious school, where they prepare for bar/bat mitzvah and confirmation. Especially on the latter occasions, questions of parental participation in the celebratory ritual arise and may become the seed bed of conflict. Rabbis are put under pressure to make the widest possible accommodation to the non-Jewish partners, in order to give them a role in the service.

This scenario is paralleled by other developments. The Responsa Committee has lately been asked questions about various kinds of non-Jewish appearances at services (e.g., Resp. 5751.14; 5753.13 and 19). which suggest a worrisome tendency toward increasing syncretism. Our decisions have held that there must be boundaries in order to assure the identity and continued health of our congregations as well as our movement. If we are everything to everyone, we are in the end nothing at all. On this, there is general agreement.

The debate begins when we try to formulate specifics and attempt to determine what is permissible and what is not. For it is not enough to say *yesh gevul*, "there must be boundaries." As our teacher Leo Baeck, *z'l*, reminded us, God is served in small increments. The fabric of Jewish life is woven of single strands.

The *she'elah* does not concern itself with the obvious, that is, with non-Jews attending Jewish services. Worshipping God in a synagogue is not dependent on the worshipper's religion. Rather, the question asks about non-Jews *leading* any part of the service or being called to the *bimah* for any singular participation which at that moment is not available to others.

It is also clear that the *she-elah* assumes that some participation of non-Jews in public ritual is possible. This responsum will consider the principles which would determine the degree and nature of such participation. Hopefully, this will provide a meaningful direction for the Reform movement.

As is our custom, we divide our answer into two parts. We first ask what Jewish tradition, as reflected in many centuries of halachic rulings and debates, has to say on the issue. If indeed there is a body of precedents we inquire whether there are any Reform principles that would lead us to suggest departing from Tradition, and if so, why and to what extent. We begin with Halachah, and then look at it in the light of contemporary insights and requirements.

I. THE VOICE OF TRADITION

When we turn to our traditional sources for guidance in this matter, we find that they do not have a great deal to say about this particular aspect of

Jewish-Gentile relations, because it is not one that would easily have arisen before the modern period. When the Temple still stood in Jerusalem, non-Israelites were permitted limited access to it and were also allowed to make offerings, including sacrifices.[3] These sacrifices, however, unlike the public offerings of the Jewish community, were entirely voluntary.

Until the modern period, non-Jewish attendance at synagogues was rare, for obvious reasons. The only period in which there were significant numbers of non-Jews regularly attending synagogues was the Roman period, when Judaism was fairly widespread in the Empire.[4] It is therefore significant that this question did not arise at that time, which was the very period during which the laws governing Jewish public worship were formalized, including laws concerning participation in public worship.

While an argument from silence is often risky, in this instance it would appear reasonable to infer that the question never arose because even the possibility of active non-Jewish participation was never admitted, and not because it was taken for granted as permitted. Just as in the Temple, participation in the form of offerings was open to all, but officiating was restricted to the *kohanim*. Similarly, participation in the form of attendance and reciting prayers in the synagogue was open to all, but leadership was still restricted, though according to different criteria. We will first consider what those criteria were.

1. Leading a service.

The liturgy of the service consists primarily of blessings and prayers whose recitation is fixed. Recital of the *shema* and its blessings, as well as the *amidah,* is considered a *mitzvah*.[5] In addition, there are individual prayers which, over the centuries, have become standard parts of the service, such as *aleinu*.[6] As such, they are by definition not obligatory upon Gentiles, whom Tradition regards as subject only to the seven Noahide laws. But, though Gentiles are free to worship with Jews, may they *lead* the service, i.e., function as *shelichei tsibbur* even though they are not obligated to recite those prayers? To answer this, we first must examine the function of the *sheliach tsibbur* (often known by the acronym *shats*), the "emissary of the congregation."

Until as late as the tenth century there was a great deal of fluidity in the language of the liturgy (although not in its overall structure). Written copies of the liturgy were rare, and many Jews, if not most, were not familiar enough with the prayers to be able to recite them by themselves. The leader, therefore, read or chanted them and the congregation had only to listen and respond Amen at the proper time, to fulfill their obligation. But the leader had to be a special kind of person. The Mishnah states:

> This is the general principle: One who is not obligated in a matter [of ritual observance] cannot enable others to fulfill their obligation [in that matter]."[8]

Hence, since non-Jews are not so obligated, they do not qualify.[9]

An additional consideration is the emphasis upon communal worship in our tradition. Because of the value placed on community, it has always been considered more meritorious to recite one's prayers with others rather than alone.[10] This is expressed halachically in the principle that certain parts of the liturgy, *devarim shebik'dushah,* "matters which [involve the] holiness [of the divine Name]," may only be recited in public.[11]

For liturgical purposes, "public" as opposed to individual, is defined through the concept of *minyan,* the minimum of ten qualified individuals required for public worship. When ten are present, they are no longer a random collection of individuals, but a community in which God is publicly worshipped.

> From where [do we learn] that an individual does not recite the *kedushah*? As it is said, "that I might be sanctified [*venikdashti*] in the midst of the Israelite people (Lev. 22:32)." All matters of holiness [*devarim shebik'dushah*] should not have fewer than ten present. How is this derived? As Ravnai the brother of R. Hiyya bar Abba taught: from [the word] 'midst' [*toch*] which comes [in two verses, and we interpret them in light of each other]. It is written here, 'that I might be sanctified in the midst of the Israelite people,' and it is written there, 'Separate yourselves from the midst of this community [*edah*]' (Num.16:21)." Just as in the latter [verse *edah* meant] ten, so in the former [verse *b'nei Yisrael* means] ten.[12]

A *minyan* is thus a minirecreation of the entire people of Israel. When a *minyan* is present, God is present. This is the rabbinic understanding of the verse, "God stands in the divine assembly [*edah*]" (Ps.82:1). The constitution of a *minyan* for worship, therefore, is a reaffirmation of the relationship between God and Israel. Within the *minyan*, Israel collectively expresses its relationship with God, and the members of the minyan reaffirm their membership in the covenant community (*b'nei b'rit*). *Minyan* thus defines a Jewish community in a spiritual sense, as opposed to an organizational or institutional sense.

When this spiritual community gathers as such for communal prayer, it must be led by one who is a full member of the community, i.e., one who is obligated to participate in fixed prayer. For this reason Tradition restricted the function of *sheliach tsibbur* to those upon whom it placed the obligation for public worship: free adult Jewish males.

2. Analogies.

While we have no exact precedent in halachic tradition that would respond to our *she-elah,* there are passages that *may* appear analogous. Even though, as we shall point out, their application as precedents for the *she-elah* submitted to us is inappropriate, we shall proceed with an extended exposition of the halachah for the sake of completeness.

In the discussion of *birkat hamazon*, we find the following statement:

> One answers "Amen" after a Jew who blesses, but one does not
> answer "Amen" after a Samaritan [*kuti*] who blesses, unless one
> hears the entire blessing.[15]

This *mishnah* clearly delineates a situation in which a non-Jew specifically, a Samaritan could recite a blessing and a Jew could fulfill a religious obligation by responding "Amen."

At the time when this *mishnah* was written, relations between Jews and Samaritans, despite their hostility, were still closer in many ways than relations between Jews and any other religious/ethnic group. Samaritans were, after all, the only other monotheists in the Greco-Roman world, and possessed the same scripture as the Jews. There was an awareness of their historical links, as well as the reasons for their separation. The rabbis of the mishnaic period therefore were at pains to delineate both the points of contact and divergence.

It was different with Gentiles, who at that time were all pagans of various sorts. During the Middle Ages, however, when Jews lived almost exclusively in Christian or Muslim lands, many areas of halachah concerning relations between Jews and non-Jews were reexamined and often modified, since most Jewish authorities clearly understood that Christians and Muslims were not idolaters in the classic sense. They continued to refer to Christians and Muslims, however, in the same terms which their talmudic predecessors had used for pagans: *goy* (Gentile), *nochri* (stranger, foreigner), or, most commonly, *akum* (acronym for *oved kochavim umazalot,* literally "one who worships stars and constellations").

Bearing these facts in mind, it is significant to find that the trend among rabbinic authorities, especially those living in Christian countries, has been to apply the provisions of the mishnah cited above to non-Jews in general. [17] The following comment by R.Yonah Gerondi (c.1200-1263)[18] is the most articulate statement on the issue:

> "A Samaritan": The reason that if one hears only the mention of God, one is not to respond "Amen" is that perhaps [the Samaritan's] intent is [still] toward *avodah zarah* (idolatry). But if one hears the entire blessing, then one should respond "Amen," since then it is proven that [the Samaritan's] intent was not toward *avodah zarah* when he said the blessing.
>
> And there are those who say that only with a Samaritan may one respond "Amen" after hearing the entire blessing, but not after any other foreigner, since it is certain that they are referring to false gods only; and now, since [the rabbis] have decreed that Samaritans are to be considered like any other foreigners, even if one hears a blessing from their lips, one is not to respond. But it appears to my teacher, may God preserve and bless him, that one should respond even after a foreigner, if one has heard him recite the entire blessing. For since we then see that he is making the blessing in this matter in God's

name, even though he does not really know God, but thinks that his false god is the Creator even so, since his intention was to praise God, and we hear the blessing from his mouth, we answer "Amen."

And a Samaritan in our day is like a foreigner in this regard, and we do respond if we have heard the entire blessing, as it says in the Palestinian Talmud: [19] "R. Berechiah said, 'I answer "Amen" after anyone who blesses, because it is written, "You shall be blessed from all peoples.'(Deut.7:14)."[20] That is to say, he used to answer "Amen" to all the other nations, because the Holy One of Blessing is in the mouths of all nations. And even though they do not recognize him, since their intent is to bless God's name, and we hear the entire blessing from their mouths, we answer "Amen" after them.

So it appears from the language of the *baraita,* "One answers 'Amen' after everyone [reciting a blessing];" for it excludes only children when they are learning [to recite the blessings], for then their intent [in reciting them] is not at all directed to God. [21]

As indicated earlier, we have listed these sources *in extenso* for the sake of completeness, and also because they throw a light on the process of the traditional halachah. When all is said, however, this discussion cannot serve our *teshuvah.* For it teaches only what to do *after* a Gentile has blessed the name of God. It is a matter of *bedi'avad,* something that has already happened, and likely by chance. R. Yonah Gerondi and R. Asher b. Yechiel (and followed by Isserles)[22] rule that we say "Amen" if we have heard the entire blessing, because at that point we are certain that his intent was toward God and not toward a pagan deity. After all, what he has said is true, and "Amen" is our attestation to the truth.

Yet we cannot infer from this that the "Amen" which we pronounce *bedi'avad,* after we have heard a Gentile's blessing, can serve as an analogy *lechatchilah* (before it is spoken). It does not treat of the subject with which we are concerned, for it says nothing about a Gentile being invited to say the blessing so that we may respond "Amen."

The logical impossibility of using these cases as a precedent in such situations is highlighted by a passage in the *Mishnah Berurah*. [23] There we find that the logic of the above-noted permission to respond "Amen" applies even when the blessing has been spoken by an apostate Jew (assuming that his intent, too, is toward the Creator). Clearly, such a ruling would never have been made *lechatchilah*. In fact, the *Aruch HaShulchan* states specifically that none of this applies to a situation when a Gentile recites a fixed *berachah*, but only when he has simply declared the praise of God. [24]

3. The public reading of Torah.

The *locus classicus* for the definition of which liturgical functions require a *minyan* is Mishnah Megillah 4:3, which explicitly includes the public reading of Torah among those functions. It did not necessarily follow, however, that only members of the *minyan* could participate in the actual reading of the Torah, and a *baraita* states:

> All may come up as part of the seven [Torah readers on Shabbat morning], even a minor or a woman; but our Sages say that a woman should not read for the sake of the honor of the congregation.[25]

It must be remembered that in the Tannaitic era the seven readers actually read from the scroll, but did not necessarily recite a blessing. The first reader recited the blessing before reading Torah; the seventh reader recited the concluding blessing.[26] The Amoraim changed this practice to require each reader to say both blessings.[27] Eventually the practice changed again, to what we are familiar with: a trained reader does the actual reading, and the seven people called to the Torah recite only the blessings.

What, exactly, is the status of public Torah reading in the hierarchy of *mitzvot*? Its origin sets it apart from the other practices in that it began as a form of public education and information, which only gradually became formalized and ritualized. This distinction becomes clear when we consider that the blessing *asher kid'shanu be-mitsvotav vetzivanu la'asok be-divrei torah* is not recited for the public Torah reading. It was, however, understood as a *takanah*, which obligated people to hear it.[28]

Since the Torah reading takes place in a liturgical context, it was inevitable that many of the same considerations came to be applied to it. The most obvious was the exclusion of women. A related consequence was that those called up for *aliyot* (that is, to recite the blessings while another person does the actual reading) were required to be members of the *minyan*.[29] Although the authorities differ among themselves on whether a boy may be called for an aliyah, there is agreement that in order to read he must have reached his majority. [30]

Summary.

Halachic tradition considers participation in communal ritual as an outflow of obligation. The absence of obligation disqualifies a Jew from leading the congregation as a *sheliach tzibbur*.

By long-standing practice, being called to the *bimah* for an *aliyah* partakes of the same principle.

II. REFORM PERSPECTIVES

1. General observations.

In its 180 years of development, the Reform movement has gone through a number of stages. It began in Europe with a pervasive concern for halachic precedent, a concern that never left it up to the destruction of continental Jewry. It remains clearly visible in the reconstituted communities as well as in the United Kingdom, and especially in its vigorous expression in Israel.

In North America, however, in a frontier environment with its loosening of traditional bonds, the movement lost many of its halachic moorings. But during the last generation, spurred on by the efforts of Rabbis Solomon B. Freehof and Walter Jacob, the presence of a developing Liberal Halachah has become evident. The CCAR's Responsa Committees were entrusted to give it voice.

During these decades the question to which our *she'elah* addresses itself has faced previous Committees in one form or another.

Thus, in 1969, R. Freehof was asked whether a non-Jewish stepfather of a bar mitzvah might receive an *aliyah* and recite Torah blessings. He suggested that the Jewish grandfather should do it instead.[31]

In 1979, the Responsa Committee was asked by the Committee on Education: "To what extent may non-Jews participate in a Jewish public service?" The answer touched on the status of non-Jews as *b'nei noach* and *gerei tzedek* and went on to say:

> We have invited non-Jews, including ministers and priests, to address our congregations during our public services...In addition, nowadays, because of intermarriage, we find the non-Jewish parent involved in a Bar/Bat Mitzvah. It would be appropriate to have that parent participate in some way in the service, but not in the same way as a Jewish parent. For example, he or she should not recite the traditional blessing over the Torah...(The Committee recommended that, instead, a special English prayer might be read by the Gentile.)

The Committee went on to speak of "essential elements of the service" which should be reserved exclusively for Jews.

> Non-Jews who fall into the category of *b'nei noach* may participate in a public service in any of the following ways: (1) through anything which may not require a specific statement from them, i.e., by standing silently witnessing whatever is taking place (e.g., as a member of a wedding party or as a pall bearer); (2) through the recitation of special prayers added to the service at non-liturgical community-wide services, commemorations, and celebrations (Thanksgiving, etc.); through the recitation of prayers for special family occasions (Bar/Bat Mitzvah of children raised as Jews, at a wedding or funeral, etc.). All such prayers and statements should reflect the mood of the service and be non-Christological in nature.[32]

In 1980, R. Freehof answered a question whether a Gentile might bless the Shabbat candles or recite the Kiddush. He answered in the negative.[33]

We will not here rehearse the principles which have become self-evident in these and in the many hundreds of responsa which have been issued over the last forty years. They advise the questioner of the view of Tradition and then ask whether there are overriding principles to which Reform subscribes which would counsel diverging from halachic precedents. For Liberal Judaism has always seen itself as part of the total flow of historic Jewish life, and its Responsa Committees have tried to maintain this connection.

Therefore, the fact that certain terms and categories of Jewish tradition are no longer familiar to most Reform Jews is a regrettable fact but in itself not decisive for the decisions we reach. It is the task of our Committee to make it clear whence we came, so that we may more securely decide where we should go.

Thus, such categories as *sheliach tzibbur* or *chiyuv* (obligation) are not on the tongues of most of our members, but they belong to the underpinnings of the very traditions upon which our movement is founded. For that reason, we have taken pains to expose them in some detail.

We live in a time of unprecedented religious freedom - a freedom that not only allows Jews to exercise their religion without restraint, but also to choose the level on which they want to be Jewish (or, for that matter, choose not iden- tify with their religion at all). The lure of a secular, non-particularistic, level- ing environment is for many Jews irresistible. The increasing incidence of mixed marriages adds to the undeniable fact that Jewish identity is being seri- ously eroded.

Questions which are asked of the Responsa Committee may appear to many Reform Jews as marginal or even irrelevant to their lives. This increas- es, rather than diminishes our responsibility. We see it as our task to stem the tide of *hefkerut*, and to cast the growth and development of our movement into a framework of continuity rather than sectarian separation. If each Jew makes *Shabbes* for him/herself, in the end no one will make *Shabbes* at all.

2. The *sheliach tzibbur* in Reform Jewish life.

It is generally understood that the rabbi has the function of leading the congregation in worship. While in theory every Jew should be capable of doing this, in practice it is the rabbi who holds the service together and gives it leadership. A similar function is assigned to the cantor, who will lead the congregation in singing and to whose recitation of prayers it will listen.

Reform Jews (like other Jews) regard these positions with special respect, even though the terminology of earlier days is no longer current or even fully understood.

Therefore, when Jews assemble for prayer and ask a rabbi or cantor to lead them, they do so in the time-honored way of placing *shelichei tzibbur* into positions of special responsibility. They represent the community and guide it in carrying out its religious obligations.

What then about the fact that in many congregations (and in earlier days, in nearly all of them) non-Jewish choristers and soloists have occupied positions which seemed to make them into *shelichei tzibbur*?

We note this fact with regret and consider it an anachronism for our time and, in retrospect, an historical error.[34] Yet we would claim that even when Gentile choirs were quite common in our temples, there was a vestige of embarrassment about that fact. How else would we explain the strange dichotomy: that the same choristers in their own Christian congregations sang as proud members of the congregation and guided it in worship, and could not only be heard but also be seen doing it. However, in Reform synagogues these same singers were carefully hidden away in choir lofts or behind screens, as if the purpose was to produce beautiful music which came from unidentified, unseen persons. One listened, so to speak, to the music and not to those who made it.

It is further noteworthy that even when the Gentile soloist stood on the *bimah*, s/he was never identified as "cantor" and certainly not as *chazan/chazzanit*. Those terms were reserved for Jews. R. Freehof ruled that Gentile choristers were not to be considered *shelichei tsibbur*.[35]

What all of this says is that the employment of Gentile singers cannot and should not be a Reform precedent for us. There may have been historical reasons for their introduction - such as the absence of equivalent musical personnel who were Jewish - but those reasons have disappeared. Even when their presence was commonplace, they were always seen as apart from the congregation. Their voices provided lovely music - but they, as persons, were never considered representatives of those present. They enhanced the esthetic environment, but they were not part of the congregation who prayed and, most important, they were not expected to pray with it. They were there to sing, and nothing else.

It is no accident that while in their Christians churches they led the congregation in singing, they did not so in our temples. We *listened* to them; and many is the rabbi or cantor who has testified to the difficulty of turning a listening congregation toward active participation in the service.

We repeat: the phenomenon of non-Jewish choristers is on its way out. It represents a phase of Reform history which no longer can serve as precedent for our *teshuvah*. The *shelichei tzibbur* must be members of the covenant community and they cannot yield this responsibility to outsiders.

3. The Torah reading and ritual.

As with regard to the *sheliach tzibbur* so here, too, the possibility of a non-Jew participating in the public Torah reading is simply beyond the pale of Tradition's imagination. Can we extrapolate from this to find an answer to our concerns?

The answer lies in the traditional acknowledgment that the public reading of Torah is an essential community act.

> Moses our teacher ordained that Israel should read from Torah
> publicly at the morning service on Shabbat, Monday, and
> Thursday, so that they would not allow more than three days to
> pass without hearing Torah.[36]

Participation in the Torah reading is one of the most potent symbols of inclusion in the Jewish community. It was precisely for that reason that Jewish women had to fight twenty years ago not only for the right to be called to the Torah and to read from it, but even to carry or even touch the scroll. The same emotional response is behind the new "tradition" of passing the Torah from family member to family member to the bar or bat mitzvah. Access to the Torah symbolizes full inclusion in the Jewish community. That is precisely why bar/bat mitzvah is celebrated in the way it is.

For this reason a non-Jew should not be called to the Torah for an *aliyah*. The reading of the Torah requires the presence of a community, because it is one of the central acts by which the community affirms its reason for existence, i.e., the covenant whose words are contained within the scroll. To be called to the Torah is to take one's position in the chain of privilege and responsibility by which the Jewish community has perpetuated itself. A non-Jew, no matter how supportive, does not share that privilege or that responsibility as long as s/he remains formally outside the Jewish community.

In many congregations the pressure to grant non-Jews *aliyot* comes in connection with the celebration of a bar/bat mitzvah. The reasons for this may be found in the ways our movement has both deliberately and unintentionally given the public Torah reading an altogether different context and meaning than the one just outlined. Relieving this pressure, therefore, is for this Committee not merely a matter of issuing clear guidelines; it is also a matter of reeducating our people to the real significance of what they are doing.

First, we must acknowledge the extent to which our movement removed the Torah reading from the public. The "Ritual Directions" in I. M. Wise's *Divine Service of American Israelites for the Day of Atonement,* for example, state:

> The sections from the Pentateuch are read in a style agreeable to modern delivery <u>and without calling any person to it</u> [emphasis added]. The minister and two officers of the congregation have to do all the *mitzvot* connected therewith.[37]

While this practice, which was widespread, may have greatly added to the decorum of the service and reduced its length, it also ensured that the individual congregant had little personal access to the Torah scroll, and learned not to view an *aliyah* as something which the regular worshipper should be honored to do. This process was reinforced for some generations by the devaluation of bar mitzvah. Thus, any common understanding of the significance of the public Torah reading atrophied, and in some cases, disappeared altogether.

Second, in far too many of our congregations, so little Torah is read, and in such a disjointed fashion, that our congregants have little or no context in which to comprehend the ritual they are watching. Most of our people, even if they attend services weekly, do not perceive the Torah as a continuous whole, which is read in a particular order and in a particular fashion. How can they, when in the vast majority of cases perhaps they hear ten verses read, excerpted randomly from the week's portion (except in parts of Leviticus, which some congregations skip completely)?

In addition, although many congregations have re-appropriated various degrees of traditional observance, the aesthetic element all too often takes precedence over the spiritual: rituals are seen to "enhance" our religious lives. Thus, any ritual becomes fair game for "enhancing" the experience of the congregation — including non-Jewish participation, if that end is served thereby.

Finally, there is the problem of bar/bat mitzvah itself. The vast majority of our children now celebrate the event. However, many of our congregations hold Shabbat morning services only when there is a bar/bat mitzvah, and in these instances many Reform Jews have come to think that a Shabbat morning service at which Torah is read is a "bar mitzvah service" — in fact, that it is "the child's and the family's service." In their eyes it resembles other family occasions, such as *b'rith milah,* engagement or wedding celebrations, where the family chooses the participants.

Since this is the popular context, it is easy to see why so many of our people consider it quite natural that non-Jews, and especially a non-Jewish parent, should be asked to take an active part on this occasion as well.

It is the view of this Committee that it is essential to preserve or recover the central elements of the Jewish service. Our members may not know the traditional categories we have adumbrated, but the rabbis should use every occasion to make them understood. Their observance safeguards the integrity of the congregation whose members are and remain representatives of the total community of Jews.

This view in no way denigrates the non-Jews in our midst. We should of course be sensitive to the Gentile parents who are committed to raising their children as Jews, and to acknowledge their commitment, but do so without violating the community's integrity.

The nature of our service can and must be communicated to them with full respect for their integrity. While they have chosen to remain non-Jews, the congregation chooses to be Jewish and sets the parameters of its services.

A child who prepares for bar/bat mitzvah must be taught to appreciate that there are boundaries and rules. They pertain to personal as well as communal life, and parents know this as a fundamental premise of education. It speaks to the essence of a child's maturation, of growing into adulthood. Are Reform Jewish parents different in that they should not teach their offspring that there are standards which define who we are, what sets us apart and lends meaning to what we do as Jews?

What the congregation can accord the Gentile worshipper is proximity and recognition. There is no reason why a non-Jewish parent should not accompany the Jewish parent to the *bimah* when the latter is called for an *aliyah*. There are ways by which the non-Jewish parent may express his/her sentiments and make them meaningful to child and congregation. Boundaries of this sort will help the celebrant understand that the sacred occasion is observed with full respect both to Jewish tradition and to the non-Jews in the child's family.[38]

There has been some discussion whether the rules enunciated above pertain also to the *aliyot* of *hagbahah* and *g'lilah*. After all, it might be argued, believing Christians too respect the Torah as part of their tradition - why then should they not be permitted to lift the scroll high and acknowledge their respect thereby?

We give the same answer because a principle is at stake: *aliyot* are reserved for the Jewish members of the worshipping congregation. In addition, there is the matter of *mar'it ayin*, that is, the question how an otherwise well-intentioned act is perceived by others. Worshippers will be hard put to make a distinction between one type of *aliyah* and another; therefore it is better to keep the lines clear, so that the essential elements of integrity and obligation not be obscured.

4. A final observation.

Many of the questions we have addressed arise in connection with bar/bat mitzvah celebrations. We are cognizant that frequently they will be seen by many if not most of those attending as a symbolic *rite de passage*. This will be especially true for celebrations in congregations which ordinarily have no

Shabbat morning service. For them, to put it boldly, the service is all too often a form of religious theatre, with actors filling prescribed roles. In Shakespeare's plays, men played the role of women; here, youngsters play the scholar - so why should non-Jews not assume the role of Jews? After all, for many participants, a "bar/bat mitzvah service" is merely a symbolic performance.

But in our view, while religious services may use symbols they are not in themselves symbolic exercises. Whether arranged specially or whether they are weekly observances, our religious services must afford those who attend an opportunity to stand in the presence of the Living God, and do so as a covenantal congregation. True, such a service may fall short of its goal, and many a service may verge on "performance" - but we may not take these aberrations as excuses to alter the very nature of Jewish worship, where despite all obstacles, the essential element of mitzvah must not be lost sight of.

There will be individuals, perhaps many of them, who will have their own reaction patterns, but it is the congregation's task to place the celebration on the common ground of Jewish tradition. That common ground, with all the respect we have for the non-Jewish parent's sensitivity, must first and foremost be the way in which a Jewish congregation expresses its love for God, Torah and Israel. It is a community in which the young person affirms his/her membership, and that community too needs constant reaffirmation and strengthening.

At the same time we treat the non-Jews in our midst with full sensitivity. They are welcome amongst us; we welcome their support and will help them to fulfill their needs as much as possible within the limits possible. (For example see footnote 38.) We are confident that in this spirit they in turn will respect our needs in these changing times.

Also, we must make a clear distinction between Jewish worship service in the narrow sense of the word, and religious observances which by definition include participation of Gentiles. Such special events as communal Thanksgiving service, held in many parts of the United States, are of a different hue. Such services do not, as such, fall under the strictures we have delineated.

A brief word should also be said on congregational membership. Where the constitution of the synagogue is not specific on the subject, Gentiles have

obtained membership as partners in a family unit. Some congregations therefore conclude that all who have the legal status of members must be entitled
to all religious privileges as well. We would disagree. Religious membership
is not the same as synagogue membership. The latter is the outflow of an institutional arrangement, the former a spiritual and historic category. Therefore,
even where non-Jewish spouses of Jews are considered full temple members,
their religious privileges and obligations derive from sources other than congregational by-laws and partake of the limitations set out above.

We are aware that there are differing views of the nature of Jewish worship and much that pertains to it.[39] However, in the view of this Committee,
there is a clear and present danger that our movement is dissolving at the
edges and is surrendering its singularity to a beckoning culture which cham-
pions the syncretistic. Jewish identity is being eroded and is in need of clear
guide lines which will define it unmistakably. To provide such markers is the
task of the Responsa Committee.[40]

The she'elah to which we responded came to us from the Reform Practices
Committee of the CCAR We hope that the Committee will create liturgical
opportunities which will reflect the principles we have discussed and thereby
provide our movement with further guidance in this complex area of Jewish
existence.

NOTES

1 See further below.

2 Rabbi Edwin Friedman describes such tensions when the parents have split up: "Bar Mitzvah
When the Parents Are No Longer Partners," Journal of Reform Judaism, Spring 1981.

3 The outermost courtyard of the Temple in Jerusalem was sometimes called the "Court of the
Gentiles," since they were not allowed to enter the innermost precincts. On contributions of sacrifices
by non-Jews see BT Menachot 73b; Yad, Ma'aseh Hakorbanot 3:2-3; also Encyclopedia Judaica 15:979,
"Temple".

4 Evidence for the attendance of large numbers of Gentiles interested in Judaism who regularly
attended synagogue comes, for example, from the letters of Paul in the New Testament. See also Salo
Baron, A Social and Religious History of the Jews, 2nd ed. (New York: Columbia University Press, 1962),
vol. I, pp. 171ff.

5 M Berachot, chapters 1 and 2, passim. The question of the exact nature of the mitzvah of the
tefillah is a complicated one, but does not need to be discussed for the sake of the issue at hand.

6 Aruch Ha-Shulchan, OC 133:1: "After U-va le-Tsiyon the shatz recites the Kaddish Titkabal, since

the Prayer is finished. However, it has been our practice to say following it the great praise of *Aleinu le-shabbe'ach*, of which the early authorities said that Joshua ben Nun instituted it at the conquest of Jericho. And the Ari of blessed memory cautioned that it should be recited following every Prayer, aloud and standing, joyously..."

7 Maimonides, *Yad*, Hilchot Melachim 8:10-11; 9:1.

8 *M* Rosh Hashanah 3:8.

9 This principle is at the crux of the Conservative movement's debates over women in the *minyan* and the investiture of women as cantors.

10 E.g.: "Said the Blessed Holy One: Everyone who engages in Torah and in the practice of deeds of loving kindness and who prays with the community —I consider such persons as if they had redeemed Me and My children from among the nations." (BT Berachot 8a)

11 BT Berachot 21b; BT Megillah 23b; *ShA* OC 55:1 The *Aruch HaShulchan* sums it up: "All matters of holiness [*kol davar shebik'dushah*] are impossible with fewer than ten free (thus excluding slaves), male, adult Jews. And therefore for *kaddish*, *kedushah*, and *barechu*, are not said if there are not ten; for the Shechinah dwells with the presence of ten." (OC 55:6)

12 BT Berachot 21b, and a fuller version Megillah 23b. Numbers 16:21 needs to be understood in the light of Num.14:26, "How long shall that wicked community [*edah*] keep muttering against Me?,"-referring to the ten spies who brought back evil reports of the Land of Israel. Thus, ten constitute an *edah*, and God is sanctified in the midst of an *edah*, which is like the whole people of Israel.

13 BT Berachot 6a.

14 Except for one who is an onen, i.e., who has just suffered the death of one of the seven immediate relatives for whom one is obligated to mourn, but the burial has not yet taken place. Such a person is not obligated to perform positive mitzvot, and hence cannot aid others to fulfill their obligations. (see *Sh.A.* YD 341:1).

15 *M* Berachot. 8:8.

16 For an excellent analysis of this process in Christian lands, see Jacob Katz, *Exclusiveness and Tolerance: Jewish-Gentile Relations in Medieval and Modern Times* (New York: Schocken Books, 1969).

17 Maimonides (*Yad*, Berachot 1:13) prohibits responding to either a Samaritan or an *akum*, under which heading he subsumes all Gentiles, although he exempts Islam (*Yad*, Ma'achalot Asurot 11:7 and *Teshuvot HaRambam*, ed. Freiman, no.369). On the other hand, he was less generous toward Christians, with their religious statuary and concept of the Trinity (see the uncensored editions of *Yad*, Avodah Zarah 9:4), probably following B. Avodah Zarah 6a and 7b, which in all MSS and in the Rashi of some of the old printed editions read our *yom echad* as *yom notzri* or *notzrim*,

R. Isaac Or Zarua of Vienna (12th- 13th century), an adherent of the pietist Hasidei Ashkenaz, also held it forbidden (*Halachot* of Alfasi to Berachot, 40a, *Shiltei haGibborim* 4). However, both Rabbenu Asher and his son R. Jacob ben Asher, author of the *Tur*, declare it permissible to answer "Amen" after a nochri ("foreigner") as long as one as heard God's name mentioned (Ibid.). In the *Shulchan Aruch* (1575), R. Joseph Karo states only that one may not respond to a *kuti*; R.Moses Isserles in his gloss adds explicitly that one does respond after an akum (by this time, just a generic term for gentiles) if one hears the entire blessing (*Sh.A.* OC 215:2). The most authoritative modern commentary on this section of the *Shulchan Aruch*, by R. Israel Meir Kagan ("the Hafetz Hayim"), written around 1900, agrees with Isserles on the grounds that when a gentile mentions God, s/he is not referring to an idol or a false god; but he also notes that an earlier commentator on the same law declared that responding after a gentile was only optional (*Mishnah Berurah* to OC. 215:2).

If one analyzes all these and other references, one sees that while a wide range of attitudes toward the religiosity of non-Jews is expressed, the trend is mostly toward acceptance. This is true even if we allow for the fact that any of these sources may have read slightly differently in original form: terms such as *kuti* and *akum* (instead of *goy*) were very often inserted by Christian censors from the sixteenth century onward.

18 R.Yonah is known as a halachist (his comments on Alfasi's *Halachot* are included in the standard editions of the latter), an early kabbalist (he was a cousin and an associate of Nahmanides), and a pietist (his famous ethical treatise is called *sha'arei Teshuvah*, "Gates of Repentance"). His fundamental conservatism was revealed in his active participation in the so-called Maimonidean controversy, on the side opposing Maimonides' philosophical thought. Furthermore, his formative years were spent studying in the *yeshivot* of southern France during the period when the Cathars (Albigensians) flourished there, and when the Church launched its Crusade against them. The spearhead of this crusade was the Dominican Order, to which the pope entrusted the Holy Office, better known as the Inquisition, which soon broadened its investigations of "heresy" to writings by Jews. R.Yonah, in other words, lived in a time and place where the Catholic Church, out of its desire for internal reform, was beginning to take serious and organized action against rabbinic literature. While it is not certain that the Dominican Inquisitors actually burned Maimonides' works in Montpellier in 1232, a huge quantity of manuscripts of the Talmud were burned in Paris in 1244 under their auspices, at the order of King Louis IX ("St.Louis"); and in 1263 Nahmanides was forced to debate the friars (led by the Jewish apostate, Pablo Christiani) before King James of Aragon in Barcelona. R.Yonah's statement is the more noteworthy when placed in this context.

19 YT Berachot 8.

20 An unusual understanding of the Hebrew, which is ordinarily rendered as "above" all peoples.

21 R.Yonah Gerondi in his commentary on Alfasi, *Halachot*, Ber.40a, s.v.*Onin amen achar yisrael hamevarech*. R.Yonah's commentary was redacted by one of students. When he speaks of R. Yonah's teacher as one of the most vociferous of Maimonides' opponents, it is likely that R. Yonah himself is meant.

22 *Sh A*. OC 215:2.

23 15:12.

24 OC 215:3.

25 BT Megillah 23a.

26 M Megillah 4:1-2.

27 BT Megillah 21b. This is the procedure prescribed by Maimonides, *Yad,* Hilchot Tefillah 12:5.

28 *Massechet Sofrim* 18:4; Be'er Hetev to *Sh. A.* OC 282:2. A takanah, literally "remedy," was a rabbinic ordinance, introduced as a measure to improve the public welfare. Since the thrice-daily recitation of the tefillah is itself a *takanah*, it partakes of the obligation; see *Yad*, Tefillah 1:5. The Rambam's source is BT. Baba Kama 82a.

29 The end result of this evolution is amply demonstrated in the lengthy discussion of the phrase *ha-kol olin le-minyan shiv'ah* found in the *Aruch Ha-shulchan*, OC 282:9-11. The phrase refers to being called to the Torah to recite the blessings while another person reads. The same is also true of the briefer pronouncement in the *Sh.A.* OC 282:2.

30 *Ibid.*

31 "Gentile Stepfather at Bar Mitzvah," CRR, no. 23, pp. 91-93.

32 ARR, no. 6, pp. 21-24.

33 "Gentiles' Part in the Sabbath Service," NRR, no. 7, pp.33-36.

34 Walter Jacob, CARR, no. 132, pp. 195-196, deals with this subject and says: "Despite their

[the choristers'] frequent use we feel that every effort should be made to use a Jewish choir...the kavvanah of such a choir will add beauty to the service." While he would allow their participation in songs which are not essential to Jewish belief or practice, this caution is surely honored only in the breach.

35 *Reform Jewish Practice*, vol. II, p.71.

36 *Yad*, Hilchot Tefillah 12:1.

37 Cincinnati: Bloch, 1891.

38 Rabbi Alexander M. Schindler, president of the Union of American Hebrew Congregations, wrote on December 7, 1993, in a letter his Board of Trustees , clarifying the intent of his address to the Union Biennial which had been held in San Francisco:

> We should be as welcoming as possible, yet boundaries need to be drawn...My colleague [Rabbi] Norman Cohen of Hopkins, MN, established a pattern which concretizes to a "T" what I have in mind:
>
> When a non-Jewish spouse is supportive of the Jewish upbringing of the children, he involves them in a number of ways in the Bar/Bat Mitzvah ceremony. While the non-Jewish partners do not actually pass the Torah, they stand with the Jewish spouse and Norman says to them quite clearly: 'The Torah is passed from your grandparents to your mother who, with the loving support of your father, passes it on to you.' And when the Jewish parent is invited to do the Torah blessing, the non-Jewish parent stands with him/her and recites the following words:
>
> 'My prayer, standing at the Torah, is that you, my son/daughter will always be worthy of this inheritance as a Jew. Know that you have my support. Take its teachings into your heart and, in turn, pass it on to your children and those who come after you. May you be a faithful Jew, searching for wisdom and truth, working for justice and peace.'
>
> In this and like manner, we can meet our two-fold obligations: to be true to the integrity of of our tradition, even as we respond to the sensitivities of those non-Jews who have not yet embraced Judaism, but who nonetheless have agreed, and indeed are determined, to rear their children as Jews.

39 Rabbi Lawrence A. Hoffman has occupied himself extensively with the nature of Jewish prayer. He speaks of categories such as "multivocality" and "performative liturgy." The bottom line of his argument may be stated as follows:

> If a congregation sees a ritual as an affirmation of its covenantal status, the ritual is reserved for Jews, and for Jews only. But if it is symbolic and affirms the spiritual worth of the participant, whether Jew or non-Jew, we may insist that all parents say it, especially a non-Jewish parent who had an easy option of denying this child's Jewish education, but did not do so. See "Non-Jew and Jewish Life-Cycle Liturgy," in *Journal of Reform Judaism*, Summer 1990, pp. 1-16. (Rabbi W. Gunther Plaut wrote a response to his exposition, *ibid.*, pp. 17-20.) See also R. Hoffman's "Worship in Common: Babel or Mixed Multitude?" in *Crosscurrents: Journal of the American Association for Religion and Intellectual Life*, 40:1 (Spring 1990).

40 Rabbi A. Stanley Dreyfus would be more accommodating to non-Jews, especially with regard to *birchot nehenin*. In view of rising mixed-marriages, he calls for such accommodation as a much needed "heroic measure."

Non-Jewish Parent as Member of Synagogue
5755.10

She'elah

Our congregation's by-laws enable the non-Jewish spouse of a Temple member to be classified as a Temple member. That non-Jewish member enjoys all membership privileges, except for holding office, voting in a congregational election, and performing ritual functions appropriate only for Jews. In the event of the death or divorce of the Jewish spouse, the non-Jewish husband or wife can continue membership if he or she so wishes. This provision was established so that the children of that marriage could continue to receive a Jewish religious education in our congregation.

Recently, a non-Jewish woman, who was married to a Jew, contacted us about joining our congregation, because at the time of her marriage she had promised to raise her children as Jews. According to our by-laws, however, because she was not a member at the time of her marriage she cannot become a member now. We also cannot grant membership to the children, since one must be eighteen years of age or older in order to join our congregation.

By denying her membership, however, we are failing to provide a religious education for her children. Is there any membership status that we can confer upon this woman so that she can fulfill her promise to raise her children as Jews? (Rabbi Samuel M. Stahl, San Antonio, TX)

Teshuvah

Granted that neither the mother nor her children qualify for synagogue membership under your by-laws, the congregation nonetheless bears a certain responsibility for the Jewish education of these young people.[1] According to tradition, the father is obligated to teach his child Torah[2] or to engage others to do so[3] (Naturally, we Reform Jews hold that this obligation is incumbent upon the mother as well as the father).[4] Should he refuse to perform this mitzvah, tradition says further, he can be coerced to fulfill his responsibility; that is, the *beit din* can seize his assets in order to provide a teacher for the child.[5] The case can be made, moreover, that in the event the parent does not meet this responsibility, the obligation falls upon the community. We find this to be the case with *milah,* another of the obligations of the father toward the son which the Talmud specifies: if the father does not discharge this duty, the court—that is, the community—must see that the boy is circumcised.[6] The community, in other words, stands *in loco parentis*. In the case before us, these children, represented by their mother,[7] have come before the congregation and asked that they be taught Torah. It would appear that you have a duty to accept them.

This does not mean that any *one* synagogue or community is obligated to accept more than its fair share of these difficult cases. On the other hand, this family has come to you; as such, your congregation carries a special responsibility toward them. We have recently addressed the question of physicians and the treatment of indigent patients. We concluded that, while doctors in a community may make any and all reasonable arrangements concerning medical treatment for the poor, the fact remains that when a person comes to a particular physician and asks for medical care, that patient should not be refused due to inability to pay.[8] The same reasoning, we suspect, applies to this case.

Having said this, how can the children be admitted to religious school when according to your congregation's by-laws neither they nor their mother qualify for membership in the Temple? We suggest the following interpretation of the rule. The mother should have the same associative status that she would enjoy were she married: she can be a "member" in the same way that she would be a "member" were she married to a Jew. Once the congregation has accepted its responsibility to educate the children, they become, if not "members", then certainly part and parcel of your congregational community. Their mother's membership would flow through them just as it would flow through a Jewish spouse. We might put this another way: were this woman a member of your congregation prior to her divorce, she would, on account of her children, retain her membership, following the divorce. In our case, since this woman has accepted upon herself the obligation to see to the Jewish education of her children, she is entitled to associate membership "so that the children of that marriage could continue to receive a Jewish religious education in our congregation."

We therefore believe that your congregation can fulfill its Jewish religious duty toward these children without transgressing the letter or spirit of its by-laws.

NOTES

1 Under the CCAR's resolution on Patrilineal Descent, the children enjoy a presumption of Jewish status. This presumption can be established "through appropriate and timely public and formal acts of identification with the Jewish faith and people." Torah study is regarded as one such act. See the text of the resolution in ARR, 550.

2 BT. Kiddushin 29a; *Yad*, Hilchot Talmud Torah 1:1; *Sh.A.*, YD 245:1.

3 *Yad*, Hilchot Talmud Torah 1:3; *Sh.A.*, YD 245:4.

4 For a Reform analysis of the traditional attitude to the study of Torah by women, see our responsum 5755.15, "Woman As a Scribe."

5 Isserles, *Sh.A*, YD 245:4.

6 BT. Kiddushin 29a; *Sh.A*, YD 261.

7 We should note that the mother, as a non-Jew, bears no halachic obligation to teach her children Torah, although she makes this request in fulfillment of a promise she made to their father, her former husband.

8 See our responsum 5754.18, "Must a Physician Treat Indigent Patients?"

Apostate in the Synagogue
5753.13

She'elah

A man, born and raised a Jew, has converted to Christianity and joined the Episcopal Church. Having earned a theological degree, he now teaches Comparative Religion at a local private school and has been "very helpful in the ecumenical dialogue between Christians and Jews." Should he be allowed to speak in a Reform synagogue? If permitted to speak, may he do so from the *bimah*? If he is permitted to speak from the *bimah*, should he be permitted to deliver a homily during Sabbath or Holiday worship? May he lead the congregation in prayer or be offered an aliyah? (Rabbi Harry Rothstein, Millertown, NY)

Teshuvah

It must be made clear that regardless of how genial this man is, regardless of his academic credentials or how honest his intentions, because he has forsaken Judaism and converted to another religion we must consider him an apostate. The issue of how we are to interact with apostates has been thoroughly covered in traditional halachic literature, as well as in our Reform responsa.[1]

Central to our she'elah is the question: Why would we even consider permitting an apostate to enter our synagogues, let alone teach or lead us in worship?

Jewish tradition has always been sensitive to the different circumstances under which a person would abandon his or her affiliation with the Jewish community. Not all apostates are lumped together. There are essential differences between one who is forced to convert during a period of religious persecution (*anus*)[2] and one whose apostasy is a matter of religious conviction and public rejection of Judaism (*mumar l'hach'is* or *meshummad*).[3]

Nonetheless, we always hope that even those who are apostates of their own volition will at some time return to the fold. For ours is not simply a religion, we Jews are also a family. We can change our name, looks and religion, but we cannot erase the familial link with the Jewish people. An oft cited passage in the Talmud reads:

> Rabbi Abba the son of Zavda said, Even though [an Israelite]
> has sinned, he is still called 'Israel.' Rabbi Abba said, there is
> a popular saying: A myrtle, though it stands among reeds, is
> still a myrtle, and so it is called.[4]

Indeed, our insistence that an apostate is still Jewish often led to grave consequences.[5] To solve some of those problems, there was an attempt by Gaonic authorities to rule that the apostate had forsaken the Jewish people and, therefore, had forfeited his or her claim for certain benefits and rights within the Jewish community.[6] But their attempts were rejected by Rashi and other leading halachic authorities.[7] Rashi takes the above-quoted statement from the Talmud and extends it to include apostates:

> The *meshummad* is a Jew in every way, as it is said: "even
> though an Israelite has sinned ...", meaning that even though
> he has sinned [or in this case, apostatized], he is a Jew."[8]

If then a *meshummad*, the willful and even provocative apostate, is still considered Jewish, are there any restrictions to his or her participation in the Jewish community? The question is an ancient one, and the answer is: yes, there are restrictions.[9]

Far from welcoming the apostate to participate in the service, the early Jewish liturgy included a *Birkat haMinim,* which explicitly cursed those Jews who abandoned their people.[10] Some authorities have even rejected or restricted communal contributions by apostates.[11] The Rabbinic decrees and ordinances against willful apostates are founded on the Torah, which established the severest of punishments against those who left the faith.[12]

Thus we have, on the one hand, the classic teaching that a Jew is always a Jew. On the other hand, tradition effectively shunned complete apostates, denying them an active role in the Jewish community. Israel of Bruna, a 15th century German Rabbi, made an attempt to resolve the conflict by teaching that even though the apostate is an Israelite, he is not a Jew, meaning that "Israelite" is the designation of one's lineage, while "Jew" refers to one's relationship with the Jewish community.[13] (The idea seems to parallel Reform Judaism's recent insistence that lineage-from either mother or father-needs to be supported by "appropriate and timely acts of identification with the Jewish faith and people.")[14]

The modern state of Israel has also ruled that an apostate, though Jewish by lineage, is not permitted to be registered as a "Jew" under the "Law of Return."[15] The Jewish community has thus been remarkably consistent in excluding apostates from active participation, all the while affirming the ancestral lineage and holding out hope for them to return. The Reform movement has similarly remained firm on the issue of the apostate Jew.

In our case, we therefore conclude that this man, who has earned a theological degree and is an active member of the Episcopal church, has willfully converted and is thus an apostate, a *meshummad*. He is thereby excluded from actively participating in Jewish worship. We would be sending the most confusing signals to our community if we permitted apostates to assume prominent roles in our synagogues and thereby blur the distinction between those who proudly declare their Jewishness and those who abandon our faith.

Consequently, this apostate should not be given the honor of ascending the *bimah*, nor should he be given the distinction of addressing the congregation before, during or after a worship service.[17] Were we to honor an apostate who, to boot, is a scholar of theology, the community would be confronted with a man who was born and raised a Jew, but determined after much study that Judaism is inferior to another religion. We must be careful to avoid conveying any message which may weaken the Jewish community.

However, we would not keep him from attending the service, because we always hold out hope that he will repent and rejoin our fold.[18]

NOTES

1 There are several Reform responsa that deal with apostasy: Solomon B. Freehof, "Status of Apostates and Burial of an Apostate," RRR no.26, pp. 120-127 and no.27, pp. 127-131; "Our Attitude to Apostates," MRR no.30, pp. 161-175. Also see Walter Jacob, "Status of a 'Completed Jew' in the Jewish Community," CARR no.68, pp. 109-112.

2 Coercion is not, of course, limited to threats of violence. Coercion can also include the combined pressures of economic welfare and professional security. See, for example, Asher Siev's article on

the strange path of an apostate Jew in *Sefer zikaron lish'mue'l kalman mirsky* (Jerusalem, 1970).

3 The *mumar l'hach'is*, literally, the "provoking apostate," is the most troublesome of those who forsake our faith. Rambam identifies this kind of willful apostate as one "who repudiates the Oral Law as a matter of personal conviction and through his reasoned opinion." (*Yad*, Mamrim, 3:3).

History has shown that it is the provoking or willful apostate who, all too often, acts in a way which denigrates Judaism and is most detrimental to the Jewish people. For evidence of the murders and oppression wrought by former co-religionists, see *The Jewish Encyclopedia*, 2:14-17; Yitzhak Baer, *A History of the Jews in Christian Spain*, Philadelphia, 1966, vol. 1, pp. 328-354) and vol. 2 (pp. 141-150, 341ff).

4 BT Sanhedrin 44a.

5 Jacob Katz details some of the "grave consequences" (in *Exclusiveness and Tolerance*, pp. 70-71), such as the cases of apostates who did not grant their wives a Jewish divorce. If they would no longer be considered Jewish, their marriages could simply be annulled. But by insisting that every apostate was still Jewish, a *get* was necessary for a true divorce. Without it, the woman could not remarry in the traditional community.

6 Katz (*ibid*, pp. 70-71) cites *Otzar HaGeonim*, VII, pp. 34-37, concerning their ruling that a widow did not have to submit to the ceremony of chalitzah with her apostate brother-in-law. In another case, some of the Geonim (*Otzar HaGeonim*, IX, pp. 28-35) and Rabbenu Gershom (*Teshuvot Rabbenu Gershom* no. 58) ruled that an apostate was no longer eligible to inherit from his Jewish relatives' estate.

7 *Teshuvot Rashi* no.173. "It was in this connection that Rashi quoted the maxim 'although he has sinned he remains a Jew,' which has, since then, become a standard ruling in connection with the definition of the status of the apostate. In its original talmudic context this sentence appears in an aggadic setting only, and not in relation to apostasy. By using it in this striking manner, Rashi ensured the almost uncontested adoption of his definition. Behind this clear-cut statement lies an emphasis on the unchangeable character of the Jew, an emphasis that would contest any possible justification for obliterating Judaism by baptism" (Katz, *ibid*, p. 71).

8 *Teshuvot Rashi* no. 173.

9 *See* for example: BT Chullin 4b-5b; *Sifra* 2.2 (Finkelstein ed., vol. II, pp. 20-21); *Vayikra Rabbah* 2.9; *Yad*, Ma'aseh HaKorbanot, 3.4; *ShA*, YD, 53.4 and OC 215.2.

10 *Tosefta*, Berachot III.25; see also Gedalia Alon, *The Jews in Their Land*, ed. Gershon Levi (Harvard Univ. Press, 1989), pp. 288 ff.

11 Rabbi Yaakov Weil, *She'elot Teshuvot: Dinim v'halachot* no.57; R. Moshe Schick, *Teshuvot Maharam Schick*, YD, no.231, cited by R. Solomon B. Freehof, *The Responsa Literature* (New York: Ktav, 1973), p. 134.

12 Deuteronomy 13:13-19.

13 *She'elot Teshuvot Mahari miBruna*, no.35; see R. Maurice Lamm in *Jewish Tradition and the Nontraditional Jew*, ed. J.J. Schachter, Northvale, NJ, 1992, pp. 169-170.

14 Resolution of the CCAR, see its *Yearbook* XCIII (1983), p.160, and the interpretation of the decision in *Rabbi's Manual* (1988), pp.225-227 (W. Gunther Plaut) and the detailed discussion in CARR, no.38, pp. 61-68. (Walter Jacob).

15 The ruling, which is known as the "Brother Daniel case," was made by the Israeli Supreme Court: 72/62, PD 16:2428-55. Cf. *Encyclopedia Judaica*, sub "Apostate."

16 See the Reform responsa on apostasy listed in the first footnote above.

17 In the words of R. Walter Jacob, CARR no. 68, pp. 109-112, "such individuals should not be accorded membership in the congregation or treated in any way which makes them appear as if they

were affiliated with the Jewish community ... We certainly do not want these individuals to speak for Judaism in any public forum."

18 This follows the CCAR's Responsa Committee's 1983 teshuvah, "Status of a 'Completed Jew' in the Jewish Community," CARR no.68, pp. 109-112. Thus, for the Committee, even "Messianic Jews" or the "Jews for Jesus" (who, because of their proclivity for proselytization, must certainly be classified as *mumarim lehachis* ("provoking apostates"), are not to be excluded from attending services or classes "for we always hold the hope that they will return to Judaism and disassociate themselves from Christianity."

Formation of a Chevra Kaddisha
5754.8

She'elah

Some members of our Reform congregation would like to establish a Chevra Kaddisha because they are dissatisfied with the local funeral directors. They have requested information concerning the traditional activities of a Chevra Kaddisha from the Orthodox perspective and are inquiring whether there are any "desirable adjustments" from a Reform point of view. (Jay Friedheim, Honolulu, HI)

Teshuvah

The Tradition. The Chevra Kaddisha is "a sacred society" of men and women who make themselves responsible for looking after the deceased and supervising the burial arrangements. It has a long and proud place in Jewish tradition. We find mention of burial organizations as early as the Talmudic era.[1]

The primary purposes of the society are *tohorah* (washing the corpse), *shemirah* (watching it) and *tachrichim* (dressing it properly).

The corpse is first thoroughly and carefully washed. Then the body is positioned for *tohorah*, the pouring of nine measures (*kavim*, approximately 24 quarts) of water in an act of ritual purification.[2] The duty of *shemirah* concerns the mitzvah of guarding the deceased. From the moment of death until burial, the corpse is not left alone.[3] Finally, the corpse is wrapped in shrouds, *tachrichim*, and is guarded until burial. At all times, the Chevra Kaddisha is scrupulous to protect the honor of the deceased (*kevod hamet*).

The responsibilities are performed with a minimum of speaking. Female members of the Chevra Kaddisha care for women, and males care for men. Membership in the Chevra is reserved for the pious, and has long been considered a great honor.

Along with many of the time-honored funeral and burial customs,[4] the rituals of the Chevra Kaddisha are considered important but not imperative by the Halachah. For instance, rabbinic authorities declare that a corpse that does not undergo the ritual of *tohorah* is still accorded all the privileges of Jewish burial:

> Heaven forbid that we should deny the person [the right] to
> be buried in a Jewish cemetery. For *tohorah* only serves to
> honor the dead [and not as a qualification for burial].[5]

The traditional reason given for the custom of *shemirah* was to protect the corpse from animals.[6] Since, in the majority of cases, this is not a concern for the modern funeral home, *shemirah* may not appear to be necessary. In fact, *shemirah* has become less a time for guarding than for reciting Psalms.

Reform Perspectives.

The functions of the Chevra Kaddisha accord with the principles of Reform Judaism. Though they have not become a part of its general practice, which has not required *tohorah, shemirah* or *tachrichim*,[7] we consider them highly desirable. In larger cities, it has become customary to engage a Jewish funeral director to be responsible for preparing the corpse for burial in order to assure traditional services. However, where there are only non-Jewish funeral directors available, or there is disregard for Jewish sensitivities and burial customs, we would encourage the community to establish either a Chevra Kaddisha or some other organization that would be involved with funeral and burial arrangements.[8] Together with a Rabbi, someone from the organization should meet with the local funeral directors (both Jewish and Gentile) to insure that they are aware of the appropriate way to handle Jewish deceased. At the very least, the Reform Chevra Kaddisha must insist that the principles of honoring the dead are being met: that the Jewish deceased are washed carefully, and that the corpse is treated with dignity in preparation for burial.

Not surprisingly, finding the right people to perform such a task has often proven to be difficult. The sources are filled with admonitions that attempt to regulate the behavior of those who are assigned the task of staying with the deceased throughout the nights and days before burial.

A Reform Chevra Kaddisha can be an important (and sometimes necessary) addition to the Jewish community. It is desirable especially when it adds to the traditional functions a concern for comforting the mourners (*nichum ave-lim*). For instance, it could establish itself as the congregational branch that is responsible for helping the family make the arrangements before and after the burial. After the funeral, the Chevra Kaddisha, or one of its auxiliaries, could see to it that the mourners will come home to a *se'udat havra'ah*, the meal of consolation. They could also help assemble a *minyan* for services during *shiva*. They could explain and make available to all Jews the traditional rituals and customs in caring for the dead.[10]

Organizationally, the Chevra might begin as a congregational or inter-congregational service, offered to members, and in time offer its services to all Jews. Even in its early, limited role, the congregational Chevra Kaddisha would make a positive contribution to the Jewish community. It should not take long for the local funeral directors to become sensitized to Jewish burial practices and customs.

Some Reform communities have successfully established a traditional Chevra Kaddisha. Others have created a related organization or committee that is responsible for helping the mourning family with burial, funeral and *shiv'a* arrangements.[11] In all cases, it is a mitzvah for friends and congregants to share in the duties and responsibilities of caring for the deceased and their grieving families. Certainly, every community would be greatly blessed by the dedication of those who help others through the pain and anguish occasioned by the loss of a loved one.

We therefore heartily endorse your intention of rendering this valuable service.

NOTES

1 BT Moed Katan 27b. The traditional duties of the Chevra Kaddisha are laid out in Hyman Goldin's *Hamadrich* (New York, 1939) and in Maurice Lamm's *The Jewish Way in Death and Mourning* (New York, 1969); see also *Encyclopedia Judaica* 8:442-446, where a brief history of the institution is given.

2 Goldin, chapter 197.

3 Goldin, chapter 194.

4 *Tur*, YD 376, in which the custom of washing the hands when returning from the cemetery and before entering the house of mourning is declared not necessary. R. Jacob b. Asher goes on to declare that many of the customs at the cemetery are for symbolic reasons only (end of 376).

5 *Kol Bo Al Avelut*, p. 89.

6 B, Berachot 18a; *Mishnah Berurah* 71.3.

7 *See Gates of Mitzvah,* p. 53.

8 Compare Walter Jacob, *NARR ,* no.167, pp. 277-278.

9 See, for instance, Chaim Benjamin Goldberg, *Mourning in Halachah,* (New York, 1992), p. 55 (especially note no.100, the reference to *Ma'avar Yabok*).

10 See also *ARR,* edited by Walter Jacob, no.100 (especially pp. 347-348).

11 For example, the Canadian Council for Reform Judaism, 36 Atkinson Avenue, Thornhill, Ontario, L4J 8C9, (905) 709-2275; Temple Beth El of Northern Westchester, 220 South Bedford Road, Chappaqua, NY, 10514, (914) 238-3928; Congregation B'nai Torah, 2789 Oak St., Highland Park, Illinois, 60035, (708) 433-7100.

Non-Traditional Sukkah
5755.4

She'elah

What is the liberal Jewish definition of the mitzvah of *sukkah*? Can a non-traditional structure (such as a tent) be considered a *sukkah* for us? Does eating meals outdoors suffice? (Rabbi Judith Z. Abrams, Houston, Texas)

Teshuvah

Like Pesach, the festival of Sukkot is the occasion for much detailed discussion in the halachic literature. In particular, a plethora of information awaits anyone seeking instruction concerning the size, shape, structure, and material for the making of *sukkot*.[1] Our task is to consider these rules in the context of contemporary Reform Jewish practice. Does Reform Judaism insist upon all the traditional requirements, or can the goals and purposes of Sukkot observance be met through the use of structures that do not meet these requirements? Indeed, does the Reform Jewish idea of the festival necessitate a physical structure of any kind?

The Halachah

We begin with the definition of a *sukkah* presented in the halachic literature. The *sukkah* is a temporary structure (*dirat ar`ai*) which becomes the functional equivalent of one's home during the festival.[2] Thus, the height of a *sukkah* may not exceed twenty cubits, since to build it that high would require that the walls be sturdy enough to support a permanent structure (*dirat keva`*).[3] Nor may the height be lower than ten handbreadths, for such a structure would be considered *dirah seruchah*, unfit for even temporary habitation.[4] The area of the *sukkah* must be sufficient to allow an individual to eat a meal within it.[5] The *'ikar,* or essence of the *sukkah* rests in the *sechach*, the material which serves as its roof or covering.[6] The *sechach* must consist of detached vegetation that cannot contract ritual impurity, and there must be enough of it so that the amount of shadow it casts exceeds the amount of sunlight which enters the *sukkah*.[7] The walls of the *sukkah* (there must be at least three), by contrast, may be constructed out of any material, so long as they are sturdy enough to withstand a normal wind.[8] The walls, if they are anchored in the roof of the *sukkah*, must extend to within three handbreadths of the ground.[9] The *sukkah* must have a roof; should the walls come together in the manner of a conical hut, the structure is not a valid *sukkah*.[10]

Reform Perspectives.

It should be obvious from the foregoing that the suggestions raised in the she'elah are not halachically acceptable. A tent, because it has neither roof nor *sechach*, is an invalid *sukkah* (*sukkah pesulah*), and eating one's meals outdoors hardly qualifies, since the minimal definition of a *sukkah* requires a structure with roof and walls. Yet the question asks us to look beyond the halachic tradition and to reexamine the very parameters of this *mitzvah*. Reform Judaism, after all, has long championed the cause of "creative ritual" and has introduced many fundamental innovations into the corpus of Jewish religious observance. Perhaps there is good reason why we ought to do so in this case.

For the sake of clarity, let us formulate the question as follows. It is a fact that many, indeed most Reform Jews, do not construct *sukkot* and thus do not fulfill the mitzvah of *sukkah* in its traditional sense. On the other hand, these Jews might well be prepared to observe the festival in some other, arguably related manner. Though not everyone will wish to purchase or erect a *sukkah*, there are those (families with young children, for example) who would find it enjoyable to eat festive meals in their camping tents. And many who are unable or unwilling to build a *sukkah* would presumably be quite willing to eat outdoors, particularly if the early fall weather is pleasant. Though their practice would be decidedly non-traditional, these individuals would be willing to leave their permanent homes to take their meals in "temporary dwellings." Would this not fulfill the mitzvah of *sukkah* for liberal Jews? Would it not meet the intent, the essential purpose of the observance, by calling to mind the miracles which God did for us when we came out of

Egypt?[11] Indeed, given that the rabbinic tradition is divided over whether God actually caused our ancestors to "dwell in booths" in the desert,[12] do we really need to construct huts in accordance with a long list of concrete halachic specifications in order to remember the wilderness experience?

The question challenges us to consider the meaning of ritual observance in Reform Judaism. Is ritual, in and of itself, ever a "necessity" for us? Does a traditional practice possess any obligatory force above and beyond the moral or religious meaning it conveys? Put in this way, we believe the answer to the question is "yes." And that means that the answer to the present *she'elah* is "no": it does not fulfill the *mitzvah* of *sukkah* to eat outdoors, or in a tent, or in some other non-traditional manner.

Jewish religious life, for us no less than for other Jews, expresses itself through the practice of concrete rituals and observances. These observances, to be sure, carry "messages" of universal moral significance, but the messages do not exist for us as Jews in the absence of the rituals. For example, shabbat communicates the values of rest, of physical and spiritual refreshment, of human dignity, of appreciation of God's creative labors and so forth. These values, which are hardly unique to Judaism, can be transmitted and taught in any number of ways. The institution of the Jewish Sabbath is our particular way of transmitting and teaching them. Marked off by kiddush and havdalah, colored by festive meals and songs that express *oneg* and *kavod*, given content by a special liturgy and by a complex of permitted and prohibited activities, Shabbat not only allows us to rehearse its "message"; it stirs us to remember who and what we are as a people. The same is true with Passover. We could absorb the message of the holiday by simply contemplating the themes of slavery and liberation. But that does not suffice for us, because our Passover is not Passover without matzah, the haggadah, the seder and its special foods and spirit. It is through these concrete observances, rituals by which the Jewish people has come to express its understanding of itself as an historical religious community, that we identify ourselves with their experience. Surely we would not suggest that liberal Jews could somehow "fulfill" the *mitzvot* of Shabbat and Passover by stripping these special times of the very rituals that make them special, that make them Jewish. And just as surely, we do not think that liberal Jews can "fulfill" the mitzvah of *sukkah* by substituting some non-traditional approximation for the age-old Jewish observance.

It is true that Reform Judaism has radically altered or done away with many traditional observances. When we have done so, however, we have tended to justify our decision on the grounds that the observance in question was fatally flawed, no longer in keeping with the spirit of modern culture and civilization, or objectionable on moral or aesthetic grounds.[13] We do not find the *mitzvah* of *sukkah* problematic by any of these considerations,[14] nor do we believe that the temper of the times demands a new, more "progressive" definition of this observance.[15] We know that it can be somewhat burdensome to build a *sukkah* or to travel to one, but this "burden" is hardly a crushing one. The availability of prefabricated *sukkot* in a variety of price ranges enables most households to erect such a structure with a minimum of muss and fuss. Moreover, synagogues and other communal institutions erect *sukkah* on their premises, making it relatively easy for those who do not have their own *sukkah* to observe the mitzvah.

None of this to to say that there is no value in non-traditional styles of observance. On the contrary: Jewish tradition recognizes that even a less-than-perfect performance of a *mitzvah* can bring merit to its doer.[16] We would by all means encourage our people to mark the seasons of the Jewish year to whatever extent they can. If one cannot build a *sukkah*, one might purchase a lulav and etrog; if one cannot do that, one can attend festival services at the synagogue. In addition, our tendency toward creative approaches to liturgy should prove that we Reform Jews certainly do not oppose the search for new and innovative ways of celebrating Jewish life. In response to the present *she'elah*, we might say that it is better for Jews to consciously and explicitly mark the occasion of Sukkot by eating outdoors or in a tent than for them to ignore the holiday entirely by doing nothing at all to observe it. But to repeat: this is not the mitzvah of *sukkah*, and it is better still for our people to come to fulfill that mitzvah in the way that Jews have over the course of many centuries come to fulfill it.

The choice, as we see it, is between two definitions of rabbinic responsibility. On the one hand, we can decide that our role is to tell our people that they may be satisfied with ersatz Jewish rituals or with whatever level of observance they are able to reach at the moment. On the other, while we validate their good intentions, we can resolve to teach, to lead, and to encourage them to adopt into their lives those forms of Jewish observance that, while resonating with our modern temperament, have become emblematic of Torah, of our people's particular religious experience in its search for God.

We think that the second alternative is the better one.

NOTES

1 The texts are centered chiefly in the Talmudic tractate *Sukkah*; the law is codified by the Rambam in *Yad*, Hilchot Shofar veSukkah veLulav, chs. 4-6, and by Karo and Isserles in *Sh.A.* OC chs. 625-669.

2 Lev. 23:42 reads: "you shall dwell in sukkot for seven days"; from this, the tradition derives that one should live in the *sukkah* precisely as one lives the rest of the year in one's home (*teishvu ke`ein taduru*; BT. Sukkah 28b).

3 This reasoning follows the opinion of Rava, Sukkah 2a, who holds that the essence of a *sukkah* is that it is a temporary structure. R. Zeira, ad loc., offers a competing theory: a *sukkah* requires shade (cf. Isaiah 4:6), and if the height of the walls exceeds twenty cubits, one dwells in the shade of the walls rather than that of the *sechach*.

4 M Sukkah 1:1; BT Sukkah 2a; *Yad*, Sukkah 4:1; *Sh.A.*, OC 633:1.

5 "The *sukkah* must contain one's head, the major part of one's body, and one's table"; this area is generally rendered as "seven square handbreadths" (BT Sukkah 3a; *Yad*, Hilchot Sukkah 4:1; OC 634:1).

6 Rashi, BT. Sukkah 2a, s.v. *veshechamatah*.

7 M Sukkah 1:1 and 1:4; *Yad*, Sukkah 5:1; *Sh.A.*, OC 629 and 631. A *sukkah* may not, as a rule, be built under a tree, since its shade will derive from that tree and its branches (M. *Sukkah* 1:2; *Yad*, *Sukkah* 5:12. For special circumstances see *Sh.A.*, OC 626:1.).

8 M Sukkah 1:1 and 1:5; *Yad*, Sukkah 4:2 and 4:16; *Sh.A.*, OC 630:1ff.

9 M Sukkah 1:9; *Yad*, Sukkah 4:4; *Sh.A.*, OC 630:9.

10 See M. Sukkah 1:11 and BT Sukkah 19b; *Yad*, Sukkah 4:7; *Sh.A.*, OC 631:10.

11 See *Sefer Ha-Hinuch*, no. 325.

12 See BT. Sukkah 11b. The dispute concerns the meaning of the sukkot mentioned in Lev. 23:43. R. Akiva reads the word in its concrete sense: "booths." But R. Eliezer understands it to mean `ananei kavod, "clouds of glory."

13 Much could be said about all of these; this is not, however, the occasion for detailed discussion. We would mention only that the phenomenon of "adjustments" in ritual practice did not start with Reform Judaism. It is in fact the very history of Jewish tradition. Our own subject is a case in point: while the original definition of the commandment to dwell in the *sukkah* required that one sleep in the *sukkah* during the entire festival, the climatic conditions of northern and eastern Europe led to the removal of this requirement. See *Aruch HaShulchan*, OC 639, pars. 11-13.

14 That a *sukkah* is not a terribly aesthetic or "nice" place for modern, upper-middle-class Jews to dine is hardly a valid objection; the whole point of "living" in a temporary dwelling is to leave our

comfortable lifestyles behind, however briefly.

15 This is not to say that we do not believe in the possibility of a progressive understanding of our tradition. Rabbi Solomon B. Freehof taught us that Reform responsa ought to be written in a "liberally affirmative" spirit. We do not share the passion of many contemporary Orthodox *poskim* to forbid new ideas or to insist upon ever-increasing levels of ritual stringency, absolute precision in measurement, etc. We interpret broadly rather than narrowly, and proudly so. In this case, however, a "broad" construction of the kind discussed would mean altering the *mitzvah* of *sukkah* beyond recognition.

16 See M Berachot 1:2: one who recites the morning *Shema* later than its appointed time nonetheless receives the reward "of one who reads (the *Shema*) in the Torah."

She'elah

We have been unable to attract enough members to our annual congregational meeting and are wondering whether it would be appropriate to hold such a meeting on a Friday evening.

Teshuvah

The question requires us to explore a number of issues. They concern the nature of Shabbat, the way we observe it as Jews, and especially as Reform Jews, and the nature of an annual congregational meeting.

Tradition, which is generally very strict about observing Shabat in all its minutiae, is surprisingly permissive when dealing with the question before us. Its proof text is Isaiah 58:13:

If you refrain from trampling Shabbat,
From pursuing your affairs on My holy day;
If you call Shabbat "delight,"
The Eternal's holy day "honored" ...

The Rabbis reasoned that "your", that is human, affairs were forbidden, but God's business was not. Hence, matters dealing with the welfare of the community were allowed to be discussed on the Sabbath.[1]

The Prophet also challenges us to the *mitzvot* of *oneg Shabbat*, Shabbat joy, and *kibbud Shabbat*, Shabbat honor, which is the subject of the Fourth Commandment.[2] These *mitzvot* give the day its distinctive character and go beyond the duty to abstain from prohibited labor. One should turn away also from those activities which, though permitted, interfere with the honoring of Shabbat and making it a time of joy. The ordinary should give way to the special and thus, congregational worship, study, and festive celebration with family and friends should be the order of the day.

For this reason, meetings of any kind are generally not scheduled for Shabbat, even though they might halachically be permitted. This abstention has become quite general in the Jewish community, which constitutes a case where popular practice (*minhag*) has become more stringent than the Halachah would demand.

Maimonides, in dealing with this type of divergence, ruled that *minhag* cannot annul that which is forbidden, but can prohibit that which is permitted.[3] As a general custom, the *minhag* of a community was respected, though of course not every *minhag* deserved that approbation. Thus, when it could be said to have been practiced and approved in error one should pay no attention to it.[4]

How does the halachic permission to hold communal meetings and the popular practice of prohibiting them fit into this schema? The answer is that the rabbinic permission was given at a time when Shabbat was strictly observed by the Jewish community, and therefore the occasional exception could be tolerated. Holding a meeting for the welfare of the community did not in anyway diminish the respect for Shabbat or its meticulous observance; it was seen for what it was: *an unusual but necessary exception.*

In our time the situation has radically changed; the community as a whole is lax in its observance of Shabbat and therefore the *minhag* of not holding meetings on that day has become a fence, meant to guard against a further erosion of Shabbat awareness and respect. Clearly, the practice of discouraging meetings on that day is designed "to keep Shabbat holy," and Jewish law would caution against overriding such a *minhag*.[5]

Rabbi Freehof was nonetheless permissive in this case. While he preferred that meetings not take place on Shabbat he reiterated the halachic rule that such meetings were indeed permissible, but at the same time he cautioned against the inclusion of financial matters in the discussions.[6]

We feel certain that, were he asked the same question today, he would rule differently and agree that the sense of Shabbat holiness has diminished so severely that every further intrusion should now be vigorously resisted--quite aside from the fact that congregational meetings have in any case a way of focusing on financial issues.

Since Rabbi Freehof published his responsum, the Reform movement has made a sustained effort to re-enforce the sense of Shabbat holiness amongst its members. To this end, the Central Conference of American Rabbis has stated:

> *Kedushah* (holiness) requires that Shabbat be singled out as different from weekdays. It must be distinguished from the other days of the week so that those who observe it will become transformed by its holiness. One ought, therefore, to do certain things which contribute to an awareness of this day's special nature, and to abstain from doing others which lessen our awareness.[7]

Congregational meetings are generally perceived as secular occasions and would by that very fact further undermine the sense that Shabbat is a special day. We should make every effort to increase rather than to diminish this sense, even in the face of good intentions. Regrettably, Reform congregations have a hard enough time to inculcate amongst their members the awareness of Shabbat holiness. Trying to involve them in greater participation in Temple business is certainly laudable, but doing it at the expense of the Shabbat spirit appears to us as counterproductive.

The problem of poor attendance at annual meetings is wide-spread and not restricted to congregations. Yet secular organizations do not hold such meetings on Shabbat, and congregations should not set the wrong example in the community by doing what popular *minhag* has so far discouraged.

NOTES

1 Here too the relevant sources were explored by Freehof in a responsum, "Congregational meeting on the Sabbath", *RR* (1950), no. 8, pp. 46-50.

2 The classic definition of these dual requirements is found in Rambam, *Yad*, Shabbat 30. One's time on Shabbat ought to be divided so that half of it is devoted to God (Torah study and worship) and half to personal rejoicing (see BT, Pesachim 68b; *Tur*, OC 242).

3 *Yad*, Shevitat-'Asor 3:3; *Responsa of R. Shelomo ben Shim'on Duran*, no. 562. (*Yad*, Issurei Bi'ah 11:14).

4 See *Yad*, Issurei Bi'ah 11:14; and cf. BT Pesachim 50b-51a; Nedarim 81b; and Tosafot to 'Eruvin 101b.

5 Further on this issue, see *Responsa of R. Yitzhak ben Sheshet,* cited in Kesef Mishneh to *Yad,* Issurei Bi'ah 11:14; see also Isserles, *Sh.A*, YD 194:1; also R. Yechezkel Landau, Responsa *Nodah Biyhudah* I, YD, no. 54.

6 *l.c.,* footnote 3 above.

7 *A Shabbat Manual* (1972), pp. 6 ff.; this sense is reiterated in *Gates of the Seasons* (1983), pp. 11 ff. See also F.A. Doppelt and D. Polish, *A Guide for Reform Jews* (1957), p. 9: "Activities which are clearly not in the spirit of Shabbat should be planned for other days."

Yoreh De'ah
Reform Jewish Practice

Testing for HIV
5750.1

She'elah

I have been informed that the Syrian-Sephardi Rabbinical Association of Brooklyn passed a resolution that they will not officiate at any marriage until they have received documentation attesting to the fact that both parties have undergone testing for the human immunodeficiency virus (HIV). Should Reform rabbis make the same requirement? There seems to be a parallel to the resolution we passed on Tay-Sachs disease. (Rabbi Alexander M. Schindler, UAHC, New York)

Teshuvah

1. Halachic Precedents

The primary role of someone officiating at a marriage (*mesadder kiddushin*, usually a rabbi[1]) is to make sure that a valid marriage is being entered into.

Circumstances may arise under which the rabbi would refuse to officiate. A well-known example is that of an inebriated groom who is unable to enter into a legal obligation. In such an instance, the rabbi's judgment not to proceed with the ceremony is not contested.[2] Since there is halachic precedent for rabbinic refusal under certain circumstances, we must now ask whether the unwillingness of the couple or one of the partners to be tested for HIV would constitute a cogent reason for the rabbi's unwillingness to officiate.

1. The rule that s/he would likely invoke is that of *piku'ach nefesh*, the protection of life. Our tradition is firm in holding that, when *piku'ach nefesh* is at stake, all *mitzvot* may be disregarded save bloodshed, idolatry and sexual transgressions (*giluy arayot*).[3] One who is too concerned with halachic propriety when life is endangered is regarded as a shedder of blood.[4]

The officiating rabbi has also another (though implied) role, namely, to prevent a transgression from being committed. In the case of HIV and the possibility that it will develop into the acquired immune deficiency syndrome (AIDS), a disease for which there is presently no cure, the command that stands in danger of being violated would be "Do not stand idly by the blood of your neighbor."[5] R. Jacob Breisch derives from this Torah proscription a specific instruction to physicians to inform the healthy party to a prospective marriage that the other partner is afflicted by a dangerous disease.[6] In instances of this kind, the person carrying it might be considered a *rodef* (literally "pursuer")[7] who, albeit unintentionally, threatens the life of an innocent person.[8]

Can R. Breisch's reasoning guide us in the question before us? Would the rabbi, like the doctor, be considered guilty of standing idly by the blood of the couple, should it turn out that indeed one of them is infected with HIV?

We believe that the precedent to which R. Breisch addressed himself is not operative here. The physician has actual knowledge of the presence of a dangerous disease and therefore is required to disclose that fact, while the rabbi has no knowledge of the couple's personal exposure and knows only that many people in society carry the virus. There is a gulf between knowledge of the actual and fear of the potential.

It is worth noting, however, that the mere potential of a life-threatening situation was dealt with by the Hatam Sofer (Rabbi Moses Schreiber/Sofer) some 150 years ago. There was a severe outbreak of cholera in Europe, and physicians had warned that fasting on Yom Kippur might make people more susceptible to the disease. In view of this medical judgment, the rabbi, who was Europe's leading halachist, permitted the consumption of food in quantities sufficient to prevent Jews from being overly weakened. Even though the violation of a direct prohibition was at issue, R. Sofer's permission (*hetteir*) functioned as a prophylactic, to prevent people from becoming ill.[9] But not all authorities agreed, and some urged their congregants to observe the fast if at all possible. Still others promoted the idea of shortening the services.[10]

As in R. Breisch's ruling, we feel that the precedent of the *Hatam Sofer* (if we were to agree with him) is not applicable to our case. For his *hetteir* was advisory and not compelling. People were free to disregard it.

More recently, this question, with specific reference to AIDS, was addressed by Rabbi Shelomo Dichovsky, a rabbinical court judge in Israel.[11] He asserts that, while the community is entitled to issue rulings (*takkanot*) in order to protect itself from various dangers, he would agree to particular measures for at-risk persons (*kevutzot sikkun*), but does not suggest that the general population be required to undergo testing.

In sum, we have not found the kind of precedent that would speak unequivocally to the *she'elah* before us. Before we go further it is well to look at an entirely different aspect, which is the right to privacy.

2. Actually, while it is not proper to speak of "rights" under Jewish law, there are numerous instances when it treats of obligations which in other legal systems might be termed "rights." Thus, a home owner may take action to protect his household against the prying eyes of neighbors;[12] or we may note the Torah's prohibition of gossip (*rechilut*).[13] Tradition goes so far as to proclaim that someone who shames another in public has no place in the world to come.[14]

R. Eliezer Waldenberg has applied the issue of *halbanat panim* (making someone blanch with embarrassment) to a medical situation and ruled that, while a physician may ordinarily bring medical students to a patient's bed, this should not be done when it causes *halbanat panim*.[15]

Thus, while the right to privacy as such has no direct precedent in Jewish law, its objective-- to safeguard the dignity of the individual-- clearly has. In the case of AIDS, an illness surrounded by popular superstitions and anxieties, the possibility of having test results revealed (to public bodies or others) poses a definite threat to privacy and arouses fears of unwarranted disclosure and slander.

In sum, for reasons set out above in (1) and (2), halachic precedents would lead us to view compulsory testing with caution.

2.   Further Considerations

What other consideration might then be brought to bear on the issue, and further, what additional guidelines might we obtain from precedents in the literature of the Reform movement?

1. The first that comes to mind is a resolution of the Central Conference of American Rabbis (CCAR) which, in 1975, called on its members

> ...to urge those couples seeking their officiating at marriage ceremonies to undergo screening for Tay-Sachs and other genetic diseases which afflict Jews to a significant degree.[16]

That resolution, however, is not fully applicable to our case. For one, Tay-Sachs is a disease which afflicts Ashkenazic Jews in significant proportions, while HIV/AIDS have no such specific identification with Jews. Secondly, the rabbis were called upon to urge, but not require, couples to undergo testing. Hence, we cannot take this resolution to guide us in our answer.

2. Various jurisdictions have instituted certain pre-marriage requirements (e.g., Wassermann tests), and rabbis in such states have an obligation to await the issuance of a license before they officiate. In Illinois, beginning January 1, 1988, all marriage applicants have been required by law to prove that they have been tested for the presence of HIV antibodies, and that the test results have been communicated to a government health agency as well as to both parties in the proposed marriage. But that law is operative only in Illinois, and since we have been asked whether rabbis should undertake a similar program for their people, we should look at the results of the Illinois statute.

In the year since the law was instituted, only 26 people out of 155,458 marriage license applicants were found to test positive. Either the incidence of HIV is very low in the state or, more likely, the figures are skewed, in that they do not take into account those prospective marriage partners who did not want to be tested and therefore went outside the state for their marriage. Under the circumstances, C. Kelly, a member of the Illinois Department of Public Health, judged the whole procedure not to be cost-effective.[17] (In fact, both HIV and Wassermann tests have since been abandoned. Ed. note.)

In the question before us, the Illinois experience would lead us to conclude,

a. that if we were to require marriage applicants to be tested for HIV, those who believe themselves at risk would search out another rabbi or functionary who does not make such a requirement;

b. that we, as rabbis, have little reason to believe that, were we to require tests, we would be more effective than the state of Illinois.

3. Since the rabbi would request only that tests be taken, not that their results be revealed to him/her,[18] the couple's privacy may not at first sight appear to have been invaded. Yet a closer look at the interplay of private concerns and public policy does give us second thoughts.

In many places the process of HIV testing itself has serious social consequences. For instance, physicians or institutions that do the testing may be obligated to register any positive finding with a government health agency, as is the case in Illinois. In our present climate of gross and unwarranted discrimination even against persons suspected of infection, the very process of testing is laden with the danger of divulging private information -- a danger which is enhanced by the potential accessibility of our electronic storage systems as well as by the still error-prone testing for the virus -- there being both "false negative" and "false positive" results. For these reasons, many persons who fear that they might have the HIV virus hesitate to submit themselves to testing.

Despite the fact that California provides the strongest protection for the preservation of confidentiality, an examination of pre-1989 legal cases indicates a serious erosion of medical privacy for HIV-infected persons.[19] A rabbinic either/or requirement might therefore lead the couple to do something that will indeed expose them to social and psychological injury and make the rabbi an unwitting party thereto.

4. In the presence of HIV/AIDS we are faced with deep "social fears," and therefore protection of the dignity of the individual must be a paramount concern.[20] This is a matter to which the CCAR has addressed itself repeatedly. In 1954 it said:

> No free society can long survive if its citizens are encouraged or
> permitted to inform indiscriminately on one another.[21]

While that resolution spoke to the concerns of the McCarthy era in the U.S., its message remains valid even when the informing arises from medical reports. In 1955 the CCAR further stated:

> The pivotal problem which confronts us today remains that of
> the proper balance between individual freedom and national
> security. Our Conference has spoken in clear and forthright
> terms on the subject.[22]

To be sure, HIV is different from the concern for national security referred to in the resolution, but the whole fabric of protection for the individual is affected when a portion of the citizenry is unduly exposed to state interference. In the 1950's as is the 1990's the individual must remain on guard against the incursion of the collective, and the rabbi should not by his/her actions diminish the protected realm of those who wish to arrange for their marriage.

5. But should we not consider the spread of AIDS a veritable plague which would sweep aside these considerations? To put it differently, does the interest of the community not require us to override our obligations to the couple and their right to privacy?

While, with regards to the spread of AIDS, the term epidemic is frequently used, it does not describe an illness against which the population cannot protect itself adequately. Rather, there are high-risk groups which are indeed gravely exposed and require urgent attention, but the majority of the population continues to experience low-prevalence exposure.[23]

6. We frequently deal with couples who are already living together and are now contemplating marriage because they wish to have children. Our responsibility should therefore be to help safeguard the health of such future offspring, and we should warn the couple that, since HIV is transmissible *in utero*, testing prior to marriage is highly advisable.

7. The question may also be asked whether Reform rabbis, who do not function in a judicial capacity, would go beyond their duties when they decide that the particular couple is not fit to be married. This kind of judgment is in any case highly problematic and should not be exercised unless very particular circumstances obtain.

8. Finally, we should also note the special characteristics of Syrian-Sephardi communities, such as the one referred to in the *she'elah*. They are tightly knit, family-like groups with strong internal controls, which observe, for instance, a stringent ban against conversions for the sake of marriage.[24] We lack that kind of disciplinary control, even if we were to contemplate exercising it.

3.   Conclusion

While halachic precedents are inconclusive or cautionary regarding a rabbinic requirement to undergo pre-marital testing, other considerations would lead us to counsel against such procedure.

Though we have every regard for the seriousness of AIDS and are committed to extending our compassionate care to those afflicted by it, we cannot state that its spread is of pandemic proportions, nor do the results of compulsory testing in Illinois convince us that rabbinic action would be successful and wise.

Advising couples about testing is one thing and is encouraged; requiring them to undergo it is not, at least at this time. Should conditions change we would be open to reconsider our position.

(Editors' note: The above responsum was written in the winter of 5750/1989-90, and the best data then available led us to our conclusion. Since then, the disease has taken on epidemic dimensions in certain parts of Africa, while in North America and other Western nations it remains confined to high-risk portions of the population. A review of up-to-date literature led Prof. Joseph Adelson of the University of Michigan to state in 1995 that AIDS will not touch most heterosexuals).[25]

NOTES

1 The emergence of the rabbi as the primary *mesadder kiddushin* has been set forth in a *teshuvah* written by R. Solomon B. Freehof and issued for the CCAR Responsa Committee; see *CCAR Yearbook*, LXV (1955), pp.85-88.

2 *Peri Megadim*, OC 573, *Mishbetzet Hazahav*, n. 11 (refusal because of inebriation); *Resp. Minchat Yitzhak*, I 10 (refusal to officiate for an apostate); *Resp. HaRambam*, Blau, n. 347 (refusal until groom, who is not known in the community, proves he is unmarried or divorces his present wife).

We might here also mention M Ketubot 7:10, which states that men with certain skin diseases are compelled to divorce their wives. The Mishnah speaks of *shechin*, which is variously understood as a skin disease in general, or leprosy, or boils. It is also identified as the *choli tsarfati*, or syphilis; see Be'er Hetev to *Sh.A.*, EH 154. The mishnaic obligation to divorce would appear to apply to a man having AIDS and thereby give the rabbi (who knows at the time of marriage of the presence of the disease) reason to refuse officiating.

3 BT, Yoma 85b; Sanhedrin 74a; *Yad*, Yesodey HaTorah 5; *Sh.A.*, YD 157.

4 *Sh. A.*, OC 328:2.

5 Leviticus 19:16.

6 *Chelkat Ya'akov*, 3:136, on the basis of his reading of *Yad*, Hilchot Rotze'ach 1:14.

7 The Halachah has made this term a legal concept , and someone so designated may be killed before s/he can kill. (In 1995 the designation by some rabbis of Yitzhak Rabin as a *rodef* became the subject of widespread controversy after the Prime Minister was assassinated. It was believed that this designation have moved the killer to commit the deed (ed. note).

8 See Bi'ur HaGera on *Sh.A.*, CM 425, n. 11.

9 *Resp. Chatam Sofer* 6, n.23.

10 See *Matteh Efrayim*, ch. 618, Elef Ha-Magen.

11 *Asya* (published by the Falk Schlesinger Institute at the Shaare Zedek Medical Center in Jerusalem), January 1989, pp. 28-32.

12 *Hezek re'iyah* is treated in Mishnah. Baba Batra 3:7; *Yad,* Hilchot Shechenim 5; *Sh.A.*, CM 154.

13 Lev. 19:16; the Rambam lists three types in an ascending order of severity, the worst offense being the spreading of news which, though true, is damaging to someone else's reputation (*Yad,* De'ot 7:2).

14 BT, Baba Metzi'a 59a; *Yad,* De'ot 6:8.

15 *Resp. Tzitz Eliezer,* vol.13, n. 81, sec. 2.

16 *CCAR Yearbook* LXXXV (1975) 79.

17 *Fifth International Conference on AIDS, Abstracts,* Montreal, June 1989, p.68.

18 We have not been asked what consequences might ensue for the rabbi should a positive test result come to his/her attention. This would raise additional halachic as well as general legal questions. A responsum on aspects of this issue was published by Walter Jacob, *Contemporary American Reform Responsa,* n. 5, "Confidential Information."

19 *Abstracts,* see above, note 16, p.945; report by Clint Hockenberry, AIDS Legal Referral Panel, San Francisco.

20 *Ibid.,* p.967; lecture by C. Aredondo, Spanish Ministry of Health.

21 *CCAR Yearbook,* LXIV (1954), p.54.

22 *Ibid.,* LXV (1955), p.65.

23 Ida Onorato, Centers for Disease Control Atlanta, *Abstracts, op. cit.*, p.78. See further *Population Reports,* published by the Population Information Program of Johns Hopkins University, Series L (Sept. 1989), especially p.4. The report covers North America as well as other areas. A survey of HIV prevalence on university campuses in the U.S. produced a rate of 0.2% (Helene Gayle, Centers for Disease Control; *Abstracts, op. cit.*, p.79). Even among homosexuals and bisexuals reported AIDS cases are leveling in selected metropolitan areas, including New York, Los Angeles and San Francisco (Ruth Berkelman, Centers for Disease Control, ibid., p.66). AIDS researcher Dr. Catherine Hankins reported that in Montreal about one in every 400 women giving birth is HIV infected. "The rates are higher than we predicted and they reflect the increasing role that heterosexual transmission of HIV is playing in Quebec" (*Globe and Mail,* Toronto, Nov. 17, 1989). The infection rate quoted, though higher than that reported in San Francisco, is still only 0.25%, which can hardly be termed epidemic. See also the latest report of the (U.S.) Federal Centers for Disease Control, reported in *The New York Times,* January 4, 1990.

24 See Moshe Zemer, "The Rabbinic Ban on Conversions in Argentina," *Judaism,* Winter 1988, pp. 84-96.

25 *Commentary,* July 1995, pp. 26-30. He bases himself primarily on E. O. Laumann a.o., *The Social Organization of Sexuality: Sexual Practices in the United States,* University of Chicago Press, 1994.

Interment of a Non-Jewish Same-Sex Partner
5752.20

She'elah

Our congregation owns and maintains a Hebrew cemetery. It has been the policy to allow the burial of non-Jewish spouses, as long as the rituals of the interment and the grave stones do not contain non-Jewish symbols. The present case involves a Jewish woman, a widow and herself, her daughter and the daughter's female, non-Jewish partner of 20 years. On what basis ought we to sell or deny her a cemetery plot for the non-Jewish significant other?

Teshuvah

1. Halachic Precedents

The Talmud provides[1] that Jews are to give charity to the non-Jewish poor together with the Jewish sick, and bury their dead together with the Jewish dead, *mipnei darchei shalom*. Reacting to the possibility that this observation lends itself to misinterpretation, Rashi hastens to point out that the non-Jewish dead may not be buried among Jews; Jews are only to *assist* in their burial in the event that non-Jewish and Jewish bodies are discovered slain side by side. R. Isaiah of Trani comments that Jews may occupy themselves with the burial of non-Jews, but Jews and non-Jews may not be buried together.

This is codified in the *Tur*,[2] and in *Shulchan Aruch*.[3] In judgmental terms reflecting the age, Caro quotes Rabbenu Nissim to the effect that under no circumstances are Jews and non-Jews to be buried together, because there is a prohibition against burying a wicked person next to a righteous person. Jews are merely to see to it that non-Jewish dead receive burial.

This position is upheld by R. David Hoffmann.[4] He deals with the case of the son of a Jew by his Gentile wife, with whom he could not contract a Jewish marriage. The son, who was neither circumcised nor immersed *leshem gerut*, died. Beyond doubt, Hoffmann insists, the child was a non-Jew, and as such as he could not be buried in a Jewish cemetery. He adds that only the Reformers and those who undermine Judaism hold that it is not sinful to bury

111

a Gentile among Jews. After reviewing the various references on the subject, he concludes that the truly observant Jews in the community must withdraw from the company of these *maddichim* (seducers) and try to establish their own cemetery.

2.   Reform Perspectives

Our question came to the attention of the Conference repeatedly between 1914 and 1919.[5] In 1916 R. Kaufmann Kohler wrote, with R. Jacob Z. Lauterbach concurring:

> I have always in my practice taken the stand that while mixed marriages should not be sanctioned by a rabbi, the civil law which declares them as valid must be recognized by us to the extent that the non-Jewish wife or husband should be entitled to the right of being buried alongside the Jewish husband or wife in the plot owned by one or the other in the Jewish cemetery.[6]

In 1919 Kohler added:

> There is no law forbidding a non-Jew to be buried in a Jewish cemetery. While there are congregations whose constitution expressly prohibits non-Jews, respectively non-Jewish wives or husbands, to be buried in their cemeteries, such restrictions were undoubtedly made with the view of preventing mixed marriage in the congregation. At the same time it cannot be denied that in the case of a Jew, whether a member of the congregation or not, his legally-married wife, though a non-Jewess, has a just claim to be buried alongside of her husband...As Rabbi of Temple Beth El in New York, I have frequently given this decision, and this view has been fully endorsed by my congregation...We have no consecrated ground which would exclude non-Jews. Each plot is consecrated by the body buried there.[7]

However, in the same *Yearbook*[8] R. Gotthard Deutsch, responding to a similar question, found no support in traditional law for the burial of non-

Jews in a Jewish cemetery, but nonetheless provided a roster of Gentiles who were in fact buried in Orthodox cemeteries. The congregation of Berlin (1883), of Leipzig (1884), and of Dresden (1897) passed resolutions permitting the non-Jewish parties in a mixed marriage to be buried in the Jewish cemetery. Similarly, while the rabbinate of Leghorn ruled against the practice, the congregation refused to accept the decision.

We have thus ample precedent both in Europe and America for the burial of non-Jewish spouses. Can that permission be extended to the burial of non-Jewish friends who have had an extended relationship with each other?

The Lesbian Aspect

If the daughter of the woman who wants to purchase a burial plot in the cemetery had been living with a non-Jewish male for twenty years in a common-law relationship, would the congregation have hesitated to grant permission for the burial of the non-Jew? We know of no congregation that requires proof of marriage before allowing the interment of the partner of a member.

R. Walter Jacob has shown that the sources rarely deal with lesbianism, perhaps because they treated it as a temporary phenomenon rather than as a permanent condition among women. Still, lesbianism was considered obscene, and the later *poskim* demanded punishment (*makkot mardut*) for the offenders.[9] Similarly, Prof. Israel Ta-Shema[10] holds that, in tradition, lesbianism was considered a form of sexual perversion and was considered included in the prohibition, "You shall not act in the way of the land of Egypt".[11]

Reform Judaism has abandoned this view and has accepted all homosexuals as persons who are to be accorded full respect and who, therefore, are accepted also as rabbis on an equal basis with heterosexuals.[12] But the same resolution which affirmed this view refrained from according homosexual unions the status of *kiddushin*. It said:

> In the Jewish tradition heterosexual, monogamous, procreative marriage is the ideal human relationship for the perpetuation of species, covenantal fulfillment, and the preservation of the Jewish people. While acknowledging that there are other human relationships which possess ethical and spiritual value and that there are some people for whom heterosexual, monog-

amous, procreative marriage is not a viable option or possibility, the majority of the committee reaffirms unequivocally the centrality of this idea and its special status as *kiddushin.*

The resolution was, in this respect, a compromise: gays and lesbians were accepted as equals in every way as *individuals,* but heterosexual marriages remained the Jewish ideal. Thus, *Reform Judaism has not recognized such unions as religiously analogous to heterosexual marriage,* and special rituals of affirmation conducted by some of our colleagues — designed to give public recognition to a loving and stable relationship which does not have the approval of conventional marriage — do not alter the official position of the movement in this regard.

The bylaws of the congregation provide that a Gentile "spouse" of a Jew may be interred in the cemetery. Promising to bury the "friend" would denote her acceptance as a "spouse" which is not an identity presently agreed to in civil law, in Jewish tradition, or in its Reform development.

This committee which interprets "Reform practice" concludes that the "friend" is by the fiat of our Conference not considered a "spouse", and the congregation would therefore be justified to refuse to sell the lot with the condition that burial would be permitted.

There were three dissenters, one of them wrote: "While we cannot consider women 'married' even if they participate in some ritual of acceptance, still we cannot overlook their long and close connection. The rule allowing non-Jewish women to be buried in the congregational cemetery should be extended in this case to permit the burial of this non-Jewish companion, certainly out of compassion as well as *mipnei darchei shalom.*"[13]

NOTES

1 BT Gittin 61a.

2 YD n. 367.

3 YD 151:12 and 367:1.

4 *Melammed Leho'il,* YD n. 127.

5 Cf. *C.C.A.R. Yearbook,* Vol. XXIV, pp 154-155; Vol. XXVI, pp 122-134; Vol. XXVII, p. 88; Vol, XXVIII, pp 117-119; Vol. XXIX, pp 77-78, 80-85.

6 *Yearbook,* Vol XXVI, pp 133-134.

7 *Yearbook,* Vol. XXIX, p 78.

8 Pp. 80-85.

9 *C ARR* n. 200, pp. 296-297.

10 *Encyclopedia Hebraica,* ed. Y. Prayer, vol. 21, col. 291.

11 See *Sifra* 18,3.

12 *CCAR Yearbook,* Vol. C, 1990, pp 107 ff.

13 A note might also be made of an essay by our colleague R. Moshe Zemer of Tel Aviv, who has discussed some of these questions and has dealt with the treatment of controversial burials *milechat chilah* and *bedi'avad* (*Ha'aretz*, 8 Adar Sheni 5744/12 March 1984).

Two caskets in One Grave
5751.8

She'elah

Recently I was asked by the management of a local Jewish cemetery if double-depth lawn crypt-burials are permitted under Jewish law. In this method of burial, a casket is lowered into a concrete lined grave several feet deeper than normal. The casket, however, is completely surrounded by earth which has been inserted into the vault. Subsequently, a second casket is buried over the first, with a layer of earth between them.

We are interested in three aspects of this method of burial.

1. Are double-depth burials (one casket over another) permissible?

2. Is crypt-burial surrounded by earth permissible?

3. Are there significant differences of opinion among the major branches of Judaism on this subject? (This particular cemetery presently serves all three branches of Judaism.)

A sketch of the proposed burial method is enclosed. (Rabbi Allan C. Tuffs, Allentown, PA)

Teshuvah

The Halachah of burial in the earth is derived from Deut. 21:23, which prescribes interment for executed criminals, and from this the Talmud derives the obligation to bury every dead person.[1]

We will deal first with the question of burying caskets on top of each other.

The traditional literature deals with bodies which are placed one above the other. The relevant passage is found in the *Shulchan Aruch* and reads: "Two caskets are not buried one over the other, but when six handbreadths of earth separate them it is allowed."[2] The Hoop Lane cemetery in London, England, which serves both a Reform and an Orthodox Sefardi constituency, permits double and triple depth burials.

What if these bodies and caskets are placed for burial in a vault (here called "crypt"),[3] a custom which is widespread in North America? Does such a vault present a problem? R. Jekuthiel Greenwald says it does and forbids it, because the vault compares to a mausoleum which is seen to delay or possibly prevent decay and thus be unmindful of the implications of the Deuteronomic passage which says, "You shall surely bury him (*kavor tikberenu*).[4] But R. Moshe Feinstein (who forbids mausoleum burial[5]) would allow the vault, because it is not designed to, nor does it, interfere with the process of decomposition, especially when the body is surrounded by earth.[6]

We hold with the latter opinion. The use of cement casings does not interfere with the purpose of interring the body, that is, returning it to the earth. It is merely the way by which many cemetery authorities prevent the ground from sinking, so that the appearance of the burial grounds is not marred and the honor paid to the dead (*kevod ha-met*) is not diminished. However, as indicated, the use of the vault might be contested by some halachic authorities.

The sketch submitted to us reveals an additional feature, in that two caskets are buried in the same casing, one on top of the other, with layers of earth surrounding each casket. This too does not represent any obstacle in our view or in the traditional Halachah.

Are there additional considerations which we might bring to bear on these issues? With cemetery space becoming scarce in many, especially larger communities, we would consider burials in a single plot, with due separation of the caskets, an acceptable alternative. Also, this would better enable survivors to carry out the mitzvah of visiting the graves of their dear ones.[6]

NOTES

1 BT Sanhedrin 46 b.

2 YD, n. 262:4. Similarly *Tur*, YD, n. 262. *Yad,* Avel 14:16, discourages the practice, apparently because of the danger that the earth separating the two bodies might not prevent the upper body from sinking and coming too close to the other; see the commentary of the Radbaz on the passage, and R. Moshe Feinstein, *Igrot Moshe,* Y.D. n. 233/234. See also R. Solomon B. Freehof, *Reform Jewish Practice*, vol I, pp. 123 ff.; *CRR,* p.148.

3 Usually a cement casing.

4 *Kol Bo al Avelut,* vol. 2, pp. 47 ff.

5 *Igrot Moshe,* YD n. 143. On this issue see R. Walter Jacob, *ARR,* n. 102, pp. 349-350.

6 *Igrot Moshe,* YD, n. 142.

7 On mausoleum burials, see Solomon B. Freehof, *RR,* n. 38, pp. 158-161.

Video Camera Affixed to Chuppah
5751.14

She-elah

Is it permissible to affix a video camera to a chuppah for the purposes of taping the wedding ceremony?

Teshuvah

Those who would allow the arrangement might draw on the tradition that it is a mitzvah to rejoice with bride and groom, and that the requested installation of a video camera could be seen as enlarging the couple's enjoyment. Those who might oppose the installation would draw on the tradition that a religious celebration has certain limits, which render intrusive devices inappropriate.

1. <u>The mitzvah to rejoice with bride and groom</u>. It is a mitzvah *der-abbanan* (instituted by the Rabbis) to accompany the couple to the chuppah and to rejoice with them.[1] Already in medieval times it became a custom to dance at weddings to the accompaniment of instrumental music[2]--even though such music making was otherwise still prohibited, as a remembrance of the Temple's destruction.[3]

By analogy, the photographing as well as audio and video taping of the ceremony have become generally acceptable as activities which, by providing happy memories of the event, enhance the wedding joy.

It is assumed that the camera is installed in such a way that it does not detract from the chuppah and its symbolism.

2. <u>Standards of propriety</u>. Already in ages past, certain limitations were placed upon merry making at weddings.[4] The custom of breaking a glass at the conclusion of the ceremony may also be seen as introducing a sober note, as was the earlier habit of placing ashes on the head of the groom, in the spot where he would normally wear his *tefillin*.[5]

There was also considerable discussion on matters of propriety, as for instance with regard to the lavishness of the wedding and the difficulties encountered when the community's leaders tried to enforce sumptuary standards.[6] In the nineteenth century, the Hatam Sofer expressed the fear that, if

119

the wedding were held in the synagogue, the customary dignity accorded to it might be diminished by excessive gaiety and the possible mingling of the sexes.[7] However, R. Moshe Feinstein ruled that the conditions on which the Hatam Sofer had based his decision no longer applied in the contemporary world, and that therefore certain customs and restrictions need no longer be observed.[8]

3. <u>Recording the ceremony</u>. This has become a custom not only in Reform but also in all other synagogues, though one objection to this practice has been raised on halachic grounds by R. Yitzhak Rudnick. He argues that tapes are frequently erased, and if blessings are recorded on them the Divine Name too is erased, which is forbidden.[9] R. Feinstein disagrees and maintains the common practice, because no actual letters are being erased; still he suggests that if erasing does take place, it be done by some automated procedure (akin to the running of Shabbat elevators, etc.).[10]

4. <u>Affixing the video camera.</u> How do these various arguments apply to our *she'elah*? Both the rules of rejoicing and limits depend on many variables. Usually the rabbi and the congregation arrive at certain standards, especially when the ceremony takes place in the sanctuary.

Since such weddings are quite common in the Reform movement it may be assumed that each synagogue has some rules and regulations-- for the participants themselves as well as for decorators, photographers and the like. In many if not most instances, the popping of flash bulbs during the ceremony is forbidden during the ceremony, so that in this regard an unobtrusively affixed camera in the chuppah is an improvement.

Still, some are cautious about a blanket permission. They point out that a chuppah, like a kiddush cup, is not just another thing, but an item which partakes of the holiness of the ritual, and that therefore its integrity should be especially safeguarded. In this view, affixing a camera to the chuppah for convenience's sake is seen as undesirable. Yet others would point to the analogous practice of many Reform (and Conservative) synagogues which place a microphone inside the Ark.

A final consideration is privacy. There are moments in life which are unsuitable for recording and photographing--even though the media frequently offend against ordinary sensitivities as, for instance, when the sorrow of bereaved persons is pictured for all to see. This caution could well apply to the question at issue. The couple are usually turned toward the Ark, away from the congregation, and only those under the chuppah can observe their intimate reactions during the ceremony. To record these may initially be thought of as a good idea, but the couple, when apprised of the implications of such procedures, will frequently opt for greater privacy and agree that some moments are best preserved in memory only.

In sum, the rabbi who asks the *she'elah* will have to consider his/her own sense of propriety, as well as the custom of the congregation and the community. Last but not least, the question ought to be raised with the bride and groom. We see no objection per se to the proposed practice.

NOTES

1 *Yad,* Avel 14:1. He derives this from the commandment to love one's neighbor and, following Hillel (BT, Shabbat 31a), concludes that we should extend this principle to making a wedding a happy occasion. Various commentaries enlarge on this ruling (see, e.g., the Vilna Gaon in his commentary on *Sh.A.* EH 65:1), and include it in the mitzvah of *hachnasat kallah* (arranging for a wedding and rejoicing with bride and groom), which the prayer book mentions as a mitzvah that accompanies us into the world-to-come (see, for instance, *Gates of Prayer,* p.235).

2 See *Tur,* OC 338: "There is no wedding joy without musical instruments."

3 The ban is found in BT Gittin. 7a and Sota 48a; Rambam, *Yad ,* Ta'aniyot 5:14. For a full discussion of musical instruments in the Halachah, see R. Eliezer Waldenberg, *Resp. Tzitz 'Eliezer,* vol. 15, n. 33.

4 See e.g. the comment of Magen Avraham on *Sh.A.* OC 560:11.

5 For a full discussion, see Prof. Jacob Zvi Lauterbach, "The Ceremony of Breaking a Glass at Weddings," in *HUCA* vol.II., pp.351-380; and R. Solomon B. Freehof, *RRR,* n. 40, pp. 182-188.

6 See R. Jacob R. Marcus, *The Jew in the Medieval World,* pp. 193-197.

7 See especially *Resp. Hatam Sofer,* EH, n. 98, whose ruling was most likely motivated by his desire to counter-act the spreading custom of Reformers to hold weddings in the synagogue. R. Isaac Halevy Herzog, *Resp. Heichal Yitzhak ,* 'EH II, n. 27, decided similarly.

8 *Resp. Igrot Moshe ,* EH, n. 93.

9 *Resp. Sedeh Yitzhak,* n. 5.

10 *Resp. Igrot Moshe,* YD, I n. 173, and II n. 142.

Practicing Judaism and Buddhism
5752.3

She'elah

A couple, who have a Jewish background and are currently practicing Buddhism as well as Judaism, want to join the temple and enroll their child in the religious school.

The wife was born Jewish; her husband was converted to Judaism as a teenager. They are presently members of a Conservative synagogue (where their Buddhist practices are apparently unknown), but now want to join a Reform temple because they consider its religious education program superior, and also because Reform Judaism seems more compatible to them.

The woman is an ordained priest in the Zen tradition. Her husband states that, by adding Tibetan Buddhist practices to his life, he has enhanced his Judaism. The two consider their Buddhism as basically non-theological and permitting synchronous religious practice. They do not missionize. (Rabbi Sheldon Ezring, Syracuse, NY)

Teshuvah

The relationship between Judaism and other religions has often been dealt with in halachic literature. While since the days of Maimonides Christianity (like Islam) was removed from the category of idolatrous faiths, responsa have nonetheless consistently taken the view that Judaism and Christianity or Islam are mutually exclusive and that Jews — whether or not born or converted to Judaism — practicing and affirming these faiths are to be considered apostates.[1] If they would wish to return to the synagogue it would be necessary for them to abjure any other faith.[2] The question arises: Is Buddhism different in this respect?

Buddhism originated in the 6th century B.C.E. and has developed into an extraordinarily variegated stream of philosophies and practices. Centered in eastern Asia, it has spread all over the globe, and national subdivisions have created additional variations.

123

The most popular form of later Buddhism has been the "Pure Land" or Amitabhist doctrine, which teaches salvation through grace in the Buddha Amitabha. There can be little question that in this form Buddhism is in fact a religion, as we use that term and concept.

While at one end of this religious spectrum one finds theistic and even clearly polytheistic beliefs, other types of Buddhism may however be called non-theistic, in that they emphasize ethics and contemplative practices. Thus, Zen Buddhism (of which there are also various streams) may generally be assigned to the latter category in that it stresses meditation and self-discipline as the path to individual enlightenment and spiritual growth. Yoga is one of its best known practices.

Tibetan Buddhism is in some respects quite different from Zen, since it has incorporated forms of the pre-Buddhist Bon cult and knows of oracular priests and concepts like divine kingship. However, it too stresses spiritual development and has developed distinct practices to achieve it.

As indicated, when Jews profess Christianity or Islam they are considered apostates. Is such judgment appropriate also when it comes to Buddhism, and is it appropriate in view of the circumstances of the present case?

If we were to deal solely with the husband we might be inclined to interpret his statement as meaning that he is engaging in meditative practices which enhance his spiritual awareness. The fact that he learned them from Buddhist teachers would seem indeed not be in competition with his Jewish identity and practice. Many Jews experiment in this fashion, which would not expose them to the charge of apostasy.

The matter is however complicated by the admission of the wife that she is a Zen Buddhist priest. Depending on the type of Zen she affirms, that could have various meanings, but we will for the moment assume that "priest" here means (like "rabbi") primarily a teacher, for Zen — the word means meditation — favors the master-to-pupil or mind-to-mind method of teaching contemplation.

But being a priest in any religion demands a special type of identification and commitment, which suggests that the devotee has embraced not only teaching practices like Yoga but also the underlying deeper philosophy.

Without in any way denying the depth of Buddhist philosophical and ethical doctrines, there are fundamental differences between them and the teachings of Jewish tradition. The latter clearly affirm this world rather than, as the majority of Buddhist traditions would, denigrate its importance. Reform Judaism especially has downplayed the salvational aspects of our religion and has taught that we have an obligation to perfect this world in all its aspects—from the environment to its social structures. Judaism is a deed-oriented rather than a contemplative religion, and while the merits of the latter are great, it reflects a basically different approach to the needs of everyday life, and therefore Rabbi Leo Baeck took the view that Judaism and Buddhism are complete opposites, "two religious polarities."[3]

To be sure, there is no conflict between Judaism and meditative practices — after all, Jewish tradition itself is familiar with it. But we see a conflict when it comes to the world-affirming view we hold and that of a world-denying Buddhism. It is therefore inappropriate to consider a Buddhist priest as eligible for membership in the congregation. The husband alone might qualify, but as a family the couple do not, as long as the mother maintains her status as a Buddhist priest.

There is also the matter of appearance (*mar'it ayin*).[4] The Jewish community would be confused by what it would conceive as an experiment in religious syncretism and a watering down of Jewish identity. The couple must be brought to realize that with all the respect we have for their Buddhist practices and beliefs, the enlargement that they think they have brought to their Judaism may fit their own personal needs but does not fit the needs of a congregation. Their request to join the congregation should therefore not be accommodated.

Yet, there is also a pastoral aspect to their situation. Since they want to be Jewish and do in fact practice Judaism on some levels, we must be sure not to push them away. In view of their meandering search for religious meaning — from Christianity (in the husband's case) to Judaism to Buddhism to Conservative and now Reform Judaism — the rabbi should engage them in counseling and help them to find their way.

As for the child, halachic tradition would consider it Jewish, even if the mother were to be considered an apostate. This view has been affirmed by a CCAR responsum.[5] In view of this, should the child be admitted to religious school?

Assuming that the congregation's by-laws permit enrolling the child of non-members, the rabbi's judgment will have to prevail. We would counsel against admitting the child if it appears that it is to be brought up in two religious traditions. R. Walter Jacob affirmed, for instance, that a child could not be a Bar Mitzvah if he is also to have a Christian confirmation.[6] The rabbi will have to evaluate the possibility that other children in the religious school may be thoroughly confused if they learn that a fellow student professes two identities. It is difficult enough to teach our children the uniqueness of Judaism and its essentials.

NOTES

[1] *ARR,* ed. R. Walter Jacob, p. 241; idem, *CARR,* n. 68, pp. 109-112, where references to earlier halachic material will also be found.

[2] *ARR,* l.c., p. 241; see also the responsum "Gentile Membership in Synagogue," by R. Solomon B. Freehof, *RRT,* n. 47, pp. 221-224.

[3] *Essence of Judaism,* rev. ed. (New York, 1948), pp. 60 f.

[4] The concept relates to a practice which is discouraged because, though by itself permissible, gives people a wrong impression in that it appears to be un-Jewish.

[5] *ARR,* l.c.

[6] *Contemporary American Reform Responsa,* n. 61, pp. 98-99.

Cosmetic Surgery
5752.7

She'elah

A woman is planning breast enlargement surgery in order, she says, to please her husband. She now wonders whether this is sufficient justification for the procedure, and she has asked my counsel. Do the same considerations apply to penile implants as well? (Rabbi Jon Haddon, Richfield, CT)

Teshuvah

The question involves the advisability of surgical procedures undertaken for cosmetic (i.e., non-medical) purposes. As such, it is essential at the outset to distinguish penile implant from breast implant surgery. Penile implantation is generally directed at correcting organic impotence and would therefore be justified on medical grounds.[1] Traditional Jewish law would favor the procedure as a means for helping a husband fulfill the mitzvot of procreation[2] and conjugal responsibilities.[3]

Breast implantation, by contrast, is undertaken for either of two broad reasons: to reconstruct the breast following a mastectomy, or to change the size of the breasts for the sake of physical appearance. The former, initiated as part of a response to disease, is generally considered a medical purpose, and so is the reduction of over-large breasts in some instances. We regard our case, in which a woman wishes to "enhance" her appearance to please her husband, as falling into the second category, that of cosmetic surgery. We are of course aware that individuals who opt for "mere" cosmetic surgery justify their choice on a variety of grounds. Our task here is to consider, from the standpoint of Jewish tradition and our own Reform perspective, whether and in which instances such procedures either violate or serve our highest religious goals.

Traditional Perspectives

We begin with the observation that, under Jewish law, it is forbidden to cause injury to one's own body without sufficient justification. The prohibition, found in the leading codes,[4] is based upon a statement of Rabbi Akiva in the Mishnah (Baba Kama 8:5). Although this ruling is somewhat controversial,[5] it reflects mainstream halachic thought as well as, to us, the better interpretation of tradition. For the gratitude which we owe God for the gift of life surely demands that we treat our bodies with the utmost reverence.

Similarly, it is forbidden to endanger one's life needlessly, a rule derived from Lev. 18:5 ("these are the mitzvot which a person shall do and live by them")[6] and from the exemption from the commandment to save the life of another (Lev. 19:16) when the attempt to do so endangers one's own life.[7] Neither of these prohibitions, however, is absolute. Rambam, for example, forbids self-injury only when it is performed for harmful or pointless ends.[8] The rule against self-endangerment does not forbid one from flying in airplanes, driving an automobile, working in construction or engaging in other potentially dangerous but worthwhile activities. In particular, the prohibition is waived in medical situations. The whole medical enterprise is suffused with risk; "that which cures one person will kill another".[9] Nonetheless, we are permitted and even commanded to administer medical and surgical measures in order to save human life.[10] One may submit to such measures when they serve legitimate and reasonable therapeutic purposes. With cosmetic surgery, then, as with other invasive procedures, the task is to reckon its inherent dangers against its hoped-for benefits: do the latter outweigh the former?

The current controversy over breast implant surgery indicates that, at least with respect to this procedure, the answer is "no". The silicone-gel-filled sacs used in this operation have long been known to deteriorate, leak, and occasionally rupture. Preliminary studies suggest that gel leakage may be associated with various health risks, including arthritis, lupus, and cancer. Widespread concern over the dangers of this surgery has led the U.S. Food and Drug Administration to place restrictions on their use.[11] The FDA has sought to distinguish between medical and non-medical need. Women undergoing reconstructive surgery after mastectomies, as well as those disfigured due to medical trauma or birth defects, will have access to breast implants; those wanting cosmetic breast enlargement can use these devices only as part of approved clinical trial programs. In one sense our answer has been determined by these events: the risks associated with breast implant surgery convince us, along with the U.S. Government, that the procedure should be restricted to bona fide medical purposes.

This answer, however, does not suffice, for the scope of the case before us extends far beyond the particulars of this one surgical procedure. The question seems to have originated at an earlier time than when the specific dangers of breast implant surgery filled the news. We are not being asked whether these dangers warrant a prohibition against this operation. We are asked instead a broader question, whether such cosmetic surgery as breast implantation, undertaken in order to "please" a spouse, ought to be permitted under our conception of Jewish teaching? Would we approve of that surgery even were it not linked to grievous health risks? In other words, supposing the absence of concerns like those surrounding breast implantation, how should we measure the potential benefits of cosmetic surgery against those factors which would persuade us to caution against it?

Orthodox halachic literature is markedly ambivalent on this subject. R. Moshe Feinstein permits cosmetic surgery to a young woman who seeks to make herself more attractive and therefore "marriageable". The prohibition against self-injury, as we have seen, applies only when the act is done for harmful or pointless ends. Cosmetic surgery undertaken for a legitimate and beneficial purpose is hardly "harmful" or "pointless", and R. Feinstein accordingly sees no reason to forbid a woman from choosing that option.[12] On the other hand, R. Eliezer Yehudah Waldenberg, in a lengthy analysis of the mitzvah of medicine,[13] concludes that physicians are permitted to perform invasive procedures only to treat conditions generally recognized as "disease". This leads him to condemn cosmetic surgery whose goal is to enhance a person's physical appearance. Such surgery serves no accepted medical goal, and R. Waldenberg sees it as evidence of hubris (an attempt to improve upon God's work) and misplaced values.[14]

Halachah supports these contradictory conclusions because, while each authority arrives at a decision which is perfectly logical, they begin their process of reasoning from opposing points of departure. R. Feinstein considers cosmetic surgery under the rubric of "benefit". Inasmuch as self-injury is permitted for a "beneficial" purpose, and since "benefits" need not be restricted to medicine, there is no reason to forbid the operation. Waldenberg, on the other hand, views the issue solely from its medical standpoint.[15] The question is one of surgery, which is generally undertaken to secure *refu'ah*, healing. Surgery which does not contribute to *refu'ah* is not, properly speaking, "surgery" at all, but willful damage to and desecration of the human body. Cosmetic surgery, which has nothing to do with medicine, thus has no justification whatsoever. Further, he bases his decision upon a value judgement which R. Feinstein does not mention, namely that the willful alteration of the human form is in itself frivolous and undesirable and in no way warrants the use of surgery which by its nature involves bodily injury.

Reform Considerations.

Reform Jews, it seems to us, must ask similar questions and make similar value judgments. If we regard cosmetic surgery first and foremost as a technology offering attractive and legitimate benefits to an individual, then we would have no real reason to caution against it, excepting those cases such as breast implants which entail significant health risks. If, on the other hand, we presume that the proper function of surgery is to contribute to healing and that enhancement of appearance is not a truly "worthwhile" goal, then we are much more likely to reject cosmetic surgery. We would, rather, affirm with Jewish tradition the sanctity of the human body and the abhorrence of capricious manipulation of its form. True, value judgments are difficult to objectify, and in a movement such as ours, which places such a high premium on freedom of personal choice, much can be said for leaving these judgments exclusively in the hands of the individuals who must make them. Religion, however, is all about value judgments, and in this case the rabbi, as a teacher of religion, is being asked for counsel as to which value judgment reflects a better and more coherent understanding of Judaism's message. To assist in the making of that judgement is the task before us.

Our answer must distinguish between the particular instance and the general rule. It is conceivable that, for some persons, "mere" cosmetic surgery may serve a useful and legitimate purpose. It may be determined, for example, that an enhanced appearance is vital to an individual's psychological and emotional well-being. This is a judgement that must be made carefully in each individual case; when it is made, these persons should not be dissuaded from this alternative. In general, however, we think this argument is too frequently raised and too easily exaggerated. We would argue the opposite: that so many people are willing to subject themselves to damaging and potentially dangerous procedures for no other reason than better looks[16] is clear evidence of the overemphasis which our materialistic culture places upon superficialities. Rabbis customarily and justly critique this distortion of values. Indeed, if Judaism means anything to us, it admonishes us to look below the surface, to concentrate upon the development of deeper and more lasting measurements of self-worth and satisfaction. When even breast reconstruction, which we tend to view as "medical" rather than "cosmetic", is not always indicated on psychological grounds,[17] the notion that purely cosmetic surgery is beneficial to mental health must as a general rule be resisted. We would therefore urge that rabbis advise against cosmetic surgery undertaken solely for the improvement of personal appearance and hoped-for marital benefits.

NOTES

1 See Jan K. Meyer in A.M. Harvey et al., eds., *The Principles and Practices of Medicine* (Norwalk, CT, 1984), p. 1404; L. Vliet and J. Meyer, "Erectile Dysfunction: Progress in Evaluation and Treatment", *The Johns Hopkins Medical Journal* 151:246-258, 1982.

2 Gen. 1:28; BT Yeb. 65b; *Yad*, Ishut 15:2

3 Ex. 21:10; BT Ketubot 61b; *Yad*, Ishut 14:1 ff.).

4 *Yad*, Chovel 5:1; *Sh. A.* HM 420:31.

5 The Talmud (Baba Kamma 91a-b) records a baraita quoting R. Akiva to the opposite effect: one is permitted to injure oneself. According to the 13th-century Spanish sage R. Meir Halevy Abulafia, the law follows the baraita (*Shitah Mekubetset*, Baba Kamma 91b). Since Rav Hisda, the latest authority found in the Talmudic discussion, seems to accept the baraita as authoritative, Abulafia invokes the rule *hilcheta kevatra'ei*, "the law is decided according to the latest authorities". All other poskim reject this ruling, inasmuch as the Talmudic sugya concludes by upholding the Mishnah's version of R. Akiva's view.

6 BT Yoma 85b; Isserles, *Sh. A.,* YD 116:5.

7 See *SA Sh. A.,* CM 426 and commentaries.

8 See note 4.

9 R. Moshe b. Nachman, *Torat Ha'adam, she`ar hasakanah* (Chavel ed., p. 43).

10 *Sh. A.,* YD 336:1.

11 Indeed, as of this writing, the leading manufacturer of silicone-gel breast implants has announced its intention to cease producing them.

12 *Resp. Igrot Moshe*, HM II, n. 66)

13 *Resp. Tzitz Eliezer*, v. 11, n. 41, end.

14 He cites Prov. 31:30—"grace is deceitful and beauty is vain".

15 He brands as "ridiculous" attempts to justify cosmetic surgery by various midrashim which speak in praise of feminine beauty. In so doing, he teaches an important lesson: traditional sources, when quoted out of context, can be made to support virtually any position.

16 According to current estimates, for example, 120,000 American women per year seek cosmetic breast enlargement (*Newsweek*, March 2, 1992, p. 75).

17 "It is rare for a husband to urge reconstruction...I can attest to the stability of married relationships after a mastectomy. I have seen only one that was significantly worse than before mastectomy, and that one was significantly bad to begin with"; T.K. Hunt, MD, in T. Gant and L. Vasconez, eds., *Post-Mastectomy Reconstruction,* Baltimore, 1981, pp. 3-4.

Private Ordination
5753.4

She'elah

A rabbi in our community declares that a young man who has studied with him is now qualified to be ordained as a rabbi. He has asked that I and another rabbinic colleague join him in granting ordination to this student. May I, as a rabbi ordained at HUC-JIR, participate in such a ceremony?

Teshuvah

This is a question of extraordinary sensitivity within the rabbinic community. Virtually all the members of the Central Conference of American Rabbis are graduates (i.e., ordinees) of the Hebrew Union College-Jewish Institute of Religion or some other established rabbinical seminary. To permit the kind of private ordination referred to in the *she'elah* is to invite a radical transformation in the way that we liberal rabbis receive our credentials to serve. An adequate response to this question must therefore address two separate issues. First, what is the nature of the ordination that we practice today? Must this ordination be granted by an officially-licensed school or agency, or is any rabbi empowered, as a matter of Jewish law, to ordain a person of his choice as a rabbi? Second, if the rabbi is so empowered, are there considerations of Jewish law, custom, and Reform Jewish practice which would argue against the use of this power?

    1. <u>Ordination, Past and Present.</u> The "ordination" customarily practiced today, a ceremony we call *semichah,* has little to do with the *semichah* described in the Talmudic sources.[1] That ancient ritual, according to rabbinic thought, elevated its recipient to the status of the biblical judge (*shofet*) and as such the latest link in a chain of Torah transmission that reached from student to teacher all the way back to Moses.[2] The ordained judges were regarded as the legal successors of the seventy elders who stood with Moses on Sinai. It was they who qualified as representatives of God(Ex. 22:7-8),[3] empowered to

133

enforce their decisions upon recalcitrant litigants;[4] it was they alone who were entitled to adjudicate all matters of law,[5] including *diney nefashot* (capital cases) and *diney kenasot* (fines).[6] Ordination was practiced only in the land of Israel. This explains why Babylonian sages were called *rav* rather than *rabbi*, the title bestowed upon the recipient of *semichah*, unless those sages themselves received *semichah* in Eretz Yisrael.[7] This semichah no longer exists, and its power has largely disappeared. In the words of R. Ya`akov b. Asher: "today, we are all lay judges (*hedyotot*) and we do not exercise the Toraitic power of jurisdiction."[8] We function as the agents of the ordained judges of old,[9] who commissioned us to exercise judgment within carefully circumscribed boundaries that exclude *diney nefashot* and *diney kenasot*. Various attempts have been made to renew the practice of *semichah* and thereby the rabbinic Sanhedrin, the supreme legislative and judicial body that can determine the authoritative interpretation of Torah to all Israel. The most notable of these efforts occurred in Safed during the 16th century; in addition, talk of the re-institution of *semichah* was common during the heady days following the establishment of the modern state of Israel. While those who advocated the restoration of *semichah* relied upon the opinion of Rambam that such an act may be halachically permissible,[10] they were rebuffed by the firm opposition of most of the rabbinic community.

What, then, is the nature of the "*semichah*" we confer upon our rabbis today? R. Moshe Isserles writes that "the purpose of the ordination commonly practiced these days is to inform the community that the student has attained the requisite knowledge to rule on matters of Jewish law (*higi`a lehora'ah*) and that he does so with the permission (*reshut*) of the rabbi who has ordained him."[11] In this view, he relies heavily upon a responsum of R. Yitzchak b. Sheshet (Rivash; late-14th century Spain and North Africa), who offers a comprehensive halachic analysis of "this *semichah* practiced in France and Germany."[12] Rivash rejects any real similarity between the original ordination and the contemporary custom, which he regards as a mere symbolic representation of the former.[13] Today's *semichah* serves only as a means of granting the student the permission to issue halachic rulings. Ordinarily, the requirement of *kevod harav*, the honor due to one's Torah teacher, prohibits a student from issuing halachic rulings during his teacher's lifetime. *Semichah* is a formal "license" which exempts the student from this prohibition.[14] It does not, however, bestow upon him the full range of powers associated with the ancient ordination ceremony. The authority of a rabbi's rulings, in this day and age, is based solely upon the willingness of the community to abide by them. And since the empowerment of rabbis flows from the people, no organized body, rabbinic or otherwise, is entitled to demand that a community engage the services of only those rabbis who have received an "approved" ordination.

2. <u>Ordination and the Qualifications of the Rabbi.</u> The foregoing suggests that today's seminaries hold no monopoly over the ordination of the rabbi. Any person acceptable to the community may serve in that position. Yet this grant of popular sovereignty is circumscribed by a vital caveat: the rabbi chosen must be sufficiently knowledgeable and qualified. All Jewish communities, including those that did not demand formal ordination, have nonetheless been concerned that their rabbis meet the criteria of learning expected of Torah scholars. And, as we have seen, the practice of ordination developed in medieval times in response to this concern.[17] Today, the widespread custom (*minhag*) is to require ordination as testimony that the individual in question is qualified to serve as a rabbi—*higi`a lehora'ah*, in Isserles' phrase—and to perform the functions generally associated with that office.[18]

Similarly, it has long been the *minhag* among the congregations and institutions of the Reform movement to recognize as "rabbi" only those individuals who have completed the prescribed curriculum at the Hebrew Union College-Jewish Institute of Religion or other comparable rabbinical school. The ordination which we have come to demand as the necessary credential for rabbinic employment is the end result of a formal, organized program of education which the community has identified as sufficient to bestow the title "rabbi" upon its graduates. This process reflects our belief that a person must be qualified—intellectually, morally, professionally, psychologically—to carry that title and that seminary education affords the best objective evaluation of his or her fitness.

True, Jewish tradition does not demand that rabbis graduate from seminaries.[19] We do not say that seminary training is the only way in which a candidate for the rabbinate can acquire the requisite learning and skills.[20] Nor do we argue that it is a foolproof method: we all know that our rabbinical schools sometimes turn away good candidates and ordain bad ones. Our seminaries can and should constantly strive to do better. Nonetheless, as a general rule, we believe that the course of education at a reputable seminary is a better preparation for the rabbinate than are the available alternatives, whether "private ordination" from an individual rabbi or attendance at a lowly-regarded rabbinical school. Unlike either of these, the seminary exposes its students to a diverse and distinguished faculty of teachers, a liberal curriculum of Jewish studies, a decent library, and a host of supervised field-work practica. Our community has chosen this means to determine whether the candidate *higi`a lehora'ah*. And Jewish tradition, which both requires that a student meet this standard and which has developed the contemporary custom of *semichah* in order to test for it, allows us to make this choice. By contrast, a "private ordination" grants the title "rabbi" to students who have not met this test. It is therefore destructive to our goal of a rabbinate that measures up to the highest attainable standards.

Moreover, in the case at hand, since the rabbi who asks this *she'elah* did not teach the student in question, he or she has no way of determining whether that young man has met the standards we expect of rabbis (*hig`a lehora'ah*). Even if it were our custom to accept "private ordination," it would be inappropriate for this rabbi to take part in the ordination ceremony. To be sure, it has long been a practice to have rabbis other than one's teachers add their names to the *semichah* document; in this way, one's credentials would appear more impressive to one's potential employers. Yet some sages have condemned this practice as senseless, a sign of the intellectual and social decline of the rabbinate.[21] It seems senseless to us as well. One who has never taught a student is in no position to testify to that student's fitness to serve as a rabbi.

3. <u>Ordination and *Kevod Harav*.</u> In addition to the determination of the student's rabbinical qualifications, we have seen that the tradition offers another reason for the contemporary practice of ordination: *semichah* is a license which permits the student to function as a rabbi without violating the principle of *kevod harav*, the duty to render honor to one's teacher. This duty implies

that the student must not engage in a disagreement (*machloket*) with his teacher over a matter of halachah.[22] The precise dimensions of this *machloket* are a matter of dispute. Some authorities hold that a student is forbidden to establish a yeshivah without his teacher's express permission.[23] Others allow the student to teach Torah but forbid him to issue halachic rulings without the express permission of his *rav*.[24] While most allow the student to debate his teacher and argue against him "should he have textual proofs for his contrary opinion," some deny him even that degree of intellectual freedom without his teacher's permission. At any rate, all authorities agree that even after ordination, the ordinee is in some way *kafuf lasomeich*, subject to the authority of the ordaining rabbi.[27] To act otherwise is detrimental to the *kavod* (honor) of one's teacher and, by extension, of the rabbinate as an institution.

Our *sho'el* asks whether a rabbi ordained at HUC-JIR may confer "private ordination" upon a student. To answer this question fully, we must consider whether and to what extent the alumni of HUC-JIR are *kefufim*, subject to the authority of those who ordained them.

On the one hand, we reject any such suggestion. Surely we are not prohibited from disagreeing with our teachers over matters of Torah. Reform Judaism proclaims our intellectual freedom, and our *semichah* is testimony to our readiness to exercise that freedom as rabbis.

Yet on the other hand we feel just as surely a sense of obligation to render honor to our rabbis, those who instilled Torah in us and prepared us for the momentous task of transmitting it to our people. We, too, recognize the principle of *kevod harav*. And this principle, if it means anything at all, must be more than mere lip-service or sentiment. It implies that we have a duty to promote the welfare of the College-Institute in any way that we can. It demands at the very least that we avoid taking actions which would undermine the centrality and integrity of the College-Institute as the agency by which North American Reform Jewry has chosen to train its rabbinic leadership in accordance with its religious world-view and its educational philosophy. Our *semichah*, whatever powers it confers, cannot entitle us to undermine the school which granted it to us. Yet "private ordination" does just that. For an ordinee of HUC-JIR to grant such an ordination, offering a shortcut to *semichah* which bypasses the rigors and requirements of a seminary curriculum, is to exceed even the most lenient interpretation of *kevod harav*. It is, quite simply, an act of *zilzul harav*, of scorn and disrespect to the teachers and the school which gave us the opportunity to become rabbis.

To repeat: we do not claim that our seminaries are perfect, nor do we say that one who has studied for "private ordination" cannot be a good rabbi. We know nothing of the details of this case. It is quite possible that the young man in question is a sincere Jew who wishes nothing more than to spend his life in service to his people. Our answer is not directed toward him as a person but rather toward a practice. It is a practice that, in our view, undermines the process by which we educate our rabbis and judge their fitness to serve in that position, endangers the survival of our rabbinical schools, and constitutes an affront to the honor of those who taught us Torah. It cannot be justified within our community, and those rabbis who engage in it do a profound disservice to the Reform rabbinate and to Reform Judaism as a whole.

For these reasons, we urge our colleagues in the strongest possible terms to refrain from awarding "private ordination."

NOTES

1 The fourth chapter of *Yad*, Sanhedrin, is a particularly useful summary of the laws of *semichah* and of the traditional understanding of that institution.

2 See BT Sanhedrin 5b and 13b.

3 BT Sanhedrin 56b.

4 BT Sanhedrin 16a; cp. Rashi to Deut. 16:18

5 See the midrash in BT Gitin 88b on Ex. 21:1: "these are the commandments which you shall place before them"— before them, and not before *hedyotot* (non-ordained judges).

6 BT Baba Kama 84a-b.

7 BT Sanhedrin 14a; *Yad*, Sanhedrin 4:6. A form of *semichah*, to be sure, was practiced in Babylonia under the auspices of the exilarch, who regarded himself in many respects the institutional equivalent of the patriarch in Palestine. See BT Sanhedrin 5a on Gen. 49:10 and *Yad*, Sanhedrin 4:13: the exilarch possessed the power to enforce his decisions, much as the ordained judges of Eretz Yisrael were entitled to enforce theirs. On the other hand, this enforcement power was seen to be based upon the recognition of the exilarch by the Gentile government. Moreover, the Babylonians understood that their *semichah* did not confer upon them the entire range of juridical power which belonged to the ordained scholar of the land of Israel. See the letter of R. Shmuel b. Eli, published in *Tarbiz* 1(1930), n. 2, 82.

8 *Tur*, CM 1.

9 *Shelichut dekama'ey avdinan*; see BT Gitin 88b and Tosafot ad loc. s.v. *bemilta*.

10 *Yad*, Sanhedrin 4:11 and *Kesef Mishneh ad loc.*

11 *Sh.A.*, YD 242:14.

12 *Resp. Rivash*, n. 271. Rivash's words testify that the practice of ordination was not recognized in Spain, ostensibly because the Sefardic communities were better organized and were able to insure the quality of their rabbinic leadership without resorting to *semichah*. For a full historical treatment, see Mordechai Breuer, "Hasemichah Ha'ashkenazit," in Zion 33 (1968), 15-46, and Jacob Katz, "*Semichah Vesamchut Rabanit Bimey Habeinayim*," in I. Twersky, *Studies in Medieval Jewish History and Literature*, Cambridge, MA, 1979, 41-56.

13 See R. Yehudah al-Barceloni (Spain, 12th cent.), *Sefer Hashetarot*, p. 131: today's ordination is but a *zecher lisemichah*. The same terminolgy is used in the late-19th cent. *Aruch HaShulchan*, CM 1:14.

14 On *kevod harav*, see M. Avot 4:12 (reverence for one's teacher is equivalent to reverence for Heaven); BT Bava Metzi`a 33a (restoring a teacher's lost object); BT Sanhedrin 109a (to dispute one's rav is tantamount to disputing the Divine Presence), and elsewhere. On the prohibition against issuing halachic rulings in the presence or during the lifetime of one's teacher, see BT Sanhedrin 5b and *Yad*, Talmud Torah 5:2-3.

15 Even should a Gentile king appoint a chief rabbi, which is entitled to do under the rubric *dina demalchuta dina*, that rabbi's rulings are null and void in the absence of community acceptance (*haskamat hakahal*); Tur, CM 3. See, in general, *Aruch Hashulchan*, CM 1:17.

16 Many medieval communities, particularly Sefardic ones, did not require ordination of their sages; see *Resp. Rivash*, n. 271, and the other sources cited in note 12, above.

17 See Isserles at note 11, above.

18 *Aruch HaShulchan*, CM 1:14: no one should preside over weddings, divorces, or chalitzot unless he possesses "the customary ordination" (*semichah* hanehugah). See also BT Kiddushin 6a and Rashi, s.v.lo *yehe lo `esek imahen.*

19 Indeed, the style of rabbinical school to which we liberal Jews are accustomed is a relatively recent innovation in Jewish life, the product of the efforts of nineteenth-century western Jewry to cope with the challenges of modern culture. On the development of modern rabbinic education, see Simon Schwarzfuchs, *A Concise History of the Rabbinate* (Cambridge, MA, Blackwell: 1993), 86ff.

20 In Babylonia during talmudic times, for example, the common method of Torah instruction was the "disciple circle"; see David Goodblatt, *Rabbinic Instruction in Sasanian Babylonia* (Leiden: Brill, 1975). Students tended to move on to study with other sages when they had mastered all that a particular teacher could give them (BT *Avodah Zarah* 19a-b and *Zevachim* 96b). This shows that even then, during "pre-seminary" times, one gained one's scholarly reputa as the disciple of many sages.

21 R. Shelomo Luria (16th-cent. Poland), *Yam shel Shelomo*, M. Baba Kama 8:58.

22 BT Sanhedrin 110a.

23 *Yad*, Talmud Torah 5:2; Bayit Chadash to *Tur*, CM 242.

24 *Kesef Mishneh* to *Yad*, loc. cit., though the concept of a "halachic ruling" is also defined rather narrowly; see *Sh.A.*, CM 242:8.

25 R. Yisrael Isserlein (15th-cent. Germany), *Pesakim Uchetavim*, n. 238, cited in Isserles, Sh.A., D 242:3; R. Ya`akov Emden (18th-cent. Germany), *She'elat Ya'avetz*, I, n. 5.

26 Siftey Kohen, YD 242, n. 3.

27 R. Yosef Kolon, *Resp. Maharik*, n. 117; *Sh.A.* YD 242:5-6.

Hiding One's Jewish Identity
5753.6

She'elah

Recently, our Confirmation class was examining what our Jewish tradition says about being Jewish in a non-Jewish world. The following question came up, and we were wondering if the Responsa Committee would address it:

Some of us go with friends to social programs of Christian youth groups. In the past, when they have realized that we are Jewish, several of our friends and/or family members have responded anti-Semtically. Should we conceal our Jewish identity from them? (Rabbi Mark Glickman, Dayton, OH)

Teshuvah

Your question has already been dealt with in Responsum no.63 of *Contemporary American Reform Responsa,* edited by Rabbi Walter Jacob. We are enclosing a photo copy.

The question which your Confirmation class asks may therefore be answered in this fashion:

We are permitted to hide our identity only under very special circumstances, and the situation to which you refer does not qualify. Instead, the students are encouraged to proclaim their Jewishness proudly and defend it with all their might. They will find out who their real friends are.

We think that you will have a very interesting session.

Selling Ritual Objects to Jews for Jesus
5754.1

She'elah

Should a synagogue gift shop knowingly sell Jewish ritual objects to anyone, Jews or Christians, involved with Jews for Jesus, and how far should we go in ascertaining a person's identity for purposes of selling any of these items? Should the gift shop knowingly sell Jewish ritual objects to Christians who say they wish to make use of them in order to "recover the Jewish roots" of their Christianity? (Rabbi Joan S. Friedman, then of Bloomington, IN)

Teshuvah

1. This Committee has repeatedly taken the position that Jews who affiliate with Jews for Jesus or with the various "Messianic Jewish" movements are apostates and should be treated as such. These individuals "should not be accorded membership in the congregation or treated in any way which makes them appear as if they were affiliated with the Jewish community, for that poses a clear danger to the Jewish community and also to its relationships with the general community."[1] If so, then it is arguable that we ought not to sell them objects which they will use to perform their pseudo-Jewish rituals. This conclusion would be based upon the verse (Leviticus 19:14) "do not place a stumbling-block before the blind," which our tradition reads as a prohibition against leading others unwittingly into transgression.[2] On the strength of this rule, one is forbidden to hand a cup of wine to a *nazir*, lest he be enticed to break the vow he has taken against drinking intoxicants.[3] Similarly, one may not hand forbidden food to an apostate Jew; despite his apostasy he remains a Jew, and the food is still prohibited to him.[4] To sell ritual objects to Jews for Jesus would aid them in the performance of religious services which amount to a renunciation of their Judaism. They are forbidden to do that, and we are forbidden to help them do that. In addition, the use of Jewish ritualia helps them create a false impression in the minds of those Jews who visit their churches. By presenting their evangelical Christian theology in Jewish garb, these movements attempt to persuade Jews in search of religious identity and spiritual fulfillment that one can be a perfectly good Jew—indeed, a "com-

pleted Jew"—by "accepting Jesus." We have every reason not to cooperate with the efforts of any Christian denomination, no matter how "Jewish" they appear, to missionize our people and to encourage them to abandon the faith of Israel.

Against this, one might argue that by selling ritual objects to Jews for Jesus we do not in fact place a "stumbling-block" before them. The sources cited above suggest that the prohibition applies only when the *nazir* or the apostate could not have committed the sin without the Jew's assistance. If he could have gotten hold of the forbidden substance on his own, he would in any event have violated the commandment. Thus, the Jew who helps him obtain it is not the exclusive agent or cause of the transgression.[5] In our case, since the ritual objects are widely available and could be purchased elsewhere, the fact that we sell them does not cause the Jews for Jesus to do anything they would not otherwise have done.

This argument, however, does not succeed. Even if our action does not technically violate the Toraitic commandment in Leviticus 19:14, rabbinic ordinance forbids us to assist other persons in committing a sin. The fact that "they would have done it anyway" is hardly a justification for our helping them do it. Moreover, Jewish tradition holds that we have a positive duty to try to prevent them from committing the transgression.[6] If we cannot dissuade them, we must at the very least refuse to involve ourselves in their act.

Still, there are other and valid arguments in favor of selling these items. The first has to do with the difficulty of determining just which unfamiliar customers are indeed Jews for Jesus. Should we push our inquiry too far,[7] we risk insulting persons with legitimate reasons for purchasing ritual objects. Should we refuse to sell ritualia to any and all persons who are unknown to us, we may appear to have something to hide. Such behavior on our part may well threaten the good relations we seek to establish with the non-Jewish community, in itself an important traditional value; the Talmud teaches that some legal requirements with respect to the Gentile world are to be relaxed "for the sake of peaceable relations" (*mipnei darchei shalom*).[8] Second, there is the factor of *dina demalchuta*, the law of the land: civil rights laws may prohibit us from refusing to sell to customers on religious grounds. Third, these purchasers, even if they are Jews for Jesus, might learn something. It is arguably better, for example, that they read a Jewish *haggadah* rather than a messianized version that turns the three matzot into the Christian Trinity, the

Pesach sacrifice into Jesus, the seder into the Last Supper and the wine and matzah into the Eucharist. It may be that a positive and open response to these people will encourage them to keep an open mind about Judaism, perhaps some day even to return to it. If our goal is that these people might one day pursue the path of *teshuvah,* we might think twice before pushing them away.

2. The second part of the question deals with Christians who wish to use Jewish ritual objects as part of their own liturgical observance. Here, the prohibition of Leviticus 19:14 does not apply. Christianity is not a form of idolatry;[9] thus, by selling Jewish ritual objects to Christians, we do not aid them in performing rites which are traditionally forbidden to the "children of Noah." We can imagine a number of legitimate purposes for which the Christian customer might want these objects: as gifts for Jewish friends and relatives, for example, or as part of an educational display. Moreover, if Christians desire to use these objects as a means of "recovering their Jewish roots," that is their business and not ours. On the other hand, we must be concerned that a Christian church which "Judaizes" its appearance may, like Jews for Jesus, give the mistaken impression that its worship service is somehow a "Jewish" one.

Conclusion.

Bearing all this in mind, our advice is as follows:

1. It is appropriate to ask a customer who is unfamiliar to us why he or she wishes to purchase a ritual item. This "inquiry" should be limited to normal conversation and "small talk."

2. If we ascertain that customers are Jews for Jesus or Christians who want to use the ritual items for purposes we deem Jewishly inappropriate, we may discourage them from making the purchase. For example, we can inform them that the gift shop exists to serve Jewish needs. We can let them know our deep feelings about the sanctity of these items, our belief that they ought to be used solely within a properly Jewish context. We can direct them to books and educational items which may serve their purposes just as well.

After this degree of discouragement and suggestion, we probably have no choice but to sell to customers who insist on buying. As long as we make the gift shop open to the community, it must be open to the entire community.

Our conclusion assumes this elemental fact: synagogue gift shops, no less than Sisterhoods, Brotherhoods, and schools, are agencies of the synagogue. They exist not simply to sell merchandise and to raise funds, but to help the synagogue fulfill its religious and educational goals. As much as is possible and practicable, the gift shop should refrain from conducting its business in ways that are inimical to basic values of Jewish life and faith as we understand them. It is therefore appropriate for the gift shop staff to take reasonable steps to discourage what we would consider the improper use of our religious objects.[10]

NOTES

1 *CARR*, n. 68, pp. 109-112. See also, n. 66, pp. 107-108 and 67, pp. 108-109; *ARR*, n. 150, pp. 471-474; and R. Walter Jacob, *NARR*, n. 110, p. 175 and 242, pp. 395-396.

2 *Sifra* to Lev. 19:14; see *Sefer Hachinuch, mitzvah* 232.

3 BT Avodah Zarah 6b.

4 Tosafot, Avodah Zarah 6b, s.v. *minyan; Hil. Harosh,* Avodah Zarah 1:2. Lev. 19:14 applies as well to non-Jews; thus, a Jew must not assist a Gentile in worshipping idolatry, which is prohibited to all people as one of the seven Noachide laws.

5 BT Avodah Zarah 6b; Tosafot and *Hil. Harosh* loc. cit.; see also Alfasi, Avodah Zarah, fol. 1b, *s.v. minayin.*

6 See the commentary of R. Nisim Gerondi to Alfasi, *loc. cit.; Tosafot,* Shabbat 3a, s.v. *bava;* R. Menachem Hame'iri, *Beit Habechirah,* Avodah Zarah 6b; *Chidushei Haritva,* Avodah Zarah 6b. The latter cites the mishnah in BT Gitin 61a, which declares that we do not aid and abet transgressors, and the rule that "all Jews are guarantors for each other (*kol yisra'el areivim zeh bazeh*; BT Sanhedrin 27b and Shevu`ot 39a), which implies a positive duty to prevent other Jews from violating the Torah. He might have cited Lev. 19:17, "you shall surely rebuke your fellow," as well.

7 There is some question as to whether we need to inquire at all. Since most of those who come to our gift shops are not apostates, we might rely upon the majority principle *(rov)* and regard those whom we do not know as members of that category. See *Tosafot,* Pesachim 3b, s.v. *ve'ana,* and Tosafot, Yevamot 47a, s.v. *bemuchzak.*

8 BT Gitin 61a; *Yad,* Matanot Aniyim 7:7 and Melachim 10:12.

9 This conclusion is the result of a long debate within Jewish legal literature, one which continues within Orthodox circles. While Maimonides (*Yad,* Avodat Kochavim 9:4 in the uncensored texts) declares Christians to be idolaters, R. Menachem Hame'iri (*Beit Habechirah,* Avodah Zarah, pp. 46, 59, and elsewhere) excludes both Christians and Muslims from this designation. Many Ashkenazic authorities rule similarly, though without noticeable enthusiasm (see *Hil. Harosh* Avodah Zarah 1:1; Isserles, OC 156). Our Reform tradition follows Hame'iri, without any hesitation. Our understanding of the nature of idolatry, of Christian teaching, and of our ethical duties toward our fellow human beings demands that we strip from Christianity any hint of the label avodah zarah. See *ARR,* n. 6, pp. 21-24, and the sources cited there.

10 See also R. Walter Jacob, *NARR,* n. 242, pp. 395-396.

Atheists, Agnostics and Conversion To Judaism
5754.15

A prospective convert expresses a strong sense of communal and historic solidarity with the Jewish experience. She finds services fulfilling insofar as they connect her to the Jewish past. She finds Shabbat to be important for its connection to the past and its role in organizing/structuring the week for her and her family. She is, however, quite unsure about the existence of God. When asked by her rabbi, "Is there any aspect of the universe other than the material?" she responds in the negative, for she believes that physical and chemical forces are responsible for the universe as we know it. Although further reading and discussion lie ahead, our question is whether an atheist committed to Jewish practice, ethics, and study can be accepted as a convert? (Rabbi Mark Dov Shapiro, Springfield, MA)

Teshuvah

<u>The Halachah</u>. The traditional procedure for conversion to Judaism was established in the Talmud. A prospective proselyte is asked: "Why do you want to become a Jew? Do you not know that Jews are frequently persecuted and oppressed?" If the proselyte persists in his or her desire to become a Jew, he/she is informed of some minor and some major mitzvot and warned of the responsibilities for observing the commandments. If prospective proselytes accept the "yoke of the commandments"(*kabbalat ol mitzvot*), then they proceed with immersion(*tevilah*) and, in the case of a male, circumcision (*milah*).[1] What needs to be emphasized is the primacy of their acceptance of the commandments.[2] A declaration to this effect before a Rabbinic court of three is the decisive act of the conversion process.[3] According to both Rambam and Joseph Karo, heading the list of the commandments to be taught to the prospective proselyte is the "essence of our faith." Using identical language they wrote,

> Inform them of the essence of the faith, which is the uniqueness (oneness) of God and the prohibition of idolatry.[4]

Belief in the Eternal as the only God and acceptance of the responsibilities of the covenant between God and the Jewish people is therefore the traditional sine qua non of conversion to Judaism. This is most clearly expressed by R. Yom Tov Lipman, who lived in the 14th and 15th centuries:

> Our faith does not depend upon circumcision but upon the heart. One [i.e., a prospective proselyte] who does not believe sincerely is not considered a Jew even though he is circumcised. But one who believes sincerely is a full Jew even if he is not circumcised.[5]

Reform Perspectives. In regard to our she'elah, we note that the Responsa Committee of the CCAR answered a similar inquiry in 1982. Our colleagues concluded that while an atheist would not be accepted, an agnostic might be accepted if the local rabbis are convinced "that her attachment to Judaism and the knowledge of it are sufficient to bring her into Judaism and to help her develop a commitment to this religion."[7] The important qualifying phrase is commitment to this religion. Reform Judaism is a religious movement, a community of faith dedicated to God. A convert must show a readiness to accept that faith in order to join our community.

Reform Judaism has long established liberal and welcoming policies toward prospective converts. The second convention of the CCAR (1891) and the third (1892) debated the requirements and rituals for conversion. Isaac Mayer Wise wrote the committee report on conversion, which concluded that it is lawful and proper to accept into the sacred covenant of Israel

> any honorable and intelligent person, who desires such affiliation, without any initiatory rite, ceremony or observance whatever; provided, such person be sufficiently acquainted with the faith, doctrine and canon of Israel; . . . and that he or she declare verbally and in a document signed and sealed before such officiating rabbi and his associates his or her intention and firm resolve:
>
> 1. To worship the One, Sole and Eternal God, and none besides Him...[8]

Thus, for Reform Judaism, a prospective convert had both to embrace the Jewish people and make a solemn declaration of faith in God, the God of our ancestors, as the one and only God. While many rabbis then and now insist on certain rituals and other obligations as incumbent upon the prospective convert (e.g. immersion, circumcision, a course of study, examinations, etc.), the sine qua non of conversion for Reform Judaism, as it is for all branches of Judaism, has always been faith in God. The centrality of God in the Reform conversion ceremony is verified by examination of the succession of rabbinic manuals published by the CCAR.

The revised edition of the Rabbi's Manual required the convert to pledge:

I,   , do herewith declare in the presence of God and the witnesses here assembled, that I, of my own free will, seek the fellowship of Israel and that I fully accept the faith of Israel. I believe that God is One, Almighty, Allwise and Most Holy. I believe that man is created in the image of God; that it is his duty to imitate the holiness of God; that he is a free-will agent, responsible to God for his actions; and that he is destined to everlasting life. I believe that Israel is God's priest-people, the world's teacher in religion and righteousness as expressed in our Bible and interpreted in the spirit of Jewish tradition ....[9]

It was deemed essential that the prospective convert clearly understood the importance of his or her commitment both to the Jewish people and to God.

The most recent CCAR rabbinic manual, published in 1988, maintains the tradition of questioning the prospective convert's belief in God. The first question asked is: "Do you choose to enter the eternal covenant between God and the people Israel and to become a Jew of your own free will?"[10] The implication is clear. To become a Jew, Reform Judaism demands that the convert affirm belief in God and the unique bond between God and the Jewish people.[11]

It must be emphasized that the declaration of faith does not demand that the *ger/giyoret* adhere to a particular God concept, but simply that he/she be able to affirm the reality of God in our religious experience. Conversion, as or movement understands it, is a religious ceremony, marking a transformation in the spiritual (as well as ethno-cultural) identity of the proselyte. We do not convert people to "secular" Judaism.

Some contend that since we find among the members of Reform congregations certain Jews who are avowed atheists or agnostics, we should not hesitate to accept a convert who falls into either category. It is true that some Jews experience crises of faith. We acknowledge the reality of the spiritual journey and struggle our brothers and sisters endure, and they remain part of us as long as they do not abandon our people or join another religion. However, that flexibility is reserved for those who are already "citizens," who already belong. It is the nature of the conversion process that the convert must meet standards that, in practice, are not demanded of the already-Jewish: a program of Jewish study, required synagogue attendance, participation in synagogue and communal activities, and the like.

The rabbi's task is to determine the convert's religious sincerity—again, a test not administered to those currently with the fold. It is a basic principle of Reform (as it is of the Halachah) that the ultimate determination of a convert's admissibility depends on rabbinic judgment, based on a personal knowledge of the candidate. One born a Jew is by definition a member of our people, but to be counted among them, a convert must first demonstrate not only a willingness to identify with us, but also an understanding and acceptance of the role of God in the continuing experience of our people.

In our case, the prospective convert demonstrates a love of the Jewish people and culture which seems to make her an attractive candidate for conversion. The problem is her ambivalence about God. It is unclear why she is classified as an agnostic and not an atheist. Atheists flatly deny the existence of God. Agnostics, by definition, maintain that anything beyond and behind the material phenomenon is simply unknowable.[12] Our *she'elah* records two of the prospective convert's opinions. She states that there is no aspect of the universe other than the material, and she maintains that "coincidence and chemistry are responsible for the universe as we see it." Her first statement is clearly atheistic. Her second could be construed as agnostic.

Consequently, if, in the opinion of the attending rabbis, she is an atheist, then the position of the Responsa Committee is well known. She is not to be accepted.[13] However, if she is, as an agnostic, simply unsure or confused, then she should be carefully instructed and introduced to the diverse theological teachings that enrich our faith. Let her be taught that we are not so arrogant as to claim to know all about God, but neither is our faith so unsure that we can fathom life without God.

Ultimately, it is imperative that the officiating rabbis are convinced that this woman can utter with clear conscience the affirmation demanded by our movement that God exists and that the Jewish people are bound to God by a sacred and eternal covenant. If the attending rabbis do not believe that she can utter such an affirmation with a full heart, then she should be given more time for study and reflection so that she will come to understand the religious significance of becoming a member of the Jewish people.

It is clear that we as Reform Jews, and particularly we as Reform rabbis, have the responsibility to establish and maintain the standards that define our movement and render applicants eligible for inclusion. This principle was recently illustrated by the case of a secular-humanist congregation which desired to join the Reform Movement. The Responsa Committee was asked whether or not a congregation that excluded God from its services could be admitted to membership in the UAHC.[14] The Committee's answer was no, and after several years of discussion, this decision was supported by an overwhelming majority of the Union's Board of Trustees.[15]

Reform Judaism is a religious movement of Jews dedicated to the covenant between God and the Jewish people. If we do not insist that the ger meet this fundamental standard and find herself ready to affirm the reality of God in Jewish religious life and experience, it would be a legitimate question whether we have any standards at all.

NOTES

1 BT Yevamot 47a-b; *Sh.A., YD* 268:3.

2 Mark Washofsky, "Halachah and Ulterior Motives," *Conversion To Judaism in Jewish Law*, edited by Walter Jacob and Moshe Zemer, Pittsburgh, 1994, page 37, note n. 1.

3 Tosafot to BT, Yevamot 45b, s.v. *mee lo tavlah*.

4 Rambam, *Yad* , Isurei Bi'ah, 14:2; *Sh.A.,* YD, 268:2. Also see, Maggid Mishneh, *s.v. keitzad mekabbelin.*.

5 *Sefer Nitzachon*:, cited by Solomon B. Freehof, "Circumcision of Proselytes," *RRT*, p.75.

6 *ARR* (1983), n. 65, pp. 209-211.

7 *Ibid.* pp. 211.

8 *Proceedings of the Third Annual Convention*, CCAR Yearbook , 1892, pp. 94-95.

9 *Rabbi's Manual*, rev. ed. (1936), pp. 31-32.

10 Pp. 201-202.

11 The candidate may choose to make his/her own clear affirmation of God and covenant.

12 *Oxford English Dictionary*, London, 1971.

13 ARR, n. 65, pp. 209-11.

14 See our responsum "Humanistic Congregation" in this volume OC (5751.4).

15 UAHC Board of Trustees, meeting in Washington, DC., June 11, 1994, voted 115-13 (with 4 abstentions) against admitting the humanist congregation, Beth Adam of Cincinnati, Ohio. See *Reform Judaism*, Winter 1994, pp. 25-27.

May a Jewish Chaplain Perform a Baptism?
5755.9

She'elah

Jewish chaplains serving in hospitals are occasionally asked to baptize children. Is it ever permissible for a Jew to perform a baptism? If so, under what circumstances? May a rabbi baptize a child? (Elena Stein, Los Angeles)

Teshuvah

The hospital chaplaincy, as it has developed in North America, can in some ways be described as an interfaith ministry. The chaplain offers pastoral care to patients of differing religious beliefs. The question must therefore arise: in providing counseling and compassion to the patients and family members in their charge, ought chaplains to ignore the principles and boundaries established by their own religious traditions? More precisely: when a patient or the family requests from the chaplain an act or a rite which will be a source of comfort to them but whose performance is at odds with the chaplain's religion, does pastoral duty demand that he or she accede to their request?

With respect to baptism, the situation might be described as follows. An infant born prematurely has been in the hospital's neonatal intensive care unit for several weeks or months. During that time, the chaplain has visited extensively with the baby's parents and has developed a close pastoral relationship with them. The infant has now taken a turn for the worse, and the parents want the child baptized. They ask the chaplain, who is Jewish, to perform the ritual. Perhaps they do not belong to a church; perhaps their relationship with their minister is distant or strained. Or perhaps they simply look upon this Jewish chaplain, who has walked with them through a most difficult period of their lives, as their pastor. For whatever reason, the parents have concluded that this ritual would be most meaningful if performed by this chaplain. Such requests are not unheard-of.[1] Should the chaplain say "yes"?

We think not. We are aware of the special bond that can exist between chaplains and those whom they serve. We recognize that the "congregation" of a hospital chaplain consists predominantly of non-Jews, and we know that in order to minister to patients and families the Jewish chaplain may need to adopt a style and manner of religious discourse that is not a particularly Jewish one. The chaplain must counsel them and pray with them in a religious language that they understand, whether or not that language accords with the chaplain's Judaism. For all that, however, it is inappropriate in the extreme for a Jewish chaplain to perform a Christian sacrament.

It is inappropriate, first of all, because some Christian communions do not recognize the efficacy of a baptism performed by a non-believer or one who is not an ordained minister of the Church.[2] A Jewish chaplain who baptizes a child may thus implant in its parents the mistaken belief that a valid sacrament has been administered. This would violate the spirit of the rule *lifney `iver lo titen michshol,* "do not place a stumbling-block before the blind" (Lev. 19:14), from which our tradition derives a general warning against deceiving those unable to discern the truth for themselves.[3] In this situation the Jewish chaplain would be the agent in the creation of a falsehood, a lie, something clearly to be discouraged.

It is also inappropriate for a Jew to baptize a member of a denomination which would recognize that act as a valid sacrament. A prime example is the Roman Catholic Church, which accepts baptisms performed by laypersons and non-Catholics. It does so because, in Catholic theology, the power of a sacrament is *ex opore operato*: its efficacy lies in the rite itself and not in the subjective disposition of the minister or of the person receiving it. The minister need not be righteous, Catholic, nor even Christian; he need only have the intention of "doing what the Church does": i.e., of administering a proper Christian sacrament.[4]

This teaching, we should point out, arose in response to events in Church history: for its own internal reasons, the Church accepts as valid those sacraments administered by non-Catholics.[5] But these reasons are irrelevant to our thinking. We are Jews; we have standards of our own by which we determine our actions. And by those standards it is inconceivable that a Jew who celebrates a baptism can possibly intend to "do what the Church does." The sacraments, we are told, are "visible signs chosen by Christ to bring to mankind the grace of His paschal ministry." Baptism, in particular, is "the sacramental representation of the death and resurrection of Jesus Christ," an absolutely necessary condition for salvation.[6] For this reason, say two leading contemporary Catholic theologians, "be he saint or sinner, so long as he intends to administer the sacrament and uses the appropriate ceremonies, it signifies...the objectively valid pledge of God's grace, the historical tangibility of his salvific will in Jesus Christ for the life of the individual and of the Church."[7] A Jew cannot believe this. Jewish faith does not hold that humankind is in need of spiritual rebirth by means of ritual acts which confer upon the recipient the salvific effects of the death of Jesus. For this reason, whatever the Roman Catholic Church thinks of baptisms performed by non-Catholics, a Jewish chaplain cannot serve as its agent in bestowing salvation. When Jewish chaplains "administer the sacrament" they perform a rite whose essence is a denial of the validity of their own religious tradition. They cannot do this and simultaneously maintain their religious integrity.

The argument can be raised, of course, that theology is irrelevant. The chaplain can assert that "what I dispense is comfort, not salvation. These people have asked me to conduct a ceremony from which they can derive spiritual strength, and as their pastor it is my duty to help them nurture that strength." To this, the obvious response is that theology does matter. Baptism is much more than the sprinkling of a few drops of water. A child's family requests baptism precisely because it is a sacrament, a rite charged with religious meaning. It speaks to them out of their own Christian religious commitment. And regardless of their level of theological sophistication, that commitment is rooted in the acknowledgement of such doctrines as original sin, the atoning death of Christ, and the power of a Church-mediated ritual to effect salvation. All of these, obviously, constitute a negation of the most basic Jewish religious self-understanding. Baptism is thus not simply an instrument of pastoral care. Its power to comfort an individual or a family lies in its evocation of a world of religious symbolism and theological doctrine which a Jewish chaplain does not share.

To say that we do not share in the basic commitments of Christian theology, is more than a bland statement of fact. We are talking about the drawing of boundaries, an activity which, however difficult it is at times for us moderns, is absolutely essential if we wish to preserve our religious distinctiveness as a people. Like Christianity, Judaism is a religious tradition which possesses its own integrity. That integrity is compromised when Jews act so as to suggest that legitimate religious boundaries do not exist. The rabbis give expression to this truth when they speak of the commandment *uvechukkoteihem lo teileichu*, "you shall not conduct yourselves according to their laws" (Lev. 18:3). The details of this principle, which adjures us not to "imitate the Gentiles" through the conscious adoption of their religious practices, are complex.[8] No objective indicator exists that will tell us precisely when the prohibition has been violated. And we Reform Jews, whose ritual innovations have often been attacked as "imitation of the Gentiles," should be extremely reticent to invoke it. Yet while we have defended ourselves from this charge, we have also recognized the importance of preserving our religious separateness. This Committee, in particular, has urged that Reform Jews take care to preserve an identifiably "Jewish" core of observance in the face of the assimilationist and syncretistic tendencies of our day.[9] For this reason, the caution of Lev. 18:3 "remains a constant and forceful warning" for us as for all.[10] In our case, this caution demands that the Jewish chaplain refrain from celebrating baptism, a rite which proclaims the central message of Christian faith. To do otherwise, to perform the baptism, is to violate the essential boundaries that distinguish the two religious traditions.

The chaplain's duty, it is true, is to offer compassion and spiritual comfort to patients and families. But this comfort must not be purchased at the cost of the chaplain's religious integrity. It is precisely when those whom we serve regard us as men and women of faith, moral fiber, and religious integrity that we—clergy in general and chaplains in particular—are able to provide comfort at all. And we barter away this integrity when we act as though theology and belief do not matter, when we celebrate rituals that declare a message that we do not and cannot accept, when we forget who and what we are. This is doubly the case when the chaplain is a rabbi, for as Jewish "clergy" we are looked upon as official spokespersons for Judaism, as models of Jewish belief and practice. It is our job to locate the boundaries, to observe them, and to point out their existence where required. If we stop doing that job, however well-meaning our intentions, we will eventually lose our standing in the eyes of our own people and cease to function as rabbis.

In saying this, we intentionally run counter to a distinct trend in North American culture. There is a tendency, due perhaps to the popular culture of secular Christianity, to view all clergy as interchangeable to some degree.[11] It emphatically does not mean, however, that we, as rabbis who have the capacity to respond to reality as well as to observe it, must acquiesce in the reduction of our role to that of interchangeable clerical parts. Such a fate does not raise our pastoral and spiritual standing among those we presume to serve; indeed, it debases it.

To repeat: a Jewish chaplain, lay or rabbinic, should not perform a baptism. He or she may take whatever steps are necessary to arrange and to facilitate the ceremony, for such is the chaplain's pastoral responsibility. He or she may (and perhaps should) be present at the baptism, provided that it is performed by another minister or lay person. It is inappropriate for the chaplain to conduct the rite or to take part in its liturgy.

NOTES

1 Phyllis B. Toback, "A Theological Reflection on Baptism by a Jewish Chaplain," *Journal of Pastoral Care* 47 (1993), pp. 315-317.

See, e.g., the *Westminster Confession of Faith*, the dominant credal expression of English-speaking Reformers and Presbyterians, sec. 27, par. 4: "there be only two sacraments ordained by Christ our Lord in the gospel, that is to say, Baptism and the Supper of the Lord: neither of which may be dispensed by any but a minister of the Word lawfully ordained."

3 *Sifra ad loc.*

4 *Catholic Encyclopedia* (New York, 1967), 12:806-812; 2:65-66.

5 The doctrine was formulated during the Donatist controversy of the patristic era and reaffirmed during the Reformation by the Council of Trent. Its intent is to proclaim that a sacrament is a valid rite of salvation solely because it is a sacrament, mediated by the Church. Its efficaciousness does not depend upon the fitness of the priest, as the Donatists argued, nor upon the faith commitment of the recipient, as many Protestants believed.

6 *Catholic Encyclopedia*, 12:806; 2:62-63.

7 Karl Rahner and Herbert Vorgimler, *Dictionary of Theology* (New York, 1981), pp. 350-351. While all this is true in theory, there is some question as to the validity of a baptism performed by a nonbeliever. "The practice today" is to rebaptize an infant when it is known that the original baptism was performed by a minister whose doctrinal and liturgical practice are incorrect; *Catholic Encyclopedia* 2:66.

8 See BT Sanhedrin 52b; *Yad,* Avodat Kochavim 11:1; *Tur* YD 178 and *Beit Yosef ad loc.*; *Resp. Maharik,* n. 88.

9 See (among others) our responsa 5754.5 (Gentile participation in Synagogue Ritual), 5753.13 (Apostate in the Synagogue), 5752.3, (Practicing Buddhism and Judaism); 5752.11 (Amazing Grace) (*CCAR Journal* 39:3 [Fall, 1992], pp. 65-66); *ARR*, n. 71, pp. 241-242 and 94; *CARR*, n. 61-68, pp. 98-112. [The cited responsa are found in this book.]

10 See CCAR Responsa Committee, no. 5751.3 ("Blessing the Fleet", p. 57), for a detailed analysis of *uvechukkoteihem lo teileichu* and its applicability to the Reform setting.

11 This tendency is reinforced by institutions such as the military chaplaincy, which serves in some important ways as an interfaith ministry, and the university chaplaincy, a position in which even a rabbi is expected to perform some functions that maintain at least the outward forms of Christian practice.

Blessing the Fleet
5751.3

She'elah

I serve a New England community and have received a request to participate in the annual ceremony of "blessing the fleet." Those involved, including Protestant and Catholic clergy, are taken on board a Coast Guard vessel into the Sound, where boats (predominantly pleasure craft) would pass by and be blessed. Is it appropriate to accept this invitation? (R. Elias J. Lieberman, Falmouth, MA)

Teshuvah

The question may be subdivided as follows:

1. What provisions and cautions in Jewish tradition and sensibility might be violated by participating in this kind of interfaith ceremony? Would it fall in the category of a gentile ritual, which the Torah forbids as *chukkat ha-goyim* (Leviticus 20:23)?

2. Is there a precedent for blessing a thing or things, as in this case, the fleet?

1. *Chukkat ha-goyim.*

At first glance the ceremony to which the rabbi has been asked would seem to be merely another civic occasion which he would share with other clergy, such as dedications, invocations, or benedictions which accompany secular functions. Reform rabbis (and not they alone) do this regularly, in part to affirm that they and their fellow Jews fully share in the life of the community. We generally take part in ceremonies which are religiously neutral and non-Christological.[1]

We have therefore come to accept certain sancta of "civil religion." Examples are prayers for the government during the service, the national flag on the *beemah*, national anthems printed in our prayer books and Haggadot, liturgies for a communal Thanksgiving and Memorial Day service, and the like.[2]

159

All of this is well founded in tradition, which bases itself on Jeremiah 29:7: "Seek the well-being of the city to which I have exiled you, and pray to the Eternal on its behalf, for your well-being depends on it." Further, there is a relevant passage in Ezra 6:10 and the oft-quoted advice of the Mishnah: "Pray for the well-being of the government, for without the fear of it we would swallow each other alive."[3] These sentiments entered the Ashkenazic liturgy by adding prayers for the government,[4] and they have become part of Diaspora ritual. This was true even when Jews did not fare well in particular countries; thus, an Orthodox *siddur* from Russia of the early twentieth century contained a prayer for Czar Nicholas II. How much more so has this custom entrenched itself in lands where Jews enjoy all civic rights.

However, despite all these precedents, the questioner clearly wonders whether there is something "un-Jewish" about blessing the fleet, which consists primarily of pleasure craft, plus some fishing vessels that contribute to the local economy. To use traditional language, does this kind of ceremony deserve the stricture of *chukkat ha-goyim*, of imitating Gentile practice?

It is well to remember that most of the ritual innovations which the Reform movement proposed in the course of its history were attacked by its opponents as *chukkat ha-goyim*, such as prayer in the vernacular, instrumental music, or gender equality. Still, the present threat of assimilation and the narrowing of Jewish religious distinctiveness and lifestyle lead us to increasing concern about melding our practices with those of the community in which we live. Therefore the question of *chukkat ha-goyim* deserves another brief look.

The biblical phrase, "you shall no walk in their ways"(u-*vechukkoteihem lo telechu*)[5] was understood as one of the negative commandments and was seen to reinforce the distinctiveness and separateness of the Jews, who are set apart from the nations (Lev. 20:26).[6] While the principle of the prohibition was never in doubt, it was understood that it had limits, but just what these were was a subject of frequent debate.

Thus, the Midrash argues that the prohibition cannot be taken to its extreme. Does this mean, it asked, that we should not build buildings or plant vineyards as Gentiles do? Rather, Scripture says, *u-vechukkoteihem...*, meaning laws and customs which are indigenous to them.[7] This led one authority to state that only idolatry and special practices enumerated by the Rabbis fall under the prohibition.[8]

According to R. Menachem ha-Me'iri the law of the Torah itself was meant as a specific caution against idolatry, and was later expanded to cover other practices as a fence against assimilation.[9] This explains the far-reaching ruling of Rambam:

> The law forbids us to walk in the ways of idolatry and from
> adopting their customs, even their means of dress and their
> social gatherings.[10]

Still, popular practice did not always abide by these prohibitions, and the earlier discussions of Talmud and Midrash were continued. Thus, R. Isaac b. Sheshet (14th century) wrote that Jews need not do away with funeral customs which reflect secular practices among Muslims.

> If you say otherwise, we might as well forbid eulogies, on the
> ground that Gentiles also eulogize their dead.[11]

Similarly, R. Joseph Kolon (15th century) permitted Jewish physicians to don distinctive medical robes worn by Gentile doctors. His wide-ranging analysis set forth these guidelines by which one could recognize what fell under the prohibition of *chukkat ha-goyim*:

> customs which Jews adopt for no other apparent reason than to
> imitate the Gentiles;
> customs which offend the rules of modest behavior.

But practices which reflect legitimate purposes or are meant as tokens of respect are not covered by the prohibition of *lo telechu*.[12] While this view was criticized by some,[13] it was endorsed by R. Moses Isserles and codified in his addenda to the *Shulchan Aruch*.[14] This in turn has become the basis for contemporary rulings.

Thus, R. Haim David Halevy permits the use of funeral flowers and the wearing of black clothing by mourners. Such practices are prohibited "only when we adopt their custom out of the desire to imitate their religious rites."[15] For this reason too he defends the Israeli custom, borrowed from Western culture, of standing for a minute of silence on *Yom Ha-Zikaron* and *Yom Ha-Sho'ah* (Remembrance Day for the fallen in Israel's wars and Holocaust Remembrance Day).[16]

The rabbi who participates in a civic ceremony does not do this in order to imitate Gentile religious practices, but rather in order to signal Jewish support for the civic well-being of the community--the kind of legitimate and purposeful motivation required by Kolon and endorsed by the Halachah. His participation would be an aspect of "civic religion."

This conclusion is fortified by another halachic consideration, found in the Talmud. There we read that even normally forbidden Gentile practices are allowed to those who are *kerovim lemalchut*, who are close to the government and must constantly deal with it.[17]

To be sure, this permission was meant for special people, like communal representatives (*shtadlanim*), and not for all members of the Jewish community, but in a democratic society all Jews may be considered *kerovim lemalchut*. Their participation in the rites of "civic religion" is therefore a proper expression of their full participation in the life of the general community.

Of course, this participation has its limits. A necessary condition would be that the ceremony be truly non-denominational and not sectarian in nature, one in which all religious believers could share.

But this should not lead us to make light of the caution against adopting *chukkat ha-goyim*. We are still under the obligation to preserve our religious separateness, and thus the caution of *lo teileichu*... in Lev. 18:3 remains a constant and forceful warning to us.[18]

2. Blessing the Fleet.

It is important to consider the terminology of the event; if it refers to an actual blessing of ships it is one thing; if it is meant as a blessing of the seafarers it is another.

We do not bless things. The blessing is, rather, an invocation of God who is the One that is *baruch*, blessed. Thus we praise God "who brings bread forth from the earth"; we do not bless the Kiddush wine but the *borei pri ha-gefen*, and the act is referred to as *lekaddesh al ha-yayin,* to make a blessing *over* the wine, and not *lekaddesh et ha-yayin*; a blessing *of* the wine, and we do not bless the Shabbat lights but rather God *asher kiddeshanu ... vetsivvanu lehadleek ner shel shabbat*.[19]

The rabbi would therefore offend Jewish tradition if his invocation aimed at sanctifying the ships themselves. While the participating Christian clergy may interpret the ceremony in accordance with their own theology, the rabbi has the same freedom and view "blessing the fleet" as referring to those "that go down to the sea in ships" (Psalm 107) and invoke upon them a way-farer's prayer, *tefillat ha-derech*.[20] The view of sailing the waters as an especial-ly dangerous enterprise has a long tradition, and though this danger has today become less pronounced, especially in comparison with other forms of loco-motion, it has not disappeared. A wayfarer's prayer retains its propriety, whether the journey is for pleasure of for earning a livelihood.

We note that the rabbi's congregation worships in a meeting house built at the end of the 18th century, which betokens a pride in the history of the community. In addition to all else, therefore, the Jewish as well as the larg-er community would expect the rabbi to be part of this history, which invokes the additional permission of acting for the sake of [communal] peace (*mipney darchey shalom*), to preserve a sense of amity and well-being among all the town's people.

We would therefore encourage the rabbi to participate in "blessing the fleet" by delivering a Wayfarer's Prayer[21] and/or read from Psalm 107, and suggest that he explain the strictures of Jewish tradition to his Christian col-leagues, and do so before the date of the actual ceremonies.

NOTES

1 See Rabbi Walter Jacob, *CARR* (1987), n.167, pp. 250-252.

2 See Rabbi Israel Bettan's 1954 responsum on the question of whether a national flag should be placed on the pulpit; *ARR*, ed. Walter Jacob, n. 21, pp. 64-66. We today might not phrase our rea-soning as Bettan did ("...our national flag speaks to us with the voice of religion"), but we would not likely come to a different conclusion.

3 M. Avot 3:2.

4 On the prayer *Ha-noten teshu'ah*, see Baer, *Avodat Yisrael* (Roedelheim 1868), p.231; *Kol Bo*, ch. 20, p.10c; *Aburdaham* (Warsaw 1878), p.47c.

5 Lev. 18:3; see also Lev. 20:23.

6 See Rambam, *Yad*, Avodat Kochavim 11:1.

7 A free translation of *chukkim ha-chakukim lahem*; *Sifra*, ed. Weiss, Acharei Mot, perishta 9, p. 85a. See also the differing interpretations of *chok* in Lev. 19:19 by Rashi and Ramban, and the tal-mudic discussion in BT Avodah Zarah 11a and Sanhedrin 52b which deal with the Gentile custom of lighting funeral pyres. The former passage permits it because it is not undertaken for religious purpos-

es, the latter because it was already mentioned by Jeremiah 34:5.

8 *Sefer Yere'im*, ch. 313. The author reads the verse according to its *peshat* and notes that only the religious practices of Egypt and Canaan are meant. This contradicts the talmudic expansion of the prohibition to imitate the "seven nations" (Exod. 20:23) to all nations (see BT Sanhedrin 52b and Avodah Zarah 11a), including those who were not idolatrous (see R. Isaac b. Sheshet, *Resp. Rivash*, n. 158). Rabbi David Zvi Hoffmann, *Resp. Melammed Leho'il*, I n. 18, therefore translates the words *avodah zarah* as *Fremder Kultus* rather than *Go3tzendienst*.

9 *Beit Ha-Bechirah*, Sanhedrin 52b.

10 *Sefer Ha-Mitzvot*, Neg. Com. n. 30; see also *Sefer Mitzvot Ha-Gadol*, neg. com. n. 50, and *Sefer Ha-Chinnuch*, n. .262.

11 *Resp. Rivash*, n. 158, and see note 5 above.

12 *Resp. Maharik*, n. 88.

13 See *Minchat Chinnuch*, comm. 262.; cf. also *Bi'ur Ha-Gera* (R. Elijah of Vilna), YD 178, n. 7.

14 *Sh.A.*, YD 178:1.

15 *Aseh Lecha Rav*, I, n. 44.

16 *Ibid.*, IV. n. 4; similarly R. Zvi Yehudah Kook, *Techumim*, v. 3 (1982), p.388; R. Yehudah Henkin, *ibid.*, v. 4,(1983), pp. 125 ff.

17 BT Bava Kama 83a, and see Rambam, *Yad*, Avodat Kochavim, 11:3.

18 R. Joseph Karo suggested that the scholars of a community should delineate the extent of the law; *Beit Yosef*, YD 178.

19 To be sure, there are certain objects which because of their nature and function are considered *keley kodesh* and are to be treated in a special fashion because they contain the Divine Name, for instance Torah scrolls, *mezuzot* and *siddurim*.

20 Such a prayer is mentioned in BT Berachot 29b-30a: "What is a prayer for wayfarers? ... *shetolicheni leshalom ve-tatz'ideni* [better, *ve-tacharizireni*] *leshalom* ... *Baruch attah Adonai, shome'a tefillah*." See also *Sh.A.*, OC, 110:4; *Siddur Otzar Tefillah*, under "*Seder Tefillat Ha-Derech*," which lists a variety of quotations and prayers; also Jacob Emden's *Siddur Beit Ya'akov*, p. 111.

21 The CCAR's *Gates of the House* (1977), p.23, brings such a newly composed prayer. [See also the CCAR's *On the Doorposts of Your House*, (1994), p. 142. Ed. note.]

Delayed *Berit Milah* on Shabbat
5755.12

She'elah

The *berit milah* of a newborn baby was delayed past his eighth day. His parents now wish to schedule that ceremony on a Shabbat, since Shabbat is a day when family and friends can attend the *simchah*. According to tradition, a delayed *berit milah* may not take place on Shabbat. Is that the position of Reform Judaism as well? (Rabbi Eric Slaton, Lexington, KY)

Teshuvah

This question, as we understand it, concerns the nature and standing of both *berit melih* and Shabbat as they are observed or ought to be observed in our communities. Is the celebration of the *mitzvah* of circumcision, truly a powerful Jewish moment, so important and central that it should supersede the restrictions that customarily define Shabbat? Or does the reverence we accord Shabbat demand that other *mitzvot*, should they interfere with its observance, be set aside? Our answer will consist of two parts: first, a brief survey of the *halachah* on the timing of the *berit melih*, and second, a look at the issue from the standpoint of our own Reform Jewish tradition.

Milah on Shabbat in Jewish Law. The Torah states twice that the ritual circumcision (*berit milah*) of a Jewish boy is performed at the age of eight days (Gen. 17:12 and Lev. 12:3). The latter verse reads: "And on the eighth day (*uvayom hashemini*) his foreskin shall be circumcised," from which the rabbis deduced that the circumcision must take place on that very day, even if it happens to fall on Shabbat.[1] The traditional expression is *milah bizemanah dochah shabbat*, "circumcision at its proper time supersedes the Shabbat": that is, we do the procedure even though it requires actions that otherwise violate the prohibitions against doing work (*melachah*) on the Sabbath. It follows that a circumcision done prior to or later than a boy's eighth day (*milah shelo bizemanah*) does not supersede the Shabbat and may not take place on that day.[2]

Of particular interest is the precise way in which circumcision at its proper time may take place on Shabbat. The Mishnah records a famous dispute over the issue.[3] According to Rabbi Eliezer, since one is permitted to perform the circumcision itself, one may also perform a variety of other actions normally prohibited on Shabbat in order to prepare for the *milah*. Thus, one may carry the *izmil*, the *mohel's* knife, through the public thoroughfare; one may even make a knife if none is available. Rabbi Akiva, however, forbids these actions according to his rule: any labor that could have been performed before Shabbat does not supersede the Shabbat, and any labor that could not have been performed earlier does supersede the Shabbat. Thus, it is forbidden to carry or prepare the knife on Shabbat, even though the circumcision cannot be performed without it, since the knife could have been brought the day before. The *halachah* follows Rabbi Akiva's more stringent position.[4] And through that determination, the tradition teaches an important point: though the performance of a *mitzvah* may entitle us to take actions that normally violate the Shabbat, we are to keep those actions to a minimum.[5] Even if it is the day of a boy's circumcision, it remains Shabbat for the entire community; Shabbat continues to make its legitimate demands upon the Jew, demands that cannot be ignored or forgotten.[6]

Reform Approaches. This Committee has consistently held to this position in questions which have come before us. Like Rabbi Akiva, we have held that Shabbat is a sacred span of time, an institution of Jewish life which makes its own legitimate demands upon us. The fact that Shabbat "conflicts" with another *mitzvah* or worthy cause does not mean that it is Shabbat which must give way. Indeed, the reverse is often the case. Put differently, Shabbat is more than merely a good day on which to schedule good deeds. It is *Shabbat kodesh*, a holy day; we do not violate or trespass upon it, even for the sake of *mitzvot*, unless those *mitzvot* must be performed on it.

In 1977, for example, the Committee was asked whether weddings might take place on Shabbat or festivals. Theoretically, there might be any number of practical reasons why a couple would wish to schedule their wedding on Shabbat, and one could even argue that, as a holy day, Shabbat is an especially meet time to hold the ceremony of marriage, which is in our tradition an act of consecration (*kiddushin*). Yet the Committee, concerned with "the sanctity of Shabbat as understood and encouraged by the Reform movement," recommended that the traditional prohibition against weddings on that day be maintained. "We encourage our members to make Shabbat a `special' day upon which we do not carry out duties and acts performed on other days. Countenancing marriages on Shabbat would detract from this objective and weaken our efforts."[7] In 1986 and again in 1993, the Committee declared that Reform synagogue groups ought not to participate in *tzedakah* projects, such as the building of houses for the poor, which take place on Shabbat. Although the importance of social action in Reform Jewish thought can hardly be overstated, the importance of Shabbat as a refuge from activity defined as work is also a sacred value to us. Since the *tzedakah* work is not an emergency and since it could be performed on another day, it ought to take place on a day other than Shabbat.[8]

Our attitude has been similar with respect to *berit milah*. We have ruled that circumcision ought to take place on the eighth day, even if another day might be more convenient to the family.[9] And we have recommended that a *berit milah* not be scheduled at night, inasmuch as tradition calls for circumcision to be performed only in the daytime.[10] In these cases, we have argued that *berit milah* is to be distinguished from "circumcision". The latter is a mere surgical procedure; the former is a ritual act whose parameters are discerned in the rules set down in the Jewish tradition. It is precisely when we conduct it according to those rules that we transform the surgical procedure into a religious observance.

There are times, of course, when *berit milah* must occur on Shabbat. This, however, is not one of those times. We recognize that it would be more convenient for the family to schedule their son's circumcision on Shabbat. But if convenience is the only justification for their request, it is, in our view, an insufficient reason to accede to it. If we are serious, as we say we are, about keeping Shabbat and observing *berit milah* within our Reform communities, we have no choice but to respect and revere the lines which define them as religious acts.

NOTES

1 BT Shabbat 132a. The word *uvayom* seems superfluous; the verse would bear the same sense had it read *uvashemini*. The rabbis reason, therefore, that the word comes to teach another detail, i.e., "on *that* day, even Shabbat."

2 *Yad*, Milah 1:9; *Sh.A.*, YD 266:2.

3 M. Shabbat 19:1.

4 See note 2.

5 Similarly, when one needs to eat or drink on Yom Kippur, "we feed him little by little", *i.e.*, the minimal amount necessary to sustain him, so as to avoid a wholesale abandonment of the commandment to fast on that day; *Hilchot HaRosh*, M. Yoma 8:13; *Sh.A.*, OC 618:7-8.

6 For the sake of thoroughness, it should be noted that even Rabbi Eliezer, who assumes a more lenient position in the mishnah, would answer our *she'elah* in the negative. The circumcision may not take place on Shabbat, since that is not the child's eighth day.

7 *ARR*, n. 136, pp. 412-415; see *Gates of Shabbat*, 58. The latter work, in particular, is evidence of our rabbinate's commitment to the observance of Shabbat as a holy day within Reform communities.

8 The responsa are, respectively, *CARR*, n. 176, pp. 265-267, and our responsum 5753.22, in this volume, "Communal Work on Shabbat."

9 *ARR*, n. 55-56, pp. 143-146.

10 See BT Megillah 20a, BT Yevamot 72b, *Yad*, Milah 1:8, *ShA*, YD 262:1; R. Walter Jacob, *NARR*, n. 99, pp. 159-161.

Communal Work on Shabbat
5753.22

She'elah

Clearly, a Reform congregation would ordinarily encourage its members to help construct a needed facility for the poor in the community. But if this mitzvah were to be performed on Shabbat, would it be a violation of Torah law and therefore be wrong in the Reform view? Or could this activity on Shabbat be considered life saving (*piku'ach nefesh*) and reflect the true spirit of Judaism and its concern for the underprivileged, and therefore be permissible? (Rabbi Leo E. Turitz, Laguna Hills, CA)

Teshuvah

The very same question was submitted to Responsa Committee in 1986 and answered by R. Walter Jacob.[1] A copy of his *teshuvah* is enclosed.

We see no reason why we would override this decision; on the contrary, it is as badly needed today as it was then. We would add a few additional observations.

1. We commend those who care for the underprivileged and are prepared to do something about it. Reform Judaism has emphasized this concern as a vital aspect of our religious obligations. At the same time, Shabbat observance remains for us a vital part of our Jewish existence, however much it has been neglected.[2]

2. We therefore have two *mitzvot* at odds with each other. Which shall be given preference? The answer is not hard to fathom: The construction can be done on any day, Shabbat cannot be moved. The old principle comes also into play, that generally we do not perform a true *mitzvah* if it is done by transgressing another command.[3]

3. The one exception is *piku'ach nefesh*. If saving of a human life is at stake, then Shabbat laws may be overlooked. Is that the case here? Surely not; there is no indication that immediate action on Shabbat is necessary, lest there be loss of life.

4. We suspect that the congregation's members did not contemplate

doing the work on Sunday, because this might offend Christian sensibilities. But would no Jewish sensibilities be offended? The very *she'elah* reveals that, by some at least, the action was considered troublesome.

5. We are certain that those who are ready to participate think that they are doing the right and religious thing, and we suspect none of them observes Shabbat as a day of rest in the accepted way. But as partners in this activity they perform the labor not as private persons; they act under the auspices of the synagogue. Jews may eat pork privately and find it both delectable and religiously acceptable, but the synagogue will refuse to serve it to them.

6. If no other day can be arranged for the building, then let the members contribute in some other manner. By doing so they will increase Gentile respect for exhibiting faithfulness to their religious tradition.

7. There is an opportunity for the Rabbi to study these *teshuvot* with the members and to explore how the sanctity of Shabbat may be strengthened in their lives. This presents an excellent opportunity for *talmud torah* and its application.[4]

NOTES

1 *CARR* (1987), n. 176, p.265 f.

2 See *Gates of Shabbat* , ed. Mark D. Shapiro (1991), pp.vii and passim.

3 See our responsum 5755.1, "Delayed Milah on Shabbat," in this volume.

4 We were informed later on that the congregation acted in the spirit of our *teshuvah* [ed note].

Abortion to Save Siblings from Suffering
5755.13

She'elah

I understand that abortion may sometimes be permissible under *Halachah* if it is done to alleviate maternal suffering. Does this extend to relieve suffering of other family members that might be affected by this birth? For example, parents might choose to abort a handicapped fetus because they are concerned that it would impose an undue hardship on their other children who would be burdened by caring for this child in the future. The distinction is that the abortion would not be done to spare the mother suffering, but rather to spare the anguish of other family members. Would this be interpreted as a permissible reason for abortion?

Teshuvah

The circumstances under which an abortion may be performed are the subject of intense debate within the *halachic* literature. The one basic principal upon which there is agreement - at least as a theoretical truth - is that fetal life has a lesser status than maternal life. This is evident from the Toraitic account[1] of a fight between two men in which a pregnant woman is accidentally injured. If the fetus is lost but the woman survives, then the aggressor is punished with a fine, but if the woman is killed it is considered a capital crime, a case of "*nefesh tachat nefesh*", demanding the life of the guilty party in recompense for the life lost.

This thinking is clearly reflected in the classic Mishnaic statement on abortion in Ohalot 7:6: "If a woman is in [life-threatening] difficulty giving birth, the one to be born is dismembered in her abdomen and then taken out limb by limb, for her life comes before its life. Once most of the child has emerged it is not to be touched, for one *nefesh* (person) is not to be put aside for another." Clearly, then, in cases where the mother's life hangs in the balance, the tradition supports abortion.

There is, however, a pivotal difference of opinion as regards the reasoning that leads to permission for abortion in such cases. Rashi states his conviction that - if the mother's life is threatened - so long as "the fetus has not emerged into the air of the world, it is not a nefesh and one is allowed to kill it in order to save its mother." Once it has emerged, it would become a case of *"nefesh tachat nefesh."*[1] Rashi plainly bases his view, that it is permitted to kill the unborn fetus, on the grounds that the fetus - though alive - does not have the status of being a nefesh, and may, therefore, be sacrificed in the interests of saving the mother who is a fully developed *nefesh*.

Maimonides, however, while arriving at the same practical conclusion, does so via a very different route. He takes up a theme - previously discounted by the rabbis in the Talmud - that the fetus who poses a threat to its mother's life should be seen as a rodef, as a pursuer coming to kill. The *halachah* encourages the killing of a *rodef* in order to prevent the *rodef* from killing. Maimonides puts it this way: "This, too, is a negative commandment: one must not take pity on the life of a *rodef*. Consequently, the sages taught: if a pregnant woman's labor becomes life threatening it is permitted to dismember the fetus in her abdomen, either by a medication or by hand, for it is like a *rodef* who is pursuing her to kill her..." Maimonides does not refer to any lesser status of the fetus; rather, he permits the killing of the fetus - so long as it has not yet emerged - because it is behaving like a rodef coming to kill its mother, and ought to be killed like any other *rodef*.[2]

Maimonides, then, has been understood by numerous judges of the *halachah* to be of the view that in those instances where the fetus is not behaving like a *rodef*, no sanction exists to kill it. The prominent halachic strand which follows this outlook holds that the only acceptable circumstances for abortion are those in which the fetus poses a direct threat to the life of the mother. It should be noted that there are those within this school of thought who include the probability of insanity in the mother as a reason for abortion, since they regard insanity as a life-threatening condition. In the twentieth century, the *halachic* consensus, as represented by such figures as Chief Rabbi I. Y. Unterman and Rabbi Moshe Feinstein, continues to be characterized by this approach.[3]

It should be noted that unlike Rashi's interpretation - which closely tracks the plain sense of the Talmud - Maimonides' reasoning process, though popular, does not so readily conform to the thrust of the text. Later halachic literature clearly has to stretch in order to explain issues raised by Maimonides' rodef explanation. For example, why does a fetus that may be aborted because it is a *rodef*, cease to be a *rodef* upon emergence from the womb?[4] It can well be argued, therefore, that those positions that are based on Rashi's explanation may be grounded in a more coherent understanding of the Talmud's intent than those which follow the stricter Maimonidean approach.

While the majority of traditionalists nevertheless adhere to the Maimonidean interpretation, a minority does base its position on Rashi's logic. Since Rashi's approval for abortion - under conditions of a threat to the mother's life - is rooted in the inferior status of the fetus, it is possible to conceive of other menacing situations where the mother's superior interests might permit abortion. This is the line of reasoning used by those who take a more permissive approach to the question of acceptable criteria for abortion.

The earliest authority to deal with abortion for reasons other than mortal danger to the mother was Rabbi Joseph Trani (1568-1639). Trani, who permits abortion in the interests of maternal health, follows Rashi's approach, without even mentioning that of Maimonides.[5] An even more direct expression of this position was given by Rabbi Jacob Emden (1697-1776), as part of a responsum on the permissibility of aborting an illegitimate fetus.[6] Emden notes that even in the case of a legitimate fetus, "there is room to permit abortion for 'great need'; so long as the birth process has not begun, even if the reason is not to save her life - even if only to save her from the 'great pain' it causes her." Emden not only plainly articulates an outlook that countenances abortion for reasons less than a threat to the life of the mother, but he also points to the central *halachic* concern of the more lenient respondents: "great pain" caused to the mother.

This "great pain" has been defined in different ways, and has been understood to incorporate both physical and psychological pain. There is an unwavering consensus, however, that if abortion is to be sanctioned then the "pain" should indeed be "great", and this has usually been understood to refer to a physical or psychological condition harboring exceptionally grave consequences, with long-term implications for the mother's 'normal' functioning. Thus Chief Rabbi Ben Zion Uziel permits abortion for a woman whose pregnancy will result in permanent deafness,[7] Rabbi Yehiel Weinberg permits abortion for a woman who contracted rubella during her first trimester,[8] and Rabbi Eliezer Waldenberg permits abortion until the end of the second trimester for a tay-sachs fetus.[9]

These permissive responsa almost always base their conclusions exclusively on considerations of maternal pain, and not on the future potential life of the fetus or any other person. It is the mother's mental or physical anguish which must be weighed, and which is acknowledged to be the sole salient factor in determining whether or not an abortion is permissible, in the view of these lenient approaches to the tradition. The impact of a potential handicap or defect in the fetus is not a consideration, as is evidenced in a 1940 Romanian responsum in the case of an epileptic mother who was concerned that she might give birth to an epileptic child:

> For fear of possible, remote danger to a future child that maybe, God forbid, he will know sickness - how can it occur to anyone actively to kill the fetus because of such a possible doubt? This seems to me very much like the laws of Lycurgus, King of Sparta, according to which every blemished child was to be put to death. ... Permission for abortion is to be granted only because of mental anguish for the mother. But for fear of what might be the child's lot? - The secrets of God are not knowable.[10]

In only one or two *teshuvot* have interests other than those of the mother been given any weight. A responsum by Rabbi Yitzchak Oelbaum from earlier this century presents an example. Rabbi Oelbaum was asked about a case in which a pregnant mother had an existent "weak" child who, according to the doctors, would not live unless it was breast-fed by its mother. The woman had noticed a change in her milk around the fourth week of pregnancy that seemed like it might be threatening to the nursing child. The mother wanted to know if she could abort the fetus in order to save the existent child. R. Oelbaum, while questioning whether the doctors were accurate in their assessment, concluded that an abortion would be permitted if the experts were of the view that the existing child would indeed be in danger.[11] Oelbaum's judgment in this matter has, however, been the subject of great caution among most poskim, who still view the halachic justification for abortion as extremis on the part of the mother.[12]

Still, Oelbaum clearly does admit of the possibility of considering the needs of others beyond the mother. It should be noted, though, that Oelbaum provides a warrant for abortion in this circumstance only as a last resort to save the child's life. He would not approve unless every other option for saving the child had been exhausted. It is difficult to imagine the conditions under which such a tragic choice would need to be made in our day. Nevertheless, the inquiry might be made as to whether Rashi's view - that reasons less than a direct threat to the mother's life may call for an abortion - could also be applied to an existing child? Could not the physical or psychological extreme distress of an existing child also be grounds for abortion? To these queries, Judaism emphatically replies in the negative. The mother is in a unique position in Jewish law because her health - physical and psychological - directly impinges on the developing fetus within her, for the fetus is a part of her, a *yerech imo*. Hence the future of mother and fetus are tied together in a way that does not exist for any other relationship. As a result, possible serious precariousness in the mother could be a reason to consider abortion in a way that would be unthinkable for any other family member. If the Jewish approach, then, is not even unanimous that the life of an existing child should be saved in preference to the fetus, then certainly an existing child's lesser need could not be agreed to as a reason for abortion.

Reform respondents have, historically, been aligned with those who are prepared to consider circumstances other than a threat to the mother's life as grounds for abortion.[13] While tending towards a preference for lenient conditions, however, the thrust of the respondents' position has been succinctly summarized with the words "we do not encourage abortion, nor favor it for trivial reasons, or sanction it 'on demand.'"[14] Indeed, all the Reform responsa concerning this subject are careful to couch their lenient rulings within the general traditional understanding of the importance of alleviating "great pain" to the mother. None of them suggest that Judaism should countenance any other reason as a valid basis for abortion.

In the *she'elah* that has been presented, the questioner definitively states that the proposed abortion "would not be to spare the mother suffering, but rather to spare the anguish of other family members." While Reform Judaism has, of course, forged new Jewish frontiers where compelling reasons deemed that a new path was the only "right and good" (*hayashar ve'hatov*) course to take, this case does not appear to warrant such action. Fetal life, though of lesser status than that of the mother, remains human life in potential, and is consequently of great significance. It can be sacrificed only for the most profound of reasons. Speculation and worry about the future are natural aspects of living, but do not themselves constitute a threat to the health of the mother sufficient to justify the termination of unborn life. Hence, Judaism could not give its assent to an abortion under these circumstances. If serious maternal anguish was the result of genuine fears over a defined handicap, then abortion could be contemplated, but certainly not for the sake of "hardship" or "quality of life" issues for other family members. It is the degree to which the mother is suffering "great pain" which remains determinative; the consideration of the anguish of others within the family is not pertinent to the question of an abortion. Perhaps, therefore, the above Romanian responsum could well be embellished as follows: "But for fear of what might be the lot of the other children? - The secrets of God for them too are not knowable."

NOTES

1 Exodus 21:22-23.
2 *Hilchot Rotzeach* 1:9.
3 *Noam* 6 (1963): 1-11; *Igerot Moshe*, CM, Vol. 2, n. 69.
4 See *Sefer Me'irat Einayim* to CM 425, n. 8.
5 *Teshuvot Maharil*, Vol. I, n. 97 and 99.
6 *Sh'eilat Ya'avetz*, n. 43.
7 *Mishpetei Uziel*, CM 3:46.
8 *Noam* 9 (1966) and *S'ridei Eish*, Vol. III, n. 127.
9 *Responsa Tzitz Eliezer*, Vol. 13, n. 102.
10 *Responsa Afrekasta D'Anya*, n. 169.
11 *Sh'eilat Yitzchak* 64.
12 See M. Stern, *HeRefuah L'Or HaHalachah*, p. 104.
13 *ARR* n. 171, pp. 541-544; *CARR* n. 16, pp. 23-27; NARR n. 155, p 253.
14 Walter Jacob, *CARR* n. 16, p. 27.

Woman as a Scribe
5755.15

She'elah

Almost two years ago, our synagogue hired a Torah scribe to clean and repair a *sefer torah* which had been rescued from the Nazis. Several of us had the opportunity to help clean the Torah and "letter" it by placing our hand over the scribe's as he wrote, thus fulfilling the commandment for every Jew to write a Torah. I became fascinated and deeply moved by this work. The feeling of standing in front of the open Torah, of sensing the spirit of the original scribe, of the generations before me who rejoiced and wept in its presence, is a powerful one. I so love this feeling of being connected to God and to my people through the Torah that I would like to learn how to be a scribe in my own right, if that is possible. I already have art and calligraphy backgrounds, and I am deeply committed to this.

Could you please reply to me in the form of a responsum on the subject of women participating in the scribal arts? If you have particular advice as to a course of study, I would appreciate hearing that, too. (Julietta Ackerman, Goldens Bridge, NY)

Teshuvah

Many of us, upon reading this question, can readily identify with your experience. We too can remember how we felt when we stood before the open *sefer torah* and sensed for the first time the power and significance of this scroll in our lives, in the way in which we define who we are. And for good reason. Jewish tradition regards the study of Torah as the means by which we discover God's will how we are to live so as to sanctify the divine name. The world, we are taught, exists for the sake of three things, one of which is Torah.[1] And the study of Torah is equivalent to the performance of all the other commandments.[2] Little wonder, then, that a child marks the occasion of reaching religious majority by being called to the Torah, for it is through participation in the life of Torah that one learns most truly just what it means to grow as a Jewish adult, to be a Jew.

The Traditional Prohibition.

Yet the fact remains that Torah as an intellectual and spiritual discipline has traditionally been reserved for males. Let us take, for example, your own experience of "fulfilling the commandment for every Jew to write a Torah", a commandment derived from Deuteronomy 31:19, "therefore, write down this poem and teach it to Israel."[3] The author of the *Sefer Hachinuch*, an important medieval work, uses exalted language to describe the purpose of this *mitzvah*:[4] "God instructed that each Jew should have a *sefer torah* readily available to study...in order to learn to revere God and to understand God's commandments, which are more precious to us than gold...". But the phrase "each Jew" is severely qualified: "This commandment is practiced in every community and in every age[5] by males, who are obligated to study the Torah and therefore to write it, and not by females."

Women, in other words, are exempt from the commandment to write a Torah scroll because they are also exempt from *talmud torah*, the requirement to study Torah. The source of this exemption is a midrash, a rabbinic legal interpretation of Deuteronomy 11:19: "you shall teach (My words) to *bene-ichem*." This Hebrew word is the second person inflection of *banim*, which means either "children" or "sons", and according to the rules of Hebrew grammar it can be rendered correctly as either "your children" or "your sons". The midrash seizes upon the latter alternative: *beneichem* means your sons and excludes your daughters. Hence, a father need not teach Torah to his daughter, nor is she required to study it on her own.[6] Since a woman is exempt from the commandment to study Torah, the rabbis deduced through the interpretive principle of *simuchin*, which draws comparisons between adjacent Torah verses or subjects, that she is also exempt from the *mitzvah* of *tefillin*.[7] And— once again through the principle of *simuchin*—if she is exempt from the requirement to wear *tefillin*, she is not qualified to write them, or to write *mezuzot* or Torah scrolls.[8] As Maimonides puts it: "Torah scrolls, *tefillin*, or *mezuzah* parchments that are written by a woman are unfit for use (*pesulin*) and should be stored away."[9] Thus does the tradition disqualify women from serving as scribes.

Critique of the Traditional View.

The position we have just described, which is the consensus view of the *halachah*, is not immune to critique. We would argue that the traditional prohibition, though strictly observed in the Orthodox community, is flawed as a matter of Jewish law. We note, first of all, that the rule which disqualifies women from serving as scribes rests upon a thoroughly arbitrary reading of the Torah. The midrash on Deuteronomy 11:19 which interprets *beneichem* as "your sons" rather than as "your children" could just as easily and correctly have chosen the alternate translation. Indeed, the *halachah* often does read *banim* and its various inflections as "children", undistinguished by gender.[10] This more inclusive reading is even adopted when the subject under discussion is a matter of ritual observance, where we would expect the rabbis to draw a distinction between men and women. A case in point is Numbers 15:38, which states: "speak to *benei yisrael* (sons/children of Israel) and tell them to make fringes (*tzitzit*) on the corners of their garments". The Talmud cites this wording to prove that only Jews (*benei yisrael*) and not Gentiles are permitted to make the ritual fringes.[11] Note that the text reads the phrase *benei yisrael* as "children", rather than "sons" of Israel; accordingly, most halachists rule that Jewish women, no less than Jewish men, are qualified to make *tzitzit*.[12] In other words, nothing prevents the rabbis from reading the Hebrew *banim* as "children" rather than "sons", including males and females alike within the terms of a *mitzvah*. They are not compelled, therefore, to interpret Deuteronomy 11:19 so as to exempt women from the *mitzvah* of Torah study and, by extension, from *tefillin* and from serving as scribes.

Why then did the rabbis of the Talmud adopt that restrictive interpretation? Clearly, the sages of late antiquity did not possess what we would call an "enlightened" view of the female mind and character. They believed it inappropriate and even dangerous for women to occupy themselves with the study of Torah. Thus, although women were not absolutely forbidden to study and even received a certain merit for doing so, "the Sages command that a father not teach Torah to his daughter, for most women are not intellectually suited to learn. Rather, due to their lack of intelligence, they are liable to interpret the words of Torah in vain and foolish ways. As the Sages teach us: `if one teaches his daughter Torah, it is as though he teaches her obscenity.'"[13] This attitude, though not the only one represented in talmudic literature, is of a piece with other rabbinic statements concerning women[14] and, as the codes indicate, it is the accepted *halachah* regarding women and Torah study. Given this intellectual and cultural reality, it is no surprise that the rabbis chose to read Deuteronomy 11:19 in the way they do.

In our age, it is hardly necessary to state that the rabbinic view of women's mental capacity does not correspond with the facts. We reject that view, therefore, not because it is politically incorrect but because it is false. And since it is *demonstrably* false, since it contradicts our own intellectual and cultural reality, one need not be a Reform Jew to recognize its falsehood. Indeed, leading traditional scholars have acknowledged that women are no less capable of learning than are men and that the rabbinic conception of female intelligence does not fit the "woman of today".[15] This is important, because the exclusion of women from the *mitzvah* of Torah study was justified largely on the basis of their supposed intellectual inadequacies. In the absence of this conception, the rabbis would not have ruled Torah study off-limits to women. And in a time when the evidence of our eyes so clearly demonstrates the collapse of that conception, no justification exists for rabbis, Orthodox or otherwise, to maintain the restrictive interpretation of Deuteronomy 11:19 which denies to women the opportunity to participate as equals in this *mitzvah*.[16]

The View of Reform Judaism.

Reform Judaism dissents sharply from this prohibition. Our movement rejects any attempt to draw distinctions in ritual practice on the basis of gender. Over the years, we have worked to remove the barriers that deny women equal access to all avenues of Jewish religious expression, learning, and leadership. Women serve our communities as rabbis, cantors, and *mohalot* (performers of ritual circumcision); there is no reason to deny them, should they possess the requisite education and skills, the opportunity to function as *soferot setam*, writers of Torah scrolls, *tefillin*, and *mezuzot*.

Since this is a matter of religious principle for us, we would maintain our dissent even if it were impossible to argue cogently on textual grounds against the traditional prohibition. Why then do we make such an argument? Obviously, we do not expect that Orthodox authorities will change their position because of anything we say. We rather seek to demonstrate that, according to *halachah* no less than on grounds of ethical principle, women ought to be obligated to study Torah and thus permitted to write sacred texts. Such to our mind is the most persuasive reading of the sources of Jewish law, one which Orthodox halachists could adopt with halachic integrity.

You, Ms. Ackerman, ought therefore to be able to serve the entire Jewish community, and not just its liberal segment, as a scribe. That some deny you this opportunity is the result of a prohibition which, as we have seen, flows from arbitrary textual interpretation and long-outdated psychology. This is a regrettable state of affairs which, we hope, will one day change. In the meantime, you should not let it hinder you from working toward your goal.

Your goal is, in fact, our goal as well. The Reform movement is deeply interested in training and producing *soferim/ot*, just as it produces rabbis, cantors, and other religious leaders. We also urge you to remember that as a scribe you will serve the community as a teacher of Torah as well as an inscriber of texts. A scribe, like a rabbi, embodies for other Jews the value of the study of Torah, the commandment that is equivalent to all the others combined. It is therefore incumbent upon the scribe, no less than upon the rabbi or other communal servants, to continue to study Torah with the greatest intensity of which he or she is capable. This study should include, at a minimum, a careful reading of the Torah itself, the weekly portions along with their *haftarot*, in the original Hebrew. In addition, you should learn the traditional *halachot*, the laws concerning the writing of Torah scrolls, *tefillin*, and *mezuzot*. A good source for these is Maimonides' *Mishneh Torah*, which contains a section devoted to this subject.

You say that it is your dream to become a scribe. We say that you have every right to pursue that dream and to serve your people thereby. We pray that God grant you the energy, perseverance, and insight to make your dream come true.[17]

NOTES

1 M Avot 1:2. And see BT Pesachim 68b: "were it not for the Torah, even heaven and the earth could not exist".

2 BT Shabbat 127a.

3 BT Sanhedrin 21b. See *Yad*, Sefer Torah 7:1: "that is to say, write for yourselves the Torah which contains this poem [in *parashat Ha'azinu*], for we write the Torah whole and not section by section."

4 *Sefer Hachinuch, mitzvah* 613.

5 *I.e.*, it is not restricted to the land of Israel or to the days when the Temple was standing.

6 BT Kiddushin 29b; *Yad*, Talmud Torah 1:1; *Sh.A.*, YD 246:6.

7 BT Kiddushin 34a. Since these two commandments are mentioned side by side (Deuteronomy 6:7-8 and 11:18-19), the rabbis learn that what is true of the one (women are exempt from Torah study) is true of the other (women are exempt from *tefillin*).

8 Since the commandment of *mezuzah* ("you shall write them on the doorposts of your house... Deuteronomy 6:9) is adjacent to the commandment of *tefillin* ("you shall bind them... Deuteronomy 6:8), what is true of "binding" (women are exempt) is true of "writing" as well; BT Menachot 42b and BT Gitin 45b. In the version of this *baraita* which appears in the printed version of *M.* Soferim 1:13, "woman" is not mentioned among the list of those who are unfit to write a *sefer torah*. However, the Gaon of Vilna reads "woman" in his text of *Soferim*; moreover, the exclusion of women seems demanded by the very logic behind this rule ("whoever does not wear *tefillin* may not write them").

9 *Yad*, Tefillin 1:13; *Sh.A.*, OC 39:1; *ShA*, YD 281:3. The *Tur*, YD 281, does not mention "woman" among those who are disqualified to write a Torah scroll. From this, some would learn that while a woman may not write tefillin she is permitted to write a sefer torah (*Derishah ad loc.*). But this is not the majority halachic position (*Siftey Kohen, Sh.A.*, YD 281, n. 6).

10 The Torah speaks of the Israelite community as benei yisrael, the "children" of Israel, a designation which almost always includes women as well as men. For example: according to all opinions the well-known statement in Leviticus 19:2 ("speak to benei yisrael and tell them: `you shall be holy...'") is addressed to the entire community and not merely to its sons.

11 BT Menachot 42a.

12 *Yad*, Hilchot Tzitzit 1:12. On the basis of BT Menachot 42a, Rambam prohibits Gentiles from making the fringes, and he does not include women within this prohibition. Tosafot, Menachot 42a, s.v. minayin and BT Tosafot, Gittin 45b, s.v. *kol*; R. Asher, Hilchot Tzitzit, n. 13; *Sh.A.*, OC 14:1; *Hagahot Maimoniot*, Tzitzit 1, n. 9. Some medieval authorities want to read *benei yisrael* in this verse as "sons of Israel", thereby disqualifying women as well as Gentiles from making *tzitzit*; see Hagahot Maimoniot ad loc. But theirs is definitely a minority opinion. Isserles, *Sh.A.*, OC 14:1, urges that *tzitzit* not be made by women, but his words are couched in the form of a prudent stringency and not as a statement that, according to the law, women are forbidden to make them.

13 *Yad*, Talmud Torah 1:13; see also *Sh.A.*, YD 246:6. The quotation is the dictum of R. Eliezer in *M* Sotah 3:4. See also *YT* Sotah 3:4: "let the Torah's words be burned rather than given over to women."

14 *E.g.*, "women are of unstable temperament" (BT Shabbat 33b and Kiddushin 80b) and "women's sole wisdom lies in the spinning of yarn" (BT Yoma 66b).

15 See *Aruch HaShulchan*, YD 246, n. 19, and *Torah Temimah*, Deut. 11:19, n. 48, end. And see, especially, R. Ben Zion Ouziel's description of "today's woman" in his *Resp. Mishpetey Ouziel*, v. 3, n. 6, where counter to the orthodox rabbinic majority he rules in favor of female suffrage. Moreover, despite women's supposed mental inferiority, halachists have long required them to study those aspects of Jewish

law which apply directly to them. See Isserles, *ShA, YD* 246:6, and *Tosafot,* BT Sotah 22b, s.v. *ben azai.*

16 One cannot defend a refusal to remove the prohibition on the basis of "hallowed tradition." The *halachah* allows contemporary rabbis to depart from the rulings of their predecessors when those rulings were based upon an observable reality that has changed since their day. See R. Eliezer Berkovits, *Hahalachah: kochah vetafkidah* (Jerusalem, 1981), 48ff.

17 Ms. Ackerman was informed of the efforts by the Union of American Hebrew Congregations to hold an institute for the teaching of scribal skills during the summer of 1996.

Even Ha-Ezer
The Jewish Family

Gossip between Husband and Wife
5750.4

She'elah

When husband and wife discuss a third person, does this constitute a permissible aspect of marital relations or does it fall under the prohibition of *lashon ha-ra'* (talking badly about someone)? Would the closeness and privacy of marriage make a difference? (Elizabeth Resnick Levine)

Teshuvah

1. The nature of *lashon ha-ra.*

Tradition repeatedly stresses the power of the spoken word, and the Midrash calls it the primary source of good and evil.[1] The biblical prohibition is found in Lev. 19:16: "You shall not go about as a talebearer."[2] The Rambam divides this law into three categories:[3]

a. *Holech rachil*, going about gossiping, even when not aimed at the degradation of another person; it is the least serious offense, but is still prohibited;

b. *Lashon ha-ra* (more properly, *leshon ha-ra*), improper speech; though true, it potentially damages another person;

c. *Motzi shem ra*, giving someone a bad name, the severest violation of the law, refers to spreading false information and slandering. The classic passage interpreting this prohibition, ascribed to the second century sage Eleazar ben Parta, relates to the report of the ten spies (Num. 13:32). They misrepresented the condition of the land, that is, its trees and stones, and for this they died and caused the entire generation who believed them to perish in the desert. If this punishment was exacted from them because they maligned inanimate objects, how much more severe is the prohibition not to malign persons.[4]

In the following we shall deal with all three categories as a unit, and do so under the general name of *lashon ha-ra.*

R. Israel Meir Ha-Kohen[5] suggested that engaging in *lashon ha-ra* violates additional commandments, such as the negative "Do not hate your broth-

187

er in your heart" (Lev. 19:17) and the positive "Love your neighbor as yourself" (Lev. 19:18).[6] Especially must one not speak of another as lacking in virtue or possessing character faults.[7] Similarly the Rambam prohibits talk that might, even though it be true, cause financial loss, physical pain, mental anguish or similar damage to the person spoken about.[8] And of course, the person listening to *lashon ha-ra* is also culpable.[9]

The importance of this subject is highlighted by its place in our prayer services. At the conclusion of the central prayer, the Amidah , a final meditation takes note of our pervasive penchant for gossip and slander and begins with the words: "O God, keep my tongue from evil and my lips from speaking guile."

2. Is *lashon ha-ra* permitted in the context of a marital relationship?

Such relationship does not of itself negate the commandment, and the Hafetz Hayyim makes it abundantly clear:

> There is no distinction made with regard to this prohibition, whether it is done of one's own or because of someone else's urging; in either case it is forbidden. Even if one's parent or teacher, whom one is required to honor and revere...were to request that one tell about so-and-so, if one knows that such telling would inevitably lead to *lashon ha-ra* or even to one of its by-products (*avak lashon ha-ra*) is forbidden to obey them.[10]

This prohibition stands even if the commandment is rabbinical (*der-abbanan*)[11] and not Toraitic (*de-oraita*) , or if a king of Israel requests that it be disregarded.[12]

There is a passage in the *Pirkei Avot* which, while it reflects a male perspective, nonetheless speaks to the question before us: "Don't indulge in idle talk with your wife."[13] What is this "idle talk"? One interpretation holds that it refers to gossip a man shares with his wife and that he, by doing so, disgraces himself. Which is to say that the marital context does not exempt a person from the prohibition of *lashon ha-ra*.[14]

Would it be different if the communication contributed to marital peace, *shelom bayit*, which is a valued tradition as well? Even God shaded the truth when speaking to Abraham about his wife,[15] and the Divine Name may be erased in the biblical "ordeal" of the Sotah in order to clear up marital suspicion.[16] And, significantly, Aaron's lasting fame rested to no small degree on his ability to establish *shelom bayit* among Israel's families.[17]

Therefore it might be argued that, since total confidence between husband and wife helps to cement the foundations of their marriage, *lashon ha-ra* could could be seen as serving a wholesome end, especially when they agree not to reveal the information to anyone.[18] But such an argument offends against the basic rule that one should not try to accomplish a *mitzvah* by committing an *averah* (transgression). There are exceptions, of course, but they deal with situations in which alternatives are impossible or severely restricted, as when there is danger to life (*pikuach nefesh*). No such exigency exists with regard to *lashon ha-ra*. There are better and more positive ways of achieving *shelom bayit* than the practice of gossip and slander which court the possibility of harming another person. The pledge of secrecy is irrelevant since gossip and slander as such constitute an offense.

To sum up: Even in special relationships which are founded on respect and bonding (parent and child, teacher and pupil, husband and wife) *lashon ha-ra* is not permitted. There are no principles in Reform Judaism that would disagree with this tradition; on the contrary, our ethics-oriented emphasis would strongly endorse it.

We are of course aware that that this position is likely to be disregarded in the marital setting. But by stating it nonetheless we are stressing the ideal, as a value in itself. We would also stress that, if people regularly engage in *lashon ha-ra* in private, they are likely to do it elsewhere as well. In practical terms, therefore, our responsum may be seen as a caution.

NOTES

1 Lev. R. 33:1; see also 16:2.

2 This is the popular understanding of the verse. But others (e.g. the translation by the Jewish Publication Society) render it: "Do not deal basely..."

3 *Yad*, Hil. De'ot, 7:1-2.

4 See *Tosefta* Arachin 2:11; *BT* Ar. 15a, which equated this sin with the combined transgression of murder, idolatry and illicit sexual behavior.

5 Often also cited as R. Israel Meir Kagan, and known by his chief work as the *Hafets Hayyim*, he laid special emphasis on pure and decent speech, *shemirat ha-lashon* (which can also be rendered "watching one's tongue").

6 See *Hafetz Hayyim*, Introduction.

7 *Ibid.,* 8:10.

8 *Yad,* Hil. De'ot 7:5. Such speech is allowed only when used for constructive purposes, such as warning someone who stands in danger of being cheated.

9 Ibid., 7:1-2; based on Exod. 23:1, Pes. 118a.

10 Hil. Lashon ha-ra' 1:5. See also the saying of R. Amram in BT Baba Batra 164b.

11 *Ibid.*, no. 8, footnote; see *Sh. A.* , YD 240:15, after Lev. 19:2 and BT, Baba Metsi'a 32a.

12 Sanh. 49a; Rambam, *Yad,* Melachim 3:9.

13 M. Avot 1:5: *ve'al tarbeh sihah im ha-ishah.* The word *ishah* may of course refer to women in general, and not toone's wife.

14 *Avot de-R. Natan* 7:3.

15 Gen. 18:12-13, and BT Baba Metzi'a 87a.

16 Num. 5:23.

17 *Avot de-R. Natan* 50.

18 Speaking kindly about another person is of course encouraged and not at issue.

Conversion and Marriage after Transsexual Surgery
5750.8

She'elah

An applicant for conversion, X, received extensive therapy at a recognized psychiatric institution which offers a sex-change psycho-therapy program. Subsequently he underwent surgery; his male genitalia were removed and a cosmetic vagina was constructed. However, this having taken place, he had a change of heart and no longer desired to be a woman. Since he had never declared himself publicly or legally as a woman, he continued his status as a man and was later married in a civil ceremony to his fiancee, a Jewish woman who is satisfied to live with him permanently, despite his mutilated condition. She supports his desire to become a Jew. The couple have been attending Shabbat services regularly. (Rabbi's name withheld, in order to prevent identification of X.)

Two questions:

1. Should we admit the 29-year old person to the Jewish information course established jointly by the Reform congregations in our city, holding out the likelihood that in the end there would be religious conversion?

2. If X is converted, should the rabbi sanctify the civil marriage through a religious ceremony (*kiddushin*)?

Teshuvah

Traditional Considerations

    1. The question of conversion. Deut. 23:2 states: "No one whose testes are crushed or whose member is cut off shall be admitted into the Congregation of the Eternal." This would appear to exclude X from membership in the Jewish people, but already Isaiah (56:3 ff.) mitigated the application of this rule when he spoke of God having special regard for the eunuchs. Subsequently, rabbinic tradition understood the intent of "No one whose testes are crushed..." to be that such a man should not marry an Israelite woman, while his status as a Jew was not affected.[1]

There is therefore no objection in principle to the conversion of a person whose genitalia are mutilated or missing altogether, even when he is a *seris adam*, one whose mutilation was effected by human hand and not by birth or illness (*seris chammah*). In these cases, immersion alone suffices for *giyur,* religious conversion. We see no reason to depart from this view and therefore hold that X's desire to become a convert has to be treated on its own merits.

The question then arises whether X, with his history of identity problems, is qualified as a prospective convert. Should we not have some concern about the mental stability of a person who, having undergone this radical and irreversible operation, now desires to be a man after all?

The Rambam deals with a convert who had been admitted without proper examination or instruction in the mitzvot.[3] But since the error has been made, he says, his conversion is deemed valid ex post facto (*be-di'avad*) though one should be troubled about the person until his sincerity is fully established. Once conversion has taken place, the presumption is in favor of the convert.[4] But <u>before</u> the event (*lechatchilah*) it is different, for the fitness of the prospective convert should be most carefully considered.

Rabbi Walter Jacob issued a *teshuvah* on the question how the mental competency of a convert might be assessed, and cautioned that "we cannot accept individuals who do not meet these prerequisites [of mental competency]."[5]

In the case before us, when could it be said that X has shown that his intention to become a Jew is firm and not likely subject to reversal? As a minimum we suggest a cautionary waiting period, like the traditional cycle of three Pilgrimage Festivals (which waiting period applies in other cases).[6] Since the conversion program in X's city lasts for eight months, let him enter the course but let him also be informed that, upon conclusion of the program, there would be a further time span, say a year, after which the rabbinic court would rule on his admissibility to conversion.

(While this is the majority opinion of the Responsa Committee, some members disagree and would not admit X to the program at all. They would consider X as a person who has already shown his instability in a matter which fundamentally affects his physical identity. They would not wish conversion to be another stage of the person's psychiatric meandering. The majority, as indicated, would leave the matter to the discretion of the *beit din*.)

2. <u>Should the rabbi officiate at X's marriage?</u> The question of admissibility to religious marriage is different from that of admissibility to conversion. In the latter, it is not necessary to deal with a presumption of X's maleness (*chezkat zachar*), because in the Reform context which treats men and women as religious equals we convert X as a human being and not as either a male or a female. But in marriage, differential gender has been the precondition.

First of all, let us look briefly at the admissibility of sex change altogether. Since the Halachah regards the mitzvah of procreation as a chief purpose of marriage, the Rabbis forbade the removal of male genitalia in the hermaphrodite (*androginos*), the person who possesses both male and female genitalia. Even more so would they forbid the removal of genitalia from an otherwise normally formed man who wishes to be a woman.[8]

Exceptions were made only occasionally. Thus, Rabbi Eliezer Waldenberg permitted transsexual surgery (from male to female) in the borderline case of an infant whose external genitalia were those of a female, though chromosome analysis and the presence of a testicle showed that the gender might be male.[9] According to Rabbi Waldenberg, the general rule is that the "visible, external organs" determine sexual identity, and in the case of X he would therefore not have allowed the surgery.

The issue before us is, however, not the permissibility of the surgery but rather, since it has already taken place, whether *kiddushin,* religiously sanctioned union, may now be celebrated.

There is a good deal of halachic discussion of the question whether the marriage of a transsexual is still a marriage and whether--if it is contracted--religious divorce (*gittin*) is necessary or redundant. When the operation has already taken place, most follow Rabbenu Asher who says that a man whose genitalia have been removed is no longer able to contract a valid marriage--even though his sexual identity may not be affected and he is still considered a man.[10] The prohibition stated in Deut. 23:2, as interpreted by Tradition, is deemed decisive.

Reform Perspectives

Are there reasons why Reform Judaism might reach a different conclusion? There might be, for it would likely view the biblical passage differently. It would see it as a time-bound response to a particular situation, namely the use of castrated men (*sarisim*) in society, and this original purpose of the law has fallen away.[11]

In addition, Reform also would accept the findings of modern science, which holds that external genitalia may not reflect the true identity of the individual. Thus, analysts have distinguished five categories which can be said to identify biological sex. They are: chromosomal configuration; gonadal sex (presence of ovaries or testes); sex-based hormones (androgen or estrogen dominance); internal reproductive structure; and external genitalia.[12] Rabbi Solomon B. Freehof was therefore ambivalent and suggested that the rabbi be guided by the attitude of the community: if the state issues a license to a transsexual it may be assumed that his/her change has the recognition of the law and therefore *kiddushin* may take place.[13] Subsequently, a CCAR Responsa Committee which dealt with the matter in some detail also allowed sex change as a permissible procedure and did not object to *kiddushin*.[14]

Despite these precedents in our movement, we remain troubled about the matter. The questioner notes that X received the best available scientific and psychological advice before his transsexual surgery was effected. Should we therefore not assume that medical evidence showed X to possess a sufficient measure of the aforementioned female characteristics? In some institutions which deal with persons like him there is a period during which the patient receives hormonal treatment and lives for a while as a woman. Only when the results of this trial period are conclusive is the surgery performed.

Was this done in X's case and was his preference for femaleness physiologically founded? The answer is not available to us and may not be available to the rabbi either. Still, we have to believe that no reputable institution would have proceeded with the surgery had there not been sufficient indications that strong female characteristics were in evidence. We would therefore consider the presumption of X's maleness to have been seriously weakened, and X to fall into the category of *safek zachar, safek nekevah*, meaning that his/her sexual identity is in doubt.[15] We would consequently advise the rabbi <u>not to proceed</u> with *kiddushin* in case X is converted to Judaism.

Of course, for those Reform rabbis who sanctify same-sex marriages, this part of our discussion is irrelevant. They will say: Here are two individuals who care for each other and who want a ceremony that recognizes their intent as holy. However, while individual rabbis have taken this position, the Reform movement as represented by the CCAR has refused to do so.

In any case, even though no religious wedding will be performed, we assume that X will be treated with all the compassion and concern which such a tormented individual desperately requires.

NOTES

1 *See* Rashi and Ibn Ezra on Deut. 23:2 . The prohibition against Ammonites and Moabites was applied only to men, while their women (like Ruth) were allowed to marry Israelite men. The matter is discussed in M. Yevamot 8:2, and BT Yevamot 76a and following.

2 Rosh, Yevamot 4:13; *Sh.A.*, YD 268:1.

3 *Yad*, Issurei Bi'ah 13:17.

4 The Mishnah (Gitt. 3:3) speaks of a man who desires to divorce his wife but, being old or ill, sends a messenger to represent him. The man is presumed alive at the time of *gittin* until the opposite is established (*bechezkat she-hu kayyam*). The same principle applies to an animal to be slaughtered. While alive it has the status of a forbidden object, for an ever *min ha-chay* may not be eaten; but once slaughtered, the presumption is that the *shechitah* was kosher until the opposite is established (*harei hee bechezkat hetteir*; BT Hullin 9a).

5 *American Reform Responsa*, ed. Walter Jacob (New York: CCAR, 1983), no. 67, pp. 215-216. The Rambam left the decision to the presiding judge; *Yad*, Edut 9:9, and Sanh. 2:1.

6 Such as the establishment of ownership of a lost object; see the Maggid Mishneh on the *Yad*, Issurei Bi'ah 13:17, who finds the case a confirmation of the uncomplimentary saying that "Converts are for Israel like a rash" (*sapachat*, Lev. 13:2). See also M. Bava Metsi'a 2:6 and commentaries.

7 Based on Lev. 22:24; BT Shabbat 110b; Rambam. ibid. 16:10. See further the study by Moshe Steinberg in '*Assiya,* vol. 1, pp. 142-145, and R. Gedaliah Felder's discussion of the way an *androginos* and *tumtum* are to be converted (*She'elat Yeshurun,* no. 23), both with extensive notes and a listing of the traditional decisors.

8 See Rabbi J. David Bleich, "Transsexual Surgery," in Fred Rosner and J. David Bleich, *Jewish Bioethics* (New York: Hebrew Publishing Company, 1983), p. 191, citing Lev. 22:24. Rabbi Solomon Freehof also says: "There seems to be no way in which Jewish tradition can permit it" [i.e., transsexual surgery, if people are born with normal genitalia]; see *MRR*, no. 22, pp. 128-133.

9 *Tzitz Eliezer*, vol. 2, no. 78.

10 So *Besamim Rosh*, no. 340. (The work is ascribed to R. Asher ben Yechiel, known as the Rosh, but was probably not authored by him.)

11 This opinion is supported by *Yalkut Me'am Lo'ez*, Devarim 866.

12 See John Money et al. in *Bulletin of the Johns Hopkins Hospital* 97 (1955), pp. 284-300; and

the article "Sexual Identity" in the *Encyclopedia of Bioethics*, vol. 3.

13 *RRT*, no. . 42, pp. 196-200.

14 See *ARR*, no. 37, pp. 416-419, and *CARR,* no. 199, pp. 293-296, both with extensive citations of source materials.

15 That uncertainty is repeatedly treated in the tradition; see *She'elat Yeshurun*, l.c.

Marrying One's Ex-Wife's Sister
5751.12

She'elah

A man who has divorced his wife now wants to marry her sister. While the traditional law of consanguinity forbids it, is it appropriate in our age to continue being strict regarding this particular relationship? If it remains objectionable and the couple are nonetheless married by civil authority, should they be accepted into the synagogue and should their children be educated in the school?

Teshuvah

The biblical prohibition regarding marrying one's ex-wife's sister (Lev. 18:18) states: *ve-ishah el achotah lo tikach litzror aleiah ... be-chayyeiah*, which the JPS translation broadly renders as "Do not marry a woman as a rival to her sister...in her lifetime." The objective of the prohibition is clearly not consanguinity but peace between the sisters. Note that the Hebrew literally says that the marriage is prohibited because its effect would be *litzror aleiah*, to make life narrow and mean for the first wife.[1] *Thus, the purpose of the law is to avoid sibling discord.*

The Talmud already posits the question whether the relationship is allowed if the first wife has been divorced, and answers that the addition "in her lifetime" prohibits this.[2] Thus, the reason for the biblical stricture is seen not as permanently inherent in the relationship itself, as it does in all other prohibitions of the chapter, but--as the codes insist--rests on plain inter-personal considerations, which disappear once the first wife is dead, but not before.[3]

To be sure, the Torah law proceeds from a stance of polygamy, forbidding a man to take sisters as wives at the same time.[4] But, as indicated, rabbinic tradition goes beyond ancient sociology and tries to avoid a situation which cannot help but create bitterness between the sisters. This configuration has not lost its potency in our time, and our *Rabbi's Manual* maintains the prohibition.[5] We therefore urge that the rabbi not officiate at the marriage.

What about membership in the synagogue if the marriage is contracted before civil authorities? Despite their flaunting of Jewish tradition the two people are and remain Jews and should therefore be admitted, and so should their children, whom we are obligated to provide with a Jewish education.

NOTES

1 So Rashi, who points out that the expression *litzror* (to make narrow) is related to *tsarah*, (trouble, misfortune).

2 BT, Yevamot 8b.

3 *Yad,* Issurei Bi'ah, 2:9; Jacob ben Asher, *Arba'ah Turim*, EH, Hilch. Pirya ve-rivya, no. 15, et al.

4 BT, Kiddushin 50b.

5 1988 ed., p. 235.

Informing a Daughter of her Mother's Death
5753.1

She'elah

An elderly woman, who has been under the care of her granddaughters, has died. There has been terrible conflict and estrangement between them and her daughter, and the granddaughters do not plan on informing their mother (the daughter of the deceased) of the death until after the funeral has taken place.

What is the obligation of the officiating rabbi in this situation? Should the daughter of the deceased be informed of the death even if her presence at the funeral will probably cause a great deal of pain and discomfort among the rest of the mourners? (Rabbi Mark Glickman, Dayton, OH)

Teshuvah

Jewish tradition considers as a mourner a person who has lost any one of seven close relatives: a spouse, a mother, a father, a son, a daughter, a brother or a sister.[1] This definition of a mourner is based on the interpretation of Leviticus 21:1-3:

"...(a priest) shall not defile himself for the dead among his
people; except for his nearest relatives: his mother, his father,
his son, his daughter, his brother; his sister. . . ."

While the Leviticus passage does not explicitly include a priest's wife among the list of "his nearest relatives" (hakarov eilav), nevertheless, Rashi maintains that the Torah implicitly instructs that a Kohen should also defile himself in order to mourn for his wife.[2] In its various guides and publications, Reform Judaism too has maintained this understanding of who is considered a primary mourner, an aveil.[3]

In reference to our case, in which the granddaughters wish to exclude their mother, it is uncontested that she, as a daughter, is a primary mourner in the legal sense. Her children may feel closer to the deceased than she does, but that does not affect her status: she has obligations as a primary mourner that her children do not have, and she must therefore be informed of her mother's death so that she can fulfill them.

Is there any reason why Reform Judaism should disagree? The CCAR's Gates of Mitzvah plainly states: "It is a mitzvah to notify all members of the family at the time of death. This applies also to cases where certain members of the family are estranged and the period of family mourning might promote reconciliation."[4] Furthermore, "the mitzvah of burying the dead is the responsibility of the person's children or spouse."[5]

Are there special considerations which would justify the children's desire to keep her from fulfilling her mitzvah? Without going into the personal details of this family's dysfunctional history, we take note of the fact that the mother and her daughters do not get along. At a previous funeral, their tempers got the best of them, and hurtful words were spoken. According to the children, it was the mother's behavior that caused the problems. Nevertheless, the mother has rights that are not abrogated by a previous contretemps. The Reform position is clear: It is a mitzvah to notify every mourner that death has occurred, and in fact, this occasion becomes frequently an opportunity for healing family wounds.

It is our judgment that the rabbi should insist that the mother be immediately it told of the death of her mother. If the granddaughters refuse to inform her, the rabbi must assume this responsibility. What we know of the past history of the family relationship does not alter this conclusion.

One member of the Responsa Committee points out that some rabbis may be under a contractual obligation to conduct a funeral upon the request of a congregant regardless of how unseemly the arrangements are. Some such contracts read: "Upon request, and consistent with established Reform Jewish practice, the Rabbi shall officiate at all funerals of members and of their families." The majority of the Responsa Committee feels that "established Reform practice" would not tolerate the exclusion of a primary mourner or the public humiliation of a mother by her children.

NOTES

1 *Sh. A.* YD 374:4.

2 Rashi to Leviticus 21:2, basing himself on the *Sifra's* interpretation, holding that the word *lesha'ero* refers to the Kohen's wife. Note also the *baraita* in BT Moed Katan 20b, which implies that the inclusion of the wife comes from the Torah (Maimonides disagrees in this respect, *Yad,* Hilchot Aveil, 2:1).

3 Cf. Solomon B. Freehof, *Reform Jewish Practice*, Vol. I (Cincinnati,1944) p. 157; David Polish and Frederic A. Doppelt, *A Guide for Reform Jews* (New York, 1957), p. 85; the CCAR's *Ma'gelei Tsedek-Rabbi's Manual*, p. 259; and the CCAR's *Gates of Mitzvah,* p. 51.

4 *Gates of Mitzvah,* p. 53.

5 *Ibid.* p. 55.

Kaddish for Adoptive and Biological Parents
5753.12

She'elah

A child was adopted in infancy by Jewish parents, converted and raised as a Jew. Subsequently, the child discovered that his or her biological parents were Jews. Does the child have *kaddish* and *yahrtzeit* obligations toward the biological parents? If so, is this obligation in addition to or in place of any similar obligation to the adoptive parents? (Rabbi Daniel K. Gottlieb, Concord, Ontario)

Teshuvah

This Committee has dealt previously with the issue of adoption.[1] The case before us differs, however, in that it raises the crucial, often explosive emotional issue which every adopted child must confront: which set of parents, the biological or the adoptive, are the "real" parents? To put the question in Jewish terms: to whom does this child owe the primary responsibility indicated by the commandment to "honor your father and your mother"? Sooner or later, say many experts in the field, every adopted child must somehow come to terms with this question, and a great deal is at stake in how he or she answers it. Accordingly, the psychological literature on adoption deals extensively with the subject. In this *teshuvah*, we want to examine the issue from the standpoint of Jewish religious tradition, a tradition we seek to understand and interpret as best we can from a contemporary liberal perspective.

Halachic Precedents. Had this child been born a Gentile, tradition would surely have regarded the adoptive parents as his or her only parents. The conversion would have severed the legal tie with the biological parents.[2] In this instance, though, the child was born to Jewish parents, and this fact matters greatly: he or she has inherited Jewish status from the biological mother and father.[3] Jewish law, moreover, regards the legal connection between Jewish parents and their biological offspring as a permanent one.

The concept of "adoption", through which a parent-child bond is created through legal means and thereby replaces the bond linking the child to

201

his or her biological parents, is not to be found in the Talmudic sources. The "adoptive" parent is always referred to as a legal guardian (*apotropos*) who raises (*megadel*) the child; that person is never called "father" or "mother". The biological parent, meanwhile, never ceases to be the parent. A number of commentators in fact hold that a child is obligated to fulfill the commandment to "honor your father and your mother" for the biological parents even if they did not care for the child during his or her lifetime. The essence of parenthood, in this view, lies in the procreation of the child, a fact which even the severest kind of parental neglect cannot erase.[4]

This theory leads to some important halachic consequences. A contemporary authority rules that "an adopted child...is obligated to honor (his biological parents) during their lifetime and upon their death, and to observe the laws of mourning and *kaddish* as any other child, even though he had no contact with those parents throughout his life."[5] The child's obligations toward the adoptive parents, by contrast, are not so strict. R. Gedaliah Felder, in an authoritative treatise on the halachot of conversion,[6] declares flatly that a person is not required to "honor" his or her adoptive parents. He hedges this conclusion somewhat with the remark that, as a matter of courtesy and good manners, one ought to show respect to those who have raised and cared for one; thus, the adoptee ought to say *kaddish* for them, unless this should somehow violate the prerogative of their biological children.[7] Similarly, R. Ovadiah Yosef rules that a person need not observe the rites of mourning (*avelut*) for the adoptive parent, nor should he say kaddish for that parent unless there are no biological children who can fulfill the requirement.[8] In short, one *may* mourn one's adoptive parents; one *must* mourn one's biological parents. In this line of reasoning, the connection between Jewish parents and their biological offspring is permanent and "real", while that forged by adoption is both artificial and less halachically compelling.

Differing Trends. There is, however, another discernible trend in Jewish legal thought, a trend composed of a number of rules, principles, decisions and customs which point in the opposite direction and portray the family relationship created by adoption as no less "real" than the biological one.

These are as follows:

1. The applicability of the commandment to honor one's parents to all biological parent-child relationships is not necessarily absolute. A Talmudic dictum holds that a parent may legitimately renounce the *kavod* (honor) owed by a child.[9] There is no more obvious case of a "waiver of rights" than a parent who has placed a child for adoption. This is not to imply that the parent's decision is cavalier, arbitrary, or thoughtless; indeed, in many circumstances that choice is a painful one which the parent nonetheless recognizes as the most responsible option available. But when a biological parent agrees to allow others to raise a child as their own and to forego all the personal and financial obligations of parenthood, it is reasonable to conclude that the parent agrees to forego "honor" as well.

2. How can parents waive this "honor" when children are required to render it to the ones who bring them into the world? The answer is suggested by the author of the *Sefer Ha-Chinuch* (mitzvah no.33), who describes the commandment to honor one's parents differently than do the authorities cited above. Its purpose, he writes, is to recognize and show compassion to those who have done kindness for us during our formative years; it teaches us to be grateful for the goodness we have received from them. He does, it is true, add that the commandment also serves as a reminder that one's father and mother are the reason for one's physical existence. Yet by equating these two purposes, he acknowledges that the essence of parenthood lies *at least as much* in the care, the love, and the teaching which the parent bestows upon the child as it does in the fact of procreation. It follows that the duty to honor our parents defines our relationship toward those who have shouldered these obligations *at least as much* as it does that toward those who supplied the genetic material from which we were conceived. Adoptive parents, that is, are also one's "real" parents, as real as the biological ones.

3. The Halachah often treats the adoptive relationship precisely as it does the biological one. R. Benzion Ouziel rules that parents are required to provide food, housing, and education for their adoptive children in the same measure as for their biological offspring. This obligation also extends to the emotional side of family life: the rabbinic court is empowered to intervene on

behalf of the adoptive children should they be treated unfairly in any way by other members of the household.[10] R. Moshe Feinstein declares that an adopt-ed child may be named "the son/daughter (*ben/bat*) of the adoptive parent" rather than of the Jewish biological parent or of "our ancestor Abraham" in the event the child was born to a Gentile mother and subsequently converted.[11] He apparently relies upon a responsum of R. Meir of Rothenburg,[12] who holds that a person may, in a legal document, legitimately refer to the child he has raised in his home as "my child." Some authorities limit this ruling, arguing that a father may call an adoptee "my child" *only* when he has no other bio-logical children; if other children exist, the document is invalid.[13] This has been explained as an attempt to avoid confusion and contention in matters of inheritance. We presume that a father would rather bequeath his property to *his* child than, say, his wife's child from a former marriage; a document that equates the two children is thus presumed a forgery.[14] Halachists are in doubt as to how the law is decided, but in our case the presumption clearly does not hold.[15]

Adoptive parents agree under civil law to treat the child in matters of property and inheritance as though he or she were their biological offspring. This agreement is valid under Jewish law as a gift made "in contemplation of death" (*matanat shechiv mera*) by which property is distributed so as to avoid the division demanded by the inheritance laws.[16] It is also binding under the doctrine "the law of the land *is* the law" (*dina demalchuta dina*), by which mon-etary obligations entered into under civil law are enforceable at Jewish law as well. Since the parents are thus obligated to their adoptive child, the objection to R. Meir's ruling is moot. A parent may refer to an adoptive child as "my child" in all respects, legal as well as emotional.

We should also refer to the issue of *yichud*. Individuals are ordinarily forbidden to be alone together with members of the opposite sex other than their spouses. Parents are exempt from this prohibition on the theory that family ties suppress any sexual inclinations they might have toward their chil-dren and other blood relations.[17] Some authorities hold that this applies only to biological children; thus, it is only with great difficulty that R. Eliezer Yehudah Waldenberg permits parents to be alone with children adopted in infancy.[18] R. Chaim David Halevy, however, takes the opposite view. Parents may be alone with and display normal physical affection to their adoptive children, for their relationship to them is exactly the same as their relationship toward biological children. The adoptees have become "like real children (*kevanim mamash*) in every respect."[19]

The matter of *yichud* illustrates an important development of halachic thought. As we have seen, Jewish tradition offers two contradictory approaches concerning the relationship between parents and their adopted children. The one defines the status of adoptees as somehow less "real" than that of biological offspring; the other regards adoptees as the "real" children of their adoptive parents. Some halachists have come to assume the second approach, at least with respect to certain issues, not because they regard the first approach as "wrong" but rather because it is irrelevant to contemporary social reality. They understand, that is, that the traditional distinctions between biological and adopted children are derived from sources which do not know of our present-day institution of adoption. When those sources speak of non-biological parenthood, they refer to situations analogous to those of step-parents or foster parents, guardians who cannot say with legal accuracy that "this is my child." They do not describe the case of adoption in which, as R. Halevy notes, the emotional differences between biological and non-biological children virtually disappear. Adoption, some authorities have come to understand, creates a "real" family relationship, characterized by the same feelings and emotions that pertain to the bond between biological parent and child. It therefore makes no sense to think about adoption as though it were the same institution as its Talmudic antecedents.[20]

Liberal Considerations. We agree, and we would go farther. We propose to apply this insight to all issues. We believe it is time that Jewish law erase all invidious distinctions between biological and adopted children. We do so not only because we regard adoption as a new phenomenon, different from legal guardianship, but because of our sense of what Jewish parenthood is truly about.

Parenthood is about family, and adoption creates family just as surely as does biology. We hold with the Talmudic sentiment that "one who raises an orphan in his home is regarded by Scripture as though he has given birth to that child."[21] We believe that those rules, principles, and customs within the tradition which portray adoptive families as "real" families are motivated by the same sentiment. And, most importantly, we agree with the *Sefer Ha-Chinuch* that the essence of parenthood does not and cannot consist of the act of procreation. Parents of adoptive children, who love them as their own, care for them, and guide them, who stand by them during the crises and the joys of their lives, who raise them to adulthood, who teach them Torah and worldly wisdom thereby become the real parents of these children. They are no less entitled to "honor" than the biological parents. Our best understanding of Jewish law and religious values demands that this simple fact be accorded full and complete recognition.

We do not hold thereby that adoption renders biology irrelevant. Indeed, the individual in our case is a Jew because the biological parents were Jewish. Had they been Gentiles, a conversion would have been necessary to create a Jewish family relationship between adoptive parents and child. Yet our case deals not with lineage but with parenthood. And though the child does not owe his or her Jewish status to the adoptive parents, they are no less entitled to love, honor, and filial devotion.

In this case, the individual may choose say to *kaddish* and observe *yahrtzeit* for the biological parents. This may be quite helpful on psychological grounds as a means for helping this person come to terms with his or her past. At the same time, however, he or she must observe the customs of mourning for the adoptive parents. Children are obligated to show their adoptive parents all the deference and honor expected of Jewish children, for indeed, these have become their parents in every respect.

NOTES

1 See *ARR,* no. 62-63, pp. 199-208.
2 "A proselyte is like a newborn"; BT Yevamot 22a and parallels.
3 M. Kiddushin 3:12; *Yad,* Hilchot Issciaei Bi'ah 19:15; *Sh.A.,* EH 8:1 ff.
4 See both the *Meshech Chochmah* and the *Ketav Sofer* to Deuteronomy 5:16.
5 R. Yonah Metzger, *Resp. Miyam Hahalachah,* v. 2, no. 18.
6 *Nachalat Zvi,* p 37. R. Felder cites approvingly the Talmudic story (BT Sotah 49a) of R. Acha bar Ya'akov, who raised his daughter's son. When the latter had grown, R. Acha said to him, "bring me some water". The young man replied, "I am not your son" (Rashi: I am not required to honor you as a son honors his father).
7 See also R. Yehudah Greenwald, *Kol Bo `al Avelut,* p. 375, who writes that the adoptee's

obligation of "honor" toward the adoptive parents is not equivalent to that owed to the biological parents.

8 *Yalkut Yosef*, v. 6, p. 100. See also R. Aaron Felder, *Yesodei Smochos*, p. 74.

9 BT Kiddushin 32a; *Yad,* Hilchot Mamrim 6:8; *Sh.A.* YD 240:19.

10 *Sha`arey Ouziel*, v. 2, pp. 184-185.

11 *Resp. Igerot Moshe,* YD, no. 161.

12 The responsum is found in the collection entitled *Teshuvot Maimoniot* printed at the conclusion of *Yad, Sefer Hamishpatim;* it is no. 48 in that collection. See also Isserles, CM 42:15.

13 R. Chayim Benveniste, *Kenesset Ha-Gedolah,* CM 42:15.

14 R. Moshe Sofer, *Resp. Chatam Sofer, EH,* v. 1, no. 76.

15 See R. Eliezer Y. Waldenberg, *Resp. Tzitz Eliezer,* v. 4, no. 22.

16 See *Yad,* Hilchot Zechiah Umatanah, ch. 9.

17 See Rashi, BT Kiddushin 81b, *s.v. ve-dar.* This theory is, of course, a presumption, valid in most (but, tragically, not in all) families.

18 *Resp. Tzitz Eliezer,* v. 6, no. 40, ch. 21.

19 *Resp. `Aseh Lecha Rav,* v. 3, no. 39. See also R. Nachum Eliezer Rabinowitz, cited in *Techumin,* v. 10, 1989, p. 317, no. 19.

20 R. Halevy (see note 19, above) significantly points to contemporary practice ("go out and see what the people are doing"; *cf.* BT Berachot 45a) to justify his decision: since adoptive parents treat their children as though they were biological offspring, there is no reason to enforce upon them an halachic distinction which has now become artificial. A popular discussion of this subject may be found in Dennis Prager, "Blood vs. Love," *Ultimate Issues* 11:2 (1995).

21 BT Sanhedrin 19b

The Absence of a *Get*
5754.06

She'elah

In a tightly knit community, where relations between Orthodox, Conservative, and Reform rabbis and congregations are very close, an Orthodox man refuses to give his civilly divorced wife a *get*, an halachically valid divorce instrument.

The wife is Orthodox and therefore unable to marry until a *get* is given her. The Orthodox colleague has asked the other rabbis in the city to support him when he imposes sanctions (withholding *aliyot*, synagogue leadership roles etc.).

What shall the Reform rabbis do when the man applies for membership in their congregation and asks to be married by them?

Should they disregard the woman's *agunah* status (i.e. a woman unable to marry halachically) and hold that she is free to be married at any time by a Reform rabbi? If that were the case, could it not be said that an *agunah* problem really does not exist because any woman in reach of a Reform rabbi has the opportunity to end her status?

Would respect for the entire Jewish community and for the woman's religious convictions demand otherwise? (Rabbis Samuel M. Stahl and Barry H. Block, San Antonio, TX)

Teshuvah

According to traditional Jewish law, a woman becomes an *agunah* when her husband is irretrievably lost and there is insufficient testimony to certify his death, or when her husband refuses to provide her with a *get* to signify the Jewish conclusion of the marriage. Under either circumstance, the woman finds herself in the situation of being an *agunah*, a "tied" woman, and may not remarry Jewishly so long as this status continues unrelieved. There is near universal agreement that there are few more tragic outcomes of Halachah. In fact so seriously was her plight viewed that time and again within the framework of Jewish law, great halachic luminaries have taken far-reaching steps to help release her.

209

The first recorded example of this trend dates back to the first century C.E. when Rabban Gamliel the Elder permitted a large number of war widows who were in danger of being classified as *agunot* to remarry. Despite the fact that the Torah required the evidence of two or of three witnesses to attest to the husband's death, Rabban Gamliel allowed remarriage on the basis of the hitherto invalid testimony of one witness, hearsay evidence, the testimony of a woman, or even of a female slave .[1] This effort has been mirrored in modern times of extremis when leading *poskim* have countenanced the remarriage of potential *agunot* - without proof of death - following the *Shoah*, Israel's wars and other instances.

Even in the more difficult circumstance of a deserted wife whose husband is clearly alive, but who refuses to divorce her, the halachah condones strong measures to move him in the direction of giving a *get*. Though in most cases a forced divorce is invalid, there are certain conditions which justify the verdict of a beit din that a man must divorce his wife.[2] He may be compelled to do so by any means, including force or even the scourge.[3] Under current Israeli law a recalcitrant husband can be imprisoned until he consents to give a *get*.[4]

While, historically, these measures have succeeded in releasing only some *agunot*, still the direction of the tradition is clear. R. Asher ben Yehiel (1250-1328) saw it in terms of a mitzvah: "One must investigate all possible avenues in order to release an *agunah*."[5] Every social and religious measure possible must be taken when such practical steps might lead to the freeing of an *agunah*.

In the light of this background, a contemporary Reform rabbi is being asked to make a choice as to how to relate to a "former" husband who has, by leaving his wife, made her into an *agunah*. Within American Reform Judaism, of course, throughout the last century, civil divorce has been accepted as effecting religious divorce. Reform Judaism has thereby effectively taken the attitude that the status of being an *agunah* should long ago have been relegated to the realm of the halachic past. One possibility, therefore, is for the rabbi to hold that this historic Reform position is applicable to the case at hand, and that - by means of the civil divorce - the man has discharged his obligations to his "former" wife, and is eligible to receive all the services afforded to any other divorced Jew. The consequences of this position would be that the man would be able to remarry in the Reform congregation, but the civilly-divorced woman - so long as she remains Orthodox - would be regarded as an *agunah*. The alternative possibility is for the Reform rabbi to participate actively in the traditional process of applying every acceptable social and religious pressure to spur the man to release his "former" wife. Should the rabbi choose this path, it would have to be decided whether the sanctions of refusing the man membership and/or marriage in the Reform congregation were appropriate measures.

Prima facie, the correct choice for the Reform rabbi may seem simple. After all, the first possibility asks the rabbi to uphold an historic Reform outlook. On the other hand, the second possibility asks the rabbi to participate in what is essentially an Orthodox practice of exerting pressure in order to obtain a traditional *get*. While the rabbi should indeed act according to Reform principles, the problem is that a closer examination reveals that there is more than one Reform Jewish principle which ought to guide the rabbi's thinking in this case.

Beyond the matter of the Reform Jewish stance on the prerequisites for Jewish divorce, the issue of pluralism is clearly central to this matter. If Reform Judaism took the attitude that there is but one form of Jewish truth that is applicable to all Jews then it would indeed be appropriate to apply that truth to all persons, no matter what the circumstances.[6] But our actual position is quite the opposite. Precisely because Reform Judaism cherishes freedom, it also holds a principled belief in pluralism; it applauds the reality that other movements within Judaism sometimes choose to see the world differently from the way that Reform Jews do.[7]

A result of this firm adherence to the principle of pluralism is that we must recognize that various principles which we have established for Reform Jews, who operate wholly within the Reform Jewish context, may not work in the same way for Jews who are not within our context. Given that individual decisions to transfer between the movements will sometimes lead to cases such as this one - wherein the application of our principles would have a direct impact on those who are outside our own context - pluralism dictates that we need to be sensitive to the repercussions of our policies beyond the borders of our own movement.

In particular, a principled Reform Jewish stance on divorce - that pronounces civil divorce to be religiously sufficient - might work very well within a Reform context where all parties are subject to the same assumptions and their consequences. But where applying our stance to the man would leave the woman unable to remarry in her Orthodox context, the use of our divorce principles would clearly lead to a lamentable outcome. To pretend that this woman could simply solve her *agunah* status by going to a Reform rabbi who would recognize her as being Jewishly divorced even without a *get*, could only be seen as a coercive position on behalf of Reform Judaism, that ignores the truth of her status as she and her rabbi see it. To take such a position would plainly and completely undermine our own stated commitment to pluralism.

Moreover, it should be remembered that this couple was married in an Orthodox synagogue. At the time of his marriage this man contracted himself to a partnership that could be finally dissolved only by an Orthodox *get*. If both parties were to agree that this element of their contracted relationship had become null and void, then he would be free of the assumptions of the contract. But since she has not agreed, to remarry him would be to assist him to evade a contractual undertaking that he had implicitly made.[8] Even though this contractual undertaking was not made within a Reform context, pluralism calls upon us to recognize the seriousness of obligations freely entered into in other Jewish jurisdictions.

In this case, therefore, respecting pluralism implies that we must respect her belief that until she is released she is an *agunah*, and only her "former" husband can change that. We may well regard her status as an *agunah* as a completely unacceptable state of affairs. Indeed we ought to continue to protest the failure of contemporary traditional *poskim* to develop a consensus around one of the proposed halachic solutions to this problem.[9] We should strenuously object to the fact that time and again the threat or reality of the woman becoming an *agunah* brings Jewish divorce procedures into disrepute both in Israel and the Diaspora. We should forthrightly rail against those who are apparently unprepared to respond to the plight of the *agunah* and to the morally indefensible results which their silence continues to bring about. But at the same time we must also acknowledge that while we do not have the power to wipe away her status as an *agunah* within the Orthodox community, we do have the power to help prolong and perhaps seal her fate as an *agunah* within that community by agreeing to remarry her husband while she remains without a *get*. The principle of pluralism shines light on both the reality and the anguish of a status that our own divorce standards can neither alter nor ameliorate.

But there is one more critical Reform Jewish principle which calls upon our conscience in a case such as this, and that is the moral mandate to strive to always support *"hayashar v'hatov,"* "the right and the good," [Deut. 6:18] as a matter of primary importance.[10] Undoubtedly, no matter what level of bitterness may have been associated with a particular divorce, no woman deserves to remain an *agunah*. Moreover, only spiteful reasons would really prevent a man from granting his civilly-divorced former wife a *get*. As the tendency of the tradition has taught us, the importance of defending our current Reform judgement - that the demand for a *get* is unnecessary - could never be compared to the moral significance of helping to release an *agunah*. This, then, is not so much a matter that pits Reform divorce principles against Orthodox divorce principles, since all would agree that fairness prescribes that the woman's status as an *agunah* be ended forthwith. Rather, this is a matter which calls upon us first to uphold *"hayashar v'hatov,"* and to help to bring about the speedy release of this woman, before turning to other considerations.

This is very much an issue of *Klal Yisrael*, and of *"Kol Yisrael arevim zeh ba-zeh,"* "all Jews are responsible for each other," which are both notions that we strongly support. We want to ensure that this man fulfills the commandment to which he obligated himself, the fulfillment of which will clearly produce the greatest good. We should cooperate with the Orthodox rabbi's call for sanctions against this man. Since we have a previous responsum which suggests that Jews who have turned towards transgression may be even more needy of synagogue influence than others,[11] and given that the Orthodox congregation has taken no steps to debar him, it would be inappropriate for us to deny this man synagogue membership. We may well wish to review his membership at some later point if the synagogue's positive influence fails to move him in the right direction.[12] However, in the interests of providing the strongest possible Jewish incentive for him to do what is right and good, it would certainly be appropriate to refuse to remarry him in a Reform synagogue. By so doing we will demonstrate our very real concern for all Jews who have been made powerless, no matter whether they have chosen our ideology or not.[13]

NOTES

1 See W. Jacob and M. Zemer (eds.), *Rabbinic-Lay Relations in Jewish Law*, (Pittsburgh, Rodef Shalom Press, 1993), pp. 60-61, and M. Zemer, *Halachah Shefuyah*, (Tel Aviv, Dvir, 1993), pp. 33-34.

2 BT Gittin 88b; Ketubot 77a; *Sh.A.* EH 154:21.

3 *Sh.A.* Hilchot Ishut 15:7; *Tur* and *Beit Yosef*, EH 154 (end).

4 See B. Schereschewsky, *Dinei Mishpachah*, 3rd ed., (Jerusalem, Rubin Mass Limited, 1984), pp. 370-372.

5 *Resp. HaRosh* 51:2.

6 One might in fact argue that this is the Orthodox position.

7 Eugene B. Borowitz, *Liberal Judaism*, (New York, Union of American Hebrew Congregations, 1984), pp. 348-349.

8 The husband made such an implicit agreement when he declared the *kiddushin* formula *kedat Moshe v'Yisrael* in an Orthodox setting. As is conveyed in BTKetubot 3a, since a Jewish man betroths a wife with the implicit acceptance of rabbinic law (*kol demekadeish ada'ata derabbanan mekadeish*), the rabbis may subsequently withdraw their consent to the marriage (in the event of his misconduct or other misfortune) and declare the relationship null and void. One aspect of this law is that the parties agree to abide by the decree of the rabbinic court (*mitzvah lishmoa divrei chachamim;* BT Baba Bathra 48a). On the basis of this implicit acceptance, the court is justified in coercing a get - physically, if need be - from the husband (BT Gittin 88a; Yad, Hilchot, *Gerushin* 2:20, and *Magid Mishneh* and *Kesef Mishneh ad loc.*). Hence, his civil divorce has clearly not released him from these implied obligations.

9 For possible *halachic* alternatives see: Ben-Zion Schereschewsky, "*Agunah*" in Menachem Elon (ed.), *The Principles of Jewish Law*, (Jerusalem, Keter Publishing House Limited, 1974), pp. 412-413 and Eliezer Berkovits, *Tenai be-Nissu'in u-ve-Get*, (Jerusalem, Mosad HaRav Kook, 1967).

10 Gunther Plaut comments on this verse: "The Rabbis developed an important ethical principle from this verse, holding that it was not sufficient to do the 'right' or legal thing, but that one needed to go beyond and do also what was 'good' or moral." -Gunther Plaut, *The Torah - A Modern Commentary* (New York, Union of American Hebrew Congregations, 1981), p. 1368. See also *Baba Metziah* 16b and Nachmanides' comment on Deuteronomy 6:18. There can be little argument that Reform Judaism has historically put great emphasis on doing that which is good, moral, and ethical.

11 Israel Bettan, "Refusing a Jew Membership," (1953), in Walter Jacob (ed.), *ARR*, (New York, Central Conference of American Rabbis, 1983), pp. 54-55.

12 This would only be done *in extremis*, based on the principle of *hara b'miuto*, that this is the less-

er of two evils. For though expelling him has negative aspects, if it leads him to take action it is clearly a lesser evil than leaving his wife an agunah for life.

13 There were two dissents, basing themselves on the unacceptable conditions and practices of halachic divorce.

A Divorced Spouse as Member of NAORRR
5754.7

She'elah

The leadership of NAORRR, the National Association of Retired Reform Rabbis, has received an application for membership from a woman who was at one time married to a rabbi, a member of the CCAR. They were divorced many years ago and the rabbi remarried. We have learned that the rabbi initiated the divorce proceedings and that he cut his first wife out of his pension. Hearsay has it that their marriage was most unpleasant. The first wife wishes to become a member of NAORRR and to attend our convention. She indicated that she would need financial assistance in order to attend the meeting.

Since widow(er)s are full-fledged members of NAORRR, this case raises a troubling question: are divorced spouses entitled to the same privileges as widow(er)s regarding membership in NAORRR, attendance at meetings, and financial aid? If so, then does that mean that after a rabbi's death, NAORRR should open its door to two or more widow(er)s of the same rabbi? (Rabbi Erwin Herman, Lake San Marcos, CA)

Teshuvah

NAORRR is a region of the CCAR and is therefore in most ways bound by the structure and by-laws of the parent body. One major exception to this rule is the status of the spouse. While spouses in the CCAR have support groups but no legal standing, NAORRR has made spouses equal members in its organization. Once a member, one remains a member for all purposes, provided that all obligations that pertain to membership are fulfilled. Therefore, if the applicant (the divorcee) was a member of NAORRR at any time, she would remain so. This, apparently, is not the case; she and her husband, while they were married, were not members of NAORRR.

217

The *she'elah* raises an important issue of rights. Is a divorced spouse of a rabbi entitled to benefits that normally accrue to spouses and widow(er)s of rabbis? We shall examine this issue in terms of the Jewish tradition concerning the legal and moral responsibilities owed toward a divorced spouse.

1. The Legal Aspect. As is the case with most legal systems, Jewish law distinguishes sharply between the legal status of the widow(er) and the divorced spouse. The texts draw this line most clearly with respect to the financial benefits that the widow (*almanah*) enjoys but which the divorcee (*gerushah*) does not. Upon the death of her husband, the widow receives the amount specified in the *ketubah*. In addition, she is supported by the husband's estate so long as she remains unmarried and so long as she does not demand her *ketubah* sum.[1] This support is called *mezonot*, but it extends beyond the narrow sense of that term as "food." The widow is entitled to live in the marital home and to be maintained at the standard of living to which she had become accustomed during her marriage.[2] These "entitlements" do not belong to the wife solely as a result of her contractual agreement with her husband, embodied in the *ketubah*. They are imposed, rather, as a *tenai beit din*, a rabbinic legislative enactment. Even if the husband did not write in the *ketubah* that "you may dwell in my home and be supported by my estate for the duration of your widowhood," the court enforces that right as though the clause were written.[3]

The widow, that is, remains the wife of the deceased in virtually all financial respects. Neither the husband nor his heirs can strip her of the claims she may legitimately make upon his estate. The divorcee, by contrast, is no longer the man's wife. Upon termination of the marriage she receives the amount specified in the *ketubah*, unless by her actions she forfeits that sum. Once she is a *gerushah*, she receives no *mezonot*.[4] Unlike the widow, she derives no benefits from the husband's estate apart from those agreed upon contractually at the time of their marriage.

2. The Moral Aspect. Based upon our Reform perspective, which holds that the financial obligations of marriage are equal for both husband and

wife, we would conclude from this discussion that the widowed spouse is entitled to the financial and social benefits which accrue to him or her by virtue of the marriage. The widow(er) therefore may become a member of NAORRR, since she or he remains the spouse of the deceased rabbi. The divorce(e), on the other hand, has no claim to financial and social benefits which stem from a marital relationship that no longer exists, and has no right to membership in NAORRR, unless he or she was a member prior to divorce.

Yet the matter is not so simple. The halachah recognizes that, even though the marriage has ended, the husband may owe something to his former wife. According to a talmudic dictum, "just as a man must show consideration for the honor of his widow, so he must show consideration for the honor of his divorcee." This notion is derived from Isaiah 58:7, "do not ignore your kin."[5] The biblical word *umibesarcha*, which the rabbis interpret to mean one's divorcee, literally means one's blood relations. Hence, in this view, a divorcee remains in some way her husband's "flesh and blood." Indeed, he is permitted and even encouraged to support her financially following the divorce.[6] Though a marriage may have ended, in other words, the halachah does not ignore the fact that a sacred bond once existed between this man and woman and that certain ethical responsibilities flow from this connection.

Of course, the fulfillment of these responsibilities is a voluntary matter, and for that reason, perhaps, R. Gershom b. Yehudah (10th-11th century Germany) issued his famous edict (*takanah*) forbidding a husband from divorcing his wife without her consent. The practical effect of this policy was to render the ketubah superfluous, since no matter what financial terms were stipulated therein a husband will have to renegotiate those terms in order to secure his wife's agreement to the divorce. This means that the divorcee now has more claim to her former husband's consideration than she had previously, under biblical and classical rabbinic law. And even after the divorce has occurred, responsibility toward one's former spouse may not be entirely left up to one's warm-heartedness and good intentions. The halachah holds that the court is entitled to coerce a person to give his or her "fair share" to *tzedakah*. Thus, were the community to determine that it is a good thing for one to display a particular degree of consideration toward a former spouse, Jewish tradition empowers the collective to see to it that the individuals involved live up to that ethical standard.

3. The Case Before Us. NAORRR, it would seem, is caught in the pull between these two sets of values. On the one hand, the distinction between "*almanah*" and "*gerushah*" continues to be of relevance. NAORRR offers continued membership and travel aid to widowed spouses of rabbis, precisely because those individuals retain their status as rabbinic spouses. The divorced spouse is no longer the spouse. If membership in NAORRR is a benefit which flows from the "estate" of the deceased rabbi, it is the widow(er) and not the divorced spouse who is entitled to derive that benefit. There are, moreover good and convincing collegial reasons why this ought to be so. NAORRR exists to insure, among other things, the continuation of community, of warm and friendly relations among retired rabbis and their spouses. Attendance of divorced spouses at meetings might well threaten this goal. It is not difficult to imagine the tension which would result if a retired rabbi's former spouse were to participate in a meeting alongside the rabbi and his or her current spouse or alongside the widow(er) of that rabbi. NAORRR would thus be justified in denying membership to divorced spouses, especially in view of the additional financial burden it would thereby assume in offering them travel aid.

On the other hand, let us imagine a different scenario. A woman has been married to a rabbi for many years. She has been, in every sense of the word, his partner, working with him side-by-side in the realization of his rabbinate. She has drawn a great deal of strength and emotional support from her status as a rabbinic spouse. And her friends, those who most truly understand her and in whom she can confide, have tended to be other rabbinic spouses, the very people she looks forward to meeting at national and regional conventions. Divorce presents some severe problems to this spouse. Should she remain a member of her husband's congregation, which is in fact her own congregation? Or should she join another community so as to avoid embarrassment? Should she be discouraged from attending CCAR functions, such as NAORRR conventions, in order to avoid causing difficulties for her former husband and, possibly, his current wife? Or do we say that, because the rabbinic community has long been her social network as well as his, she has every right to maintain her place in it? Do we, as an organization of rabbis, necessarily emphasize the personal and emotional needs of rabbis over those of persons who were at one time related to these rabbis? Is this an unavoidable social tragedy, simply "one of those things that can't be helped"? Or do we bear some kind of ethical responsibility to a human being who has invested a great deal of herself in the rabbinate as an institution?

These are difficult questions, not just for NAORRR, obviously, but for the Conference as a whole. The growing incidence of rabbinic divorce confronts our profession with a singular array of difficult challenges. The way we choose to respond to these challenges will do much to enhance or to diminish our reputation as pastors, as counselors, as religious leaders. There are no easy, simple answers. But we believe that a sufficient and satisfying answer must begin with the recognition of a complex reality: the Reform rabbinate is simultaneously a professional body and a community, a family. As a professional body, its institutions exist first and foremost to serve the needs of its members. Spouses of rabbis may derive benefit from this membership, but only to the extent that they are and remain spouses of rabbis. When divorce has put an end to the relationship between a rabbi and a spouse, that spouse has no legal right to demand continued membership in a rabbinic organization. As a community, however, as a family, our institutions serve as meeting places where life-long friends and acquaintances may come together, feel at home with each other, and share interests and memories that are the product of years of warm association. A divorced spouse surely has no legal right to demand entry into such a meeting place. But, just as surely, the CCAR and NAORRR should be the last to cut off rabbinic spouses from life-long friends and associates, whether or not such spouses are widowed or divorced.

Conclusion. We recommend, therefore, that the *she'elah* be resolved by an approach which recognizes two distinct levels of spousal membership in the Reform rabbinic community.

1. *Legal membership* is a matter of entitlement, flowing from marriage to a rabbi who is or was a member. In our case, the applicant is not now the spouse of a rabbi and was not a member of NAORRR when she was married to the rabbi. She is therefore not entitled to membership in NAORRR.

2. *Collegial membership* is of a different and less formal nature. It is not a matter of entitlement but of recognition; that is, when a former spouse of a rabbi is understood to be and accepted as a member of the Reform rabbinic family even in the absence of a "legal" right to join one of our organizations. This recognition is a form of *tzedakah*, since it is based upon the conviction that our values of justice and righteousness may demand that a particular person who is no longer a rabbinic spouse be accorded membership in our organizations. Like all questions of *tzedakah*, those which pertain to this category of membership should be handled confidentially, on a case-by-case basis.

We are in no position to decide whether the divorced spouse in this case ought to be granted the status of "collegial member". That determination must be left to NAORRR and its constituent bodies. We know that those who are granted the privilege of making such difficult decisions will keep in mind the needs of both NAORRR and the applicant.

NOTES

1 M. Ketubot 11:1; *Yad,* Ishut 18:1.

2 BT Ketubot 103a: "she enjoys the use of the home as she did during her husband's life, the servants as she did during her husband's life, the household furnishings as she did during her husband's life,

etc." See Yad, Ishut 18 on her rights and her corresponding obligations toward her husband's heirs.

3 M. Ketubot 4:12; BT Ketubot 52b; *Sh.A.* EH 93:3.

4 BT Ketubot 97b; *Yad*, Ishut 21:17 and Magid Mishneh *ad loc.*; Sh.A. EH 82:6.

5 YT Ketubot 11:3 (34b). The specific halachic issue there concerns the degree to which a man should want to spare his former wife the humiliation of appearing in court to sell her *ketubah* in order to support herself.

6 *Hagahot Maimoniot, Yad*, Isurei Bi'ah 21, no. 70. Isserles codifies this rule in *Sh.A.* EH 119:8: "a man is permitted to provide maintenance to his divorcee. To do so is to fulfill a greater mitzvah than one fulfills by supporting other poor persons."

Marriage and Financial Duress
5754.9

She'elah

A couple in my congregation met one another at a support group for those battling multiple sclerosis. They have had to postpone their decision to be married, based on some very serious medical and economic problems. If one of them becomes fully disabled, full-time nursing care in the home or in a nursing home would be required. The government would insist that the spouse pay for such care and the family would be driven to destitution. Therefore, they cannot share in a wedding ceremony. Does Jewish law offer any guidance to them? (Rabbi Martin S. Weiner, San Francisco)

Teshuvah

Our tradition has the greatest regard for marriage as an institution, an aspiration, and a natural state of existence. The rabbis praise marriage as a quintessential source of joy, blessing, and goodness whose value stands at the summit of Jewish religious obligations.[1] One is permitted to sell a Torah scroll in order to raise funds for only three purposes: to study Torah, to redeem captives, and to marry.[2] Marriage is thus equated with the study of Torah, which itself is equal to all the other mitzvot combined,[3] and the redemption of captives, compared to which "there is no greater mitzvah."[4] In this day and age, when the promotion of Jewish marriage and family life is a communal priority of the highest order, it is most unfortunate when a couple is denied the opportunity of marriage for financial reasons. Such, we are told, is the case before us. What practical guidance does Jewish tradition offer to this couple who wish to live their lives together but, for clear and compelling reasons, fear economic ruin should they choose to stand under the *chupah*?

We begin by noting that Jewish tradition is sensitive to financial obstacles to marriage and has taken steps to help overcome them. As noted, it is permitted to sell a *sefer Torah*, a Jew's most cherished possession, to acquire the funds needed to begin married life. Moreover, Jewish communities throughout history have sought to provide assistance to those who, for reasons of economic hardship, find it difficult to marry. This is the act of *hachnasat kalah*, which our tradition classifies under the heading of *gemilut chasadim*, deeds of lovingkindness, itself a rabbinic mitzvah whose roots lie in the Biblical injunction to "love your neighbor as yourself."[8] Such aid is called the most sublime form of *tzedakah*.[7] Thus, from a Jewish perspective the problems faced by this couple are not simply their own problems. Since *tzedakah* is not a voluntary act of alms-giving but rather an obligation which can be enforced on grounds of social justice,[8] they have a legitimate claim to the assistance of the Jewish community. Helping this couple deal with their situation is emphatically a communal responsibility.

This, of course, is easier said than done. Communities face many different responsibilities. Like all public bodies, Jewish communal agencies must wrestle with severe budget restraints to provide for a host of religious, cultural, and social needs. They may decide that, given the many pressing demands upon their resources, they cannot grant the kind or amount of assistance that this couple seek. The general community, meanwhile, has determined that the primary financial responsibility for long-term nursing care must be borne by one's spouse and family. We might protest this state of affairs and argue that the United States must enact reforms in its health-care system that would provide for this need. We may argue, too, that the Jewish community should reconsider its funding priorities and devote more of its substance to long-term nursing care.[9] These policy arguments, however, do not solve the problem facing this couple, here and now. What counsel can we offer them?

We cannot recommend that they live together without benefit of marriage. Although this would afford them a semblance of marital life while allowing them to shelter their assets, cohabitation is not and cannot be a valid moral substitute for *kiddushin*, a marital union consecrated in a spirit of holiness and reverence, created out of "a willingness to enter wholeheartedly into a sacred covenant with another person."[10] We recognize that

this couple, by entering into marriage, will subject themselves to a significant financial sacrifice imposed by the civil law. But the absence of this or
that governmental or communal benefit does not offer a moral justification
for an act that denies the sanctity of Jewish marriage.

Still, there may exist legal means by which this couple can marry and
yet protect themselves financially. Such a means is precedented in Jewish
law.

One of the monetary obligations owed by the husband to the wife is
that of *refu'ah*, the duty to provide for her medical expenses.[11] Yet the very
mishnah which specifies this requirement places an important limitation
upon it: "The husband is entitled to say: `Here is her *get* and her *ketubah*;
let her heal herself.'"[12] The husband, that is, may divorce his wife and
thereby limit his liability for her medical bills to the total amount of her
ketubah. This is a controversial device, to say the least. Some early decisors
deny a husband the right to divorce his wife who is seriously ill.[13] Others
say he has that right but add that it is unethical for him to use it.[14] Still
others rule that although this right exists in theory it is no longer
enforced.[15] At any rate, the discussion shows that the rabbis were vitally
concerned with the issue in our case: does marriage require a person to risk
financial ruin to provide for the spouse's medical expenses?

The Responsa Committee has dealt with a somewhat related issue.[16]
There, the wife of an Alzheimer's patient asked whether she was entitled to
divorce her husband in order to protect her assets and to keep from falling
into poverty. Since we interpret Jewish marital law in an egalitarian manner, the Committee found the legal material in the preceding paragraph to
be relevant to the wife as well as to the husband. It concluded that it would
be immoral, a violation of the spirit of *kiddushin* for the wife to divorce her
husband for this reason. It also noted, however, that Jewish law permits a
spouse to gain financial independence by renouncing the reciprocal duties
of the partner.[17] In addition, the *beit din* is empowered to seize the husband's estate in the event of his mental incapacity in order to provide for

his wife's support.[18] As we understand this rule, it implies that whatever disabilities befall one partner in a marriage, that condition cannot deny the other partner's inherent right of financial sustenance.

However, our case differs in a crucial respect. We are not talking about the divorce of an incapacitated spouse. The couple are not yet married; they can make legal arrangements to protect each one's assets and financial independence on a mutual basis, before either has reached a critical medical stage. Thus, we find no ethical objection to the drafting of a prenuptial agreement to this effect, to the extent that such is permitted under civil law.

We hope that a solution will be found that will encourage this couple to "build a household in Israel," affording them the fulfillment of the sacred union of marriage which our tradition calls *kiddushin*.

NOTES

1 BT Yebamot 62b-63a; *Tur*, EH 1.

2 *Sh.A.* and Isserles, YD 270:1.

3 BT Shabbat 127a; *Yad*, Talmud Torah 3:3.

4 *Yad*, Matanot Aniyim 8:10; see BT Bava Batra 8a-b.

5 *See* BT Ketubot 67b and *Sh.A.* YD 250:1-2.

6 Lev. 19:18; *Yad*, Avel 14:1.

7 R. Yosef Kolon (15th century), *Resp. Maharik, shoresh* 123; *Sh.A.* YD 249:15.

8 BT Ketubot 49a and Bava Batra 8a; *Yad*, Matanot Aniyim 7:10; *Sh.A.* YD 248:1.

9 The question of priorities in the distribution of community resources is a complex rubric in Jewish legal literature. This responsum is not the setting to analyze those texts, but it would certainly be appropriate for this Committee or other rabbinic bodies to discuss them as part of a more general consideration of issues of social welfare and economic justice.

10 *Gates of Mitzvah*, p. 29; see also *ARR*, no. 133 and 154.

11 M. Ketubot 4:9 (51a); *Yad*, Ishut 12:2. The requirement is derived from the obligation to provide food (mezonot); BT Ketubot 52b.

12 M. Ketubot *ad loc.*

13 This is the opinion of R. Avraham b. David, the Rabad, who bases it upon *Sifre*, Deut. 21:14 (ch. 214), which states that the Israelite soldier may not send away his female captive of war while she is seriously ill. If this limitation applies to the captive, Rabad reasons, then a man's wife certainly enjoys the same protection. He restricts the *mishnah's* rule to cases where the wife is not suffering from a serious illness. *See* Rashba, Ritva, and Meiri to BT Ket. 52b and R. Nissim to Alfasi, Ketubot, fol. 19a.

14 *Yad*, Ishut 14:17 (Magid Mishneh *ad loc.*: it is "obvious" that for the husband to exercise this lawful power is a violation of *derech erets*); SA EHE 79:3.

15 R. Shelomo Luria, cited by Bayit Chadash to *Tur*, EH 79, fol. 102b, and *Beit Shmuel* to SA, EHE 79, no. 4. The argument is that should this power be recognized the husband would be able to violate the decree of Rabbeinu Gershom (10th-11th c.) forbidding him to divorce his wife without her consent.

16 *CARR*, no. 86.

17 BT Ketubot 58b; *Yad*, Ishut 12:4. The wife renounces the right to sustenance (*mezonot*) from her husband and thereby receives full use of her income. Again, we would apply this formula regardless of gender.

18 *Yad*, Ishut 12:17.

Substitutes for Wine Under the *Chupah*
5755.16

She'elah

A couple are planning their wedding in the near future. The man has disclosed to me that he is a recovering alcoholic, now six months sober. He is making great efforts to stay away from alcohol. I of course encouraged and supported him. When it came to the wedding ceremony, however, I had to inform him that the use of wine is an integral part of the service. I indicated to him that he could use grape juice instead of wine. He told me that he was so unsure of his sobriety that even grape juice would test his resolve and that he would prefer not to use it. Is there a solution to this problem that will simultaneously preserve the structure of the traditional ceremony yet not hazard his sobriety? (Rabbi Kenneth D. Roseman, Dallas, TX)

Teshuvah

There is no denying the powerful symbolic importance of wine in Jewish observance. In biblical times it was noted that "wine gladdens the human heart" (Psalms 104:15). The Talmud adds that today, in the absence of the Temple and the sacrifices, "there is no joy without wine."[1] This means that at special festive moments of our lives as Jews we express the happiness we feel through the drinking of wine.[2] We welcome Shabbat with *kiddush* and bid it farewell with *havdalah*, both of which are recited over wine. Wine helps us fulfill the mitzvah to rejoice during festivals.[3] We drink four cups of wine at the Pesach seder to celebrate our liberation from bondage.[4] Indeed, wine is so essential at that occasion that "one who does not accustomed to drinking wine because he dislikes it or because it causes him pain should force himself to drink it, to fulfill the mitzvah of the four cups."[5] At moments of personal joy, such as a wedding and *berit milah*, the appropriate blessings are recited over a cup of wine. Due to its intrinsic importance, wine receives its own benedic-

231

tion (*borei peri hagafen*) at those moments, even though we use it for purely ritual purposes and not for consumption.[6]

All the above serves to emphasize both the centrality of wine in Jewish ceremonial observance and the problem which faces the man who is the subject of this *she'elah*. He wishes to celebrate his great moment of personal joy as a Jew, under the *chuppah*, when the officiating rabbi recites the betrothal and wedding benedictions. But he does not want this ritual to endanger his continuing recovery from alcoholism. For our part, we certainly want to encourage this man in what will be a life-long struggle against this disease, and we think it would be ironic and tragic were a ritual of the Jewish tradition, which we regard as a source of life, to act as a stumbling block to his recovery. The question, as you note, is one of options: does the tradition require the use of wine or grape juice at a wedding? If it does not, does it offer alternatives for wine under the *chuppah* so as to maintain "the structure of the traditional ceremony?" Can a wedding, that is, be conducted without wine and yet remain, in form and feeling, a Jewish wedding? And if such alternatives do exist, which would we consider to be the best one from our Reform perspective?

Is Wine a Requirement at Weddings?

We begin by noting that, although wine plays a central ceremonial role in Judaism, the tradition never establishes the drinking of wine as an absolute ritual requirement no matter how severe its effect upon one's health. It is well known that the *halachah* permits a Jew to set aside almost all mitzvot for the sake of *pikuach nefesh*, when their performance would endanger one's life.[7] Moreover, this warrant can apply even when the danger is less than mortal. Wine is an excellent case in point. We find that, although the drinking of four cups at the Pesach seder is a rabbinically-ordained mitzvah, a person may refrain from drinking wine should it make him seriously ill.[8] The prospective bridegroom, as a recovering alcoholic, has every reason to fear that by consuming wine or grape juice he runs the risk of serious medical consequences. Under Jewish law, therefore, he is in no way required to drink wine under the *chuppah*.

Moreover, wine is not an absolute ritual requirement under the *chuppah*. We utilize two cups of wine at the wedding, one for each of the two distinct legal ceremonies taking place at that time. The betrothal benediction (*birkat erusin*) is recited over a cup of wine and is thus preceded by *borei peri hagafen*. The six wedding benedictions (*birkat chatanim*) are recited over a separate cup of wine; they are preceded, again, by *borei peri hagafen*, making a total of seven benedictions (hence, the "*sheva berachot*"). Suppose no wine is available? The halachic consensus with respect to both sets of benedictions is that some other alcoholic beverage (*sheichar*) should be used and the blessing *shehakol nihyah bidevaro* recited. If no intoxicant can be obtained, then according to all opinions the *birkat erusin* can be recited by itself, without a cup, since wine is not regarded as an indispensable element of the erusin ceremony.[9] Concerning the wedding benedictions, however, there is a dispute. Some say that wine or a suitable substitute is absolutely required, that the *sheva berachot* can be recited only "over a cup."[10] Others, meanwhile, rule that the benedictions may if necessary be recited without any beverage at all.[11] While the *Shulchan Aruch* follows the more stringent view,[12] the disagreement continues among the later authorities.[13]

Non-Alcoholic Alternatives to Wine.

We have seen that, while some authorities do not require wine under the *chuppah*, others do. Yet even the latter permit the use of *sheichar*, an alternative, though alcoholic, beverage. This reflects the halachic concept of *chamar medinah*, literally "local wine," the choicest drink of a particular locality, the beverage "that most people drink" (other than water). *Chamar medinah* is not necessarily grape wine, yet even so may be used in place of wine in certain ritual settings. Thus, we read that *havdalah* may be recited over *sheichar* if that is indeed the "local wine."[14] The question whether such a beverage can be used for *kiddush* is, again, a subject of dispute.[15] The Talmud speaks of "wine" as a requirement for *kiddush*.[16] Some do not read this requirement literally. They argue that the sanctification of a holy day surely ought to be performed over the most desirable beverage available, even if this is not grape wine. Others, however, do read the Talmud's word *yayin* as excluding the use of any beverage other than wine. As a means of resolving this dispute, it has become the traditional practice to require grape wine at the evening *kiddush* which commences the Sabbath or a festival but to permit other beverages for *kiddusha raba*, the sanctification recited at the noon meal the next day, so long as these beverages are regarded as *chamar medinah*.[17]

If *chamar medinah* can be used in place of wine at *kiddush* (or, at least, *kiddusha raba*) and at *havdalah*, the recitation of which is a Toraitic requirement,[18] then surely it may be used at a wedding, where the "cup" serves only a customary function and fulfills no biblical or rabbinic mitzvah. And, indeed, those who require that the wedding benedictions be recited "over a cup" permit the use of *chamar medinah* in place of wine.[19] The question is whether "local wine" must be an alcoholic beverage; the answer, it would seem, is "no." At least one contemporary Israeli halachic authority rules that for purposes of the wedding benedictions "pure, fresh citrus juice is considered *chamar medinah* in the land of Israel."[20] That is to say, in Israel "the fruit of goodly trees" is as honored as a beverage for consumption as is fermented grape juice. There is every reason to argue that the same is true in America, for here, too, pure fruit juice is regarded in many circles and at many occasions as the beverage of choice.

Reform Considerations.

Tradition, therefore, permits the use of a non-alcoholic beverage as a substitute for wine at weddings. To this, we would add the following note. The halachic sources discuss this issue in the context of an unusual or "emergency" case where wine is not available. The present situation is a qualitatively different one, and it demands a qualitatively different response. While traditional literature does address the subject of drunkenness, it says little if anything about the disease we call alcoholism. In itself, this is not surprising. Our consciousness of alcoholism, of its medical dimensions and its human tragedy, far outstrips that of former generations. Given that consciousness, it is incumbent upon us to confront this disease directly and openly, and to do whatever we can to aid those who come to us in their struggle for recovery. In our case, a recovering alcoholic seeks to celebrate his wedding as a Jew, as a full and participating member of the community of Israel. We owe him no less consideration, surely, than we show to the disabled members of our congregations whom we seek actively to bring into the circle of Jewish life and observance.[21] Therefore, while we recognize the real and special symbolic importance of wine in Jewish ritual experience, it is our ethical obligation to emphasize that non-alcoholic beverages are not to be thought of as inferior alternatives to wine for ceremonial purposes. This is a declaration we make in general, in all cases and not just emergency ones, a declaration we state as forcefully as we can.

NOTES

1 BT Pesachim 109a.

2 BT Pesachim 106a, on "Remember the Sabbath day...". Havdalah may be recited over another beverage; see below, on the discussion of *chamar medinah*.

3 Deut. 16:14; *BT* Pesachim 109a; *Yad*, Yom Tov 6:17.

4 M. Pesachim 10:1, and Rashi *ad loc.* (99b); *Sh.A.* OC 472:8 ff.

5 *Sh.A.* OC 472:10, from *Resp. Rashba*, I, 238. And see YT Shekalim 3:2 (47c): when Rabbi Yonah drank the four cups of wine at the seder, even though the wine would leave him with a headache that lasted until Shavuot!

6 *BT* Berachot 42a and Rashi, s.v. degoreim berachah le`atzmo; *Sh.A.* OC 174:1.

7 *BT* Yoma 85b and Sanhedrin 74a; *Yad*, Yesodey Hatorah 5:1-3; *Sh.A.* YD 157:1.

8 See *Mishnah Berurah*, OC 472, no. 35: one should not drink wine should it cause one "to take to his bed." The *Sha`ar Hatziyun ad loc.* explains the reason: we drink wine at the seder to emphasize our liberation, and to cause ourselves illness is hardly "the way of freedom." *See also Aruch Hashulchan*, OC 472, no. 14, and R. *Ovadyah Yosef*, Resp. Chazon Ovadyah, I, no. 4.

9 *Sh.A.* EH 34:2. Rav Nisim Gaon, cited in Hilchot Harosh, Ketubot 1:16, says that the use of wine at erusin is not, properly speaking, an obligation (*lav mitzvah min hamuvchar hu*).

10 Rav Nisim Gaon in *Hil. Harosh loc. cit.*; *Tur* EH 62.

11 Yad, Ishut 10:4 and *Magid Mishneh ad loc.*

12 Sh.A. EH 62:1.

13 *Chelkat Mechokek* and *Beit Shmuel*, EH 62:1. The Aruch Hashulchan, EH 62, no. 6, requires wine or sheichar; R. Ya`akov Emden, *Siddur Beit Ya`akov, Dinei Birkat Erusin veNisu'in*, does not.

14 BT Pesachim 107a. The precise definition of *chamar medinah* remains somewhat unclear. Some say that a beverage qualifies as "local wine" only when grape wine is completely unavailable in a particular locale. Others say that when wine is available but can be obtained only with great difficulty, a substitute beverage can be chamar medinah. Still others require only that the grape wine that is available be significantly inferior to the other favored beverage. See *Aruch Hashulchan*, OC 272, no. 13-14.

15 The leading disputants are R. Asher b. Yechiel, who permits *kiddush* over *chamar medinah* (*Hil.*

Harosh, Pesachim 10:17), and Rambam (*Yad,* Shabbat 29:17, and see *Maggid Mishneh ad loc.*), who does not.

16 *BT* Pesachim 106a, on Ex. 20:8.

17 *Sh.A.* OC 272:9, following R. Asher. Isserles ad loc., *Turei Zahav,* no. 6, and *Aruch Hashulchan loc. cit.* all note that the prevalent Ashkenazic custom is to say *kiddusha raba* over an alcoholic beverage other than grape wine.

18 BT Pesachim 106a. The requirement is to "remember" (zachor) the Sabbath day, i.e., to declare it holy through words of sanctification. Rambam holds that *havdalah* is included in this Toraitic requirement to "remember" the Sabbath; *Yad,* Shabbat 29:1 and *Maggid Mishneh ad loc.*

19 *Sh.A.* EH 62:1.

20 R. Yitzchak Yosef, *Sove`a Semachot,* 1988, p. 67.

21 See our responsum 5752.5, on the treatment of the disabled within our communities.

Blessing a Mixed Marriage
5754.10

She'elah

I have been asked to give a "blessing" to a couple following their civil intermarriage. Would you advise me to do so? (Rabbi Mark J. Mahler, Pittsburgh, PA)

Teshuvah

When rabbis officiate at marriages they are not engaged in the dispensation of their own blessings. Any *berachah* they pronounce are prayers that God might issue a blessing.

Yet, in the day-to-day parlance of our people, "giving a blessing" has a less precise meaning. It means also "to approve", as in the phrase, "I give my blessing to that kind of arrangement".

Therefore a rabbi who officiates at mixed marriages is not asked merely to pronounce a blessing. By officiating, rabbinic approval (however hesitant it might be) is implied. On the other hand, a person like yourself, who does not so officiate, can certainly give no approval and hence no "blessing" in either a religious or popular sense. In fact, to say so would constitute an oxymoron.

But having said all of this, we recognize that there is also a legitimate desire which underlies the very question that has been asked of you: to have the rabbi — even the one who refuses to perform the ceremony — participate in some fashion. If he/she cannot do so by participating in the marriage ceremony itself, then perhaps there is some other way in which the rabbi can show that the people who have engaged in this act are not excluded from the community. We believe that Reform rabbis have no hesitation in supporting that desire. We do want to draw them in, even if we did not officiate.

One member of our committee recounts his own practice: "After having explained to the couple that I personally could not, as a representative of the community, agree to officiate, I tell them that I have no prejudice against the

237

non-Jewish partner as a human being. I therefore counsel them — seeing that they are definitely committed to proceeding with the marriage — to have a civil marriage and afterwards, if they so choose they may come to me private-ly, and I will pray for their personal welfare in their relationship. In this way I show my respect for them as human beings and my desire to remain close to them without transgressing my traditional role as representative of the com-munity. I do not reject them as human beings, and I invite them to stay close to the synagogue.

"Thus I do not give them a 'blessing', and I make that perfectly clear. A number of those to whom I make this suggestion choose to come to me after-wards and ask me to pray for their welfare. Many others do not. But I make the offer and that is as far as I would go."

We transmit this to you for your consideration.

Naming of an adopted child who will not be raised as a Jew
5754.16

She'elah

A child of non-Jewish parentage has been adopted by an interfaith couple. An adoption stipulation was imposed upon the couple requiring them to raise the child with "no religion." However, the adopting mother of the child, who is Jewish, would like to give the child a Hebrew name without a ceremony. The Jewish grandmother presented the request to the rabbi, stating that it would give her and her daughter "peace of mind" if this child could be given the Hebrew name of a deceased relative. Would it be appropriate for the rabbi to help the woman select such a name, especially considering that it is given that this child will not be raised as a Jew? (Rabbi Dena Feingold, Kenosha, WI)

Teshuvah

The traditional Halachah would consider this child as non-Jewish, and only it's conversion would make it into a Jew. Giving it a Hebrew name would in itself do nothing to alter its status.

The Reform Movement views this situation in a somewhat different way. The child of non-Jewish natural parents has entered a new envionment, and it might be said that its status becomes *potentially* Jewish and may be likened to that of a child from a mixed marriage. If so, this would trigger the application of the CCAR's decision on patrilineal descent.[1] Would the bestowal of a Hebrew name:

a. satisfy the conditions of the patrilineal decision and confer Jewish indentity upon the child, and

b. violate the agreement entered upon at the time of adoption?

Regarding (a), neither a public or private naming would be sufficient to satisfy the intent of the CCAR resolution, in view of the fact that the child will not be raised as a Jew. Giving the child a Jewish name would not afect its

238.1

status.

Regarding (b), the mother's lawyer should be consulted to determine whether bestowing a Hebrew name on the infant would be a violation of the agreement that governed the adoption.

Should the answer be negative and the naming be deemed permissible, we would have to ask whether such naming should be contemplated by the rabbi altogether, even though no particular ceremony has been asked for.

After all, the adopting mother has agreed to violate a basic Jewish duty, which is to teach Torah to one's children. The name-giving might therefore appear as if the rabbi acquiesces in the situation. Nonetheless, though the naming cannot undo the violation or repair its damage there is room for compassion.

The mother has, no doubt, had a desperate desire to have a child, and was therefore willing to accept the unpalatable condition. While she may not raise the child as a Jew, she is looking for some way by which she can confer a small measure of Jewish inentity upon it and, in the process, help to remember a deceased relative.

While discouraging a public naming as inappropriate, we wouldconsider a private naming, in form of a prayer, to be a compassionate possibility. But, we repeat, whatever is done shoulod be cleared with an expert in civil law.

NOTES

1. Adopted in 1983; see Rabbi's Manual, 1988/5748, p. 226.

Naming a Child Without Mentioning the Father
5752.1

She'elah

An unmarried woman is about to give birth. She knows that she will have a son and does not want the natural father's name to be noted when the Mohel gives the child a name at the *berit milah*. What name should be given? (Dr. Peter Torren, Lafayette Hill, PA)

Teshuvah

The matter has been dealt with repeatedly in the Halachah, especially when the identity of the father was either unknown, or not revealed by the mother, or when he was an apostate. In the latter case, the *Shulchan Aruch* says that the name of the child's grandfather should be substituted for that of the father.[1] This was done, in part, because calling the child merely by the name of the mother would at once testify to the fact that the son was not born into a normal family and thereby shame the mother in public.[2]

The cultural environment of our day, of course, has changed significantly, and many a woman would not mind at all to have it acknowledged publicly that her child was born extra-maritally, and therefore to mention only the mother's Hebrew name would be acceptable and sufficient. (This too has ample halachic sanction.) However, no one knows at this point how the son will feel about this in later years, and so I would deem it advisable to add a patronymic to the child's name. Giving him the mother's father's name would be in accordance with halachic tradition.

The same would apply if the actual father's name is unknown or if he is a Gentile.

In sum, we suggest that the child be named XYZ, son of .... (grandfather's name) and ... (mother's name). If the woman does not wish to use her father's name, she may (according to talmudic precedent) choose the name of a much admired personality, biblical or other.

239

NOTES

1 OC 134:3.

2 See the survey of this whole issue by Rabbi Solomon B. Freehof, *CRR*, "Naming the Child of an Unmarried Mother," no. 20 pp. 91-97.)

Hatafat Dam Berit for a Three-Year-Old Child of a
Mixed Marriage
5752.2

She'elah

A Reform mohel was asked to perform the *berit milah* of a newborn child and, on the same occasion, give a name to the child's three-year-old brother. This latter ceremony raises the *she'elah*. For upon arriving at the synagogue, where *milah* and naming were to take place, the mohel discovered two pertinent facts: 1) the father of these children is Jewish and the mother is a Gentile; 2) the three-year-old had been circumcised in the hospital with no religious ceremony prior to the eighth day of his life. The mohel performed the naming ceremony by reciting parts of the *milah* liturgy, making appropriate changes. Still, since the older child had not undergone the actual *milah* ceremony at its proper time, the mohel now wonders whether he should have taken the ritual drop of blood (*hatafat dam berit*) in order to symbolize the child's entry into the covenant of Abraham.

Teshuvah

Our responsum must consider three separate, yet related issues: 1) the Jewish status of the three-year-old child; 2) the halachah concerning *hatafat dam berit* for a male who was circumcised prior to his eighth day; 3) other issues which might affect our decision.

I. The child's Jewish status. Were we to regard this child as a non-Jew there would be no question of the ritual validity of his circumcision. His *milah* would have been performed for the purpose of converting him to Judaism (*leshem gerut*), while the requirement for circumcision on the eighth day applies only to infants who are Jewish by birth.[1] For us, however, the three-year-old child qualifies for the "presumption" of Jewish identity under the "patrilineal descent" resolution of the CCAR.[2] The resolution specifies that this presumption must be established through "appropriate and timely public and formal

acts of identification with the Jewish faith and people," an example of which
is "the acquisition of a Hebrew name." The naming ceremony performed by
the mohel thus confirms that this child has been Jewish from birth. We are
dealing therefore with the *milah* not of a convert but of a Jewish child:[3] does
a circumcision performed prior to the eighth day of his life fulfill the requirements of ritual circumcision, or must a drop of blood be taken in order to
invest the surgical procedure with religious significance?

II. Halachic Considerations. According to Jewish law, a male infant is
to be circumcised on the eighth day of his life, during daylight hours from
sunrise on.[4] In our case, the circumcision took place before the eighth day; has
the mitzvah of circumcision been fulfilled thereby? The 14th-century authority R. Asher b. Yechiel rules that *hatafat dam berit* is not required when a boy
is circumcised prior to his eighth day. He learns this from the statement in the
Talmud that if a child whose eighth day falls on Shabbat is mistakenly circumcised the day before, "the Sabbath cannot be overridden" to take the drop
of blood from him.[5] This contrasts with the well-known rule that a circumcision performed at its proper time (*i.e.*, the eighth day) does take place on
Shabbat.[6] This means, says a later authority, that the premature circumcision
is ritually acceptable, for otherwise the *hatafat dam berit* would be considered
the actual fulfillment of the mitzvah and, if it occurred on the eighth day,
would override Shabbat. Since the taking of a drop of blood does not, however, override the Shabbat, "you must conclude that circumcision performed
prior to the eighth day is not unfit and does not require *hatafah*."[7] This position is codified by the 16th-century *poskim* R. Moshe Isserles and R. Shelomo
Luria.[8]

On the other hand, R. Shabetai Kohen, a leading 17th-century commentator to the *Shulchan Aruch*, rejects the position of R. Asher, Isserles, and
Luria. He argues that the fact that *hatafat dam berit* does not override the
Shabbat is no proof that a circumcision which takes place prior to the eighth
day is ritually fit. In his view it is only the actual procedure of circumcision,
and *not* its ritual substitute, which is permitted on Shabbat if that is the boy's
eighth day. Nonetheless, a premature circumcision does not fulfill the mitzvah
and a drop of blood must be taken, albeit on a weekday.[9] A prominent later

authority, however, upholds the logic of those who do not require *hatafat dam berit*: if the premature circumcision did not fulfill the mitzvah, then the taking of a drop of blood surely does perform that requirement and ought to be allowed on Shabbat if that is the boy's eighth day. There is no reason to distinguish between the procedures. If one fulfills the mitzvah thereby, one ought to be allowed to do so on Shabbat. But inasmuch as all agree that *hatafat dam berit* does not override Shabbat, we conclude that the mitzvah has been fulfilled by the earlier circumcision.[10]

We might explain the dispute between the two positions in the following manner. Those who rule stringently see the requirement that *milah* be done at its proper time as a condition of the commandment. There is no mitzvah to circumcise prior to the child's eighth day, and a circumcision performed during that time fulfills no commandment. The ritual obligation of *berit milah* must still be met through *hatafat dam berit*. Those who rule leniently agree, of course, that *milah* ought to occur on the eighth day. But if the circumcision is done prematurely, the obligation to perform that procedure no longer exists, and no ritual substitute is required. Just as one is exempt from the obligation of *tzitzit* if one does not wear a four-cornered garment and from the commandment to remove leaven from the house before Pesach if one possesses no chametz, so too is one exempt from the mitzvah of *milah* on the eighth day if the child has already been circumcised.[11]

There are, in other words, two alternative interpretations of the halachah on this point. Contemporary Orthodox opinion favors the more stringent position.[12] We disagree.[13] The stringent position is based almost exclusively upon the ruling of R. Shabetai Kohen, which as we have seen has been refuted by later authorities. It is not demanded by the talmudic sources, which have led a number of poskim to rule that *hatafat dam berit* is not required in this case.[14] It is merely a *chumra*, a stringency imposed upon Jewish ritual practice either by those who are unable to decide which interpretation of the sources is correct[15] or by those who deem it necessary for reasons of religious policy. Whether such a stringency is in fact justified on policy grounds we shall consider below. In the meantime, we conclude that the *halachah* does not require *hatafat dam berit* for a Jewish child circumcised prior to the eighth day of his life.

III. Other Considerations. We now inquire into those "reasons of religious policy." Do any exist which speak to us, which would persuade us that this child should be made to undergo *hatafat dam*? An argument of this type is advanced by the late R. Isaac Klein, one of the leading halachists of the Conservative movement. Noting that many circumcisions take place prior to the eighth day "through ignorance or for convenience," he rules that "in order to discourage this practice, we would insist that such circumcisions are valid only if a drop of blood is drawn on the eighth day." As a matter of general principle, we share with our Conservative colleagues this concern that *milah* be performed on the eighth day.[17] Indeed, it is precisely when circumcision is conducted according to Jewish ritual requirements that it is transformed from a purely surgical procedure into *berit milah*, a sign of this child's entry into the covenant, a religious act undertaken with the proper spiritual intention, an acknowledgement of our continuing bond with the tradition of Israel.

Nothing in this responsum, therefore, should be construed as expressing our approval of circumcision performed prior to the eighth day. On the other hand, we cannot lose sight of the fact that the child in our case is not eight days but three years old; for him, as well as for his family, the experience of *hatafat dam berit* would likely be traumatic and terrifying. Given that Jewish law does not require this ritual of a child circumcised before the eighth day, we believe that the negative repercussions of imposing stringency in this case would far outweigh any benefits we might hope to gain thereby. While we strongly encourage Jewish parents to have their sons circumcised on the eighth day in accordance with Jewish tradition and Reform practice, no good purpose would be served by requiring that a child in a case such as ours undergo the ritual drawing of a drop of blood.

We conclude that the mohel's actions were proper[18] and that they displayed the sensitivity and the learning which we would hope to find in all Jewish professionals. He brings credit to himself as a Reform mohel and to our movement as a whole.

Excursus

(See note 3, above) Were this child born a non-Jew (and traditional *halachah* does so regard him), we would need to consider whether *hatafat dam berit* was required to convert him to Judaism (*leshem gerut*), inasmuch as his circumcision was not performed for that purpose.[19] In our Reform tradition, this question is addressed by an 1892 resolution of the CCAR which permits a Reform rabbi to perform conversions "without any initiatory rite, ceremony, or observance whatever."[20] This clearly dispenses with circumcision, *hatafat dam berit*, and immersion as essential ritual prerequisites for conversion. The question has been raised: what does this century-old resolution mean to us, rabbis operating in a vastly different religious climate? Are we still bound by its provisions? If so, how does this affect the guidance which this Committee may offer on *she'elot* that touch upon conversion to Judaism?

It is true that the resolution's accompanying argumentation, authored by Rabbi Isaac Mayer Wise, is couched in language and expresses ideas which strike many of us as outdated.[21] Nonetheless, it remains the official statement of the policy of the Central Conference until such time as it is amended or repealed. This Committee, unlike individual Reform Jews, rabbis, or congregations, is an agency of the Conference and in that sense is bound by explicit statements of Conference policy. At the same time, in judging how such a resolution should be applied in practice, we need to look not only to its wording but also to the history of its interpretation. We need to get a sense of how this statement has been implemented in Reform Jewish religious life for the past hundred years: how have Reform rabbis (and the Responsa Committee) understood its terms and provisions.[22]

When we consider the matter from this perspective, we find that Reform rabbis have not entirely dispensed with ritual requirements for conversion. Virtually every member of the Conference, when performing conversions, accompanies them with some ritual or "initiatory rite". Such a ceremony is included in our *Rabbi's Manual,* which provides for both *milah* and *tevilah* (ritual immersion) for proselytes. While these are not mandatory, "nevertheless, we recognize today that there are social, psychological, and religious values associated with the traditional initiatory rites, and therefore recommend that the rabbi acquaint prospective converts with the halachic background and rationale for *berit milah, hatafat dam berit*, and *tevilah* and offer them the opportunity to observe these rites. In Israel, Canada, and various communities elsewhere, *giyur* [conversion] is performed by our colleagues in accordance with traditional halachic practice."[23] Our Committee, too, has dealt with *milah* and *tevilah* as serious, relevant options for conversion under Reform auspices.[24] Both these responsa and the *Manual* take note of the 1892 resolution but add that it is customary among many Reform communities to require these rites of converts. This is not a case of local custom superseding formal law;[25] rather, what has happened in our communities is an example of the age-old tendency of minhag to operate within "neutral spaces" in the law, defining the authoritative practice where none exists[26] or where the formal halachah is either vague or equivocal.[27] Our practice, in other words, has determined that the 1892 resolution does not demand the elimination of ritual requirements for conversion and that the restoration of these requirements violates neither the letter of the resolution nor the spirit of Reform Judaism.

The Committee's approach to this subject should keep this nuanced reality in mind. So long as the 1892 resolution remains on the books, we should remind our correspondents that circumcision and immersion are not required for conversion. They have, however, become the norm in many of our communities, for good and sufficient cause.[28] If such is the practice of those who submit inquiries to us, we shall answer them within the context of their own *minhag*.

NOTES

1 *See* R. David Zvi Hoffman, *Resp. Melammed Leho`il,* YD, no. 82: *hatafat dam berit* is not required for the adult son of a Jewish father and a non-Jewish mother who was circumcised at birth but not immersed for purposes of circumcision. Significantly, this applies even when the mohel was under the mistaken impression that the child was born Jewish. Hoffman argues that the milah in any event was done for the purpose of *mitzvah*, since all Jewish males, whether Jews by birth or by choice, must be circumcised. Thus, the requisite intent to perform *mitzvat milah* was present, and the child (now an adult) need only ratify his status as a proselyte with ritual immersion.

2 *CCAR Yearbook*, 93 (1983), 157-160.

3 Our responsum speaks to the situation of Jewish communities which recognize patrilineal descent. Other Jewish communities will regard this child of a non-Jewish mother as a non-Jew who would require conversion. While it is reasonable to assume that Reform *mohelim* will act in accordance with the Reform interpretation of Jewish law and tradition, they along with rabbis have a moral obligation to inform parents in cases such as this that other streams of Judaism do not accept this _milah_ as the circumcision of a *Jewish* child. Honesty and integrity demand that we stand for our own beliefs; they also demand that we offer all who come before us the same opportunity to make informed decisions con-

cerning their Jewish lives. On the requirement of *milah* for conversion, see *Excursus*.

4 Genesis 17:12 and Leviticus 12:3; BT Pesachim 4a and Yevamot 72b; Megillah 20a and *Rashi ad loc.*, s.v. *ad hanets hachamah.*

5 Hilchot HaRosh, Shabba*t* 19:5; the talmudic statement is found in BT Shabbat 137b.

6 BT Shabbat 132a; *Yad*, Hilchot Milah 1:9.

7 R. Yoel Sirkes, *Bayit Chadash* to *Tur*, YD 262.

8 Isserles in *Sh. A*, YD 262:1; Luria in *Yam Shel Shelomo, Yevamot* 8:6. As noted by both *Siftey Kohen* and *Turey Zahav* to *Sh.A.*, YD 262:1, Isserles seems to contradict himself in this very paragraph when he rules that a circumcision that takes place at night is invalid and requires hatafat dam berit. But see Isserles in his *Darkey Moshe, Tur* YD 262: the prohibition against performing a circumcision at night is more strenuous than the one forbidding the ceremony prior to the eighth day. Meanwhile, two other *poskim* (Luria, loc. cit., and Perishah, *Tur* YD 262) resolve the contradiction by ruling that a circumcision that takes place at night, like the one that takes place prior to the eighth day, is ritually fit and does not require *hatafat dam berit.*

9 Siftey Kohen, *Sh.A.*, YD 262, no. 2.

10 R. Aryeh Lev b. Asher (18th cent.), *Resp. Sha'agat Aryeh*, no. 52.

11 This explanation is advanced by R. Yosef Babad (19th cent.), *Minchat Chinuch, mitzvah 2.* See also *Sha'agat Aryeh*, who calls circumcision before the eighth day an "irreparable error"; compensation in the form of *hatafat dam* is neither required nor efficacious.

12 See *Aruch HaShulchan*, YD 262, par. 5. Most authoritative halachic compendia on *berit milah* acknowledge that there is a dispute over this issue; see R. Asher Greenwald, *Zocher Haberit* (Hungary, 1931), ch. 4, no. 9. Some popular works, however, tend to ignore the lenient opinion altogether and give the false impression that all authorities require *hatafat dam*. Examples are R. Paysach Krohn, *Bris Milah* (Brooklyn, Mesorah Artscroll Series, 1985), 92, and R. Eugene J. Cohen, *Guide to Ritual Circumcision* (New York, 1984), 9. In general, readers should be advised to utilize such popular Orthodox guides with appropriate caution.

13 See *ARR*, no. 56, pp. 145-146.

14 See notes 5, 8, 10 and 11. *Sha'agat Aryeh*, no. 54, adds Maimonides to this list. He deduces this from *Yad*, Hilchot Milah 2:1, where Rambam rules that while a circumcision may not be performed by a non-Jew there is no need to take a drop of blood to validate the procedure. This implies, says R. Aryeh Lev, that Rambam subscribes to the "irreparable error" theory (see note 11) and would apply it to the case of premature circumcision.

15 *Bayit Chadash* (see note 7).

16 R. Isaac Klein, *A Guide to Jewish Religious Practice* (New York, 1979), 425.

17 *CARR*, no. 28, p. 48; *Gates of Mitzvah*, 14.

18 One member of our Committee dissented. He would require *hatafat dam* in this case, for reasons that parallel those cited by Rabbi Klein (see note 16).

19 Shabbat 135a; Alfasi *ad loc.*; *Yad*, Hilchot Milah 1:7; *Sh A*, YD 268:1.

20 *CCAR Yearbook*, 3 (1893), 94-95; *ARR*, 236-237.

21 See the critique by R. Solomon B. Freehof, *RRT*, no. 15, pp. 71-79.

22 In a similar way, our Committee has issued a number of decisions pertaining to the Patrilineal Descent resolution. These decisions are part of the "annotated edition" of the resolution, part of a tradition of interpretation which over time will determine its actual parameters.

23 *Rabbi's Manual* (New York, CCAR, 1988), 232. The ceremony for conversion is at 199ff.

24 *ARR*, no. 57, pp. 146-149 and no. 69, pp. 238-239; *CARR*, no. 44, pp. 74-76; no. 45,

pp. 76-79; no. 47, pp. 83-85; and no. 49, 83-85.

25 *Minhag mevatel halachah*; see Y. Baba Metsi`a 7:1.

26 *Yad,* Hilchot Shevitat Asor 3:3: minhag is valid when it constitutes a choice between several options permitted by halachah.

27 See the famous incident between Hillel and the Beney Beteira (Pesachim 66a). On the relationship between *minhag* and halachah in general see Menachem Elon, *Jewish Law* (Philadelphia, 1994), pp. 880-944.

28 This may involve a desire to emphasize that, in accepting proselytes, the community sees itself as representing not only the Reform movement but the Jewish people as a historical entity; it therefore adopts the same conversion procedure utilized by all Jewish communities.

Naming a Child of a Mixed Marriage
5755.2

She'elah

A child from a Jewish father and Gentile mother has been converted and has undergone immersion in the mikveh. What parental Hebrew names should be inscribed on the certificate? (Rabbi Alejandro Lilienthal, Rio de Janeiro, Brazil)

Teshuvah

The way we name a child is a matter of custom and not of law, as is set forth in a *teshuvah* issued by R. Walter Jacob.[1]

Since the child has a Jewish father, the only question that arises concerns the name of the child's mother. As a general practice, we do not assign a Hebrew name to the non-Jewish parent.[2] If it seems desirable to add such a name, you might wish to use that of our ancestor, Sarah.

NOTES

1 *NARR*, p. 182. (The *teshuvah* was enclosed with our letter.)
2 *CARR*, ed. R. Walter Jacob, p. .57.

The Dual Religion Family and Patrilineal Descent
5755.17

She'elah

A Jewish man applies for membership in a congregation for himself and his young son, and wishes to enroll the boy in our religious school. The prospective member is married to a Catholic woman, and they also have a daughter who is being raised as a Catholic. Should the congregation accept the applicant as a Temple member? Would the *teshuvah* be different if it was a Jewish mother and a Catholic father, and the mother was applying for membership? (Rabbi Martin Zinkow, Saint Paul, Minnesota)

Teshuvah

The North American Reform movement has long distinguished itself by its efforts to welcome interfaith families as members of our congregations. These efforts are based upon the belief that a firm and unwavering commitment to "outreach," to programs aimed at bringing Jews heretofore on the margins of the community into the mainstream of Jewish religious life, is essential to insure the long-term survival of American Jewry. The resolution on patrilineal descent, adopted by the Central Conference of American Rabbis in 1983, is one of the more prominent expressions of this attitude. With that doctrine, which extends the presumption of Jewish status to the child of one Jewish parent, we say to the children of mixed marriage that we will accept them as Jews, without the need for conversion, so long as they establish their claim to Jewishness through the procedures specified by the resolution.[1]

Yet this stance of openness has never been without its limits. While we "reach out" to the interfaith couple and welcome them into our midst, we do not forget that we are a *Jewish* religious community and that our goal is the encouragement of *Jewish* religious life. For this reason, we do not look upon mixed marriage as a desirable or "normal" situation for our people. Our hope is that the interfaith marriage shall one day cease to be such, that the non-Jewish spouse will choose to become a Jew. In the meantime, we call upon the couple to establish a Jewish home, and we insist that the children be raised exclusively in the Jewish tradition.[2]

The case before us poses a severe test to these limits. We confront a mixed marriage in which the non-Jewish spouse remains an active and practicing member of her faith. Moreover, by their decision to raise one of their children as a Catholic and the other as a Jew, they have insured that their home is not a "Jewish" one, a home in which Judaism is the exclusive religious identity of the family. The *she'elah* asks whether the Jewish father ought to be accepted as a member of the congregation, even though his acquiescence in the creation of a dual-religion household runs sharply counter to the most basic Jewish religious principles. In addition, the question's wording raises the issue of the son's religious status. By suggesting the possibility that the answer might "be different if it was a Jewish mother and a Catholic father, and the mother was applying for membership," it invites us to consider whether a child raised in such a religious environment qualifies for a presumption of Jewishness under the doctrine of patrilineal descent.

1. The Father as Member of the Synagogue. This applicant is a Jew, identifying as such; he is not an apostate. For this reason there is no justification for denying synagogue membership to him.[3] Although he has chosen a lifestyle that is contrary to the ideals of our people, he is permitted to associate with the Jewish religious community. Indeed, our commitment to outreach and the furtherance of Jewish life demands a positive and active approach. He should be welcomed into the congregation and encouraged to build, step by step, a Jewish home. We Reform Jews, moreover, make no distinction in this regard based upon the gender of the applicant. On the other hand, though this man is welcomed as a member, his decision to allow his child to be raised as a Catholic raises doubts concerning his commitment to the most elemental Jewish responsibilities (*veshinantam livanecha*). It is therefore inappropriate for him to serve as a congregational officer, board member, committee chairperson, religious school teacher, or to hold any other significant communal position, since we look upon our leaders as Jewish role mod-

els, as exemplars of the kind of committed Jew that we want all our people to be.[4]

2. The Limits of Patrilineality. We must now consider the status of this man's son. Does the child qualify for Jewish status under the CCAR's doctrine of patrilineal descent? Or does the family's religious environment render his religious identity so doubtful or unsettled as to require that he undergo conversion prior to his admission into the congregation?

The text of the 1983 resolution states:[5]

> The Central Conference of American Rabbis declares that the child of one Jewish parent is under the presumption of Jewish descent.
>
> This presumption of Jewish status of the offspring of any mixed marriage is to be established through appropriate and timely public and formal acts of identification with the Jewish faith and people. The performance of these mitzvot serves to commit those who participate in them, both parent and child, to Jewish life.

The resolution goes on to enumerate some of the "public and formal acts" which might establish the child's "positive and exclusive Jewish identity." One of these is "Torah study," which would include a child's enrollment in and successful completion of a congregation's religious school curriculum.

Some might argue that the child in our case enjoys a presumption of Jewish status. He is, first of all, the offspring of one Jewish parent, and his parents state that it is their intention to raise him as a Jew. Moreover, the father wishes to enroll his son in religious school, which the resolution cites as an example of a "public and formal" act of Jewish identification. And although more than one religion is practiced in the home, that fact might be regarded as irrelevant to the boy's Jewishness. The resolution, after all, speaks of the "presumption of Jewish status of the offspring of any mixed marriage (emphasis added)," a terminology which does not explicitly exclude the child raised in a dual-religion household. This might be said to follow upon the Conference's previous statement on the subject, which pronounces the child of a Jewish father and a non-Jewish mother to be Jewish "if he attends a Jewish school and follows a course of studies leading to Confirmation. Such a procedure is regarded as sufficient evidence that the parents and the child himself intend that he shall live as a Jew."[6] Cited in the Resolution on Patrilineal Descent, this statement, too, makes no explicit exception for the child raised in a dual-religion environment.

The difficulty with this argument, however, lies in its assumption that under the 1983 resolution a child *automatically* qualifies for Jewish status when he or she has one Jewish parent and when the parents declare their intention to raise the child as a Jew. We reject that assumption. We would note that the resolution speaks of a *presumption* of Jewish status, a presumption established by the performance of certain "public and formal acts" which testify to the child's "positive and exclusive Jewish identity." This wording is key to a proper understanding of the document as a whole. It demands the conclusion that, while acts of Jewish identification can serve to confirm a child's Jewishness, they do not *inevitably* do so. That is to say, the child of one Jewish parent does not necessarily become a Jew upon *berit milah*,[7] acquisition of a Hebrew name, or attending religious school. These acts "establish" the presumption of Jewishness because they serve as evidence that the presumption was a correct one, that Judaism is the child's *positive* and *exclusive* religious identification. It follows that, in a situation in which the performance of these acts does not offer proof of exclusive Jewish identification—as in a case where the child's religious identity is torn, conflicted, or confused—then they cannot and do not establish that the child is in fact a Jew.

The thrust of the resolution, it must be remembered, was not simply to "equalize" the role of the father to that of the mother in determining the Jewishness of the child, but rather to limit the effect of genealogy in making that determination. Under its terms, the child of a Jewish mother and a Gentile father is no longer *ipso facto* a Jew, just as the offspring of a Gentile mother and Jewish father is no longer *ipso facto* a Gentile. In both cases, the child is presumed to be a Jew, but this presumption must be validated "through subsequent and meaningful acts of identification."[8] That is to say, the conferral of Jewish status in cases of mixed marriage now depends as much if not more upon the quality of the child's religious upbringing as it does upon the circumstances of his or her birth. These acts of Jewish identification, though "public and formal," are more than mere public formalities. To be "meaningful," they must offer evidence that the child in fact identifies as a Jew and that the parents are willing and able to transmit a sense of Jewishness to their son or daughter. If they offer no such evidence, then they become meaning*less*, mere words and empty ceremony that tell us nothing of the depth of a child's Jewish identification or of the parents' capacity or sincerity in fulfilling their promise to raise the child as a Jew.

To summarize: patrilineal descent does not confer Jewish status automatically. Whether the child of a mixed marriage is in fact Jewish is a matter of judgment. It depends upon an evaluation of his or her conduct and commitment, a finding that the child's acts of identification with Judaism are sufficiently "meaningful" to remove any doubt as to the genuineness of his or her Jewish identity.

In the case before us, we are convinced that this judgment must yield a negative conclusion. We are dealing here, not with an ordinary mixed marriage, but with a dual-religion household. Dividing itself equally and intentionally between Catholics and Jews, the family has determined that theirs shall not be a Jewish home but one that is as Catholic as it is Jewish. Christian holidays and observances will be prominent in the home, not merely as "Mother's" private religious expression but as family celebrations that are as much "ours" as the Jewish ones. It is far from obvious that the "Jewish" child of such a couple, no matter what the parents' stated intent, will develop a true Jewish religious identification. We question, therefore, whether such a family is capable of transmitting an exclusive Jewish identity to one of its children.

Our position flows from Reform Judaism's categorical rejection of the concept of religious syncretism, the notion that a child can be raised simultaneously in more than one religious tradition.[9] We hold that Judaism is an exclusive religious identification, that one is either a Jew or one is not, that one cannot successfully be a Jew and something else. For this reason, in the case of a mixed marriage, until there exist in the family a firm and discernible intent and ability to raise the child as a Jew, that child is not regarded by us as Jewish. Indeed, given the family situation, it makes as much sense to say that the child has a claim to Gentile status as it is to talk about a presumption of Jewishness. It is up to the parents, through a sincere and credible commitment, to decide which of these claims to validate. And if there is any doubt as to the choice they have made, the child does not qualify as a Jew under the doctrine of patrilineal descent.[10]

The dual-religion household is one in which two religions have a legitimate claim to equal status. This distinguishes our case from one in which the non-Jewish parent agrees that the home shall be Jewish and that the children—all of them—will be raised as Jews. A child raised in a dual-religion environment cannot help but be confused as to his or her true religious identity. Therefore, though his parents declare that they intend to raise him as a Jew and though he undertake "appropriate and timely public and formal acts" of Jewish identification, he does not enjoy a claim to Jewish status under the CCAR's resolution on patrilineal descent. In a situation such as this, a child's Jewish status can be established only through the process of conversion.[11]

Conclusion. We suggest that the father be accepted as a member of the congregation. His son, on the other hand, is a Gentile and can qualify for Jewish status through the process of conversion. The son should be admitted to religious school, so that he may begin a program of study that will help strengthen his sense of Jewish identity. Some members of the Committee believe that the child should be converted prior to his entry into religious school, as a means of removing all doubt as to his Jewish status. Other members feel that the conversion should be postponed until such time as the child can make a more mature choice for Judaism.[12] In any event, while the child's readiness to choose Judaism is a matter to be determined by the rabbi in the particular case,[13] conversion must occur before the child is permitted to celebrate becoming a Bar Mitzvah. We would add, in answer to the sho'el's query, that under the current position of the CCAR, the same procedure would apply were this boy the child of a Jewish mother and Gentile father.

Addendum. Our decision in the matter of the son is based upon our interpretation of the text of the CCAR's 1983 resolution on patrilineal descent. Although, as we mentioned above, one could draw a different set of conclusions from that text, we believe that our interpretation, which leads to stringency in this case, reflects the best and most accurate understanding of it. To interpret Jewish tradition, along with the traditions and precedents of our own movement, is the task of our Committee. But while we are certainly willing to perform that task, we would be remiss if we did not call attention to the particular difficulties inherent in this issue. The question of Jewish status is a most serious and sensitive one, especially in a community such as ours where mixed marriage is on the rise, where assimilation poses a constant challenge, and where the danger of religious syncretism is rife. Questions such as the one we address here will become more frequent over time. And it is unlikely that they will be firmly and finally resolved without a concerted effort on the part of the Conference as a whole to re-examine the question of Jewish status in a thorough and thoughtful way.

We do not wish to be misunderstood. It is not our role to advocate either for or against the resolution on patrilineal descent or for or against its amendment. That resolution reflects the policy of the Conference to which this Committee adheres. We simply want to suggest to our colleagues that the time has come to look carefully at the way in which this policy is practiced in our communities and to consider the effects of the resolution, which was controversial when it was adopted and remains so today, upon our congregations and upon the wider Jewish world.

NOTES

1 See: Report of the Committee on Patrilineal Descent on the Status of Children of Mixed Marriages, *CCAR Yearbook* 93 (1983), 157-160; *ARR*, 547-550.

2 See below, in the discussion of the resolution on patrilineal descent.

3 Were he in fact an apostate, a convert to another religion, the situation would differ radically. See CCAR Responsum 5753.13 in this book. In this case, however, we would simply note the famous rabbinic dictum, based upon BT Sanhedrin 44a, that "a Jew, even though he sins, remains a Jew." On the halachic implications of this principle, see *Teshuvot Rashi,* ed. Elfenbein, no. 171, 173, 175, and 246.

4 On the qualifications for holding office in the synagogue, see R. Solomon B. Freehof, *TRR*, no. 51, and Responsa Committee, no. 5754.17 in this book.

5 *ARR*, 550.

6 *Rabbi's Manual*, Rev. ed. (New York, CCAR, 1961), 112.

7 The language of the resolution refers to "entry into the Covenant." This cannot refer to conversion, since a child presumed to be Jewish under the doctrine of Patrilineal Descent does not require conversion. The "entry" ceremony spoken of here is either *berit milah* or *berit banot*, rituals performed for children who are Jewish by birth.

8 *Ma`gele Tsedek: Rabbi's Manual* (New York, CCAR, 1988), 227.

9 *CARR*, no. 61, pp. 98-99; R. Walter Jacob, *NARR*, no. 88, pp. 138-139 and 109, pp. 173-174.

In cases of mixed marriage where the parents have decided to raise their child simultaneously in Judaism and in another religious tradition, the Committee has ruled that those children are Gentiles: they do not qualify for a presumption of Jewish identity under the doctrine of patrilineal descent, and they must undergo conversion if they wish to be recognized as Jews.

10 R. Walter Jacob, NARR, no. 111, pp. 176-177.

11 One member of the Committee, although agreeing that the child in this case should be required to undergo conversion, believes that the determination of the Jewishness of children of dual-religion households must be left to the judgment of the rabbi of the congregation on a case-by-case basis. The majority of the Committee, as indicated by the text, holds that the presumption of Jewishness under the doctrine of Patrilineal Descent can *never* apply to the child of a dual-religion household such as the one described in this *she'elah*.

12 The Halachah provides for the conversion of minor children, but they retain the right to renounce the conversion upon reaching majority (BT Ketubot 11a; *Yad*, Melachim 10:3; *Sh.A.* YD 268:7).

13 "In matters of conversion, the determination is left to the discretion of the court;" R. Yosef Karo, *Beit Yosef* YD 268.

Conversion of a "Matrilineal" Jew
5754.13

She'elah

Recently, a woman in her mid-twenties has come to me seeking conversion. Her maternal grandmother had been a practicing Jew. Her mother was raised as a Jew but converted to Christianity when she married. The woman in question was baptized as a Lutheran and brought up in that church. Her sister has meanwhile maintained a Jewish identity and refused to undergo confirmation as a Lutheran. Their father's sister, while maintaining her native Christianity, married a Jewish man. Thus, there has always been a Jewish influence in this family, most evident at Passover, when the entire family would attend seder at their uncle's home. The woman in question has met a Jewish man whom she wishes to marry. Is she a Jew by the traditional, "matrilineal" definition? Even should this be the case, I believe that a full conversion is warranted, given that she was raised and confirmed as a Christian. (Rabbi Marvin Schwab, Orangevale, CA)

Teshuvah

We agree with your decision to require a conversion for this woman. Under the definition adopted by the Central Conference of American Rabbis at its convention in 1983,[1] "the child of one Jewish parent is under the presumption of Jewish descent. This presumption...is to be established through appropriate and timely public and formal acts of identification with the Jewish faith and people...Depending on circumstances, *mitzvot* leading toward a positive and exclusive Jewish identity will include entry into the covenant, acquisition of a Hebrew name, Torah study, *Bar/Bat Mitzvah*, and *Kabbalat Torah* (Confirmation). For those beyond childhood claiming Jewish identity, other public acts or declarations may be added or substituted after consultation with their rabbi."

The last sentence is the governing rule in our case. This Committee has taken the view that the adult child of one Jewish parent requires conversion when that child has never previously identified as a Jew.[2] In the case at hand, the woman was baptized and raised as a Christian. That is her religious identity; the Jewish identification of her sister and uncle are irrelevant under the terms of our Resolution. We hold that she has forfeited her claim to Jewish status by way of descent; like any non-Jew who wishes to join us, she may undergo the process of conversion.

We should also note that though this woman qualifies as a Jew under the traditional "matrilineal" principle,[3] halachic practice would likely demand some formal ceremony to mark her return to Judaism. While under Torah law (*dina de'oraita*) she does not require ritual immersion, it is often customary to have the repenting apostate immerse in a *mikveh* in the presence of a *beit din*.[4] Some authorities do not impose this requirement. A returning apostate, they stress, is a Jew and should be treated as such; no ceremonies connected with the conversion process should be performed for this person.[5] A Jew, after all, "even though he sin, nonetheless remains a Jew."[6] Still, the dispute over this issue indicates that not all authorities agree that an apostate remains a Jew, come what may. Some geonim, for example, view such a person as a non-Jew for purposes of levirate marriage and inheritance law.[7] The conferral of Jewish status is therefore not necessarily an automatic thing. The response of rabbinic authorities to the phenomenon of apostasy has been varied, reflecting in all probability the varying attitudes of Jewish communities over the course of time toward those who abandon Judaism and those who return to it.

To repeat: we agree that this woman requires conversion before she can be accepted as a member of the Jewish people.

NOTES

1 Report of the Committee on Patrilineal Descent on the Status of Children of Mixed Marriages, in *ARR*, 550.

2 *CARR*, no. 39, pp. 68-69, 42 (end), pp.71-72, and 59, pp. 95-96.

3 Learned by implication from the words of M. Kiddushin 3:12.

4 *Hiddushei Ha-Ritba*, Yebamot 47b; *Nimukei Yosef*, Alfasi Yebamot, fol. 16b; Isserles to Sh.A., YD 268:12.

5 R. Shelomo b. Shimeon Duran, *Resp. Rashbash*, no. 89, urges that those forced into baptism (*anusim*) who seek to return should be "drawn with cords of love". For other sources, see CARR, no. 64, pp. 104-105. While there can be no exact comparison between American Jews in our day and the *anusim*

of yore, it can be argued that this woman, whose mother was an apostate, was an "involuntary" convert to Christianity.

6 BT Sanhedrin 44a, after Joshua 7:11. Rashi is recognized as the authority who first lent halachic force to this aggadic saying; see *Teshuvot Rashi*, ed. Elfenbein, no. 171, 173, and 175.

7 *Otzar HeGeonim*, Yebamot 22a and Kiddushin 18a.

Child Raised in Two Religions
5754.3

She'elah

A Jewish father, whose wife is Christian, has two sons for whom he would like to arrange Bar Mitzvah ceremonies. On alternate weeks the children receive one hour of Jewish education in an informal setting. Throughout the year they attend synagogue services with their father at regular intervals, and on Sundays go with their mother to church school and services. The parents say that they want the children to learn about both traditions, with the intent of permitting them to choose their affiliation when they grow up.

Inasmuch as the children have not made a commitment to be Jewish, nor have the parents made a commitment to raise them as Jews, should the children participate in Jewish life cycle events such as Bar Mitzvah?

In a similar vein, if the parents claim that they are raising their children to be "both Jewish and Christian" (i.e., if there are simultaneous Jewish and Christian commitments)), are such children entitled to celebrate their Bar Mitzvah? (Rabbi Amy R. Scheinerman, Baltimore, MD)

Teshuvah

Since the children have a Jewish father and a Christian mother they are considered Gentile in the traditional Halachah, while the 1983 resolution of the CCAR would consider them to be potential Jews. We acknowledge their Jewish status if and when a *public* affirmation of their identity has been made through a formal act.[1]

A Bar Mitzvah celebration is precisely this: an affirmation of identity, when a boy becomes subject to the mitzvot and assumes the obligations of Jewish life. If he has not as yet resolved the question of his identity, such a celebration would suffer from an inherent contradiction, and to carry it out nonetheless would be a sham, pretending to something the celebrant and his parents do not want it to be.

Rabbi Walter Jacob issued a *teshuvah* on this very question.[2] It deals with a child who was born of a Jewish *mother* and, although baptized as an infant, was halachically considered still to be a Jew. Even so, Rabbi Jacob would not admit him to the Bar Mitzvah course and emphasized that parents and child must reach a decision on the boy's Jewish identity before he could contemplate a Bar Mitzvah.

This ruling applies, *al achat kama vechama*, to the instant case. The rabbi should counsel the parents about the possibility of a delayed or even adult Bar Mitzvah; but at this time, when the boys' religious future is still undecided, a Bar Mitzvah is out of the question. The celebration is a confirmatory act, not a trial run. It may please parents and grandparents, but its observance under present circumstances would be a denial of its essence.

NOTES

1 CCAR, *Ma'agelei Tzedek--Rabbi's Manual*, (1988) pp. 225-227.
2 *CARR*, 1987, no. 61, pp. 98-99.

Rejecting One's Infant Conversion
5753.20

She'elah

I have always informed parents of children who were converted as infants when their parent became a Jew, that their children have a right to reject their conversion when they reached maturity, which I have considered to be the eighteenth year. How does Reform Judaism review this issue? (Rabbi Thomas P. Liebschutz, Winston-Salem, N.C.)

Teshuvah

The matter has been discussed by Rabbis Solomon B. Freehof and Walter Jacob.[1] You will find both *teshuvot* attached. They have followed the traditional view that a person may repudiate his/her conversion as a child. We note however, the dissent of Rabbi Moses Schreiber (the Hatam Sofer) who said that when a parent is converted along with the child, no repudiation is possible.[2]

As Liberals, we would hold with the mainstream ruling that persons converted in childhood — with or without their parents converting at the same time — have a right to reject Judaism upon reaching maturity.

When is the *terminus ad quem* when such a rejection must be effected? Traditionally, the age has been 13, but we believe that your position is preferable, namely to postpone this *terminus* until the age of 18.

To be sure, this creates an awkward situation when such a child becomes bar/bat mitzvah or is confirmed. Both acts serve as a confirmation of Jewishness. The parents, along with the rabbi, will have to explain to the child that the mitzvot will be accepted at this time in accordance with his/her understanding of Judaism, but that at maturity, he/she may re-evaluate that decision. We thus would consider the earlier asseveration as provisional in view of the immaturity of the person at that time. Obviously, this matter has to be handled with considerable sensitivity.

NOTES

1 Freehof, *CuRR* (1969) no. 20, pp. 80-83; Jacob, *CARR*, no. 47, pp. 80-81.

2 For the repudiation, see BT Ketubot 11a; *Sh.A.*, YD 268:7; and for the Hatam Sofer, see his *Pitchei Teshuvah* to YD 268:7.

Funeral of a Child of Mixed Marriage
5751.7

She'elah

A rabbi has been asked to co-officiate with Christian clergy at the funeral of a 16-year old boy who died tragically in an automobile accident. His mother is Catholic and his father Jewish. The boy was enrolled for a few years in religious school, but was never called to the Torah as a bar mitzvah. His parents are not currently members of the congregation. The clergyman has assured the rabbi that, at the request of the family, the service would be non-sectarian and that nothing would be said to offend Jewish ears. The cemetery, too, is non-sectarian.

The rabbi has been was invited to lead the mourners' Kaddish and has asked whether it was proper for him to co-officiate in this manner.

Teshuvah

The following questions arise:
1. Is this the funeral of a Jewish or Gentile child?
2. When should rabbis agree to co-officiate with non-Jewish clergy?
3. What other considerations should be addressed?

1. The religious status of the child is not in doubt. The Halachah would consider him a Gentile since he was born of a Gentile mother and was not converted. Neither would the boy meet the requirements of the patrilineal definition of the CCAR, for while he attended a Jewish religious school for a while he did not affirm his Jewishness in a "timely public and formal fashion," as required of him in order to be acknowledged a a Jew.[1]

2. If the rabbi had been asked to be the sole officiant at the funeral, the propriety of his/her accepting this task would not have been in question. That constellation was first discussed with regard to non-Jewish spouses, and there were no obstacles to the rabbi's participation.[2] Rabbis have also officiated on

other occasions in keeping with the Talmudic dictum to keep peace with the gentile community, *mipnei darchei shalom*, a rule which has been incorporated in the codes.[3] Nor is there an objection with regard to reciting the Kaddish for a Gentile.[4] The whole matter was explored in detail by R. Solomon B. Freehof in a responsum published in 1957.[5] We see to it that the dead are buried with dignity and that the mourners are consoled.

Does the matter of co-officiating alter these conclusions?

A funeral is not an "interfaith service" of a civic nature, in which Reform rabbis generally participate.[6] Rather, it is a service which performs a specific religious rite and thereby focuses on the identity of the deceased.

In the case of the burial of a non-Jewish spouse the deceased's identity is not at issue, and the rabbi's participation is understood as an act of comforting the surviving partner. Here, however, the dead boy's religious identity is unclear and the rabbi's co-officiating gives rise to the impression that the boy had two religious identities, the existence of which we have declared inadmissible.[7]

Further, another long-established principle comes into play. What we do must not only be right, but also should be perceived as being right. We should not act in a manner which will create false impressions (*mipnei mar'it ayin*). The rabbi's participation would appear to affirm the Jewishness of the child, along with his Christian identity. Therefore, even if the service does not contain specific christological references the rabbi should *not* co-officate. We draw a definite line between ourselves and Christian practice. In an age in which boundaries were not as blurred as they increasingly tend to be in our time, it might have been possible to arrive at a different answer, but for us the setting of boundaries has become an important aspect in the maintenance of our Jewish identity. Participation in the ritual would give the appearance that the child was considered Jewish.

3. However, we do not counsel the rabbi to turn away from a family that is in the throes of bitter tragedy. On the contrary, we believe that there is a meaningful role for Jewish spiritual guidance and participation.

Responding to the invitation to participate in the ritual, the rabbi might give the following answer: I find myself unable to co-officiate in the ritual, but I will assist the father in fulfilling his own religious duty to say Kaddish for his son. I will sit with him in the pew and help him to perform the mitzvah.

In this way, religious boundaries are observed, as are the two principles of *mipnei mar'it 'ayin* and *mipnei darchei shalom*. The presence of the rabbi provides a measure of consolation to the father, and the father himself is encouraged to express his feelings in a Jewish way.

NOTES

1 See *Rabbi's Manual* (1988), p. 226.

2 *ARR*, ed. Walter Jacob, no. 95, pp. 323-335.

3 Based on BT Gittin 61a; *Tur* YD 367 rephrases the law to read: *mishtadlim bikevuratam kemo she-mishtadlim bikevurat yisra'el*, "we participate in their burials as if they were Jews." See also *Yad*, Hilchot Avel 14:12, and Hilkhot Melachim 10:12, supporting his position with references to Ps. 145:9 and Prov. 3:17. There is some speculation on the meaning of Rashi's interpretation of the Gittin passage; see Rashba and R. Nissim Gerondi (commentary on Alfasi, folio 28a).

4 Oshry, pp. 69 ff.

5 *ARR*, no. 124, pp. 387-390.

7 See *CARR*, ed. Walter Jacob, no. 167, pp. 250-252.

8 *Ibid.*, no. 61, pp. 98-99.

Choshen Mishpat
Social Issues

Nuclear War
5750.2

She'elah

The Justice and Peace Committee of the CCAR feels that many of the resolutions which deal with social issues and which the Conference ultimately adopts are not as thoroughly grounded in rabbinic thought as they might be. Our Committee wishes to make a particular contribution to the Religious Action Center by assessing some of these issues from the perspective of Jewish law, and therefore calls on the Responsa Committee for assistance. At this time, matters dealing with nuclear weapons are of continuing concern and we therefore ask the following: How can we deal with nuclear war from within the Jewish tradition? (Rabbi Douglas E. Krantz, Chair)

Teshuvah

The Responsa Committee warmly welcomes the spirit of the question and has attempted to frame an answer that will meet the needs of the Committee. However, let it be said at the beginning, we cannot treat this question as we would other *she'elot*.

The problem we face lies in the nature of the traditional *teshuvah*, which aims at answering a specific question with a straightforward (or occasionally a conditional) yes or no. When this cannot be done, the question is said to lack justifiability, that is to say, it is not meant for a responsum, though of course it may be meant for ethical and moral considerations. The resolutions on nuclear war which the CCAR has issued proceed from a sense of strong moral concern, chief of which is the deep-rooted Jewish perception of what constitutes *kiddush ha-chayim*, the sanctity of life.

Responsa, however, aim at a different level of consideration. They are halachic in nature and conclude that a certain matter does or does not satisfy the standards of Halachah, adding thereto the particular principles of the Reform movement. A responsum therefore resembles a judicial opinion which,

273

though it may not find that the law deals with the matter precisely, applies its language and intent to the case at hand and thereby arrives at a conclusion. This conclusion is usually not the only one that could be drawn, and in fact another court may vitiate it. Yet it must always be issued *from within the law*, which is to say, it must constitute a judicial and not a legislative act. If, after the exercise of judicial methods, the law cannot be seen as addressing itself to a certain question, judges will as a rule conclude that it cannot receive a judicial answer and, instead, would require a legislative response. Of course, whether or not there ought to be a legislative response is for the legislature to determine. Until that happens, the law, being silent on the specific issue, may be said to be neutral.

The problem with Jewish law is, to be sure, of a somewhat different nature. We lack a legislative body, for with the coming into existence of the Torah the basic law was proclaimed once and for all, and what followed could only be interpretation. The Halachah came to fill the void. In its scheme, laws are therefore either Torah or rabbinic laws (*de-oraita or de-rabbanan*), with the latter being quasi-legislative and, in the Tradition, fully compelling.

The Reform movement arose because this process of authoritative interpretation had lost its creativity and did not meet the needs of the modern age. In time the CCAR, through resolutions, platforms, and such publications as *Sha'arei Mitzvah* attempted to play a quasi-legislative role (although the term "legislative" was consciously avoided).

The Responsa Committee of the CCAR bridges these two poles. It begins with the dicta of Halachah and then asks whether there is any reason why Reform should disagree with them. That, in fact, is the nature of Reform Judaism itself: it begins with tradition and, if necessary, develops it further, according to its best insights.

There are some broad and contentious issues which can indeed be approached from the point of view of the Halachah and are therefore justiciable. Euthanasia and abortion are two of them; they can be dealt with from within the legal framework of Jewish tradition. But other questions cannot be treated in this fashion, at least not in their entirety. Thus, we derive from the totality of our tradition the moral imperative to alleviate the lot of the poor and disadvantaged, or to fight racism in all its forms. But that does not mean that a Responsa Committee can rule that our Jewish sources require us to support the California grape boycott or the principle of school busing. There is a fine but real distinction between the free-wheeling application of moral demands and the narrower exposition of halachic precedents. The former will best be met by resolutions and the like, the latter by responsa. The two approaches together weave the fabric of our movement.

To take an example closer to the *she'elah* at hand, the stockpiling of nuclear weapons represents to some a distinct and identifiable ecological hazard. Others, who approve of such stockpiling, will argue that it is necessary in order to deter another power from launching a nuclear attack. Both points of view are justifiable in the Halachah. One is the preservation of nature and its gifts, expressed in the principle of *bal tashchit* (Deut. 20:19-20); and the other is the need for self-defense, expressed in the principle of the "law of pursuit" (see below). It depends ultimately on a political judgment which of the two is to prevail in a given case. The Halachah can delineate only the underlying principles and precedents, and one hopes that Jewish decision makers will keep them in mind.[1]

We therefore proceed to outline some of the halachic considerations which deal with the issue of war in general and, specifically, with nuclear war.

1. The permissibility of war.

It is the responsibility of each individual to respect and guard the life of other human beings (based on the injunction *va-chay bahem*, Lev. 18:5), and the saving of a single life is reckoned as if it were the saving of the whole world.[2] Therefore, human beings have no inherent right to kill others, except by divine command, and God alone can give permission to go to war. This is derived from the interpretation of *Adonai 'ish milchamah*, which was understood as "God is the master of war" (see Rashi on Exod. 15:3), that is to say, God alone determines whether a war and the concomitant killing of human beings is permissible.

Jewish tradition distinguishes two types of war, an obligatory war (*milchemet mitzvah*, such as the defense of Eretz Yisrael), and a discretionary war (*milchemet reshut*, such as the enlargement of borders). The latter required God's permission, which was obtained through the Urim and Tumim, and later with the consent of the Sanhedrin. With these authorities no longer available, the gap between obligatory and discretionary wars has become larger, in that a discretionary war is hemmed in with greater restraints.

On the other hand, self-defense is a right given to all human beings. Tradition derived it from Exod. 22:1-2 and encapsulated it in the so-called "law of pursuit": *ha-ba' lehorgecha, hashkem le-horgo*, if someone is after your life you may prevent being killed by slaying the person first. Unfortunately, in the process of defending oneself others may be endangered. Rabbi J. David Bleich comments on this problem:

> War almost inevitably results in civilian casualties as well as the loss of combatants. Yet the taking of innocent lives certainly cannot be justified on the basis of the law of pursuit. The life of the pursuer is forfeit in order that the life of the intended victim be preserved. However, should it be impossible to eliminate the pursuer other than by also causing the death of an innocent bystander, the law of pursuit cannot be invoked even by the intended victim, much less so by a third party who himself is not personally endangered. Since the law of pursuit is designed to preserve the life of the innocent victim, it is only logical that it is forbidden to cause the death of a bystander in the process, since to do so would only entail the loss of another innocent life. In such situations the talmudic principle,[4] "How do you know that your blood is sweeter [lit. redder] than the blood of your fellow?" is fully applicable.[5]

The Halachah has developed various rules concerning the waging of war: regarding military service; the safeguarding of the environment; the treatment of the inhabitants of a beleaguered city; and restrictions on harming non-belligerents in general. These may be brought to bear on specific issues.

2. Nuclear War.

By its very nature nuclear war is indiscriminate and even unpredictable in the size and nature of the destruction it causes. While of course the Halachah has no comment on a weapon which is so new and revolutionary, it does treat of large-scale killing in war time.

Such discussion has focused on a rather obscure phrase in the Talmud. There, the Sages debate which words are to be considered "holy" (and therefore may not be erased from a text) and which are "profane." The name of Solomon fits the former category, with the exception of its occurrence in the Song of Songs 8:12 and, some say, also in 3:7. In order to prove the point, an opinion of the Amora Samuel is adduced who quotes the Song in support of an entirely different matter — and it is the latter which, in this round-about way, refers to large-scale war. Samuel is quoted as saying:

A government which [during warfare] kills one sixth of the population *be'alma* is not held culpable.[7]

A literal reading of this cryptic pronouncement would seem to suggest that killing of up to one sixth of the world's population might be permissible, but the meaning of the Aramaic text is not at all certain. Some believe that *be'alma* refers to the warring nation's own realm and indicates the number of soldiers that might be killed in combat;[8] while others hold that Samuel referred to a Jewish state and wanted to provide a limitation on conducting a *milchemet reshut*. The Hatam Sofer goes even farther and concludes that what Samuel was driving at was the very opposite, namely, that such extensive killing (or potential killing) was *prohibited altogether*—both in the national and the international context.[9]

This whole discussion reveals much about the traditional technique of finding support for a certain point of view: it desires to trace our natural concern over uncontrollable warfare to ancient sources and thereby give it added authority. While the way of achieving this end is tortuous and tenuous, it does arrive at a judgment: *indiscriminate warfare in a discretionary war is against Jewish tradition*. And even if one were to read the talmudic text literally, there is little assurance that in a nuclear confrontation "only" a sixth of the world's population would be annihilated.[10]

Questions of this sort would doubtless be raised in Israel, where halachic opinions were expressed regarding the Lebanese War of 1982, because it was seen as a discretionary war. In such a case, the prohibition of killing innocent bystanders is applicable, while in an obligatory war matters would be quite different. If the very survival of Israel were at stake, the latter category would, halachically speaking, give the government much greater freedom when waging war.

But the Justice and Peace Committee does not wish us to rule on Israel; rather we are asked to speak about Jewish obligations in the Diaspora. Here, it must be clear that the category of *milchemet mitzvah* does not apply, and that in consequence we are in the realm of greater restrictions. And even though the decision to wage war does not lie in Jewish hands alone, we who want to abide by the principles of our religion feel obligated to take a stand, either supporting or opposing a particular government policy.

However, it is the opinion of our Committee that such a stand best be taken not by way of a CCAR responsum but through Conference resolutions which, to be sure, ought to keep in mind the general principles adumbrated above.

We wish to emphasize that we do not thereby close the door to future inquiries. But it is desirable that they be specific and refer to an identifiable situation and not be couched in broad, general terms. This would also give our Committee the opportunity to assess whether there are particular Reform principles that should be taken into consideration.

Finally, it might be argued that this kind of investigation does not deal with real life, since persons who have their fingers on nuclear buttons are not likely to pay attention to halachic issues. Still, in a democracy these same persons act in a context of perceived popular approval or disapproval, and therefore a delineation of moral principles prior to nuclear crises may render decision makers hesitant to disregard ethical positions which are embraced by the majority. This is true for Israel as well as the Diaspora. Responsa can help to shape the attitudes of Jews and, through them, of the nation.

NOTES

1 Our emphasis on "Jewish decision makers" does not, of course, affect the responsibility of non-Jews to abide by moral injunctions. In halachic terms, this responsibility falls under the rubric of "Noachide laws" (see Rabbi J. David Bleich, "War and Non-Jews," in *Contemporary Halachic Problems*, vol. II, New York: Ktav/Yeshiva University Press, 1983, pp. 159-166). These considerations, and the attitude which Reform Judaism would bring to them, exceed the limits of our *teshuvah*.

2 M Sanhedrin 4:5. The commonly quoted passage reads *kol ha-mekayyem nefesh achat mi-benei adam*...(whoever saves a human life...), but another version has ...*nefesh achat mi-yisra'el*...(whoever saves the life of an Israelite...).

3 BT Sanhedrin 72a.

4 BT Sanhedrin 74a.

5 *Contemporary Halachic Problems*, vol. III (1989), pp. 5-6. R. Bleich argues that the principle is incumbent on all human beings; see footnote 1, *ibid.*, with sources.

6 BT Shevuot 35b.

7 The connection is made as follows: The Song of Songs (8:12), in a poetic vein and quite unrelated to warfare, mentions the figures 1,000 and 200. The former was seen, in typically allegorical fashion, to apply to ordinary people who live to observe the Torah, and the 200 to soldiers who are exposed to death and therefore likely to die. The total is 1,200, and the soldiers form one sixth of the number.

8 Rashi, commenting on the talmudic passage, understands it to refer to a labor levy (*angaria avodat ha-melech*, forced service to the king).

9 *Teshuvot*, OC, no. 208.

10 This point is made specifically by R. Bleich, op. cit. , vol. III, p.10.

Gun on Temple Property
5753.24

She'elah

Is it proper for our Temple superintendent, a non-Jew who lives on the synagogue premises, to keep a gun in his apartment? Though the temple already has an electronic security system in place, he wants the added protection of a gun for his own personal safety. Some members of our Board have expressed reservation about the matter of safety as well as about the symbolism of a gun on temple property. (Rabbi Jonathan Stein, Indianapolis, IN)

Teshuvah

A number of issues must be considered:

1. Self-defense. Both Torah and tradition deal with the principle at stake. The basic law is Exod. 22:1-2, which speaks of a thief engaged in housebreaking. It provides that if he does so *bamachteret*, literally, while tunneling [under the wall] and is surprised in the act, may be slain, and the owner incurs no guilt in doing so. By extension, this was applied to any attempted robbery perpetrated at night, but when it is done during daylight hours, killing the intruder is not permitted under ordinary circumstances and the owner is held responsible for manslaughter.

The Rabbis took these verses as the basis for extended legal considerations and said: When our life is threatened--and a nighttime robbery suggests that possibility--we may take action in self-defense, even if this requires that we shed blood. This was derived from Exodus 22:1.[1]

Thus they ask whether the killing stipulated in Exod. 22:1 may also be done on Shabbat, and the answer is affirmative, because a superior principle is at stake: break the Shabbat laws that ordinarily would prohibit the use of arms.

A general rule is then adduced: When someone threatens to kill you, you may prevent being killed by slaying the person before harm befalls you. This applies even if there is no certainty that the intruder means to kill you. For, coming at night and knowing that you will defend your property, the robber is likely armed and therefore must be considered dangerous. This applies on Shabbat as well, even though you are not really certain that the person is in fact armed. The rule is: If there is any reasonable doubt about your personal safety, defending it has priority over everything, even Shabbat. Self-defense by any appropriate means is therefore considered legitimate, and the locus of the defense (whether outside or inside the temple) is immaterial. (Your state's civil and criminal law will have additional parameters.)

2. Security. Is there any justified worry about security on the temple's premises or in the neighborhood? This is a question your Board will have to answer, and obviously the superintendent must be consulted about the reasons why he feels threatened.

Security has another aspect: is the superintendent properly trained to handle a gun, and is he thoroughly familiar with the laws that govern self-defense in your state? The Board must make sure to institute all reasonable precautions against misuse of the weapon.

3. Temple as a model. Board members are worried about the image of a gun located on Temple property at a time when there are already too many guns in the community.. Citizens are arming themselves, and the introduction of a weapon by an institution like yours may help to feed public hysteria. The Board of the Temple quite naturally would not wish to contribute to this already highly charged climate. Gun use is not merely a defensive enterprise, it is also a kind of communicable disease. The more guns the more shooting, and your members are right to be concerned about this. If it is generally known that the Temple too is infected with this anxiety virus, other members of the community may feel that they too must take similar precautions.

In sum, your leadership will have to make a reasoned assessment of the circumstances that cause the superintendent to request a gun in the first place. If the answer is that a potential danger exists and the superintendent's precaution is judged reasonable, Jewish tradition and sensibility will not oppose that conclusion.

NOTES

1 The Talmud went on to conclude that for the sake of saving life we may violate the prohibition of work on Shabbat; BT Yoma 85b and Sanhedrin 72a-b.

Confidentiality and Threatened Suicide
5750.3

She'elah

Counselor A. has a client (B.) and has been informed by the latter that she is bringing a malpractice suit against a certain physician. Meanwhile, A. has learned that a psychiatrist has diagnosed B. as a schizophrenic and borderline retarded person. Counselor A. believes that, were B.'s attorney to know of this diagnosis, he would drop the suit, which by its very nature would be damaging to the physician's reputation. Knowing this, may (or should) the counselor break the rule of confidentiality and tell the attorney of B.'s medical history? The matter is further complicated by B.'s threat that, were she to lose the law suit, she would commit suicide. Counselor A. has now come to me to ask me whether Judaism can give her some guidance in the matter. (Rabbi Elbert L. Sapinsley, Raleigh, NC)

Teshuvah

1. Confidentiality.

While today confidentiality is a hallmark of certain professions, especially clergy, physicians, counselors, and lawyers, the Halachah does not know of a special category of "professional ethics." In this regard, professionals are under the same obligations as any lay person.

Therefore, the laws prohibiting slander and talebearing or gossip (*leshon ha-ra* and *rechilut*) apply to all Jews, professional or otherwise. There are exceptions, however, when information that is vital to a third party may be divulged. Thus, every Jew is commanded to come forward with testimony that benefits another.[1] Failure to do so constitutes violation of the mitzvah *Lo ta'amod al dam re'echa*, "Do not stand idly by the blood of your neighbor."[2]

The latter commandment on occasion may come in conflict with the Hippocratic oath a physician has sworn, or with the accepted canon of a counselor's discipline (which, while not formally an oath, is nonetheless assumed by every client to be the basis of counseling). Does such an oath or canon of confidentiality override the obligation to testify to someone's benefit?

In Jewish law, an oath that obligates an individual to violate a mitzvah is generally invalid on its face. Since one is commanded to testify in court, an oath that forbids the swearer from revealing testimony which s/he is otherwise obligated to give would be a false oath, *shevu'at shav.*[3]

Counselor A.'s oath (or equivalent) has, of course, not obligated her specifically to keep confidential information from a court, rather, her discipline requires of her to keep it from *anyone*. This is analogous to the *shevu'at kolel*, an inclusive oath which, since it appertains to most persons may also be valid with regard to judges.[4] Thus, the counselor, because she is forbidden to reveal her information to the patient's relatives or friends or to anyone, would by extension also appear to be prohibited from revealing it to the court.

R. Eliezer Waldenberg tried to find a way out of this dilemma. He argued that a physician, when swearing the Hippocratic oath, never intended thereby to violate another commandment. Hence, says R. Waldenberg, the doctor may testify in court despite that oath, and in the face of any lingering doubts about it should apply to a *beit din* to be exempted in this instance from the generality of the oath.[5]

This consideration would certainly apply to a counselor who has assumed certain professional obligations without swearing a formal oath. The counselor, when taking upon herself such discipline, never intended to harm a third party. Any person is obligated to come forward with important information in order to avert the damage that a traumatic and expensive law suit would entail for an innocent party. A counselor is not relieved from this responsibility.

Counselor A., by asking the rabbi for guidance, reveals her sensitivity to both Jewish law and to the importance of confidentiality. Indeed, many persons would refrain from seeking medical, psychological, legal or religious counseling without the assurance that their conversations will not be revealed . If, nonetheless, a decision to violate confidentiality is made by a counselor it will have to be based on very sound reasons. Are these present in the case before us, so that we would advise Counselor A. to give preference to the mitzvah of *lo ta'amod* (and divulge the information she has) over the prohibitions of *rechilut* and *lashon ha-ra* (and say nothing)'?

In order to make a judgment, the following considerations would come into play:

a. Counselor A. has learned (we do not know how) that B. has been diagnosed by a psychiatrist as a schizophrenic and borderline retarded person, and she asks whether she may reveal this information to A.'s lawyer. Now, schizophrenia remains a somewhat imprecise term for a state of mind that is still not fully understood; and "borderline" retardation could be of various kinds and limit a person in one respect but not in another. Further, the fact that B. has been diagnosed in this fashion does not by and of itself say anything about the justification of her lawsuit. Malpractice may indeed have occurred, and Counselor A. should not place herself in a position where she would weaken her client's case *ab initio*. And even if the lawyer, learning of the information, were to abandon the case, B. would doubtlessly find another one. Would A. search out each lawyer and disclose her information? This is an unlikely and disagreeable scenario.

b. If a discovery process takes place,[6] it will in any case tend to uncover B.'s medical history, since such inquiries are made routinely in medical malpractice cases. Should we advise A. to breach her confidence in order to reveal something that legal procedure would reveal anyway?

c. We do not know what the law of confidentiality is in the state where A. practices. She has to respect the principle of *dina' de-malchuta dina*, the halachic requirement to observe civic law.[7] In addition, she may very well expose herself to a lawsuit for breach of confidentiality and unprofessional conduct.

d. The lawsuit against the doctor has already been launched and a certain degree of initial trauma has undoubtedly been suffered. The trial will bring out the facts, and if B.'s suit is malicious, that will be exposed in time. If it is not, then the Counselor's interference would be harmful to her client. The court now becomes the judge of the doctor's competence, and A. is not a in a good position to substitute her own judgment for the court's.

In view of these doubts and uncertainties we do not believe that in this case the prohibitions against *rechilut* and *leshon ha-ra'* should be overridden by the mitzvah of *lo' ta'amod*. Counselor A. should not come forward with the information she has.

2. The issue of threatened suicide.

Since we would advise A. not to interfere in the matter, might that conclusion possibly be different in view B.'s threat of committing suicide should her lawsuit fail? It is well to take a brief look at the halachic issues involved.[8]

R. David Zvi Hoffmann wrote a responsum concerning a student who was enrolled in business school. The young man's father ordered him to attend scheduled classes on Shabbat; the young man refused and a family crisis ensued. The student's mother warned him that, were he not to relent and obey his father, she would commit suicide.

Hoffmann ruled that our primary duty to save our or someone's life (*pikuach nefesh*) was not at issue, because the mother had no right to request her son to violate the mitzvah of Shabbat observance. If we were to decide otherwise, then anyone wishing to turn Jews away from Torah could threaten suicide if we did not accept his/her heresy.[9]

In the conflict between the duties to honor one's parents and to honor Shabbat, R. Hoffmann gave the latter priority, even though the mother might carry out her threat. He feared that ruling otherwise would set a dangerous precedent.

We cannot, of course, say whether R. Hoffmann would have ruled similarly in our case. The mitzvah of *Lo ta'amod* is not as clearly circumscribed as that of Shabbat observance. We will therefore not speculate on how he might have decided in this particular conflict of mitzvot.

However, in another case, also involving threat of suicide, R. Walter Jacob did reach a different conclusion.[10] At issue was the potentially fatal illness of a bride whose fiance was unaware of her condition. The bride, confiding the matter to the rabbi, stated that, if her condition were revealed to the groom, she would kill herself.

R. Jacob applied the mitzvah of *Lo ta'amod* to the safeguarding of the woman's life. He cited the Hafetz Hayyim in a similar case[11] and said:

In this specific instance the rabbi must weigh the danger of the woman committing suicide against the problem of not providing adequate information to the fiance. The quotation "Do not stand idly by the blood of your neighbor" weighs heavily on the side of the woman. If the rabbi is convinced that the threat of suicide is real he may *not* divulge the information.[12]

Thus, R. Jacob left it to the rabbi to decide whether the threat of suicide was sufficiently serious, in which case the information was not to be revealed. Applied to our case, we would draw the following conclusions:

a. If Counselor A. believes that B.'s threat of suicide is real, she should not disclose her information and threaten the success of her client's law suit. That would confirm the conclusion we reached on the basis of other considerations, enumerated above under (1).

b. But what if A. were convinced that B.'s threat of suicide was *not* serious? Basing ourselves on the considerations outlined above under (1) we would say No in this instance as well.

Conclusion.

While the Halachah would permit or even require disclosure of confidential information *under certain circumstances*, we do not believe that such circumstances exist in our case. Counselor A. should not break the confidence placed in her by her client.

We are advised that the lawsuit faces considerable delay. Meanwhile, the counselor might help her client abandon her suicidal threats and explore ways and means to settle her legal claims in a non-adversarial manner.

NOTES

1 Lev. 5:1; BT, Baba Kamma 56a; *Sh.A.*, CM 28:1.

2 Lev. 19:16; also understood as "do not profit from the blood of your neighbor. See also *Sifra*, Kedoshim 2:4.

3 BT Shevuot 29a; Rambam, *Yad* , Hilchot Shevu'ot 5:14-15.

4 *Netivot ha-Mishpat*, CM 28, n. i.

5 *Resp. Tzitz Eliezer*, v. 13, n.81, part 2; see also Jacob Breisch, *Chelkat Ya'akov* 3, n. 136. However, R. Baruch Rakover deems the Hippocratic oath to have priority (*No'am,* vol 2).

6 A legal procedure which takes place before the court hearing. It is designed to acquaint both parties with the general documentary and other evidence upon which they expect to rely. Discovery thereby saves court time later on.

7 This rule obtains in most cases, unless it requires Jews to transgress Jewish principles.

8 On the laws governing suicide, see Y.M. Tukzinsky, *Gesher Ha-hayyim,* 2nd ed. (Jerusalem 1961), vol. I, pp.169-273.

9 Resp. *Melammed Le-Ho'il,* part 1, no. 61.

10 *CARR,* no. 5.

11 *Sefer Hafetz Hayyim*, Hilchot Rechilut, no. 9.

12 Of course, R. Jacob decided a specific case and did not attempt to make a general rule.

Temple Board Member Accused of Cheating
5754.17

She'elah

A member of the congregation complains that a Trustee of the synagogue has cheated him in a professional manner and owes him a significant sum of money. The member contends that synagogue Board members should be reputable and representative of the best in our tradition, and he feels that this Trustee has shown a character flaw serious enough to warrant removal from the Board. He has asked the Board to take action. The synagogue Constitution, which governs the selection of Trustees, does not address the issue. If the facts are established beyond dispute, what course of action should be taken?

Teshuvah

We begin this responsum by stating our operating presumptions. We presume that any individual named to a position of leadership in a synagogue is of high moral character. We presume that an individual who already serves on a synagogue board has not thus far given the congregation any reason to suspect that he or she possesses serious character flaws or that he or she may even be guilty of criminal activity. And we presume that the serious allegations mentioned in this *she'elah* are just that: allegations, not yet proven. We will therefore respond to this question not with a general pronouncement on the fitness of communal officials, but with a very specific pronouncement on what to do if a currently serving board member is definitely found to have acted unethically in a matter not connected to his or her synagogue responsibilities.

We note, first of all, the absence of specific precedents. The structure of Jewish communal leadership has changed over the centuries, and in the premodern Jewish communities within which most halachic activity took place there was no position exactly equivalent to the modern synagogue board member. Historically, too, the ability of the Jewish community to police itself was severely hampered at times by both internal and external circumstances. Internally, real authority often rested with lay leadership rather than with rabbinic scholars, thereby rendering purely halachic considerations irrelevant; externally, the interference of Gentile governments often removed Jews from the jurisdiction of the Jewish community. Nevertheless, there are significant indirect precedents.

Halachic Precedents

Rabbinic literature discusses several types of communal officials, including the *parnas*, the *gabbai tzedakah*, and the *sheliach tzibur*. References to the *parnas*, the community's chief official, stress the importance of high moral conduct; virtually all these references, however, are aggadic in character.[1] Generally, comments about the *parnas* are silent on the individual's personal character and conduct, with the notable exception of *Yoma* 22b: "We appoint as *parnas* over the community only one who has a basket of crawling creatures hung at his back [i.e., who has some improper or unsavory aspect to his past], so that if he becomes too overbearing, we may say to him: look behind you." The implication here is that a *parnas* is not necessarily a person of blameless moral character.[2]

On the other hand, the *sheliach tzibur* (*shatz*) is supposed to be an individual of spotless character. "The *sheliach tzibur* should be worthy [*hagun*]. What is worthy? One who is free of sin and about whom an evil report has not circulated, even in his youth. He should be humble and pleasing to people; he should have a pleasant voice and should be accustomed to reading Torah, Prophets, and Writings."[3] The reason for emphasizing the worthiness of the *shatz*, of course, is that he is the community's representative in prayer.[4] As the *Mishnah Berurah* comments:[5] "Many books have discoursed at length about the shame caused by appointing an unworthy *shatz*, for thereby good fortune is denied to Israel." An unworthy *shatz* causes great harm because God does not respond well to the prayer of the unrighteous. Good character in a *shatz* is preferable to a good voice.[6]

For the third type of communal official, the *gabbai tzedakah*, good character is also essential.[7] On the other hand, he is understood to be subject to extraordinary temptation. For this reason, the halachah builds in numerous safeguards to remove every possible opportunity for dishonesty, as well as situations that could give rise to rumors of dishonesty in the community.[8] If less-than-upstanding individuals do hold this office, they must have obtained it through high-handed tactics, perhaps even bringing the power of the Gentile government to bear on Jewish communal affairs.[9]

While there is no mention of removal of a *parnas* for any reason, there is considerable discussion of removal of an unworthy *shatz* or a *gabbai tzedakah* suspected of financial malfeasance. The halachah is far more restrictive with respect to a *shatz*, though the penalties are mitigated somewhat by means of repentance.[10] If the *shatz* is already serving in that position, he cannot be removed for something he did before he was appointed; nonetheless, should there arise even a rumor that he has done something inappropriate since assuming the position, "even if it is the smallest thing, then even one person can protest and have him removed."[11] This opinion is expanded in the *Aruch Hashulchan*:[12]

> When we say we do not appoint someone who is the subject of an evil report, this means appointing him a priori. But if an evil report goes out concerning an incumbent *shatz*, we do not remove him, for one does not remove a person from his position on the strength of a mere rumor. But if the rumor is persistent, and we know that his enemies have not planted it...then we do remove him. Even a single individual may protest and have him removed, as long as we know that person's motivation is sincere.

However, if the *shatz* does repent of this transgression, he is not to be removed.[13]

The idea that repentance suffices to prevent a *shatz* from losing his position, even if he has committed deliberate and grave sins, is found in the *Aruch Hashulchan* in a comment upon the words of R. Moshe Isserles. It has the effect of nullifying virtually any dismissal of a *shatz*, except in cases of flagrant and unrepented wrongdoing:[14]

> It must be, therefore, that [Isserles] does not mean an accidental transgressor who sins only once; for even a deliberate sinner who sins only once and then repents may be appointed *shatz*, for if he repents then his bad reputation is immediately cancelled. His disqualification as a deliberate sinner is only if he sins a number of times. And if he transgresses a num-

ber of times accidentally, in this case he is still fit.

In the case of a *gabbai tzedakah* the issue is somewhat muddled. Clearly there is concern that a *gabbai* might violate the trust of his office; this is obviously the reason why he may be required to render an accounting. This is how the *Siftey Kohen* understands Isserles' gloss to Sh.A., YD 257:2. Isserles states: "And in any case, in order that they be 'clean before God and Israel,' it is desirable that they render an accounting. This applies to worthy *gabbaim,* but not to one who is unworthy, or who obtained his position through coercive means..." *Siftey Kohen* explains that "one who is unworthy" is "one who was appointed with consent of the community and is then accused of malfeasance serious enough to be examined by a judge."[15]

It is not explicitly stated what the consequences are if he is found to have acted improperly. Isserles states: "If the community wishes, they may dismiss the *gabbai* and replace him with another, and this does not cast suspicion upon [the one dismissed]. The same is true for other officials."[16] *Siftey Kohen* explains that individuals serve for set terms, and therefore if the community chooses someone else to fill the position at term's end this should not be taken as a slap at the former office holder. He is concerned, however, because Isserles seems to imply that "within the time of service the community cannot dismiss them because of suspicion of impropriety. And this is not explained as well as it should be in the words of Isserles."[17]

Siftey Kohen's difficulty is noted and incorporated by the *Aruch Hashulchan,* which ignores any possibility that a *gabbai* cannot be replaced mid-term for wrong-doing and cites *Siftey Kohen* in such a way as to take for granted that a *gabbai* can be removed if he has violated the trust of his office.[18]

The case at hand. In the present case, again, we are dealing with an incident *be-di'avad,* after the fact. We are not deciding whether an ethically dubious character should be appointed to a synagogue board, but whether, *if* an accusation against a person hitherto considered blameless is proven, that individual should be forced to resign.

First of all, a synagogue board member is not a *parnas.* He or she is not the administrative head of an autonomous or semi-autonomous corporate Jewish community, nor do we live in a time and place in which oligarchical rule and its abuses are accepted as norms. The absence of halachic strictures concerning the character of a *parnas* or his removal from office should not be taken as a sign that we should tolerate unethical conduct among today's communal leaders.

There is also no direct parallel between the position of synagogue trustee and the *sheliach tzibur*. The position of trustee involves responsibility for the welfare of the congregation, including a great degree of fiscal responsibility, but it certainly does not carry the same theological weight as that of *shatz*.

And there is no precise analogy to be drawn between the modern-day board member and the *gabbai tzedakah*. While the halachah concerning the latter speaks at length about financial probity, this always refers to communal funds, not personal business dealings. It does not call for the dismissal of a communal official for financial wrongdoing against a member of the community, though we may wish that it did.

Nevertheless, the lack of a specific precedent should not mean that there is nothing to be done in this situation. With regard to all three communal officials there is a basic assumption of righteous and ethical conduct. The *parnas* is not to govern in an oppressive fashion. A member of the community may protest against the *shatz* when the latter has committed some misdeed. And the *gabbai tzedakah* is subject to elaborate procedures and strictures to avoid even the appearance of financial wrongdoing in office.[19] The people must be able to trust in their institutions and the individuals who administer them. It is therefore imperative that, when a congregant has contested an individual's moral or ethical fitness to serve as a board member, the complaint be resolved speedily and fairly.

In our case, the congregant charges that the board member "has cheated him in a professional matter and owes him a significant sum of money." The language of the complaint is vague and is open to three interpretations: 1) the accused actually violated civil or criminal law in taking money that belonged to the accuser; 2) no law was broken but the accused acted in a manner that was morally culpable; 3) the accused and the accuser were involved in an unfortunate dispute where no law was broken and neither side's action was morally superior.

If the case is one of the third type, then there would certainly be no compelling reason to compel the trustee to step down, although the local rabbi might take steps to mediate the dispute or to encourage the parties to seek professional mediation.

We hasten to add this note: it is of vital importance that the rabbi and the congregation respect the rights of the board member as well as those of his accuser. The board member, whose reputation and good name are at stake, is as entitled to his "day in court" as is the congregant who is charging him with dishonesty. Mere accusation is not sufficient to disqualify a person from communal office. If it is found, after a careful and responsible investigation of the facts, that the board member has not committed the ethical infraction of which he is accused, he deserves public exoneration from the synagogue and a public apology from his accuser.

If, however, the case is of either the first or second type, then the Jewish legal and ethical tradition demands that prompt action be taken to safeguard the standards of moral conduct that our leaders ought to exemplify. As a first step, the rabbi and the congregational leadership through sensitive intervention might convince the board member to do teshuvah, to admit his wrong and to make restitution to his accuser. Should the board member respond favorably to this request, then he should remain on the board even if the accuser refuses to be mollified.[20]

The members of the Committee are divided as to the course of action to be pursued if the trustee refuses the opportunity to be persuaded to step down from the board voluntarily. We say "voluntarily" because as we have seen, tradition does not demand the removal of a communal official for misdeeds unrelated to his office.[21] Others hold that the moral gravity of the situation demands the immediate dismissal of the trustee.[22] We all agree, however, that misdeeds remain misdeeds, even if they are not impeachable offenses. The board member who has committed such a misdeed and who refuses to make restitution is unfit to hold communal office. Even if he remains in that position until the conclusion of his term, he should not be appointed to any position of leadership in the congregation once his term expires, and no congregational honors should be extended to him in the future unless he repents and makes restitution.

Modern political tradition, especially in the British Commonwealth, suggests yet another solution : When a cabinet minister faces a serious accusation of misbehavior, he/she steps down temporarily until the matter is cleared up. This is one of the rare instances where we can learn from political precedent.

NOTES

1 For example: "One who is engaged in the needs of the community is like one who engages in the study of Torah" (YT Berachot 5:1). "There are four who cannot be tolerated.. .and a *parnas* who lords it over the community without cause" (Pesachim 113b). "Who are those that terrorize the land of the living? R. Hisda said: This is the *parnas* who intimidates the community when not for the sake of Heaven. R. Yehudah said in the name of Rav: A *parnas* who intimidates the community when not for the sake of Heaven will never have a son who is a Torah scholar" (BT Rosh Hashanah 17a). "Our rabbis taught: There are three for whom the Holy One weeps every day...and for a *parnas* who lords it over the community" (BT Hagigah 5b).

2 However, Rashi *ad loc.* explains this as referring to some family blemish (*dofi ba-mishpacha*).

3 *Sh.A.* OC 53:4.

4 Jewish tradition has understood the *sheliach tzibur* (abbreviated as *shatz*) to be quite literally the "representative of the community" in prayer, who chants the prayers on behalf of the congregation, acting as their agent. This is expressed physically by having the *shatz* face the Ark, and not the congregation, during prayer. The role of the *shatz* was largely eliminated from Reform worship.

5 *Sh.A.* OC 53:5.

6 *Sh.A.* OC 53:5.

7 The *gabbai tzedakah* was the communal official responsible for collecting, counting, and distributing charitable funds. See *Yad*, Matanot Aniyim 9:1: those in charge of *tzedakah* must be "well known and trustworthy."

8 See, e.g., M. Shekalim 3:2; Shekalim 7a, 9a; *Sh.A.* YD 257:1, 2, 6.

9 See Isserles to YD 257:2: the *gabbai tzedakah* must render an accounting of his actions in office "if he obtained his position through coercive or violent means."

10 See *Mishnah Berurah* 53, nos. 14 and 16.

11 *Mishnah Berurah* 15 ad loc.

12 *Aruch Hashulchan* OC 53:7

13 *Mishnah Berurah* 53, no. 15.

14 *Aruch Hashulchan*, OC 53, par. 8.

15 *Shach*, YD 257, no. 3.

16 YD 257:2, citing the *Kol Bo.*

17 *Shach*, YD 257, no. 4.

18 *Aruch Hashulchan,* YD 257, par. 13.

19 The principle is *neki'im tih'yu me-Adonai ume-Yisrael*; Num. 32:22; M. Shekalim 3:2, YD 257:2.

20 It is axiomatic that, when those who have wronged us seek to repent and make amends, we accept their effort as we would have them accept ours. B. Yoma 87a-b; *Yad,* Teshuvah 2:9; YD 606:1.

21 The position of *shatz*, of course, is an exception to this rule: as the representative of the com-

munity before God, all aspects of the character of the *shatz* relate directly to his (and — today — her) fitness for office. This is not true of the *gabbai tzedakah*, whose position affords the closest analogy to that of synagogue trustee.

22 We should note that the by-laws of the congregation apply here. If the by-laws do not explicitly provide that a sitting board member may be dismissed before the conclusion of his or her term, such a course of action carries its own set of difficulties.

Disabled Persons
5752.5

She'elah

What are the obligations of the community, and specifically of congregations, toward physically and mentally disabled persons? (CCAR Committee on Justice and Peace)

Teshuvah

Jewish tradition speaks repeatedly of the role that elderly, deaf, blind, mentally and physically handicapped persons play in the ritual and ceremonial realm, but there is little discussion of the community's obligation toward such persons. What follows is a brief overview of the relevant attitudes found in the biblical and rabbinic sources, and the Reform perspectives we might bring to them.*

1. Blind Persons.

We are obligated to treat a blind person (*ivver*) with special consideration. For example, the Torah prohibits putting a stumbling block before the blind and warns, "Cursed be the one who causes the blind to wander out of the way."[1]

However, tradition saw the blind as lacking certain legal and ritual capacities,[2] and a talmudic passage contains different opinions about issues affecting the sightless. What is remarkable about it is that, at its end, a blind Torah scholar's reaction to the discussion becomes "the last word" on the matter.

> R. Joseph [who was blind] stated: Formerly I used to say: "If someone would tell me that the halachah is in accordance with R. Judah who declared that a blind person is exempt from the commandments, I would make a feast for our Rabbis, because though I am not obligated I still perform commandments."

But I have heard the statement of R. Hanina, who said that greater is the reward of those who are commanded to do [mitzvot] than of those who without being commanded [but merely do them of their own free will]. If someone would tell me that the halachah is [after all] not in accordance with R. Judah, I would make a feast for our Rabbis, because if I am enjoined to perform commandments the reward will be greater for me.[3]

In general, the halachah goes with R. Hanina and obligates the blind to observe all the commandments, though there were numerous discussions about it.[4] Thus, while the *Shulchan Aruch* rules that the blind may not say the blessing over the havdalah candles, other authorities permit them to recite all the benedictions for the ceremony.[5] Further, the blind are obligated to wear *tzitzit*, even though the wording of Numbers 15:39 would seem to demand eyesight for the fulfillment of this mitzvah.[6] We also learn that two blind rabbis recited the Pesach Haggadah for themselves as well as others.[7]

2. Deaf Persons.

The deaf person (*cheresh*) is dealt with in the Mishnah:

We have learnt: "Wherever the Sages speak of *cheresh*, [it means] one who can neither hear nor speak." This [would imply] that he who can speak but not hear, or hear but not speak is obligated [to do all mitzvot]. We have [thus] learnt what our Rabbis taught: One who can speak but not hear is termed *cheresh:* one who can hear but not speak is termed *illeim* [mute]; both are deemed sensible in all that relates to them.

This passage is contradictory in that it offers two definitions of the word *cheresh*, one who is a deaf-mute and one who is simply deaf.

Said Ravina, and according to others, Rava: [Our mishnah] is defective and should read thus: All are bound to appear [at the Temple] and to rejoice (Deuteronomy 16:14), except a *cheresh* that can speak but not hear, [or] hear but not speak, who is exempt from appearing [at the Temple]; but though he is exempt from appearing, he is obligated to rejoice. One, however, that can neither hear nor speak (as well as a *shoteh* [simpleton]) and a minor are exempt from rejoicing, since they are exempt from all the precepts stated in the Torah.[8]

In our day, R. Eliezer Waldenberg holds that anyone who can hear anything at all, including using a hearing aid and that anyone who can speak is considered *pikei'ach* (as if without disability) and therefore obligated regarding all mitzvot, except those that require hearing. They are married *d'oraita* (based on Torah law directly) and require biblically ordained divorce.[9] Under this very limited definition of *cheresh*, most people with hearing and speaking disabilities will be considered as having no handicap.

Similarly, R. David Bleich maintains that the ability to speak, no matter how acquired and even if the speech acquired is imperfect, is sufficient to establish full competence in all areas of halachah.[10] However, he notes that the status of a normal person who subsequently becomes a deaf-mute is the subject of controversy among halachic authorities. Some consider them to be like congenital deaf-mutes, while others hold that such persons are not to be regarded as legally incompetent.[11]

The development of schools for the deaf was one of the greatest factors in liberalizing halachic thinking regarding deaf and mute persons. R. Isaac Herzog, chief rabbi of Israel until 1959, ruled that, "those [rabbis] who remain in the ivory tower and say the schools [for the deaf] are not good enough do not realize the techniques that have been developed in the schools." He goes on to describe the techniques used in the schools and suggests that once they are known, one's point of view must change. You have got to do so and then remove all limitations that still exist surrounding the technically deaf-mute.[12]

3. Otherwise Physically Disabled Persons.

Little systematic consideration is found in rabbinic sources regarding their needs. Such handicapped persons are permitted to recite the Megillah while standing or sitting. We find a discussion about prostheses worn on Shabbat, and such exceptional circumstances as a woman's ability to perform *chalitzah* (the removal of a shoe from her brother-in-law who refuses to marry her)[13] when her hand was amputated. The Sages generally attempted to include handicapped or disfigured individuals in public ceremonies, except when their participation would cause people to gawk at them rather than concentrate on worship.[14]

4. Mentally Disabled Persons.

The word *shoteh* ("simpleton," "imbecile" or "idiot") has generally been taken to refer to a mentally disabled individual. However, close examination of the use of the word in the Mishnah and Talmud reveals that there are two basic kinds of *shotim*:

(1) the mentally ill and the retarded (little distinction is made between the two), and

(2) the morally deficient who do not act in accordance with the communal ethos, though having the intelligence to do so.

Tradition identified particular types of behavior as falling in category (1) of the definition: One that goes out alone at night, spends the night in a cemetery, tears his garments, or always loses things.[15] Clearly, these activities were meant to characterize the mentally ill rather than the retarded.

In our day, R. Moshe Feinstein differentiated between a *peti* (the mentally retarded whom the community must provide with an education once s/he has reached the understanding of a six-year-old) and the *shoteh*. He urged the welcoming of the *peti* to synagogue worship once s/he has reached majority (12 or 13 years of age) and would count such a person in a minyan. On the other hand, he would not include a *shoteh* who might be diagnosed as severely mentally ill and truly unaware of, or unable to relate to a worship service. Even so, such persons should be encouraged to join as much as possible in the life of the community, to the degree that they can do so without being disruptive to others or are themselves unhappy.[16]

5. Reform Perspectives.

We should be sensitive to the fact that disabled persons, particularly the deaf, have traditionally been regarded in light of what they can not do, rather than considering positively the unique capabilities they have. We should encourage the inclusion of all disabled persons in our congregations and, where indicated, encourage the formation of special support groups.

Our *she'elah* asks whether the community or congregation has an express "obligation" in this respect. The answer is yes with regard to the principle. We deal here with a mitzvah and include it under the obligations we have with regard to our fellow human beings (*mitzvot bein adam l'chaveiro*), and the important part such mitzvot play in Reform Jewish life and theology.[17]

Of course, their application must be considered in the context of the congregation's and rabbi's resources. We cannot obligate any rabbi or congregation to provide special services to all disabled persons who come within their purview, but the obligation to be of whatever service possible has the status of a mitzvah. Without stating what is or what is not possible in a particular community, the following opportunities may serve as examples:

When we include the disabled in our *minyanim*, we must attempt to include them fully and facilitate their participation in the spiritual life of the community. For instance, large-print and Braille prayer books and texts, hearing aids, sign-language interpreters, wheelchair access to all parts of the synagogue building and sanctuary, fall under the rubric of mitzvah and present the community with challenges and opportunities. New technologies will facilitate in-home electronic participation in services and classes. Sometimes, aesthetics and mitzvah may seem to clash: a ramp for wheel chair access to the pulpit may present a visual detraction, but it will also be inspiring for the congregation to know that its religious obligations toward the handicapped have been fulfilled. And obviously, where new buildings are constructed, the needs of the disabled must be taken into consideration in the planning. As Reform Jews, we should allow for a creative interpretation of the mitzvot that would help to incorporate disabled persons into the congregation in every respect.[18]

In addition to providing physical facilities, we must provide the handicapped with the education that they will need to participate fully, or as fully as they can, in the life of the congregation. Where necessary, several congregations in the city should combine their resources to make this possible.

The aim of inclusion of the disabled is their complete participation in Jewish life. Therefore, we would, for instance, permit a blind student to read the Torah portion from a Braille Bible, if not from the Torah scroll itself, though this would not constitute a halachically sanctioned reading, it may not be done from memory.[19] We see the mitzvah of including the disabled as overriding the traditional prohibition.

A deaf bar/bat mitzvah student, depending on his/her capacity, could read from the Torah, or write a speech and have someone else deliver it, or deliver it in sign language him/herself and have an interpreter speak it to the congregation.[20]

Mentally disabled persons could be encouraged to do as much as possible.

Many of these issues are not only similar to, but directly concern, elderly individuals. Indeed, hearing, visual, mental and physical disabilities often come as part of the aging process. Just as the Jewish community has gone out of its way to provide proper facilities for the aged, so should it make adequate resources available for the mentally and physically disabled of all ages. The fate of the tablets of the Decalogue describes our obligation: "The tablets and the broken fragments of the tablets were deposited in the Ark."[21] There was no separate ark for the broken tablets: they were kept together with the whole ones.

In sum, our worth as human beings is based not on what we can do but on the fact that we are created in God's image.[22] We should aim for the maximum inclusion of the disabled in the life of our communities.

NOTES

*See also, Carl Astor, *Who Makes People Different?* (New York: United Synagogue of America, 1985) for an even more in-depth analysis of this topic.

1 Leviticus 19:14 and Deuteronomy 27:18.

2 For example, BT Gittin 2:5, 22b prohibits a blind person from delivering a get (the religious divorce document). M Terumot 1:6 does not allow a blind person to separate *terumah* (a special donation to priests and sanctuary). M Megillah 3:6 and BT Megillah 24a teach that a person blind from birth may not recite the *Shema* and its blessings for the congregation since s/he would not have experienced the light mentioned in the morning prayer, but this is overruled by the Gemara.

3 BT Baba Kamma 86b.

4 Tosafot on BT Baba Kamma 87a. Others argue that even if the law does not require the blind to observe the commandments, their own desire to observe them becomes, in effect, an obligation to do so. See *Chiddushey HaRashba,* BT Baba Kamma 87a. However, Rambam disqualifies blind persons from serving as witnesses (*Yad,* Hilchot Edut, 9:12; *Sh. A.,* HM 35:12; *Resp. Tashbetz,* v.3, no. 6. See also R. Asher b. Yechiel, *Resp. Ha-Rosh* 4:21, R. Shelomo Luria, *Yam shel Shelomo,* Baba Kamma 8:20, Meiri to BT Baba Kamma 87a and Mishnah Berurah to *Sh. A.,* OC 53, 41.

5 The reason for denying them the privilege arises from the argument that, in order to say a blessing over light, one must be able to enjoy its benefits.

6 *Numbers Rabbah*, Sh'lach Lecha 17:5, BT Menachot 43a-b, and *Sh. A.*, OC 17:1.

7 R. Sheshet and the above-cited R. Joseph; BT Pesachim 116b.

8 BT Hagiga 2a; he cited passage is from *M*. Terumot 1:2.

9 Resp. *Tzitz Eliezer*, 15, no. 46, p. 120 ff.

10 "Survey of Recent Halachic Periodical Literature: Status of the Deaf-Mute in Jewish Law", *Tradition*, 16 (5): 79-84, Fall, 1977, p. 80.

11 Ibid. Note that Bach, *Sh. A.*, YD 1; Shach, *Sh. A.*, YD 1:22; and Divrei Chaim, II, EH, no. 72, take the former position, and Rambam and Bertinoro (in their commentaries on M Terumot 1:2) adopt the latter.

12 Jerome D. Schein and Lester J. Waldman, eds. *The Deaf Jew in the Modern World* (New York, 1986), p 17.

13 BT Shabbat 65b and Yevamot 105a. The latter tractate is devoted to this biblically ordained ceremony, which obtained when a married man died before he could sire a child. His brother was then obligated to marry the widow in order to "build up a name" for his deceased brother. In modern Israel, the brother is no longer permitted to marry his sister-in-law, but the ceremony of *chalitzah* is still necessary in order to release her so that she can marry again.

14 *See, e.g.*, the question of whether a priest whose hands are discolored may lift them in blessing the congregation; BT Megillah 24b.

15 BT Hagiga 3b-4a. The discussion revolves around the question whether any one of these acts is enough to characterize one as a *shoteh*. *Sh. A.*, YD 1:5, deems one of these actions sufficient.

16 "The Difference Between 'Shoteh' and 'Peti' and the Obligation of Keeping Commandments and Learning Torah in Relation to a 'Peti'," *Behavioral Sciences and Mental Health*, Paul Kahn, special issue editor (New York: Sepher Hermon Press, 1984), p.229.

17 *See Gates of Mitzvah*, Simeon J. Maslin, editor (New York: CCAR, 1979), pp. 97-115 for a discussion of the role of mitzvot in Reform Judaism

18 Rabbi Joseph Glaser recounts an example of such creativity: a deaf, and basically speechless, boy calligraphed his Torah portion, incorporating its theme (the burning bush) into the artwork (personal communication, 1991).

19 BT Gittin 60b, Rambam, Hilchot Tefillah 12:8, *Sh. A.*, OC 53:14 and YD 139:3, cited in J. David Bleich, *Contemporary Halachic Problems*, Volume II (New York, 1983), p. 30. Though the *Sh.A.* rules that a blind person may not be called to the Torah, since one is not permitted to read it from memory (OC 139:3), this ruling is challenged by a number of authorities who hold that the obligation of the one called up to read the Torah portion personally no longer applies (Maharil, quoted by Isserles ad loc.; Mordechai Yaffe, *Levush*, OC 141:3; Bayit Chadash to *Tur*, OC 141; Magen Avraham, OC 139, n. 4; *Turei Zahav*, OC 141, no. 3; *Mishnah Berurah*, OC 139, no. 12). The Conservative Movement issued a responsum in 1964 regarding a blind man's wish to read the Torah for the congregation on Shabbat using Braille. The responsum, signed by Ben Zion Bokser, then Chairman of the Committee on Jewish Law and Standards, states, "We would not regard it appropriate for a person to read the Torah from Braille. Such reading would have the same status as reading from the printed text of Humash, which is not regarded as valid." However, a blind man may bless the reading of the Torah when it is read on his behalf by a reader. The bar mitzvah may, according to some authorities, recite the haftarah from memory or from a Braille text, while others require that a sighted reader repeat the haftarah prior to the final blessings over the reading by the Bar mitzvah.

Mark Washofsky notes: "R. Binyamin Slonick, a student of R. Moshe Isserles in the 16th century, in *Resp. Mas'at Benyamin,* no. 62, addresses the question whether a blind person may be called to the Torah. In doing so, he remarks that he himself has become blind in his old age and that those such as R. Yosef Karo (*Beit Yosef,* OC 141) who prohibit this practice would 'expel me from God's portion, the Torah of Truth and eternal life.' His language testifies not only to his ultimate halachic conclusion that the blind are in fact permitted to be called to the Torah, but also to his fervent wish that the law not be otherwise. His is not an attitude of resignation, a passive readiness to accept whatever lot assigned to him by the Torah; he actively desires that halachah not exclude him from a ritual which has long been a source of much satisfaction to him." ("Some Notes on the Rights of the Disabled"; unpublished paper, 1991)

20 Such a student might be reminded of Moses' speech impediment, which did not hinder him from becoming Judaism's greatest leader. He or she might also want to read Les Gruber's article, "Moses: His Speech Impediment and Behavior Therapy," *Journal of Psychology and Judaism* 10:5-13 (Spring/Summer, 1986), pp. 5-13. He takes Moses' description of himself as *k'vad peh u-chevad lashon* (Exodus 4:10) to mean that he stuttered and that the Torah account accurately describes the sort of therapy stutterers use today to overcome their disability.

21 *Numbers Rabbah,* Bamidbar 4:20.

22 M Sanhedrin 4:5, BT Sanhedrin 37a.

Linkage Analysis
5752.6

She'elah

A new form of genetic testing—called linkage analysis—makes use of genetic markers near the gene of interest, to make predictions about the probability that the fetus has inherited a genetic disorder. This has been used for the prenatal prediction of a number of childhood disorders (such as cystic fibrosis, the muscular distrophies) and to predict such conditions as Huntington Disease and susceptibility to chronic diseases (cardiovascular, neuropsychiatric, cancerous) that may develop at a later stage of the individual's life. The following questions have been asked by the researcher:

1. Should such a testing procedure—which only provides probability of odds and does not establish definite diagnoses—be used for the prenatal detection of genetic diseases and possible abortion of fetuses found to have a high likelihood of having inherited the disorder?

2. Successful use of the technique often requires the genetic testing of other members of the family in order to determine what markers are present and how they are organized in the individual seeking information. Do other family members have an obligation to participate in this testing when, as a result, they may discover that they are a carrier or likely to develop a genetic disorder?

3. Should genetic testing be done for disorders that develop later in a person's life and for which there is currently no effective treatment or cure as in Huntington Disease or Alzheimer's Disease? (Rabbi Richard Rosenthal, Tacona, WA)

Teshuvah

New trends in scientific research about the components of the human genome and of their organization and function are laying the foundation for considerable scientific advances and, at the same time, engage our concern about their impact on social and individual ethics. The field of new medical

305

frontiers is constantly expanding, and whatever answers we may be able to provide will themselves raise additional questions.[1] We do not, in this *teshuvah,* aim at a comprehensive analysis of all the issues involved, but will rather attempt to set them into the framework of Jewish concerns.

Summary of Halachic Precedents.

We stand in the tradition of the Rambam (Moses Maimonides, 1135-1204) who set the model for combining Jewish insights with scientific and metaphysical inquiry. He stressed wonder and modesty as starting points of any inquiry:

> When we reflect on these [wondrous] things...and realize the divine wisdom manifested in them all, our love for God will increase, the soul, the very flesh will yearn to love God. We will be filled with fear and trembling as we become conscious of our own lowly condition.[2]

Basing himself on scriptural verses and talmudic precedents, he reaffirmed our obligation to apply the divine gift of human intelligence to explore nature and use its resources for the art of medicine, and that it was a mitzvah to heal and to be healed.[3]

Physicians are therefore expected to use their art to heal through the means provided to them by nature. Indeed, to refuse to heal was compared to shedding blood.[4] In this way the pursuit of modern science to widen the opportunities for healing are urged upon us as a mitzvah, and Liberal Judaism fully supports this traditional demand.[5]

Response to the Questions.

1. The acquisition of new medical insights therefore has solid support. Even though the result of testing provides us currently and perhaps inherently not with certainties but only with odds, we consider this an important and permissible inquiry. Knowledge is open-ended, and because human foresight will always be limited, certainties will elude us in any case in most areas of knowledge.

But, asks the questioner, how do we deal with the added probability that the odds will stimulate people's desire for children with a minimum of medical problems and therefore will choose abortion if there is any question?

Jewish tradition countenances abortion under certain conditions,[6] and Reform tradition has dealt with it on a number of occasions.[7] Thus, we have permitted abortion when results of aminocentesis for Tay-Sachs Disease suggested its desirability.[8]

Generally, we would support decisions on an individual basis. Some families thrive on crisis situations, others break down; one woman reacts differently from another. The possibility that the test results may lead to some abortions is not, in our view, reason to abstain from research in this area altogether. As its methods are refined and the odds for accurate predictions increase, the necessity for more and more difficult moral decisions will also increase. Indeed, the application of new knowledge will frequently present us with new problems.

2. Members of the family, like all members of the human family, have an obligation to save life. The Rambam phrased it succinctly:

A person who is able to save another and does not do so transgresses the commandment "Do not stand idly by the blood of your neighbor" (Lev. 19:16).[9]

But the saving of life is not at stake here. In linkage analysis the family would be asked to undergo testing so that the physician can more accurately analyze the genetic markers and so that, thereupon, one or several members of the family might make an informed decision about unborn children. This can hardly be classified as saving life; hence no one is obligated to participate in the testing.

We would consider it the physician's duty to inform all members of the family about the process and, if they do consent to participate, the doctor in turn would be obligated to make the results of the testing available to them if they wish it.[10] Thus, they may consent to be tested, yet not desire to know the outcome. They have a right to this refusal, for linkage analysis does not at this point provide them with opportunities for bettering their own health (in which case the answer could be different).

3. As long as there is no effective treatment for certain diseases, testing would provide information only, and little more. Some persons may wish to obtain it, but with resources already limited we doubt that it would be freely available under such circumstances. If, on the other hand, there are familial links to people who have been tested positively, the situation might change. In such cases the information might serve the mental well being of the patient seeking the information. Healing through information may in fact become a new frontier of the medical arts.

NOTES

1 See H. J.. Evans, "New Trends in Human Genetic Research--an Introduction and an Overview," *Experientia*, 42:10, p. 1069. Funding for the Human Genome Project has recently been curtailed in the United States, but it remains a formidable project. See Marc Lapp, "Genetics, Neuroscience and Biotechnology," *Hastings Center Review*, Nov./Dec. 1990, p.21.

2 *Yad*, Yesodei Ha-Torah 4:12; see also Maharil (R. Jacob b. Moses of Moelln), *Netivot Olam*, 14.

3 The biblical proof text is usually found in Exod. 21:19, where the double use of the word "heal" (*rappo yerappe*) is taken to mean "he shall surely heal" However, the Rambam preferred to rely instead on Deut. 22:2; see his commentary on M. Nedarim 4:4.

4 *Sh. A.*, YD 336:1, and see Turei Zahav.

5 We may note here the problem which medieval scholars faced when they were confronted with certain medical practices of Babylon which are recorded in the Talmud. Could such prescriptions be overridden in the light of newer medical insights? They managed to set aside the rules of the ancients by saying that they were no longer understood. See, for instance, the question whether bleeding is beneficial: BT, Shabbat 129a; *Yad*, Hilchot De'ot, 4:18; and also the Rambam's "Responsum on the Length of Life."

6 See Fred Rosner, *Modern Medicine and Jewish Ethics*, pp. 161-171.

7 See Walter Jacob, *Contemporary American Reform Responsa*, no. 16, pp. 23-27. We will not here rehearse these discussions. To be sure, our generally liberal attitude as to what constitutes "a threat to the mother's health" (which is the prerequisite for permission to abort) would favor the mother's right to make an informed choice, but this is not equivalent to endorsing the unlimited Pro-Choice position in the current political controversy.

8 R. Eliezer Waldenberg, *Tzitz Eliezer*, vol. 13, no. 102, also takes this position, but would not permit abortion when the presence of Down's Syndrome is discovered in the fetus.

9 *Yad*, Hilchot Rotze'ach 1:14. While the biblical verse was usually understood in this manner (so, for instance, does Rashi), there is some doubt as to its real meaning. The translation of the Jewish Publication Society suggests that the Hebrew probably means that we should not profit from our neighbor's misfortune.

10 See A. S. Avraham, *Nishmat Avraham*, YD 338, no. 3; also Prof. Shimeon Glueck in *Sefer Asya*, April 1987, pp. 8-11.

Medical Confidentiality, Malpractice, and Moral Responsibility
5753.2

She'elah

Some years ago, twenty-two patients at a hospital, all of them children, accidentally received transfusions with blood contaminated by the AIDS virus. When the hospital subsequently discovered the error, its administration withheld this fact from the patients and their families for four years. The hospital justified this action on the grounds that to release this information would cause widespread panic and would be "extremely dangerous." The patients who subsequently contracted AIDS sued the hospital for damages and compensation for medical expenses resulting from their infection. These suits have failed, due primarily to the courts' finding that the hospital "met the standards of the time" in its blood-testing procedures and was therefore not guilty of negligence.

From the standpoint of Jewish law and tradition, was the hospital justified in withholding from the patients the information concerning the HIV contamination of the blood supply? And does the hospital have a responsibility to provide treatment to the children who received the infected blood? (Rabbi E. Robert Kraus, Camarillo, CA)

Teshuvah

We will address these questions from the perspective of the Jewish law of medical malpractice and medical confidentiality. To what extent are physicians and the medical establishment as a whole liable to compensate patients injured as a result of their care? Is the physician or hospital required to inform a patient of his or her condition when in the considered opinion of the doctors such information would likely be harmful to the patient? We shall also consider these issues in the light of the halachah's higher aspirations. That is to say, should the technical law (*din*) absolve the hospital of responsibility in this matter, and is there a basis in the tradition to hold its administration liable to a more stringent standard of ethical conduct?

309

1. Medical Malpractice in Jewish Law. The practice of medicine is considered a mitzvah, a commanded act.[1] For this reason, the physician enjoys wide immunity from monetary liability for damages caused by errors of professional judgment. We find this idea in its classic form in the writings of R. Moshe ben Nachman (Ramban, 13th-cent. Spain),[2] who writes that the Talmudic law of the judge (*dayan*) provides a proper analogy to that of the physician (*rofei*). Like the physician, the judge is in the position of handing down instructions which, if incorrect, can result in depriving a person unfairly of property or life. Were one to be held liable for these damages, the person knowledgeable in the law would likely refuse to serve as a judge. Therefore, the halachah protects them from liability, so long as they perform this judicial function in a conscientious manner.[3] The halachah, argues Ramban, offers similar protection to physicians, so that they will not refrain from practicing medicine out of fear that they will be held liable for damages caused to a patient as a result of the treatment. As long as the physician performs the medical function in a conscientious manner (that is, "provided that all proper precautions are taken and no harm comes to the patient through negligence"), he or she cannot be sued in court for damages. While Ramban believes that the physician does bear a moral obligation to pay compensation for damages,[4] even this limited notion of the physician's responsibility does not go unchallenged. Some authorities hold that the moral obligation of which the Ramban speaks applies only to the surgeon who injures the patient with a knife, but not to the physician who causes damage by means of administering medications.[5] Others, meanwhile, exempt the physician altogether from even a moral obligation to pay damages, precisely on the grounds that medical practice is a mitzvah and that doctors should not be held liable for an unintentional error resulting from an act that they are commanded to perform.[6]

All this suggests that Jewish law takes an openly protective stance towards physicians, shielding them from legal liability and perhaps even from moral liability for medical error that leads to a patient's injury or death. This protection, of course, is not absolute. As Ramban emphasizes, physicians who commit out-and-out negligence (*peshi`a*), defined as conduct which a reasonable person (in this case, a trained professional) can be expected to know will lead to damage,[7] are indeed required to compensate their victims. In our case, however, the courts have found that the hospital "met the standards of the time" in its blood-testing procedures and observed all the safeguards then accepted in the medical community. In other words, no negligence was involved. We could conclude that despite the tragic consequences of the blood transfusions, the hospital bears no responsibility, legal or moral, to compensate the children or to provide them treatment should they develop the AIDS virus.

2. Medical Confidentiality. Did the hospital act improperly in withholding the information about the contaminated blood from the patients? Recall that this decision was defended on the grounds that release of the news would induce "panic," in the patients themselves and, presumably, in the wider community. To the extent that this fear was a reasonable one, the hospital can make a persuasive case under Jewish law in favor of its position. The predominant halachic view is that a patient in critical condition should not be informed of this fact.[8] The notion here is that a patient's optimism and hope are vital factors in his recovery and that to deprive the patient of this hope is therefore likely to hasten his or her death. Nor should the patient's relatives be informed of his condition if we fear that their sorrow will lead the patient to despair and to abandon the struggle for life. To the argument that one has "the right to know" of one's medical condition, the halachists who take this view would respond that the preservation of life, and not some abstract concept of rights and liberty, is the paramount concern of the physician. The medical team is therefore duty-bound to conceal from the patient any information which, in their professional judgment, would contribute to a deterioration in his or her condition. In our case, again, the hospital could claim that the "panic" that would result from revelation of the fact of the tainted blood would be injurious to the patients. Thus, from a Jewish legal standpoint, the hospital can make a strong case in defense of its actions.

3. The Higher Aspirations of Jewish Law. Despite all of this, it can be argued—and we think persuasively—that a higher standard of conduct was demanded of the hospital in this case. That argument rests upon upon what

we would term the higher aspirations of Jewish law, the deeper significance that lies behind the concrete details and precedents of halachic history and which binds them together in a framework of meaning and purpose.

Let us consider, first of all, the question of medical malpractice. We have seen that halachah offers a wide immunity to physicians from the requirement to compensate patients for damages. We have also seen that this immunity is justified, not out of special sympathy with the physician, but on the grounds that medicine is a mitzvah, the way in which we as a community fulfill the commandment of *pikuach nefesh*, the responsibility to preserve human life.[9] We exempt physicians from damages precisely in order to insure that this mitzvah will be performed. We exempt them because, if we held them liable, they would refrain from practicing medicine out of fear of financial ruin. We exempt them, in other words, *mipnei tikun olam*, out of concern for the betterment of public life and the welfare of all.[10] It is this concept, therefore, which expresses the higher aspirations of Jewish law as these relate to the practice of medicine. That is to say, the very definition of medicine, the structure of the medical profession and the rules concerning the relationship between physician and patient are determined by the demand that medicine serve the public interest, promote the general welfare, and achieve the goal of *tikun olam*. It is *tikun olam* which declares the higher aspirations of Jewish medical law, which provides the background and the justification for the varied rulings and precedents in halachic history. It is because of this principle that, as we have seen, the law on occasion assumes a lenient, "favorable" stance toward medical practitioners.[11]

But just as surely, there are times when this same principle demands from us a very different kind of response. The halachah, after all, does not exempt physicians from liability for damages caused either maliciously or through gross negligence, for to protect them in such cases would be to endanger society, not to better it; it would frustrate the goal of *tikun olam*. Indeed, whenever the physician acts in a way that is contrary to this principle, he or she ceases to practice "medicine" in the halachic understanding of that term. Similarly, whenever the medical profession acts in a way that undermines our conception of *tikun olam*, it forfeits our respect and our trust, and it no longer serves as our agent in the fulfillment of the mitzvah of *pikuach nefesh*.

Given this understanding of the higher aspirations of Jewish medical law, our evaluation of the hospital's actions in this case takes on a very different tone. Granted that the hospital did not act "negligently" in that it met "the standards of the time"; but did it act *properly*? Did it act according to its responsibility to contribute toward a better world? Was it an agent for the realization of *tikun olam*? Our answer is no. It is not enough that physicians and hospitals adhere to the letter of the law (the *din*) and thereby excuse themselves of monetary liability, for the medical profession must be held to standards that go beyond the norm. Even as a physician is not just another professional, the hospital is no ordinary business. The hospital is the place where human beings confront death and suffering, hope and mortality. It is a place where lives are saved, where the mitzvah of *pikuach nefesh* is performed; but as the tragic consequences of this case teach us yet again, our dealings with the hospital can be suffused with terrible pain and anguish. It is for this reason that the medical profession has come in the past several decades to realize what we Jews have always known: that doctors must heal the soul as well as the body. Hospitals today regularly employ chaplains and social workers, because they are aware of the vital spiritual dimension of their responsibility to care for their patients. The hospital must therefore conduct itself in all matters so as to retain the public's trust and the confidence, for once it loses these, it loses with them the ability to provide the necessary care for the emotional and spiritual side of illness.

In our case, we find that this hospital, by studiously ignoring for several years the effects of its actions upon these innocent children, abused its trust. Its conduct, though legally blameless, was at best morally insensitive, at worst repugnant. Its actions, though they may have met the "standards of the time" as recognized by law, seriously weakened the public's trust in the medical establishment and in its ability to perform faithfully the mitzvah of *pikuach nefesh*. The hospital, in short, did not live up to its obligation, as defined in Jewish tradition, to go beyond the minimum legal requirement, to contribute to *tikun olam*.

Let us now turn to the hospital's decision to conceal the fact of the tainted transfusions from the patients and their families. For the sake of argument, we shall grant that the hospital is being truthful when it defends this concealment on the grounds that it wished to avoid the spreading of panic. Still, despite the precedents cited above which appear to support a physician's decision to withhold "bad news" from a patient, the hospital's conduct in this case cannot be justified. We say this, again, because the higher aspirations of Jewish law require such a response. As we have seen, the halachic approach to medical confidentiality is based upon the paramount value of medical care: the welfare of the patient. The authorities who hold that physicians may conceal information concerning a patient's critical condition do so precisely because they believe that the communication of any news which will lead to depression, despair, and the consequent weakening of the patient's will to live is medically harmful. Such news, therefore, like unnecessary drugs or surgeries, should not be "administered" to the patient. It follows that, in cases where it is clearly to the advantage of the patient to know the truth of his situation, that truth ought to be revealed. Medical thought today, proceeding from our heightened understanding of the importance of the spiritual dimension of medical care, has come to see that it is generally to the advantage of the patient to be well informed of all aspects of his or her condition. A feeling of control over one's fate, a sense that one is able to make informed decisions about one's medical treatment, can be a powerful source of strength to a patient, a boost to morale and an antidote to depression.[12] The higher aspirations of the halachah, which would have us look beyond the specific rulings and precedents in order to comprehend the ultimate goals and purposes of Jewish law, would therefore lead us to conclude that, while each case must be judged on its individual merits, in general "honesty is the best policy."[13]

What about the merits of *our* case? For our part, we can see no defensible reason for withholding the news of the contaminated blood. Concealment cannot in any way have been beneficial to the patients. On the contrary: what was called for was immediate monitoring of their medical condition so that treatment, if necessary, could begin as quickly as possible. Nor was concealment helpful to the general public. In most cases, news such as this eventually leaks out. And then, not only might the "panic" the hospital feared actually ensue, but the public also loses respect for and confidence in those entrusted with its health and safety. The higher aspirations of Jewish law, in other words, forbid the hospital from hiding behind this or that halachic decision as a way of avoiding its responsibility.

4. Reform Considerations. Our own Reform tradition, with its emphasis upon social justice, would clearly demand that physicians and medical institutions be held to a high standard of ethical conduct, regardless of the narrow assessment of legal liability. And our stress upon the value of personal autonomy would certainly argue against the concealment from the patients of news concerning their condition, particularly in a case where such concealment offers no tangible benefits to them or to the community as a whole. Moreover, we consider it our special responsibility as Reform Jews who interpret Torah in order to apply its teachings to daily life to allow those teachings to speak to us in their best and noblest voice. In our understanding, the true message of Jewish law lies not in the precise holdings of this or that rabbi or in the consensus opinion of the current leading Orthodox scholars, but rather in the principles and insights which give meaning to the individual rulings and which serve as the moral and religious goal toward which all halachic decision ought to strive. Put differently, we do not believe that the halachah can exist separately and apart from its higher aspirations. In this case, those aspirations surely demand from us the answer we have reached.

5. Conclusion. The hospital was not justified in concealing the facts of this case from the patients, their families, or the public. Moreover, it bears a significant moral responsibility to offer treatment to these children, even if the courts have not found them liable for monetary damages. How this responsibility should be met is an issue to be worked out among the parties. It is only by meeting its responsibility that the hospital can live up to the standards demanded of it by the higher aspirations of Jewish law.

NOTES

1 *Tur* and *Sh.A,.* YD 336:1, drawing from Nachmanides (see below, n. 2), consider medicine a species of the commandment to save life (*pikuach nefesh;* Lev. 18:5 and BT Yoma 85b). Maimonides, on the other hand, learns the mitzvah of medical practice from Deut. 22:2, inasmuch as the commandment to restore a fellow's lost object is expanded to include the restoration (saving) of his life (BT Sanhedrin 73a; Rambam, *Commentary* to M. Nedarim 4:4).

2 Ramban, *Torat Ha'Adam,* Inyan Hasakanah (ed. Chavel, 41-42).

3 BT Sanhedrin 6b (and Rashi ad loc.), a midrash on II Chr. 19:6. The operative rule is *ein lo ladayan ela mah she`einav ro'ot,* "the judge can rule only on the basis of the evidence before him"; *i.e.,* so long as the judge's ruling corresponds to the facts and the law as he sees and understands them, he is absolved of blame should other evidence which he could not have been expected to know demand a different ruling.

4 Ramban cites *Tosefta* Baba Kama 6:6: the trained and licensed physician who causes damage to a patient is exempt under earthly law (*patur midinei adam*) but remains obligated under the law of heaven (*chayav bedinei shamayim*).

5 R. Shimeon b. Tzemach Duran (15th century North Africa), *Resp. Tashbetz,* v. 3, no. 82. Duran argues that injury caused with a metal implement is under Torah law a more obvious case of *chabalah* (physical damage) than is injury caused by medication. Given what we know about poisons and dangerous chemicals, however, this is a difficult distinction to maintain. See R. Eliezer Waldenberg, Resp. *Tzitz Eliezer,* v. 4, no. 13.

6 R. Nissim b. Gerondi, *Chidushim,* Sanhedrin 84b; Waldenberg, op. cit.

7 *De'iba`ei leh la'asokei ada`ata;* BT Baba Kama 21b, 52a, 52b and elsewhere.

8 Ramban, *Torat Ha'Adam,* ed. Chavel, 46; *Sh.A* YD 338:1; *Siftei Kohen,* YD 338, no. 1; *Bayit Chadash,* YD 338; R. Betzalel Stern, *Resp. Betzel Hachochmah,* v. 2, no. 55; R. Moshe Feinstein, *Moriah,* Elul 5744, 53; R. Immanuel Jakobovits, *Jewish Medical Ethics* (New York, 1959), 120-121; R. Shelomo Aviner, in *Asya* 3 (1983), 336-340; R. Yitzchak Zilberstein, in *Emek Halachah—Asya* (Jerusalem, 1986), 163.

9 See at note 1, above.

10 The phrase *mipnei tikun olam* is applied to doctors in *Tosefta,* Gitin 3:13; that passage, in turn, is cited by *Tashbetz,* note 5, above.

11 A similar case is that of doctors' fees. Although one should not be paid for performing a *mitzvah* (BT Bechorot 29a), the *halachah* permits physicians (like rabbis) to be compensated for their expenses and for the value of their time and training. To do otherwise would deter people from practicing medicine and thus frustrate the goal of *tikun olam.* See Ramban,

Torat Ha'adam (Chavel ed.), 44-45; *Tur* and *Sh.A* YD 336:2.

12 See the essay of and the literature cited by Dr. Shimeon Glick in *Asya* 42-43 (1987), 8-15.

13 Orthodox halachists, too, show signs of coming to this conclusion; see R. Yigal Shafran, *"Amirat ha'emet lacholeh `al matzavo,"* *Asya* 42-43 (1987), 15ff.

Endangered Species
5753.3

She'elah

I am a religious school teacher and have been asked by my fourth grade class about the protection of endangered species. What does Judaism say about this? (Paula J. Dugan, Saratoga Springs, NY)

Teshuvah

The question that your class has raised has no simple answer. However, you may wish to share with your students the following basic considerations:

While according to the Torah the human species is given mastery over the world (Genesis 1:28), that mastery has never been considered absolute. Cruelty to animals is prohibited several times, and fruit trees are protected from wanton destruction even during warfare (see Deuteronomy 20:19).*

Still, human beings may use God's creation in order to satisfy their legitimate needs. Thus, animals may be used for food, but the killing must be done humanely. And Judaism has never approved of hunting for sport.

Our post-biblical tradition elaborated the basic principle of respecting all creatures and in fact all creation. Waste was considered a contradiction of God's purpose, and a special term was created for it (*bal tashchit*, do not destroy or spoil).

It is quite clear from this that we are here confronted with two principles which may occasionally or even frequently confront each other. On the one hand Judaism strongly confirms the need for environmental concerns, but on the other it also confirms the need of human beings to lead normal lives (which includes making a livelihood).

Traditionally, Reform Judaism has leaned strongly toward enlarging our concerns for the environment, but at the same time we are also deeply aware of human needs in a complex society.

Some would say that many species of plants and animals have been extinguished by the forces of nature (like dinosaurs), and no doubt this process will continue. Are we forbidden to contribute to it?

We cannot answer the question categorically, and think it is important to let the class know that not all questions, however important or well phrased, have clear yes-or-no answers. Each case has to be decided individually and on its merits. As with many ethical questions, some form of accommodation might be found that satisfies both sides. For instance, a special refuge may be found for the Spotted Owl, if indeed the destruction of the trees in question is in itself environmentally permissible.

In sum, it will be important for your students to realize that deciding a case in favor of one side or the other does not mean ethical insensitivity. Two scholars, both deeply aware of the issues, might very well come to different conclusions. In Judaism, the search is very often part of our growth. Each case must be considered on its own merit.

* The teacher was referred to *The Torah - A Modern Commentary,* ed. W. G. Plaut (9th ed. 1994), pp.1478 and 1487; and to *Die Lehren des Judentums.* ed. S. Bernfeld and F. Bamberger (1928), Part II, Section IX, pp 417-423, for further references.

On the Redemption of Captives
5753.5

She'elah

What does Jewish tradition teach us concerning the ransom of captives? Specifically, both Maimonides (*Yad*, Matanot Aniyim 8:10) and the *Shulchan Aruch* (Yoreh De`ah 252:3) indicate that we must pay the ransom and negotiate with those who take hostages. What can we learn from these teachings that might help us shape an appropriate response to those who would kidnap Jews for any purpose? (Rabbi Douglas E. Krantz, Armonk, NY).

Teshuvah

Jewish tradition indeed speaks directly to this issue which is, regrettably, of more than theoretical interest to the Jewish community, whether in Israel or elsewhere.

The Talmud refers to the redemption of captives (*pidyon shevuyim*) as a high obligation, greater even than that of *tzedakah*.[1] Maimonides, in the passage cited above, expresses the Talmudic law as follows: "The redemption of captives takes precedence over supporting the poor...One who ignores the responsibility to redeem the captive violates the following negative commandments: 'do not harden your heart and do not shut your hand (from your brother in need)' (Deut. 15:7); 'do not stand idly by the blood of your neighbor' (Lev. 19:16); 'he (the master) shall not rule rigorously over him (the indentured servant)' (Lev. 25:33). One similarly annuls a number of positive commandments: 'you shall surely open your hand to him' (Deut. 15:8); 'your brother shall live with you' (Lev. 25:36); `you shall love your neighbor as yourself' (Lev. 19:18)... There is no mitzvah as great as the redemption of captives." The *Shulchan Aruch* notes: "each instant that one fails to redeem captives when it is possible to do so, it is as though one has shed blood."[2]

Yet despite its exalted status, this obligation is not without limits. The Mishnah[3] rules that we are not to redeem captives "for more than their

321

monetary value" (*yoter al kedey demeyhen*)[4] on account of "the welfare of society" (*mipney tikun ha'olam*). What could "welfare" mean in this context? The Talmud[5] offers two explanations: payment of exorbitant ransoms might bankrupt the community; alternately, the knowledge that the Jews will pay dearly to redeem their captives might tempt would-be kidnappers to seize more Jewish hostages.

There is a significant halachic difference between these two explanations. Should we conclude that ransoms are limited due to the crushing burden they impose upon community treasuries, then there would be no restriction imposed upon the amount that wealthy individuals may pay out of their own funds to redeem their relatives. On the other hand, should we adopt the second theory, concern that high ransom payments encourage further kidnappings, then even the wealthy would be prohibited from paying more than the limit set by the Mishnah.[6]

The Talmud does not resolve this issue, and the halachic authorities are in dispute. The Rambam declares that ransoms are limited in order to discourage future kidnappings.[7] R. Asher ben Yechiel,[8] by contrast, rules that a private individual may exceed the ransom limit in order to redeem himself, his wife,[9] or a Torah scholar.[10] Others expand the permit, allowing an individual to redeem any family member at any price.[11] Such lenient rulings would imply that the limitation was instituted to safeguard the public treasury. The *Shulchan Aruch* strikes a balance between these alternatives: it simultaneously accepts Rambam's explanation for the ransom limitation and R. Asher's exceptions to the rule.[12]

While some, if not all, of these authorities permit individuals to exceed the Mishnah's limitation upon ransom payments, none of them allows the community to do so. This distinction between the private and the public realms is eminently reasonable. The primary ethical responsibility of individuals, when confronting the captivity of loved ones, is to the captives themselves; that duty may be said to take precedence over their responsibilities toward society at large. Governments, meanwhile, may not set such priorities; they are charged with the protection of the entire community. As such, they are forbidden to yield to the extortionate sums demanded by the kidnappers, for to do so would encourage future attempts at hostage-taking and thereby expose the rest of their citizens to danger.

The government of Israel, in its dealings with hostage-takers, wrestles with the very dynamic described in the rabbinic sources. Though the question may not involve the "monetary value" of captives, it does go to the issue of price: at what point do the demands of the kidnappers become "unreasonable", so that the government, which is ultimately responsible for the security of the people as a whole, must refuse to give in to them? In return for prisoners of war or civilian hostages, captors will set an exorbitant price, often the release of hundreds of imprisoned terrorists or criminals for each liberated Israeli. To yield to this demand might well entice other potential kidnappers to seize captives in the future; the freed prisoners, in addition, would pose a serious security risk to the Israeli public. The government may regard this price as excessive and, faced with a choice between the lives and freedom of its captive citizens and the safety of its population as a whole, refuse to pay it. Difficult as this decision must be, it is well in keeping with the Jewish legal tradition which, in the name of *tikun ha-olam*, sets limits on what communities may pay to redeem their captives.

Still, a case can be made for the opposing view, that no demand is too excessive or unreasonable when the lives of the captives are at stake. Some authorities rule that the limits imposed upon ransom payments apply only when the captors are interested solely in money. When they threaten to kill their hostages, however, the commandment to save life (*pikuach nefesh*) takes precedence over all else. While others disagree,[14] this theory has been adopted by a leading contemporary halachist, R.Ovadyah Yosef,[15] who argues that in such instances the clear and present danger (*vadai sakanah*) to the lives of the hostages outweighs the potential danger (*safek sakanah*) to the rest of the population should the ransom be paid. On this basis R. Yosef concludes that Israel ought to pay the price, whatever it may be, that terrorists demand for the release of its captive citizens.

His opinion, however, is subject to a number of criticisms. First, it is by no means clear under Jewish law that individuals or societies are required (or even permitted) to subject themselves to *safek sakanah* in order to rescue those in *vadai sakanah*.[16]

Second, it is arguable that the danger posed to society by the payment of exorbitant ransoms, while not as direct as that to the hostages, is no less "certain."[17]

Third, R. Yosef bases his argument in part upon his claim that by giving in to terrorist demands we do not thereby invite further intimidation, since the terrorists are committed to a campaign of violence and murder against Israel and its people whether we give in to their demands or not. He may be right; still, much political and strategic thinking disputes him, holding that surrender to the demands of hostage-takers *does* encourage future acts of violence.

Fourth, R. Yosef does not consider the fact that Israel is a sovereign nation in a state of war with its neighbors. Since its enemies have shown themselves willing to pursue this war against its civilian population, it is not unreasonable for Israel to regard all its citizens as soldiers in the conflict. If soldiers are called upon to risk their lives in defense of the nation, Israel's civilian hostages may be said to share that duty. R. Yosef's ruling is, to be sure, a compassionate one; he would place the safe return of hostages in the first rank of Israeli security priorities. In so doing, however, he would tie the hands of Israel's civilian and military leaders who must somehow, in painful dilemmas such as these, strike an acceptable balance between the lives of the hostages and the welfare of an entire nation.

This balance, we think, can be established solely on a case-by-case basis. In any hostage situation, the government must determine whether and to what extent payment of the ransom demanded by the kidnappers would threaten the safety of the rest of the population. In some situations the government will decide that to pay the ransom is the lesser of two evils, that to obtain the freedom of its captives justifies whatever danger the public may face at some later date.[18] In others, it will conclude that the price is too high. In each case, the decision must reflect, on the strength of careful consultation with military, diplomatic, and political experts, the best available judgement as to the likely results of either course of action.[19]

This is no guarantee that mistakes will not be made; experts, like the rest of us, can be wrong. It is, however, the surest means by which the government of Israel (and indeed, any government or communal authority) can hope to discharge its ethical responsibilities to its people against the backdrop of one of the harshest realities of our time.

NOTES

1 BT Baba Batra 8a-b.

2 YD 252:3. The source is *Resp. R. Yosef Kolon* (Maharik, 15th-cent. Italy), no. 7.

3 Gitin 4:6.

4 How to determine the "monetary value" of captives is a subject of some dispute. Some (*Chidushey ha-Ritba*, Gitin 45a) set the amount according to the price the individual would fetch on the slave market (or the estimated price, should slavery no longer be in practice; *Resp. Maharam Lublin*, no. 15). Others (*Resp. R. David ibn Zimra Ha-Chadashot*, no. 40) measure the ransom price against that which is normally paid to kidnappers. Still others (R. Menachem Ha-Meiri, *Beit Ha-Bechirah*, Ketubot 52b) set the price according to the captive's social status.

5 BT Gitin 45a.

6 Rashi, Gitin 45a, s.v. *o' dilma*.

7 *Yad*, Matanot Aniyim 8:12. Alfasi, Ketubot 52b (fol. 19a), rules that a husband may not redeem his captive wife "for more than her monetary value." This suggests that Alfasi, too, accepts the reasoning that the limits are set in order to discourage future kidnappings and that even a private individual may not exceed those restrictions; see Rabbeinu Nissim *ad loc.*, as well as *Chiddushey Ha-Rashba*, Gitin 45a. This position is adopted as well by the Gaon of Vilna (*Bi'ur Ha-Gra*, YD 252, no. 6).

8 Gitin 4:44, following Tosafot, Gitin 45a, s.v. dela. See also R. Asher to Ketubot 5:22, in the name of R. Meir Halevy Abulafia.

9 See BT Ketubot 52a-b.

10 See BT Gitin 58a, where R. Yehoshua pays a high price to redeem a child from captivity, because he realizes that the child is learned and will one day become a great halachic sage. "How much the more so," says R. Asher, "does this apply to one who is already a *talmid chacham*."

11 See R. Yoel Sirkes, *Bayit Chadash* to *Tur*, YD 252, who notes that such is common practice "to which no one objects", and R. Shabtai Cohen, *Siftey Kohen*, YD 252, no. 4.

12 YD 252:4. In Even Ha`Ezer 78:2, we read: "the husband *is not obligated* to redeem his wife at a price greater than her monetary value...". This suggests that he *may* do so if he wishes.

13 A similar order of priorities is established with regard to the giving of *tzedakah*. See BT Baba Metsi`a 71a (on Ex. 22:24); *Yad*, Matanot Aniyim 7:13; *SA*, YD 251:3.

14 See the responsa cited in *Pitchey Teshuvah*, YD 252, no. 4.

15 In *Torah She-be`al Peh* 19 (1977), 9-39.

16 See, in general, *Journal of Reform Judaism* 36 (Winter, 1989), 53-65, and the sources cited there. R. Yosef may have the better argument on this point, yet given the long-standing dispute over the issue, it is a shaky halachic foundation upon which to advocate that Israel cave in to extortionate ransom demands.

17 R. Ezekiel Katzenellenbogen, *Resp. Kenesset Yechezkel*, no. 38.

18 And, contrary to popular impression, Israel has never adhered to a "no negotiations—ever" policy with respect to hostages. Its recent willingness to deal for the release of Western captives in Beirut

and (thus far unsuccessfully) for its pilot Ron Arad, held by the Hezbollah in Lebanon, are cases in point.

19 This is essentially the position taken by a number of contemporary authorities. See R. Shaul Yisraeli in *Torah She-be`al Peh* 17 (1975), 69-76, R. Yehudah Gershuni in *Ha-Darom* (1971), 27-37, and our colleague R. Moshe Zemer in *Ha'Aretz,* December 13, 1983.

Beneficial Options
5753.21

She'elah

Beneficial Options is a company which finds investors willing to buy the life insurance policies of AIDS patients who are not expected to live more than twenty-four months. The patient gets cash with which to pay medical and living expenses (most life insurance policies do not pay out during the life time of the insured). The investor, who becomes the beneficiary of the policy, receives the death benefit upon the death of the insured. The company receives a fee for its management services.

From the standpoint of Jewish tradition is there something unethical about this business arrangement?

Teshuvah

Beneficial Options is a company which essentially profits from a matching service. They enable AIDS patients - who are clearly *in extremis* - to sell the rights to a precious contract in order to provide some immediate monetary assistance or relief at a most difficult time. A close analog in Jewish law to this situation arises with the sale of a *ketubah*.

In the Shulchan Aruch[1] it is stated that a woman may sell the benefits of her *ketubah* - either wholly or in part - to others, and that the recipients of the *ketubah* benefits receive payment from its monetary provisions if she is widowed or divorced. Of course, if she dies while the husband is still alive, they would receive nothing. The *ketubah* acts as a promissory note which the wife (creditor) holds against the husband (debtor) and his estate. Like other such notes, the *ketubah* may be used in a variety of business transactions. The wife may sell it in order to raise cash. She obviously cannot sell it for much, since the buyer would collect the money only if the wife survives her husband or is divorced. Should the husband survive the wife, the buyer would get nothing. Plainly, the potential investor would only pay a "minimal amount"[2] for such a risky proposition.

In the present case, the investor can certainly expect better returns since the AIDS patient is terminal. The buyer will indeed collect on the policy; hence, he/she will be prepared to pay a greater sum for it. The company believes this to be a better deal for the patient as well, since he/she will collect a significant amount of desperately-needed cash which, without this buyer, would be unavailable.

Of interest to our question is the fact that the traditional literature condemns neither the wife nor the buyer of her *ketubah* for committing an unethical act. To be sure, it recognizes that the wife would sell the *ketubah* only under severe financial duress.[3] Yet this does not invalidate the transaction. In discussing the theory behind the law of sale, the Talmud notes that "nobody would sell anything were they not under some degree of compulsion; still the sale is valid." Thus, as the *Gemara* explicitly states, "if they hang him (from a tree) until he sells, his sale is a sale".[4] The point is that a financial decision made under duress is not necessarily irrational; indeed it may be the best option available under a very difficult set of circumstances.

In the contemporary AIDS circumstances, no human agency is doing the "hanging." The patient has a terminal disease; he/she needs money, and this device allows him/her to raise cash at no cost to him/herself. This is a rational plan. It is also quite arguably ethical: by enabling a person to purchase medical care, that individual may well be purchasing an extension of life. As a result, it might cogently be maintained that there is an element of *piku'ach nefesh* (saving a life) here which cannot be ignored. Hence, we ought not to condemn the Beneficial Options proposal lightly.

On the other hand, it is inaccurate to say that "nobody gets hurt" under this proposal. The patient has beneficiaries, loved ones who stand to collect the death benefits of his/her policy. The point of life insurance, after all, is to purchase protection for those who are dependent upon the insured financially. If Beneficial Options advocates the sale of the entire face value of the policy, the beneficiaries of the AIDS patient will be denied this protection.

Here too, the *ketubah* analogy is helpful. *Halachah* prescribes that the wife who sells her *ketubah* does not lose the benefits which customarily accrue to her as a result of marriage. In addition to the food, raiment and conjugal rights provisions detailed in the Torah,[5] she continues to receive most of the benefits of the *ketubah* that were ordained by the rabbis.[6] These include the requirement that the husband ransom his wife should she be taken captive and provide her medical expenses should she fall ill. They also include the provision that the wife's sons from this marriage (*i.e.,* excluding her husband's sons from other marriages) will inherit the sum of the *ketubah*, as well as the rule that her daughters from this marriage will be supported from their father's estate until they themselves are married. In other words, neither the wife nor her "beneficiaries" lose the essential protections afforded by the *ketubah* in the event that she decides to sell it.

Similarly, we might say that the proposal of Beneficial Options is both legal and ethical in the eyes of Jewish tradition, provided that the beneficiaries of the insured are not stripped of necessary protections by the sale of the policy. In many cases the heirs will need money to pay medical bills, and in some instances to provide for their own minimum care. In actuality, it is, of course, extremely difficult to achieve an appropriate balance between the needs of the patient and those of the beneficiaries. If the beneficiaries were so inclined, they could, presumably, waive their rights on behalf of the buyer, but if the beneficiaries are minors this would obviously be inappropriate. In practice, therefore, it would usually mean that the beneficiaries would have to be guaranteed at least some of the death benefit, and this, in turn, would make the deal less attractive to potential investors. Nevertheless, if the Beneficial Options proposal is to be regarded as ethical, it must include some formula which acts to encourage the safeguarding of the financial needs of any beneficiaries.

Of course, the Beneficial Options proposal must also be seen to operate ethically in practice. For clearly there are two potential sources of duress operating in a given sale: a) the duress brought about by the illness, which makes the sale conceivable in the first place, and b) the duress brought about by an enthusiastic salesperson who may be over-eager to conclude a transaction. Naturally, the patient must be protected against any pressure tactics, so that a reasoned, rational decision can be made on the merits of the proposal.

Based on the principle that we "do not place a stumbling-block before the blind,"[7] Jewish law advocates a position prohibiting the salesperson from providing ill-suited advice - particularly to a vulnerable individual - in order to make a sale.[8] Moreover, in these circumstances, we would surely expect the salesperson to act "*lifnim mishurat hadin,*" "beyond the strict letter of the law" in ensuring that proper advice and a reasonable period for thoughtful consideration was provided. A brief mandatory waiting-period may well be desirable between the initial proposal and the conclusion of the transaction, in order that family-members and advisers might be consulted. Further, just as for the *ketubah*, it should be expected that the transaction will be appropriately witnessed as being the "voluntary", free act of the patient who decides to sell part of the value of his/her policy.

Provided then that the legitimate interests of the beneficiaries are protected, and that the terminally ill individual is not pressured to make a poorly-advised decision, such a business arrangement would be considered ethical from a Jewish standpoint.

NOTES

1 Even Ha-Ezer 105:1.
2 Rashi, Baba Kama, 89a.
3 Ketubot 53a.
4 Baba Metziah 47b; see Hoshen Mishpat 205:1 for the limitations to this rule.
5 Exodus 21:10.
6 See Mishnah Ketubot 4:7-12.
7 Leviticus 25:17.
8 *Yad*, Rotzeach, 12:14.

Responsum on Smoking[1]
5753.23

She'elah

In view of the fact that it has been proven that tobacco smoking is extremely dangerous to human health, what should be the policies of the synagogue regarding smoking on its premises, including the offices? Should synagogues and rabbis take any action with regard to smoking of its members and others in the community off premises?

Teshuvah

Until a few years ago, the hazardous nature of smoking was not on the public or Jewish agenda. On the contrary, there were rabbis who thought that smoking was beneficial because of its curative properties. This was the claim of the famed Rabbi Jacob Emden (1697-1776): "Tobacco is a healthful substance for the body ... its natural action is important in helping to digest food, cleanse the mouth, separate the humours, and help the movement of essential functions and blood circulation which are the root of health ... It is indeed beneficial to every healthy man, not only because of the pleasure and enjoyment it affords, but because it preserves one's health and medical fitness."[2]

Eventually, the position of halachic decisions on smoking changed. At the turn of this century, their opposition was not a matter of health, but of propriety. Rabbi David Hoffmann (1843-1921), head of the Hildesheimer Rabbinic Seminary in Berlin, stated in response to a query : "It is known that the Gentiles are very punctilious and forbid smoking in their houses of worship, and therefore, it might appear, God forbid, as a desecration of the Divine Name if we should permit it", and therefore forbade it for synagogues.[3]

As a result of more recent medical revelations on the health dangers of smoking, most rabbis came to the conclusion that not only is it without beneficial qualities, but on the contrary, the tobacco habit may be dangerous and even fatal. They dealt with two major issues : the danger to the non-smoker

331

(in medical parlance: passive smoking) and the danger to the smoker himself/herself.

Danger to the Non-Smoker

A prominent halachic authority, R. Moshe Feinstein of New York, forbade the widespread practice of smoking in rabbinical academies (*yeshivot*). He ignored studies claiming that the deleterious effect of smoking had not been conclusively proved and ruled it should be prohibited even if it were not injurious to the health of others studying in the same room, but only disturbed them. He rejected the argument that cigarette smoking helped students to concentrate. On the contrary, he considered leaving for a puff a waste of time that could be spent in the study of Torah (*bitul talmud torah*). He also criticized the claim that since the room was already full of smoke, each smoker was adding only an insignificant amount. R. Feinstein retorted that each smoker was responsible for his portion of all of the smoke in the room and therefore for the discomfort of all those present who suffer from his habit.[4]

R. Eliezer Waldenberg of the Israel Chief Rabbinate Council went a step further, forbidding a host to smoke in his own home, if this habit bothers or harms his guests or members of the family, and especially children who might be present.[5]

Danger to the Smoker

Rabbinic respondents have been divided on the question of whether available medical evidence is sufficient to ban smoking as dangerous in the view of Jewish religious law.

R. Feinstein would concede only that, since "we may be wary of the danger of becoming ill from smoking, it would be better to be cautious."

However, in his view, it is impossible to forbid smoking for two reasons :

1. Tobacco is in very wide use and has become an entrenched popular practice. The Talmud states about such a habit : "Since the multitude are accustomed to it, 'the Lord will protect the foolish.'"[6]
2. "We must especially note that some of the great Torah scholars in past generations were smokers and still are in our day."

The only thing that may be done is to advise against acquiring the habit and especially against allowing one's children to learn to smoke. Nevertheless, in his opinion, the Torah does not rule out offering a light or matches to a smoker.[7]

The sephardic chief rabbi of Tel Aviv, R. Haim David Halevi, disagreed with this ruling. A youngster asked him whether he must obey his father who sent him out to buy a pack of cigarettes. R. Halevi responded : "In view of the fact that physicians have universally warned against the great danger of smoking to human health, and since, in my opinion, it is forbidden by the Torah which commands : "You shall carefully preserve your lives" (Deuteronomy 4:15), you are not permitted to buy him cigarettes. Furthermore, whenever you see him with a cigarette in his mouth, say to him, 'Father, see what we are warned in the Torah about preserving life and we know that smoking is very harmful' - in the hope that he will understand, overcome and refrain."[8]

As a foremost expert on medicine in Jewish law, R. Eliezer Waldenberg accepts the findings of medical experts and proclaims that "smoking is the number one killer of humanity!" Disagreeing with R. Feinstein's position, he declares "that there is no reason to congratulate oneself ... and to rule that since smoking is widespread there is no reason to prohibit it." R. Waldenberg points to medical findings that "cigarette smoking is the main cause of death from cancer ... therefore it is certainly absurd to turn a blind eye on all this and to blithely conclude that (in a case like this) 'The Lord will protect the foolish.'"[9]

The reality is that scientific evidence has conclusively proven that smoking is dangerous and even fatal. The United States Surgeon General has issued a 300 to 500 page volume every year on the dangers of smoking.[10] There can no longer be any reasonable doubt about it.

Many smokers today see their habit as a strictly private matter, asserting that no one has a right to interfere or tell them to stop. Many modern rabbinic respondents reply by quoting Maimonides: "The Sages forbade many things which involve mortal danger, and anyone who did so saying : 'Look, I am endangering myself and what does it matter to others' or 'I don't care', is beaten by the rabbinic court."[11] For according to the Halachah, we have stewardship rather than ownership of the body given to us by our Creator, and therefore may not jeopardize our life.

To whom, then, does one's body and life belong? R. Moses Ribkes (17th century) taught : "The reason the Torah warned us about preservation of life is that God graciously created the world to benefit His creatures so that they may be aware of His greatness and may work in His service by observing His mitzvot.[12]

What are the operative conclusions of these rabbinic verdicts for the smoking Jew of our day? There is almost universal agreement that this habit involves *pikuah nefesh*. A consensus of halachic opinion may be summarized as follows :

(a) Smoking near anyone who may be disturbed or harmed by smoke is prohibited.

(b) It is forbidden to harm oneself by smoking. (If a smoker cannot stop immediately, then he must make every effort to reduce the number of cigarettes smoked per day and to receive help to be cured of the habit.)

(c) Children and adolescents are forbidden to begin or to become accustomed to smoking. Adults may not help or encourage them to acquire the habit.

(d) Encouraging smokers in their habit, by offering a cigarette or a light, is prohibited.

(e) Synagogues and rabbis should be involved in a serious educational campaign to convince congregants and members of the community. They should help to set up smoking cure groups.

(f) Synagogues and rabbinic organizations should counteract the smoking advertisements sponsored by the tobacco industry (especially with their minuscule notice of the danger to health.) More people die of smoking than of gun-shot wounds or AIDS, yet the public awareness is weaker than it ought to be.

The above sources indicate that the Halachah can and must be a developmental and dynamic phenomenon which has taken cognizance of the discoveries of medical science. Jewish law in its position on smoking has progressed from the 18th century rabbinic view that "tobacco is healthful for the body" to the present day opinion : "Smoking is the number one killer of mankind." The Reform movement welcomes this halachic progression.

NOTES

1 Written by R. Moshe Zemer, a member of our Responsa Committee. It was previously published in Israel (in Hebrew) and was not part of our process, but has been included because of its importance.

2 *Mor u-ketzi'ah*, O.H. section 511.

3 *Responsa Melamed Leho'il* O.H. no. 15.

4 *Responsa Igrot Mosheh*, H.M. pt. 2, no. 18.

5 *Responsa Tzitz Eliezer* vo. 15, no. 39.

6 BT Shabbat 129b; Psalms 116, 6.

7 *Responsa Igrot Mosheh*, YD, pt. 2, no. 49.

8 *Responsa Aseh Lecha Rav* v.6, no. 59.

9 *Op. cit.*

10 These have included, among others, volumes on *Smoking and Health*, 1964; *The Health Consequences of Smoking*, 1972; *Smoking and Cancer*, 1982; *Smoking and Cardiovascular Diseases*, 1983.

11 *Yad,* Hilchot Rotzeach 11:5.

12 *Be'er Golah* H.M. 427, letter 90.

On the Treatment of the Terminally Ill
5754.14

She'elah

A Jewish couple is providing care to two relatives with end-stage neurological disease.

Naomi, the couple's 16-month-old daughter, has Canavan's Disease, a rare progressive brain disease similar to Tay-Sachs, though the potential exists for the child to survive into teenage. She recognizes her family, smiles and laughs, but she cannot roll over, grasp objects, or hold up her head. Her vision is worsening towards blindness. She is not gaining weight. Her parents are concerned for her "quality of life": how much discomfort and pain should she suffer, enduring the medical procedures that might be introduced, for the kind of future that she will inevitably have?

Esther is the husband's 95-year-old grandmother and a patient at a nursing home. She has had Alzheimer's Disease for over ten years. She can feed herself and roll over in bed but needs help with everything else. She does not recognize her family but smiles with some activities. Based upon her previously stated wishes, life-prolonging medical care will be withheld, including antibiotics, hospitalization, and tube feedings.

What approach to medical care is most appropriate for Naomi? Is it justifiable to treat her in the same manner as a 95-year-old with Alzheimer's and withhold life-prolonging measures? Does her current "happiness" mandate some or all efforts to extend her life as long as possible? Does her future quantity or quality of life justify painful medical interventions? What differentiates these two cases? (Rabbi Norman M. Cohen, Hopkins, MN)

Teshuvah

I. On Euthanasia and Assisted Suicide. It is undeniably difficult to speak to the situation that confronts these parents. We know that whatever counsel we can offer will be inadequate in the face of the heartbreak they endure as they watch their daughter's deterioration toward an early, inevitable

337

death. Yet they ask us to explore the resources of the Jewish tradition and derive from them a response to her illness that is both compassionate and ethical: compassionate in that it spares her unnecessary pain, ethical in that it meets our moral duty toward a human life that is infinitely precious in God's sight. How might they best achieve both these goals, striking a proper balance between them?

The parents do not suggest euthanasia, or "mercy killing," as an option for either Naomi or Esther. For that reason alone, we might be justified in ignoring the subject altogether. Yet it cannot be ignored; the issue of euthanasia and assisted suicide has lately become a hotly-debated one within our culture. In particular, some prominent Reform rabbis have proposed that we rethink our long-standing opposition to euthanasia.[1] Therefore, though it is not directly relevant to this case, we believe it to be our responsibility to examine that question, if briefly, as an essential first step in the consideration of the broader question of the treatment of the terminally ill.

Jewish tradition, as is well known, prohibits suicide, if by "suicide" we mean a rational, premeditated act of self-killing.[2] The prohibition flows from the tradition's affirmation of the sanctity, the inviolability of human life. This affirmation, in turn, assumes the doctrine that life belongs to God, Who has the final say in its disposal.[3] This implies that the individual has no right of "ownership" over his/her life, no authority to bring that life to an illegitimately premature end. For this reason, the court may not execute a criminal on the strength of his own confession, "for the human life is not the property of man but of God... one's confession cannot be accepted with respect to a matter that does not lie within his power...(for) one is not entitled to commit suicide."[4] Similarly, Jewish law prohibits euthanasia, or mercy killing. Inasmuch as human life remains sacred and inviolable until the final moment of its existence, the sources uniformly reject any distinction in this regard between the dying person (*goses*) and any other. "The dying person is like a living person in all respects" (*Semachot* 1:1). Though he or she lies in a moribund state in which death is imminent,[5] a person is still a person, a human being created in the image of God. This life is to be treasured and protected; even though the prognosis is hopeless, he or she deserves all appropriate care. Just as the laws prohibiting work on Shabbat may be violated in order to save life (*pikuach nefesh*), so do we violate them on behalf of the *goses*. We set aside the Shabbat in order to treat this person, despite the fact that this is a life we cannot "save."[6] The one who kills the *goses* is guilty of murder.[7] The dying person is compared to a flickering flame: the slightest touch will extinguish his life. It is forbidden to take any action that hastens the death of the *goses*; "whoever touches him commits bloodshed,"[8] even though this act is taken out of compassion, in order to relieve him of terrible pain and suffering. If such is the case with the *goses,* then it is surely so concerning patients such as Naomi and Esther who, though incurably ill, have not yet reached the very end of life.[9]

On the other hand, the prohibition against suicide is not absolute. One major exception to the rule is the case of martyrdom: a Jew is obligated to accept death rather than to transgress the Toraitic commandments against murder, idolatry, and sexual immorality. Thus does one fulfill the commandment of *kiddush hashem*, of sanctifying the Divine Name through one's decision to die.[10] Some suggest that this requirement extends to active suicide: one who fears that the persecutors will, through excruciating torture, coerce him into violating the Torah may take his life in order to avoid committing that act.[11] Of special interest to our question is the fact that the sources look with considerable understanding upon individuals who commit suicide in extreme straits. A classic case is that of King Saul, who falls upon his sword rather than suffer a degrading death at the hands of the enemy (I Samuel 31:4). Saul, writes one commentator, "committed no sin in taking his own life" under these circumstances.[12] Some authorities derive from Saul's example that, while such an act is not "permitted," one who takes his or her life out of a desire to escape terrible pain and degradation (*oni uvizayon*) is not in fact a "suicide." Such a person has in effect been coerced by overpowering circumstances into this most extreme measure; that action is not the "rational, premeditated act of self-killing" forbidden by halachah.[13] This judgment coheres with the rabbinic tendency to exploit every available pretext in order to declare that a person, though he has died at his own hand, may receive all the customary rites of mourning normally denied to the suicide: "it is most unlikely that a person of sound mind would take such a horrible step."[14]

If the tradition responds with compassion and empathy to those who commit suicide, some contemporary observers go farther. Citing as a proof text the story of the death of Saul, as well as the talmudic narratives surrounding the deaths of Rabbi Chanina ben Teradyon and Rabbi Yehudah Hanasi, they argue that Judaism actually permits suicide and mercy killing for those who face the pain and agony of terminal illness. In doing so, however, the Rabbis face an interesting problem in interpretation. On the one hand, it is certainly true that these stories might plausibly be read so as to support the option of active euthanasia. On the other hand, through the long history of the Jewish study of the Bible and the Talmud, the texts in question have not been understood in this way (see Excursus). This is a point of no little importance to our discussion. We wish to know, after all, whether the "Jewish tradition" offers evidence in support of active euthanasia. It is for this reason that advocates of mercy killing cite these stories in the first place. Yet we find that the very *tradition* of learning which created these passages and which has studied them for fifteen centuries and more as sources of moral meaning declares consistently and unequivocally *against* euthanasia. Indeed, the message which emerges from traditional halachic thought on this subject is quite clear and uniform: we do almost anything to relieve the suffering of the terminally-ill, but we do not kill them and we do not help them kill themselves. It is always possible to read these texts differently than they have ever been read by the Jewish religious community, to discover in them levels of meaning that generations of rabbis and *talmidey chachamim* may have missed. Still, the unequivocal voice of the halachic literature renders it is most difficult to sustain an argument, based upon the citation of a few stories from the Bible and the Talmud, that the "Jewish tradition" permits euthanasia.[15]

As Reform Jews, of course, we consider ourselves free to ascribe "new" Jewish meanings to our texts, to depart from tradition when we think it necessary to secure an essential religious or moral value. In this case, though, we fail to see why we should do so.[16] We see no good reason, first of all, to abandon the traditional Jewish teaching concerning the inestimable value of human life. If the doctrine of life's essential holiness means anything at all, it means that we must stand in reverence before the very fact of life, the gift of

God that renders us human. And this reverence does not diminish as human strength declines, for the dying person still possesses life, a life stamped indelibly with the image of God until the moment of death. It is an awesome and awful responsibility we take upon ourselves when we determine to kill a human being, even when our intentions are good and merciful. Such an action is the ultimate arrogance, for it declares that we are masters over the one thing--life itself--that our faith has always taught must be protected against our all-too-human tendency to manipulate, to mutilate, and to destroy.

Second, we do not believe that the existence of pain and suffering constitutes a sufficient Jewish justification for killing a human being in the name of compassion. It is true that none of us wants to endure a state of physical or psychological agony, and none of us wants this for our loved ones. We have every right to administer treatment to relieve pain. In addition, we are under no obligation to take every conceivable measure to prolong a life of suffering; on all this, see below. It remains a fact, however, that pain and suffering are part and parcel of the human condition. We do not cease to be human, that is, when we experience suffering, even that of a terminal illness. The choice we face when we are ill is essentially the same choice we confront at every other moment of our lives: to determine what we, human beings in covenant with God, propose to do with the time and the strength available to us on this earth. All of life, its end no less than its beginning and its middle, is the arena in which we act out our humanity. Judaism, for its part, bids us to respond to the challenges of life by *choosing* life, to praise God whether that life brings us joy or sorrow.[17] Even in debilitating illness, when our freedom of action is severely limited, we yet sanctify the divine name by *living* our relationship with God, by striving toward nobility of conduct and of purpose, by confronting our suffering with courage. To say this is not to ignore the agony of the dying but to recognize a fundamental truth: that even when we are dying we have the power to choose how we shall live. We can kill ourselves, thereby accepting the counsel of despair, or we can choose life, declaring through our actions that despite everything life--all of it--is blessed with the promise of ultimate meaning and fulfillment.

Third, we are uncomfortable with arguments for assisted suicide that proceed from judgments concerning the "quality of life." While this standard may be persuasive to many, the quality of life by its nature is virtually impossible to determine. That is to say, the decision that "my life is no longer worth living" is an inescapably subjective one; it cannot be quantified, verified, or tested against any principle other than the conviction that one's suffering is no longer tolerable. For example, it is often suggested that the life of a patient in a protracted coma or persistent vegetative state lacks a minimal element of "quality" and that the patient is therefore justified in giving advance authorization for his or her euthanized death. Yet there is nothing inherent in such a condition that demands suicide or euthanasia; the sole "objective" warrant for mercy killing in this instance is the patient's stated desire to die. If so, on what grounds can we deny the "right to suicide" to other persons who state that desire, to persons who are paralyzed, severely depressed, aged and infirm? Are they not entitled to decide that their lives lack "quality"? Once we have adopted "quality of life" as our standard, we have no principled reason to oppose the suicide of *any* person (with the possible exception of children and the insane, who by definition cannot make a "responsible" choice), no matter how flimsy the justification, whether undertaken in response to terminal illness, or to chronic illness, or to psychological or emotional distress. So long as a person concludes that "I do not want to live like this," we would have no right to oppose that decision.

Indeed, what of persons such as the psychotic, the senile, the defective newborn, who have not made or cannot make their own decisions but about whom we can say with confidence that "no one should have to live like this"? Shall we declare for involuntary euthanasia on their behalf, in service of their "human dignity"? The experience of the Netherlands in this regard is both instructive and frightening. In that country, where euthanasia and physician-assisted suicide are officially tolerated, government figures record at least 1000 cases annually of active involuntary euthanasia, defined as "deliberate action to terminate life without the patient's consent." Private observers believe that the real figure is much higher, that it should include the approximately 5000 persons killed per year by lethal dose of morphine but whose deaths are current-

ly classified as "pain relief." All this has occurred despite the fact that euthanasia in Holland is supposed to be "voluntary," authorized by the patient. In its
study of the Dutch experience, the Board of Trustees of the American Medical
Association warns that such non-observance of the rules is inevitable once
physicians, the guardians of life, become dispensers of death. Predicting similar (and worse) numbers should these practices become legal in the United
States, the Board warns that "meaningful control by a society of (the practice
of euthanasia) is illusionary once the physician-patient relationship has been so
changed that death becomes an accepted prescription for pain and suffering."[18]
Indeed, the move from voluntary to involuntary euthanasia is a natural one; for
once we have convinced ourselves that the absence of an identifiable standard
of quality of life justifies the destruction of that life, why should we hold ourselves back from acting upon our belief?

Our duty to the sick is to heal them or, when this is no longer possible, to care for them; it is not to kill them. The sick, the terminally-ill, have
a right to expect compassion from us, for such flows from the respect we ought
to display to ourselves and to others as children of God. But they are not entitled to ask that we take their lives, and should they make that request, we are
not entitled to grant it. For when we define "compassion" so as to include the
killing of human beings, we have transgressed the most elemental of Jewish
moral standards and the most basic teachings of Jewish tradition as we understand it. We believe that compassion toward the dying is a moral responsibility. But we also believe that this responsibility can and must be discharged
without resort to assisted suicide and active euthanasia.

II. The Cessation of Medical Treatment for Terminal Patients. Jewish
tradition teaches that we achieve this compassion through two means: measures aimed at the relief of pain, and the cessation of unnecessary medical
treatment for the terminally ill. For example, the same tradition which rejects
suicide and euthanasia also bids us to strive to alleviate the suffering of the sick
and the dying. Patients may undergo risky surgery to relieve pain, even
though the surgery may hasten their death; such surgery is, after all, legitimate medicine.[19] Physicians may administer powerful anti-pain medications

such as morphine to dying patients, even though such a course of treatment may shorten the patients' lives, for pain itself is a disease and its relief is a proper medical objective.[20]

In addition to permitting such active measures, the halachah also supports the withdrawal of medical treatment under some circumstances from terminal patients. The classic source for the discussion of this issue is the comment of R. Moshe Isserles in *Shulchan Aruch* Yore De`ah 339:1. Drawing upon material from the 13th-century *Sefer Chasidim*,[21] Isserles rules that while it is forbidden to take any measure that would hasten the death of the *goses* (e.g., by moving him or by moving the pillow or mattress from beneath him), "if there exists any factor which prevents the soul from departing, such as the sound of a woodcutter near the house or salt on the patient's tongue...it is permitted to remove that factor. This is not considered a positive act (*ma`aseh*) but merely the removal of an impediment." While the realia mentioned in this passage hardly resemble what we recognize as science, Isserles and *Sefer Chasidim* deal here with an issue familiar to all students of contemporary medical ethics. They distinguish between "active euthanasia", defined as the application of any factor such as physical contact which would hasten the patient's death, and "letting nature take its course," the removal of any existing factor which serves only to impede the patient's otherwise imminent death. The former is forbidden; the latter is permitted. Should we draw the analogy between the technologies of the Middle Ages--the birdfeathers, woodcutters, and salt--and those of our own day, we would discover traditional support for the discontinuation of medical treatment ("turning off the machines") when that treatment can be viewed as "useless", an impediment to death.

A problem with this analogy is that the line which separates active euthanasia from the removal of an impediment to death is not always clear. Indeed, Isserles apparently contradicts himself on this point. On the one hand, he forbids the removal of the mattress from beneath the patient, an action taken on the grounds that "some people say that certain birdfeathers have the property of delaying a patient's death," because to do so involves physical contact with the patient which hastens his death. On the other hand, he allows the removal of salt from the tongue, which also involves physical contact with the patient and thus presumably hastens his death, because this is merely the "removal of an impediment." What is the difference between the two? Why may we remove the salt but not the mattress? Halachic authorities have addressed this contradiction in various ways. Some, opting for extreme caution, declare Isserles wrong and prohibit the removal of the salt altogether.[22] Others allow the removal of the salt as but an "insignificant" contact with the patient.[23] A third approach is provided by R. Yehoshua Boaz b. Baruch, the 16th-century author of the *Shiltey Giborim* commentary to Alfasi.[24] He notes that while it is forbidden to hasten the death of the *goses* it is likewise forbidden to take any action that unnecessarily impedes it.[25] Salt, which cannot bring healing but only impede the patient's death, should never have been put on his tongue. Whoever put it there has acted improperly; thus, its removal, even though it involves physical contact, is permitted as the restoration of the correct *status quo ante*.

The advantage of the *Shiltey Giborim's* analysis is that it turns our attention away from blurry distinctions between "active" and "passive" measures and toward the nature and purpose of those actions. The essential issue is the medical efficacy of the factor we seek to remove. Certain measures must never be applied to the *goses* because they lack any trace of therapeutic value. Offering no hope of cure or successful treatment, they serve only to delay his or her otherwise imminent death. Since it is forbidden to do this, to unnecessarily prolong the death of the dying person, these measures may be discontinued even if we must touch the patient's body in order to do so.[26]

This theory helps to translate the medieval language of the texts into a usable contemporary vernacular. Does there not come a point in a patient's condition when, despite their obvious life-saving powers, the sophisticated technologies of modern medicine--the mechanical respirator, for example, or the heart-lung machine--become nothing more than mere "salt on the tongue," mechanisms which maintain the patient's vital signs long after all hope of recovery has vanished? Answering "yes" to this question, some contemporary *poskim* allow the respirator to be disconnected when a patient is clearly and irrevocably unable to sustain independent heartbeat and respiration. Even though the machine is considered part of routine medical therapy (for patients are as a matter of course connected to it during emergency-room and surgical procedures), it has at this juncture ceased to serve any therapeutic function. They can no longer aid in the preservation or prolongation of life.[27] Once their therapeutic function is exhausted, the machines "merely prolong in an artificial way the process of dying. We must disconnect the patient from the machines, leaving him in his natural state until the soul departs."[28]

III. The Duty to Heal. Other authorities, it is true, reject the comparison of modern medical technologies to those mentioned by Isserles. Birdfeathers, woodchoppers, and salt on the tongue fall into the category of *segulah*, something mystical or metaphysical in nature, whose properties are not subject to scientific verification.[29] Moreover, even if we accept the designation of the respirator and other end-stage technologies and therapies as "impediments to death," Isserles describes a situation at the last moments of life, a point at which we are certain that "the soul is struggling to depart the body," when death is imminent and would occur almost instantaneously should the impediment be removed.[30] Even if it is possible to determine precisely when a patient has reached this final extremity (and we are well aware that medicine is not precise in this respect), the patients who concern us here clearly have *not* reached it. A *goses*, particularly one at the very last instant of life, is not the same as a terminally-ill patient, who may have weeks, months, or even years to live. Neither Naomi nor Esther is a *goseset*. The medical treatments they are receiving are, to be sure, keeping them alive, but since neither lies at the very doorstep of death, these treatments do not qualify as "impediments" to imminent death as the tradition understands that concept. If we view their situation according to the criteria of Yore De`ah 339, therefore, we must conclude that we are not justified in withholding these treatments.

Jewish tradition, however, offers another conceptual framework for thinking about the terminally-ill patient whose death is not yet imminent. Under this framework, we consider not only the patient's specific prognosis but also (and primarily) the nature of the practice of medicine itself. The questions addressed are: what is the Toraitic source of the commandment to heal? How does Jewish law understand "medicine" as an ethical obligation? And, most importantly for our case, does the obligation to provide medical care change or cease altogether when the patient's illness enters a terminal stage and when hope for successful treatment has vanished? Should the answer to this latter question be "yes", it might follow that some types of medical care may be withdrawn from a patient even before he or she has arrived at the very last moments of life.

The commandment to heal the sick is never stated explicitly in the Torah and is addressed but obliquely in rabbinic literature. A midrash on Exodus 21:19, which speaks of the tort-feasor's obligation to pay the medical expenses for the person whom he has injured, declares that "from here we derive that a physician has permission (*reshut*) to practice medicine."[31] It is Nachmanides who raises this "*reshut*", a term that implies a voluntary act, to the level of a mitzvah, a religious and moral obligation. He bases this deduction upon a logical inference: since we rely upon the physician's diagnosis to determine whether and when to set aside the laws of Shabbat and Yom Kippur on behalf of the sick, it is obvious that medicine is an integral part of the commandment to save life (*pikuach nefesh*).[32] Maimonides, on the other hand, also believes that medicine is a mitzvah, but he derives the commandment from Deuteronomy 22:2, a verse which, according to the Talmud, imposes upon us a positive duty to rescue a person from mortal danger.[33] Both approaches see the obligation to practice medicine as a subset of the more general commandment to save life. It follows that the obligation to heal should be understood according to the definition of that more general mitzvah. And, say the rabbis, fundamental to that definition is the element of *ability*. That is to say, one is required to take action to save life (and, conversely, one is liable if one does not take such action) only when the action has a reasonable chance of success. Thus, as Maimonides puts it, "whoever is able to save another (*kol hayachol lehatzil*) and does not do so has violated the commandment: You shall not stand idly by the blood of your neighbor."[34] One is under no obligation to undertake useless actions, actions which clearly do not contribute to the rescue of another person, for such measures are not to be defined as "the saving of human life."

The same principle would apply to the practice of medicine: As with lifesaving in general, the obligation to practice medicine holds only when "one sees another in danger and one is able to save that person (*veyachol lehatzilo*)" by medical means.[35] Put differently, the point and the essence of medicine is to heal. It is for this reason, and only for this reason, that we are permitted to administer harsh drugs and invasive surgical procedures which, under non-therapeutic conditions, would be strictly prohibited as *chabalah*, the causing of unnecessary physical harm to the human body.[36] This would imply that once a medical treatment ceases to be effective and beneficial it ceases to be "medicine" as that practice is conceived by Jewish tradition. A physician is obligated to administer those measures which in the judgment of the profession are therapeutic: *i.e.*, they are regarded in medical opinion as contributing to the successful treatment of the disease. On the other hand, treatments which do not effect "healing" are not *medicine* and thus are not required. While we may be entitled to administer such treatments we are not commanded to do so, inasmuch as they do not partake in the saving of life.

This distinction is of great practical significance in the halachic discussion of some familiar problems of medical ethics. As we have seen, halachists rule that a terminally-ill patient may be given powerful pain-killing medications such as morphine, even though these drugs may actually hasten the patient's death, because the treatment of pain is a legitimate goal of medical practice.[37] Then there is the question whether a person has the right to refuse medical treatment. On the one hand, since medicine is viewed as a mitzvah and suicide is prohibited, it stands to reason that a person is obligated to accept medical treatment for illness. One leading authority deals with the case of an individual who refuses treatment on the apparently admirable ground that the preparation of the medicine would involve a violation of the laws of Shabbat. Such a person, he responds, "is a pious fool (*chasid shoteh*). This is not an act of piety but of suicide. He is therefore compelled to do what the physicians prescribe,"[38] that is, to accept proper therapeutic treatment for disease is an act of *pikuach nefesh*; it is a commandment, to which one has no right to say "no." This standard would apply, however, only to medical procedures classified as *refu'ah vada'it* or *bedukah*, tested and proven remedies which offer a reasonably certain prospect of successful treatment. On the other hand, should a particular remedy be experimental in nature, if its therapeutic effect upon the disease is uncertain at best, then the patient is not required to accept it.[39] Under such circumstances, the treatment is no longer classified as "life-saving" and is therefore no longer obligatory. While physician and patient have the permission (*reshut*) to utilize it, there is no moral requirement (mitz-vah) that they do so.[40]

On this basis, halachists can permit the cessation of medical treatment for end-stage patients who have not arrived at brain death or to the point of *gesisah*, the very last moments of life. R. Moshe Feinstein rules that "when the physicians see that a person cannot recover from his illness but can only continue to live in a state of suffering; and when the treatment they prescribe serves only to prolong his life as it is now, filled with suffering; they must not administer the treatments but leave him alone." To support his decision, he cites the story of the last days of R. Yehudah Hanasi, or Rabbi, discussed above. Rabbi's maidservant, to use modern terminology, "pulled the plug" on prayers which had lost their therapeutic value.[41] Thus, we learn that there is a significant difference between healing (*refu'ah*) and medical procedures that needlessly prolong a patient's suffering; the former is obligatory, the latter is not.[42] R. Immanuel Jakobovits, too, rules that "there is no obligation to pro-long the life and the suffering of a clearly terminal patient." He permits a dia-betic who develops terminal, inoperable cancer to cease taking insulin. Although the insulin is a successful treatment for the diabetes, it can now only prolong his suffering and delay his death. This is true "even though he is not yet a *goses*; since the whole point of medicine is to restore a person's health, (the insulin) is no longer obligatory but merely voluntary."[43]

The standard of therapeutic effectiveness, as a tool by which to make judgments concerning medical treatment, allows us to draw some conclusions with moral confidence. Under the heading "therapeutic" and "successful" treat-ments we would certainly include all medical and surgical procedures, such as antibiotics and routine surgeries, which physicians expect will lead to a cure for the illness in question. These treatments are "obligatory" under the tradi-tional Jewish conception of medicine. Other therapies, though they do not produce a cure, would nonetheless fall under this category because they are able to control the disease and allow the patient a reasonable degree of function. Included here are such therapies as insulin for diabetes (so long as the patient has not developed another, terminal illness; see above) and dialysis for chronic renal disease. These procedures can be unpleasant, true, and they do not offer a cure, but they do offer life; they are to be considered as *pikuach nefesh*. When, however, a patient has entered the final stages of terminal disease, medical treatments and procedures which serve only to maintain this state of existence are not required. A cancer patient, for example, would accept radiation and/or chemotherapy so long as according to informed medical judgment these offer a reasonable prospect of curing, reversing, or controlling the cancer. Once this prospect has disappeared and the therapies can serve only to increase suffering by prolonging the patient's inevitable death from the disease, they are no longer to be regarded as medicine and may therefore be withdrawn.

While this standard is useful in helping to direct our thinking, it is by no means free of difficulty. Terms such as "therapeutic" and "successful treatment" are inherently vague and impossible to define with precision. In many situations it will be problematic if not impossible to determine when or even if the prescribed regime of therapy has lost its medical value. Yet the decision to continue or to cease the treatment must nonetheless be made, and those who must make it will confront an element of doubt and uncertainty that cannot be entirely resolved. Every such decision is inherently a matter of choice, a choice between two or more alternatives when none is the obviously correct one. This kind of uncertainty is disturbing to many, who believe (as do we all) that fundamental issues of life and death must be handled with an attitude of reverence and caution. Yet their laudable search for moral certainty has led some authorities toward an extremist position, rejecting the very possibility that treatment can ever be withdrawn from a dying patient. Says one: "every person is obligated in every case to seek out medical treatment, even though he believes that the treatment will not heal him but only prolong his suffering; for we must hope for and await God's deliverance to the very last moment of our lives."[44] This conviction is based upon the reasoning that, inasmuch as medicine is not a precise science, even the most definitive medical prognosis is a matter of *safek*, of doubt. We must work to preserve life until the very end, for while it can never be established with certainty that a patient has absolutely no hope for recovery, it is indeed certain that, should we withdraw medical care, the patient will die.[45]

To this argument we would simply ask: is this truly "medicine" as we conceive it? Our answer, as liberal Jews who seek guidance from our tradition in facing the moral dilemmas of our age, is "no". We do not adopt the simplistic approach, advocated by some, which holds that Jewish sacred texts have nothing to say to the challenges posed by contemporary medical reality. But we cannot and do not believe that those texts, which bid us to heal the sick and to preserve life, demand that in fulfilling these duties we apply in indiscriminate fashion every available technological device to prolong the death of a dying person. Medical science has made immeasurable advances during recent times, and we are thankful for that fact. Doctors today are able to prevent and to cure disease, to offer hope to the sick and disabled to an extent that past generations could scarcely imagine. Yet there comes a point in time when all the technologies, the chemicals, the surgeries, and the machines that comprise the lifesaving arsenal of modern medicine become counterproductive, a point when all that medical science can effectively do for a patient is to indefinitely delay his inevitable death. This is not *pikuach nefesh*; this is not medicine; this is not what physicians, as agents of healing, are supposed to do. There is neither meaning nor purpose in maintaining these treatments. They are salt on the tongue and the sound of a woodchopper. They are not *refu'ah*; no commandments are fulfilled thereby. Yes, life is a precious thing, and every moment of it should be regarded as God's gift. But we are not required under any reading of the tradition that makes sense to us to buy additional moments of life by undertaking useless and pointless medical treatment.

If this conviction leaves us in doubt as to the "right" answer for particular patients, then it is well to remember that moral, religious, and halachic truth can never be a matter of absolute certainty. There will always be more than one plausibly correct answer, more than one possible application of our texts and our values to the case at hand. Our task is to determine the best answer, the one that most closely corresponds to our understanding of the tradition as a whole. That search must be conducted by means of analysis, interpretation, and argument. Its outcome will never enjoy the finality of the solution to a mathematical equation; its conclusions will be subject to challenge and critique. Yet this is no reason to shrink from moral argument; it means rather that we have no choice but to enter the fray, to confront difficult cases, and to do the best we can. We may never be absolutely sure that we are "right"; but if we are thorough in our thinking, if we read the texts, consider the case, and conduct our argument carefully and prayerfully, then we can be sure that we have done our job.

IV. <u>The Cases Before Us.</u> We begin with Naomi. Canavan's Disease, a "spongy degeneration" of the central nervous system, usually occurs in infants of East European Jewish ancestry. It is characterized by progressive mental deterioration, spasticity, and blindness. Due to diminished chest muscle function, the child will often develop respiratory tract disease. Death will occur in most cases before the age of five. No means presently exist to cure or control the illness; "treatment is symptomatic and supportive."[46]

Based upon the analysis developed in the foregoing sections of this *teshuvah*, we turn our attention to the nature and extent of this "symptomatic and supportive" treatment. Since Naomi's disease is a progressive one and can neither be reversed nor arrested, any measure that might be adduced to prolong her life is essentially an artificial and improper delay of her death and has no therapeutic value. For example, should she develop a respiratory tract disease, the goal of treatment need not be to "cure" that disease, since it is an integral part of a terminal illness which cannot be cured. She should receive treatments directed at relief of physical pain and suffering, so long as those treatments are not themselves so invasive as to increase her suffering. Naomi's parents are under no Jewish moral obligation to resort to any measures whose purpose it is to lengthen her life.

As for Esther, whose terminal illness has brought her to the very end of her life, it is clear that the family has no duty to administer "life-prolonging measures." By this we certainly mean "painful medical interventions," that offer no hope of arresting or controlling her Alzheimer's Disease. The issue of antibiotics is somewhat more difficult. On the one hand, these drugs do not affect the course of the Alzheimer's, which is causing her death; on the other hand, they would be considered "successful" treatments for the particular infections that afflict her. In this particular case, we would take the position advocated by Rabbi Jakobovits[47] and counsel that the antibiotics not be administered. We should remember that when we practice medicine, we are treating the *patient* and not this or that disease. The successful treatment of a particular infection in a terminal patient does not change the fact that the patient remains terminal and that death is inevitable. Antibiotics may be justified in cases where the patient's death is not imminent or when those drugs offer the prospect of restoring the patient to a reasonable degree of function. This latter judgment must, again, be measured not by the drug's effectiveness in controlling a specific, identifiable syndrome but rather in the context of the patient's total medical situation. Esther's advanced age and medical condition offer convincing evidence *both* that she is "terminal" and that death is relatively near. For such a patient, the antibiotics serve no reasonable therapeutic function; they are but pointless hindrances to her death.

V. <u>On Artificial Nutrition and Hydration</u>. The conclusion that medical treatment may be withdrawn or withheld raises a difficult question with respect to artificial nutrition and hydration. A terminal patient may be kept alive partially or even primarily by means of food and water supplied through tubes inserted into the veins, nose, or stomach. May we discontinue the supply of nutrients or disconnect the tubes altogether on the grounds that, as all hope for recovery or satisfactory control of the illness has vanished, this feeding serves only to prolong the patient's death?

The answer to this question depends upon whether we regard artificial nutrition and hydration as a "medical treatment." As we have seen, Jewish tradition offers strong support for the cessation of medical treatments for the terminally-ill when these treatments have lost their therapeutic effectiveness. We are not commanded to do medicine when our actions are *not* medicine, when they do not heal. We violate no moral obligation if we refuse to offer a patient drugs or technologies that are medically useless. By contrast, we do violate such an obligation under normal circumstances when we withhold food and water and thereby starve that person to death. Though we might respond that a dying patient fed through a tube hardly constitutes a "normal circumstance," artificial feeding differs from other hospital procedures in one crucial aspect: it can be argued that the feeding tube has nothing to do with "medicine" at all. Its function is not to treat the disease but to provide essential nutrients to the patient, and so long as the patient is capable of digesting these nutrients, the tube is successfully performing its task. In this analysis, artificial nutrition and hydration are not medical treatments, do not lose any "therapeutic" effectiveness, and therefore may not be withdrawn.

One could argue that artificial feeding devices are indeed "medical", a response to disease. They are utilized precisely because a patient is unable to ingest nutrients in the "normal" manner. As such they are medical interventions and can be withdrawn when the intervention is no longer medically justified. There is no reason to distinguish between feeding tubes and other, indisputable "medical" procedures such as cardiopulmonary resuscitation: both keep the terminal patient alive, and the withholding of either will result in death from the very disease that warranted its introduction in the first place. On the other hand, unlike sophisticated medical procedures, food and water are universal human needs. All of us, whether sick or well, require food and water in order to survive. Moreover, the fact that these nutrients are supplied by a machine does not transform them into exotic medical substances; we all receive our food at the end of a long chain of production, transportation, and distribution technologies. A real and desirable distinction can therefore be made between artificial feeding and medical treatment.

Opinions on this question are deeply divided. A broad coalition that includes medical ethicists, the American Medical Association,[50] and the United States Supreme Court[51] supports the definition of artificial nutrition and hydration as a medical procedure that may be withdrawn from terminal patients. On the other hand, this "emerging medical, ethical and legal consensus"[52] has been challenged by some ethicists who argue that the withdrawal of nutrition resembles killing more than it does the cessation of purely "medical" treatment.[53] The dispute among halachic scholars is the mirror image of that among ethicists. Most authorities prohibit the withdrawal of food and water; "the reason, quite simply, is that eating is a normal physiological process, required to sustain life, necessary for all, including those who are healthy."[54] Food and water are not, therefore, medicine; their presence cannot be defined as medically illegitimate.[55] At the same time, some halachists have suggested the opposite, that artificial nutrition is a medical procedure and may be withdrawn.[56] Reform halachic opinion is also split: one responsum opposes the removal of the feeding tube,[57] though several others permit it.[58]

Given this division of opinion, we cannot claim that Jewish tradition categorically prohibits the withdrawal of food and water from dying patients. It can be plausibly argued that artificial nutrition and hydration are medical interventions which, on the Judaic grounds that we have cited in the previous two sections of this *teshuvah*, may be discontinued upon a competent finding that they no longer provide therapeutic benefit to the patient. At the same time, we stress the plausibility of the opposing argument. Food and water, no matter how they are delivered, are the very staff of life (*lechem chuki*) for the human being. They sustain us at every moment of our lives, in health as well as in illness. It is therefore not at all obvious that we should look upon these substances as "medicine" merely because they come to us in the form of a tube inserted by medical professionals.[59] Moreover, the moral stakes in removing the feeding tube are considerable. As one authority who rules permissively admits, "there is something which is, minimally, highly unaesthetic" about withholding food and water from terminal patients.[60] We agree. Indeed, some of us would use stronger adjectives, for--let us neither mince words nor hide behind comforting euphemisms--we cannot overlook the fact that by removing them we are starving these human beings to death.[61]

We would therefore caution at the very least that the removal of artificial nutrition and hydration should never become a routine procedure. It is preferable that artificial feeding of terminal patients be maintained so that, when death comes, it will not have come because we have caused it by starvation. Nonetheless, because we cannot declare that cessation of artificial nutrition and hydration is categorically forbidden by Jewish moral thought, the patient and the family must ultimately let their conscience guide them in the choice between these two alternatives.

Excursus

As previously noted, supporters of euthanasia will cite various biblical and talmudic passages as evidence that the Jewish tradition supports a permissive stance toward mercy killing or, as it is called these days, physician-assisted suicide. We indicated in brief that the "tradition" does *not* so interpret those texts. That is to say, however Jews have read and understood the narratives of the deaths of King Saul, R. Chaninah ben Teradyon, and R. Yehudah Hanasi ("Rabbi"), these episodes have not tended to serve as "proof" that a terminally-ill patient may take active steps to end his or her life to avoid the sufferings of illness or that others may do so on behalf of the patient. We now want to examine this issue in some detail.

A. The Death of King Saul. While many commentators go to great lengths to justify Saul's suicide, they do so in a way which makes it difficult to use his case as a model for today's terminally-ill patient. Some write that Saul, as king of Israel, was a unique case, subject by the nature of his office to special ethical and political obligations that make it difficult to draw an analogy from his situation to any other. There was the concern, for example, that should Saul be captured alive the Israelites would have felt bound to attempt to rescue him, an attempt that would have entailed a severe loss of life and a further weakening of Israel's already-precarious military situation.[62] Others suggest that Saul took his life out of fear that his captors would torture him into committing the sin of idolatry; his death was thus an act of martyrdom and not simply an attempt to avoid suffering.[63] Still others reject the whole tradition which exonerates Saul: he committed suicide, and bears the guilt of sin.[64]

B. The Death of R. Chaninah b. Teradyon. R. Chanina b. Teradyon died a martyr's death at the hands of the Romans during the Hadrianic persecutions of the second century C.E.[65] According to the story, the Romans burned R. Chanina at the stake, wrapped in the parchment of a *sefer Torah*, and they placed wet woolen rags around him in order to retard the flames and to prolong his agony. He nonetheless refuses to open his mouth and let the fire enter, in order to hasten his death; "it is better that the One who gives life take it away than for a person to bring harm upon himself." Yet when a Roman guard asks: "Rabbi, if I increase the flame and remove the rags, will you guarantee me life in the world to come?", R. Chanina answers "yes," and the guard did so.

Since the guard's action hastens R. Chanina's death, it is sometimes suggested that this narrative proves that we are permitted to do the same for the terminally ill. Yet if this is the case, if one may ask another to speed one's inevitable end, why does Chanina himself not commit suicide? We cannot argue that an individual is forbidden to kill himself but may request others to do so, for such a conclusion runs counter to the most fundamental conceptions of moral responsibility. If I am forbidden to kill myself, I am not entitled to appoint another to kill me.[66] How then may R. Chanina empower the guard to take this lethal action? Traditional commentators resolve this contradiction by reminding us that the story of R. Chanina is a case of martyrdom, for which, as we have seen, special rules apply.[67] The guard is not R. Chanina's agent but his executioner; the rabbi cannot "appoint" the guard to do anything. The guard is the agent of the Roman authorities, who have the discretion to kill R. Chanina according to their law or by any means they desire. The manner of R. Chaninah's death is not the "will of Heaven," "natural law," or any such thing; it is not up to him or subject to his decision. If the executioner decides to kill him more quickly, that is entirely the executioner's choice. What is up to R. Chaninah is the decision to participate directly in the hastening of his death, either by his own hand or through an agent; and this he does *not* do. This set of facts radically distinguishes the case of a martyr from that of the terminally-ill patient.

C. The Death of R. Yehudah Hanasi (Rabbi). When Rabbi is near death, his students gather to pray for his recovery.[68] His maidservant, who at first is sympathetic to their efforts, soon realizes that Rabbi is beyond the point of healing; the time of his death is nigh, and the prayers serve only to prolong his suffering. She therefore prays that Rabbi die quickly. When she sees that the students will not cease their own prayers, she casts a glass vessel from the attic of the house to the ground; the startling sound interrupts the prayers, and Rabbi dies.

Again, some read the story as an example of mercy killing; therefore, they argue that this story provides support for the practice of euthanasia for those like Rabbi suffering the end-stage of terminal disease. The rabbinic tradition, as we have seen,[69] adopts a different interpretation: the maidservant did not kill Rabbi but rather removed an inappropriate impediment to his death. Advocates of mercy killing reject this distinction as excessively formalistic. They claim there is no significant moral difference between taking action to hasten a person's death and withdrawing treatment so as to allow death to occur; both of these are positive actions which speed the death of the patient. We would reject this claim on two grounds. First, Jewish ethical thought does see a significant difference between action that directly kills a person and inaction which allows him to die.[70] And second, as we have argued above, the removal of an impediment is not an act of killing at all, even passive killing, but in fact a corrective measure taken against a situation that we have wrongly allowed to occur. For while Jewish tradition forbids us to kill a terminal patient it also forbids us to delay her death unnecessarily. It is therefore permitted to remove factors which contribute to that delay. To permit mercy killing, however, would be to permit the taking of a life even in the absence of "impediments" (machines, medications, etc.) that serve no therapeutic effect other than to delay death. Such killing is qualitatively distinct from the removal of an impediment.

NOTES

1 See the essays by Rabbis Leonard Kravitz and Peter Knobel in Walter Jacob and Moshe Zemer, eds., *Death and Euthanasia in Jewish Law* (Pittsburgh and Tel Aviv, 1995).

2 This is evident from the Hebrew term for "suicide": *hame'abed atsmo leda'at*; see *Sh.A.* YD 345:2-3 and commentaries *ad loc.*

3 See *Yad*, Hilchot Rotzeach 1:4.

4 See the commentary of R. David ibn Zimra to *Yad*, Sanhedrin 18:6, printed editions. For the prohibition of suicide, see BT Baba Kama 91b (the midrash on Gen. 9:5, and see Rashi, *ad loc.*) and *Yad*, Hilchot Rozseach 2:2-3. For that matter, one is not entitled to subject his/her body to physical damage (*chabalah*), a principle so well established that the permissibility of cosmetic surgery is a matter of no lit-

tle controversy within the legal literature. BT Baba Kama 90b; *Yad,* Hilchot Chovel 5:1; *Sh.A.*, CM 420:31.

5 See Rambam, Commentary to M. `Arachin 1:3.

6 *Sh.A., YD* 329:4. This ruling seems odd at first glance because the permit to violate the laws of Shabbat is based upon Leviticus 18:5: "these are the laws...which a person shall perform and *live by the*M..." (BT Yoma 85b). Surely the *goses,* who stands at the brink of death, cannot "live" by these laws for more than a few hours or, at the very most, days. Yet see *Mishnah Berurah, Be'ur Halachah, s.v. 'ela lefi sh.a.`ah*: we violate Shabbat for the goses because the Torah places inestimable value upon even the briefest span of human life.

7 BT Sanhedrin 78a; *Yad,* Hilchot Rotzeach 2:7.

8 M. Semachot 1:4; *Yad,* Hilchot Avel 4:5; *Alfasi,* BT Mo`ed Katan, fol. 16b; *Sh.A.* YD 339:1.

9 Some authorities point to the *tereifah,* the person who is terminally ill and should die within one year, as a major exception to this rule: according to Jewish law, the one who kills a *tereifah* is not punished by death as is the killer of the *goses.* However we try to resolve this apparent contradiction, we should not forget that while the killer of the tereifah is exempt from execution by the earthly court, he has still committed a serious moral offense that will presumably bring heavenly retribution in its wake. It is arguably possible to rank the *tereifah* lower than the healthy person on a scale of priorities in *pikuach nefesh*; i.e., I may be entitled to save the healthy person before I aid the *tereifah.* Still, it is *not permitted* to kill the *tereifah,* a point of no little significance in the debate over euthanasia. See BT Sanh. 78a and *Yad,* Hilchot Rotzeach 2:7-9.

10 BT Sanhedrin 74a-b and parallels; *Yad,* Hilchot Yesodey HaTorah 5:1-4; YD 157:1. The sources add that during a time of religious persecution a Jew must accept martyrdom rather than transgress even the smallest detail of customary Jewish observance. Some authorities permit an individual to accept martyrdom even in situations where the law does not require one to do so; see *Hil. HaRosh,* Avodah Zarah 2:9.

11 Rabbeinu Tam in Tosafot, Avodah Zarah 18a, s.v. ve`al, citing the story of the captive children in BT Gittin 57b (and see Tosafot Gittin 57b, *s.v. kaftsu*). By the early fourteenth century, such acts of suicide had been approved by leading rabbinic authorities; see *Hiddushey HaRitva,* Avodah Zarah 18a. See, in general, R. Yosef Karo's Bedek HaBayit to *Tur YD* 157.

12 R. David Kimchi *ad loc.*, citing Bereshit Rabah 34:13, which exempts cases "like that of King Saul" from the prohibition against suicide derived from Genesis 9:5 (see note 4, above).

13 *Sh.A.*, YD 345:3. See also *R. Shalom Schwadron, Resp. Maharsham,* v. 6, YD, no. 123, who explicitly rejects the opposing view of the Hatam Sofer (*Responsa,* YD, no. 326). A similar position is taken by two of Sofer's early 19th-century contemporaries: R. Efraim Margoliot, *Resp. Beit Efraim,* YD, no. 76, and R. Mordechai Benet, *Resp. Parashat Mordechai,* YD, no. 25-26.

14 *Aruch HaShulchan,* YD 345, no. 5: Saul's suicide was a case of emotional coercion (ones) and not a rational choice. See in general *SA, YD* 345:3 and *Pitchey Teshuvah,* no. 3.

15 Those who advocate euthanasia sometimes attempt to distinguish between an "agadic tradition" which tells stories that support mercy killing and a "halachic tradition" which opposes it. We think this attempt is fruitless. Both literary genres are the product of the same religious culture; the rabbis who tell the stories are the same rabbis who read them to learn the law. And it is those rabbis who prohibit euthanasia.

16 Our own Reform responsa tradition, it should be noted, has consistently rejected euthanasia as a morally acceptable response to terminal illness. See the *teshuvot* of R. Israel Bettan (*ARR,* no. 78, pp.

261-271), R. Solomon B. Freehof (*ARR*, no. 77, pp.257-260 ; *Reform Responsa*, no. 27, pp. 117-122; *Modern Reform Responsa*, no. 34, pp. 188-197, 35, pp. 197-203), R. Walter Jacob (*ARR*, no. 79, pp. 271-274; *CARR*, no. 81, pp. 135-136, 83, pp. 138-140; *Questions and Reform Jewish Answers*, no. 145, pp. , 157, pp. 259-262), R. Moshe Zemer (*Halachah Shefuyah*, pp. 295-298).

17 Hence, the blessing *dayan ha'emet*, "blessed be...the True Judge," traditionally recited at the death of a relative or when one receives evil tidings. See M. Berachot 9:5: the commandment to love God "with all your strength" (Deut. 6:5) implies that we are to give expression to this love come what may. See also *Yad*, Hilchot Berachot 10:3, and *Sh.A.*, OC 222:2. This does not mean that we must accept sorrow and tragedy in passivity; the numerous stories of Jewish heroes who "argue with God" against the evil in the world are sufficient proof of that. It does suggest, however, that the experience of evil does not bring an end to the very relationship with God in which a meaningful argument can take place.

18 Report of the Board of Trustees of the American Medical Association in *Issues in Law and Medicine* 10:1 (Summer, 1994), pp. 89ff, at p. 91. See also at p. 81: "The Board of Trustees recommends that the American Medical Association reject euthanasia and physician-assisted suicide as being incompatible with the nature and purposes of the healing arts." While Dutch observers report that there is some controversy over these statistics, that controversy in no way lessens the moral gravity of the situation. On the case of the Netherlands, see the article by Joop Al in *Jewish Law Annual*, v. 12.

19 R. Ya`akov Emden (18th century), *Mor uKetzi`ah*, ch. 328.

20 R. Eliezer Waldenberg, *Resp. Tzitz Eliezer*, v. 13, no. 87. Waldenberg cautions that the intent of the procedure must be to relieve pain and not to hasten the patient's death, a point made as well by Emden, note 19, above.

21 ch. 723 (= ch. 315, Wistinetzki-Freimann ed.)

22 *Turey Zahav*, YD *ad loc.* He notes that Karo's ruling, to which Isserles does not object, prohibits even the closing of the patient's eyelids at the moment of death. The slightest amount of contact, therefore, must be seen as the hastening of death.

23 *Nekudot HaKesef ad loc.*

24 *Shiltey Giborim* to Rif, Mo`ed Katan, fol. 16. It should be noted that R. Yehoshua Boaz, an older contemporary of Isserles, never saw the latter's ruling. He is addressing the same contradiction as it appears in *Sefer Chasidim*. The thrust of his comment is applied to Isserles by *Beit Lechem Yehudah*, YD 339.

25 *Sefer Chasidim loc. cit.*

26 For this reason, too, the *Shiltey Giborim* supports the prohibition against moving the mattress. Even though the feathers may serve to impede the patient's death, the mattress itself is supposed to be there; it plays a legitimate role in the care of the *goses*, and is thus not solely an impediment that must be removed.

27 See R. Eliezer Yehudah Waldenberg, *Resp. Tzitz Eliezer*, vol. 13, no. 89. Waldenberg conditions this permit upon the performance of extensive test which show that the patient cannot recover independent respiration. See also R. Chaim David Halevy, *Aseh Lecha Rav*, v. 5, no. 29.

28 Rabbi B. Rabinovits, *Sefer Asya*, 1976, pp. 197-198.

29 Dr. Ya`akov Levy, *No`am*, vol. 16, 1973, pp. 53ff.

30 Thus, Waldenberg (see above, n. 24) stresses that his permission to turn off the respirator applies only at the very end of life (*gemer kalot hanefesh*).

31 BT Baba Kama 85a. "Permission" is necessary, according to Nachmanides (see n. 29, below), for two reasons: in order to protect the physician from claims of liability should he cause injury to the

patient, and in order to allow the practice of healing even when it seems to contradict the Divine will ("if God smites a person, who am I to heal him?").

32 Ramban, *Torat Ha'Adam,* Chavel ed., pp. 41-42. His discussion forms the basis of the Tur, YD 336, on the laws of medicine. On *pikuach nefesh* see Lev. 18:5 and BT Yoma 85b.

33 Rambam, *Commentary to the Mishnah,* Nedarim 4:4. The verse declares that we are obligated to restore a lost object to its rightful owner; the midrash cites a linguistic peculiarity in the verse to extend this duty to the "restoration/rescue of a person's life" (hashevat gufo; BT Sanhedrin 73a). See the discussion in our responsum 5754.18. "Physicians and Indigent Patients," below.

34 *Yad,* Rotzeach 1:14. On "not standing idly by..." see Lev. 19:16 and BT Sanhedrin 73a.

35 Maimonides, *Commentary to the Mishnah ad loc.*

36 M. Baba Kama 8:5; BT Baba Kama 91a-b; *Yad,* Hilchot Chovel 5:1; *Sh.A., CM* 420:31. See, in general, our responsum 5752.7, "On the Permissibility of Cosmetic Surgery," above.

37 See at note 19, above.

38 *Resp. R. David ibn Zimra* (16th-c. Egypt), v. 1, no. 1139.

39 R. Ya`kov Emden, *Mor uKetzi`ah,* 328; R. Moshe Raziel, *"Kefi'at choleh lekabel tipul refu'i,"* *Techumin* 2 (1981), 335-336.

40 See R. Ya`akov b. Shmuel (Prussia, 17th century), *Resp. Beit Ya`akov,* no. 59. R. Ya`akov Reischer (Germany, 18th century) in his *Resp. Shevut Ya`akov,* OC no. 13, disputes the *Beit Ya`akov,* but only in that he regards it permissible (*mutar*) for a physician to administer medications that delay death. He does not claim that it is obligatory to do so.

41 R. Nissim Gerondi, *Commentary to* BT *Nedarim* 40a, also cited this story as an halachic precedent, but in a more restrictive sense: since the maidservant, seeing Rabbi in excruciating pain, had previously prayed for his speedy death, R. Nissim learns that there are times when one is permitted to pray for the death of a suffering patient. Feinstein goes farther, suggesting that the story serves as a precedent for the cessation of medical treatment.

42 *Resp. Igrot Moshe,* CM, v. 2, no. 73-74.

43 Rabbi I. Jakobovits, in *HaPardes* 31 (1957), no. 3, pp. 18-19.

44 R. Natan Zvi Friedman, *Resp. Netser Mata`i,* no. 30. See also R. Eliezer Yehudah Waldenberg, *Resp. Tzitz Eliezer,* vol. 5, Ramat Rachel, no. 28, and J. D. Bleich, "The Quinlan Case: A Jewish Perspective," in Fred Rosner and J. David Bleich, eds., *Jewish Bioethics* (New York, 1979), pp. 266-276.

45 See R. Avraham Yitschak Hakohen Kook, *Resp. Da`at Kohen,* no. 142; *Resp. Chatam Sofer,* YD, no. 158.

46 J.G. Theone, *Physicians' Guide to Rare Diseases* (Montvale, NJ: 1992), pp. 373-374. See also J.B. Wyngaarden and C.H. Smith, Jr., eds., *The Cecil Textbook of Medicine,* 18th edition (Philadelphia, 1988), p. 2216.

47 At note 43, above.

48 BT Sanhedrin 77a and *Rashi ad loc.*; *Yad,* Hilchot Rotseach 3:9-10.

49 President's Commission for the Study of Ethical Problems in Medicine and Biomedical and Behavioral Research, *Withholding or Withdrawing Life-Prolonging Treatment* (Washington, DC: 1983), p. 88; Tom L. Beauchamp and James F. Childress, *Principles of Biomedical Ethics* (New York, 1989), pp. 163-169; Hastings Center, *Guidelines on the Termination of Life-Sustaining Treatment* (Briarcliff Manor, NY: 1987); and numerous others.

50 Council on Ethical and Judicial Affairs of the American Medical Association, *Opinions* (Chicago: 1986), Opinion 2:20.

51 *Cruzan v. Director, Missouri Department of Health*, 497 U.S. 261 (1990).

52 The term is that of Robert Steinbrook and Bernard Lo, "Artificial Feeding--Solid Ground, Not a Slippery Slope," *New England Journal of Medicine* 319 (1988), p. 288.

53 See Patrick G. Derr, "Why Food and Fluids Can Never Be Denied," *Hastings Center Report* 16 (February, 1986), pp. 28-30; Gilbert Mailaender, "On Removing Food and Water: Against the Stream," *Hastings Center Report* 14 (December, 1984), pp. 11-13; Daniel Callahan, "On Feeding the Dying," *Hastings Center Report* 13 (October, 1983), p. 22.

54 R. Moshe Feinstein, *Resp. Igrot Moshe*, CM, v. 2, no. 74, sec. 3.

55 See *Nishmat Avraham*, YD 339, pp. 245-246; Avraham Steinberg in *Sefer Asya* 3 (1983), p. 448; R. Immanuel Jakobovits in *HaPardes* 31:3 (1957), pp. 18-19. Among Conservative thinkers see R. David Feldman, *Health and Medicine in the Jewish Tradition* (New York, 1986), p. 95, and R. Avram Reisner in *Conservative Judaism* 43:3 (1991), pp. 52 ff.

56 For Orthodox opinion, see R. Zev Schostak, "Jewish Ethical Guidelines for Resuscitation and Artificial Nutrition and Hydration of the Dying Elderly," *Journal of Medical Ethics* 20:2 (June, 1994), p. 98, and R. Zalman Goldberg in *Emek Halachah* (*Asya*) (Jerusalem, 1986), p. 78 (but see note 13 ad loc.). An important Conservative responsum in this vein is authored by R. Elliot N. Dorff in *Conservative Judaism* 43:3 (1991), pp. 36-39.

57 See "Hospital Patient Beyond Recovery," below.

58 R. Walter Jacob, *Questions and Reform Jewish Answers*, no. 159, pp. 263-269; R. Mark N. Staitman in Jacob and Zemer, *Death and Euthanasia*, pp. 1-10. See also R. Solomon Freehof, in *ARR*, no. 77, pp. 257-260, who permits the physician to refrain from connecting or refilling the nutrition apparatus of a dying patient.

59 The argument, advanced by some, that we are not obligated to provide artificial nutrition because it is essentially different from "eating" in the normal sense is hard to understand. In either case, whether we prevent a healthy person from eating or withdraw artificial nutrition from a patient, we are withholding nutrients that are necessary for survival and starving that person to death.

60 *Dorff*, note 56, above, at 38.

61 The *Cruzan* case (see n. 51, above) is instructive here. Though Ms. Cruzan's parents sought to discontinue artificial feeding, they did not ask for the removal of the feeding tube, which they wanted left in place so that medications might be administered to reduce seizures as their daughter died. That is to say, they did not ask to discontinue her medical treatment so that "nature" might take its course; they asked that food and water be withheld so as to cause her death by starvation.

62 See R. Shelomo Luria, *Yam shel Shelomo*, Baba Kama, ch. 8, no. 59.

63 *Hiddushey HaRitva*, Avodah Zarah 18a. See above at notes 10 and 11.

64 See R. Yosef Karo, Bedek HaBayit, *Tur* YD 157.

65 BT Avodah Zarah 18a.

66 The operative principle is *shelucho shel adam kemoto*, "one's agent is the legal equivalent of oneself". A person's legal representative, who carries that person's "power of attorney", is endowed with only those rights enjoyed by the one who appointed him or her. A corollary is the statement *ein shaliach ledevar aveirah:* "an agent cannot legally perform a transgression." Should I instruct my agent to do something prohibited by the Torah, those instructions are null and void; BT Kiddushin 41b-42b and parallels.

67 See above at notes 10 and 11.

68 BT Ketubot 104a.

69 See above, at notes 41-42.

70 The classic example is the case in BT Sanhedrin 74a, where one has been told: kill so-and-so; if you refuse, we will kill you. The ruling in that instance: let yourself be killed. How do you know that your blood is redder than his? Perhaps his blood is redder. That is, the lives of both are equally precious to God. One life will be destroyed in either event; do not compound the tragedy by committing the sin of murder (see Rashi *ad loc.*). The only proper moral stance is *shev ve'al ta'aseh,* inaction, for positive action can but make the situation worse.

Hospital Patient Beyond Recovery
5750.5

She'elah

A man in his seventies suffered a stroke, but was expected to recover. During this period he received his nourishment through a feeding tube. However, recovery did not take place and for the past four or five months he has been in a semi-comatose condition, with no hope for improvement. Family and doctor wonder whether it is permissible to withdraw the feeding tube and let him die. (Rabbi Sheldon Ezring, Syracuse, NY)

Teshuvah*

In order to consider the *she'elah* some additional information about the patient and his condition was solicited and was supplied by the attending physician:

The patient had been an intellectually and psychologically sound septuagenarian who developed a massive left sided cerebravascular accident secondary to emergency thoracic surgery. A nasogastric feeding tube was placed early after the onset of his stroke as all thought that a "meaningful recovery" would ensue. It did not. He remains mute and usually asleep. He barely responds to his name spoken — he might slowly and in a delayed fashion move his head toward the speaker. Occasionally he would be found rubbing his scalp. When his eyes are open, his stare is almost always "blank." At most, he makes brief eye contact. There is no consistent response to voice command such as appropriately moving an extremity.

All of this remains the case greater than 4-5 months past onset of his stroke. His CT scan demonstrates massive left brain permanent damage.

The physician then posed some questions and proceeded to answer them:

1. Does he fulfill the criteria of persistent vegetative state? No! [sic]
2. What is his quality of life? As we can ascertain it, close to zero.
3. Will any further measures be undertaken besides oxygen or feeding tube? No.
4. Would he have wanted to be kept alive at this "level" based on pre-admission conversations? No.
5. Does the family view his quality of life as meaningful? No.
6. Can they ethically bring him home and stop feeding him through a feeding tube?? [sic; the doctor added the extra question mark and did not venture an answer.]

Withdrawal of life support systems.

The matter of withdrawing life support systems from a dying patient has been dealt with in a responsum by R. Solomon B. Freehof.[1] The question put to him was as follows:

A terminal patient was dying as a result of a series of strokes. Two physicians, one of whom was the patient's son, decided — with the consent of the family — to hasten the end by withdrawing all medication and fluids given intravenously. Is such procedure permitted by Jewish law?

In a wide-ranging discussion Freehof drew, *inter alia,* on Joshua Boaz who stated that while one must not do anything to hasten death, one may remove the causes of the delay of death.[2] Freehof concluded:

If the physician actively attempts to hasten the death, that is against the ethics of Jewish law. In the case as described "to hasten death" is perhaps not correct, or at least should be modified. The physician is not really hastening the death; he has simply ceased his efforts to delay it.

We see no reason to depart from Freehof's decision, but must raise two questions:

a. whether our patient may be considered terminal;

b. if so, whether the nasogastric tube, which was originally a means of hoped-for recovery, may now be considered a "heroic measure" which might be discontinued.

Is the patient considered terminal?

Ad a. The physician's letter does not suggest that the patient is near death, that is, in halachic parlance, a *goses*. The writer denies that the patient's state can be described as "persistent vegetative," (sub 1) but also does not affirm that death is imminent or even near and merely says that no further measures, beyond oxygen and feeding tube, will be undertaken (sub 3). We therefore deal with a patient who is not facing imminent death but may be considered hopeless as far as recovery is concerned. In this regard his condition is similar to that of the Quinn girl in New Jersey some years ago.[3]

Ad b. Since the patient is not at death's door the question becomes moot.

We must therefore conclude that Freehof's discussion and teshuvah, which deal with a *goses*, do not to apply to the *she'elah* before us. Rather. we deal with a different question: May a feeding tube be withdrawn from a patient who, without such action, might remain alive for an unknown time? The *she'elah* is therefore about the permissibility of euthanasia.

Euthanasia and Jewish law.

This question too has been discussed with both in traditional sources and Reform responsa.

A *teshuvah* by the CCAR Responsa Committee (1980) dealt with a patient who had sunk into a deep coma and was kept alive solely by artificial means. The Committee was of the opinion that it would be permissible to remove life support systems once all signs of "natural independent life" had disappeared and brain death, as defined by the ad hoc committee of the Harvard Medical School, had occurred. The ruling concluded by saying: "We would not endorse any positive steps leading toward death...We would reject any general endorsement of euthanasia..."[4]

This was in keeping with an earlier report to the CCAR by a special committee, chaired by R. Israel Bettan (1950), which studied the permissibility of euthanasia in general terms and, reaffirming the Jewish ideal of the sanctity of human life and the supreme value of the individual soul, considered euthanasia "contrary to the moral law." A spirited floor debate followed in which contrary opinions were brought forth. The Conference itself did not vote to endorse the report, but instead merely received it and referred it to the Executive Committee.[5] This meant, in effect, that the report stands as the opinion of the Bettan committee but not as a resolution of the Conference. In that respect, it has the same standing as a report of the Responsa Committee.

We are dealing with a patient who is neither dying nor even in a deep coma. On a greatly reduced level, he still responds to some external stimuli. In all precedent considerations of similar conditions, the removal of the feeding tube would be seen as an act of euthanasia.

But what of the argument, contained in question 5 of the physician's letter, that, in the opinion of the family, there is no further "meaningful quality" to the patient's life, and that therefore the family would endorse removal of the tube? A more recent responsum by the CCAR Responsa Committee dealt with this very question (1985), when it addressed itself to the case of a person who was unable to communicate because a segment of the brain which provided intelligence seemed to be damaged beyond repair.

> Judaism does not define human life only in terms of mental activity. Every person has been created in the image of God, and so even those individuals who may be defective...have always been considered as equally created in the image of God; their life is as precious as any other. It is necessary to guard their life and protect it just as any other human life. This is also true of an elderly individual who has lost some... mental ability or power of communication....[6]

The underlying concern of this *teshuvah* was that we really do not know what "quality of life" really means. Furthermore, we still have an incomplete understanding of what goes on in the mind of the paralyzed patient who is unable to communicate properly. We are prone to assume that he would not wish to keep on living and may in fact have talked about such a situation at some previous time (*Doctor's question no. 4*). It is indeed possible that he now wishes to die and then again, he may wish to live, either because he still hopes to recover or because he has an active mental life of which we know little. As long as this uncertainty exists we need not address the question of whether we would have a right to help our patient die if indeed he wished to end his life.

To be sure, there is also the emotional and financial drain on the family, a drain that is undoubtedly severe. But this responsum can hardly be expected to rule on a person's life and death on such grounds. The responsibility for the former remains the family's, and for the latter rests to a significant degree with society at large, which must provide a safety net for catastrophic illness.

In sum, since the patient is not dying, the withdrawal of the feeding tube is not permissible in the light of Jewish tradition, as confirmed by precedent responsa. Though we have the deepest empathy with the unfortunate circumstances, we have no choice but to confirm a larger principle.

NOTES

* Many of the issues raised in this responsum are discussed in greater detail in our *teshuvah* 5754.14, "Treatment of the Terminally Ill," above.

1 *CCAR Yearbook* LXXIX (1969) pp. 118-121, reprinted in full in *American Reform Responsa*, ed. Walter Jacob (New York: CCAR, 1983), no. 77 pp. 257-260.

2 *Shiltey Ha-giborim*, commentary on BT Mo'ed Katan, ch.3 (16b in Vilna ed., Alfasi).

3 In that case a court permitted the parents to cease "heroic" measures. This was subsequently done, though intravenous feeding was not ended. It was expected that the girl would die shortly, but to everyone's surprise she lived on for some months, sustained merely by the feeding device.

4 *American Reform Responsa*, op. cit., no. 79, 271-274.

5 *Ibid.*, no. 78, pp. 261-271.

6 Walter Jacob, *Contemporary American Reform Responsa*, (New York: CCAR, 1987), no. . 83, pp 138-140.

Sexual Proclivity of an MS Patient
5750.9

She-elah

A thirty-year old male with end-stage multiple sclerosis (MS) is a resident in skilled care facility. Though he is confined to a wheelchair and can do virtually nothing for himself, he is still alert and oriented, and quite capable of conversation with others. It is quite doubtful whether he could begin and sustain a relationship with a woman, due to his condition and prognosis.

Yet he is constantly thinking about women, and has begun to address and touch the female nursing staff in inappropriate ways. He cannot engage in sexual intercourse. Because of his disability, auto-eroticism is not an option, but he is probably able to achieve orgasm if aroused in other ways.

Given his condition, what Jewishly acceptable options for sexual release does this person have? (Rabbi Cary D. Kozberg, Columbus, OH)

Teshuvah

The problem which the MS patient faces is as old as human sexuality and has in fact already been mentioned in the Talmud. There,[1] we find the case of a man who is so lovesick that he is overcome by his erotic dreams about a certain woman. What should be done with him or for him? One rabbi suggested that maybe if the woman were to appear naked before him his desire might be stilled. Needless to say, this was rejected as were other "solutions." We cite this because it shows that cases of this kind were taken seriously, and our patient deserves the same attention.

An extensive treatment of the question would involve a general discussion of human sexuality in the light of Tradition, and of Reform Judaism in particular. It might, for instance, treat of such matters as masturbation, use of prostitutes, and the like.

But it must also lead us to consider whether the illness of MS which afflicts the patient excuses him from observing time-hallowed restraints on

371

our sexual behavior. In our opinion it does not. He must be told that nurses have the right to be treated properly as does everyone else, and that MS does not give him an excuse to harass them.

However, we have great sympathy for this unfortunate person who is frustrated in so many ways. Since we do not know any details of his medical condition or of his personal circumstances, we cannot make any useful prescription which could be deemed unexceptionable.

Consequently, we would leave it to you as the man's rabbi and counselor, together with the medical authorities involved, to devise a course of help for him. If you arrive at such a proposed procedure and wish to correspond further with us about it, please do not hesitate to write.

NOTES
1 BT Sanhedrin 75a.

Physicians and Indigent Patients
5754.18

She'elah

Many of the Jews from the former Soviet Union who have settled in our community are now dependent upon government assistance for their health care. Frequently when they call physicians in the community to secure appointments, they are told that these physicians do not see patients who are without private insurance coverage. While our local Jewish Family Service has had some success in making individual appeals to physicians active in our congregations to provide care for these newcomers, a broader question remains. Under our tradition, may a Jewish physician refuse to treat a patient because he or she lacks medical coverage? (Rabbi Melanie Aron, Los Gatos, CA)

Teshuvah

This question addresses the situation in the United States, where as of this writing health care is largely a private matter rather than a right guaranteed by the community to all citizens or residents. Yet it also has application in countries where health care is state-sponsored and where physicians and other medical professionals have been known to go on strike against what they regard as inadequate funding, poor compensation, and the like. In both cases, the issue is essentially the same: may physicians refuse for economic reasons to provide medical service?

The Mitzvah of Medical Practice.

We begin our discussion by noting that Jewish tradition regards the practice of medicine as a mitzvah, a religious obligation which imposes duties upon doctor and patient alike.

This attitude was not unanimous; a number of texts express a highly negative stance toward medicine, physicians, and those who resort to them. This critical viewpoint proceeds from the doctrine that God is the Source of

373

both illness and healing.[1] If disease is understood as a sign of God's displeasure, as punishment for our misdeeds, it follows that the correct response to it is prayer and repentance. When one turns instead to the practitioners of the medical arts, one betrays both a desire to frustrate the divine decree and a fundamental lack of trust in God. Thus, King Asa of Judah is criticized in that "in his sickness he sought not God but rather physicians,"[2] while King Hezekiah wins praise for hiding away a medical book so that people would learn to pray for healing rather than seek medical help.[3] The Talmud declares that one who does engage the services of a medical practitioner should pray: "May it be Your will...that this procedure restore my health...You are a faithful and healing God, whose healing is true. As for human beings, they have no power to heal; rather, it has become a habit with them." The implication, says Rashi, is that human beings "should never have become involved with medicine; instead, they should have learned to seek God's mercy."[4] This way of thinking finds its classic expression in the commentary of Nachmanides (Ramban) to Leviticus 26:11. He writes that the blessings promised in that chapter as a reward for our obedience to God are all miracles, suspensions of the natural order of the world. This teaches that when Israel is at one with God, it is exempted from the normal workings of nature and merits special providence. Medicine is irrelevant to the community of the righteous, for whom disease is a matter not of the body but of the spirit. Cures are effected by repentance and prayer, for God "will bless your food and your water and remove all disease from your midst" (Ex. 23:25).[5] Had Israel maintained its trust in God, it never would have needed physicians and medicine; since, however, "it has become a habit with them," the Torah grudgingly permits the physician to practice his art.[6] Yet this "habit" continues to separate us from God; were we to walk in God's ways, we should have nothing to do with physicians.

Despite these opinions, the tradition developed a positive and affirming conception of medicine. This fact is most obvious in the large number of rabbinic scholars who were also physicians, as well as in the significant medical literature produced by rabbinic writers, most notably Maimonides.[7] The Talmud tells us that "one who is in pain should go to the physician" and for-

bids a scholar from residing in a town that lacks a doctor.[8] The apparently negative statements on medicine receive different explanations.[9] Nachmanides
himself argues that the "permit" to practice medicine is in fact a mitzvah,
falling under the rubric of *pikuach nefesh*, the saving of life.[10] The saving of life
overrides the prohibitions connected with Shabbat and Yom Kippur,[11] and
Ramban notes that we often set aside these prohibitions on the strength of a
doctor's diagnosis.[12] Maimonides, meanwhile, derives the commandment to
practice medicine from Deut 22:2, the obligation to restore lost objects which,
say the rabbis, extends to the saving of life.[13] Whatever its Scriptural basis,
the *Tur* and the *Shulchan Aruch* formulate the obligation to practice medicine
as halachah:[14] the patient is required to resort to the physician, and the physician is required to heal. Whoever delays or refrains from meeting this obligation is considered as having shed blood.

From this, it would follow that a Jewish physician is not entitled to
refuse treatment to a patient for financial reasons. A religious obligation does
not cease being a religious obligation on account of its expense. And since the
practice of medicine is an enterprise of *pikuach nefesh*, a duty which outweighs
virtually all others, we would conclude that the physician must surely provide
life-sustaining treatment to patients regardless of their ability to pay. Indeed,
are we not taught that the physician who refuses to treat the indigent is
deserving of everlasting punishment?[15] While doctors may press their reasonable financial demands, therefore, they cannot shirk the duty imposed upon
them by the Torah.[16]

The Physician and Economic Freedom.

The matter, however, is not so simple. Like all human beings, the
physician is possessed of an essential dignity which the community cannot
ignore. Fundamental to this dignity is what we moderns might term economic freedom. The traditional basis for this principle is the verse (Lev. 25:55): "for
the people of Israel are My servants," to which the rabbis add: "and not the servants of servants."[17] The free man or woman ought not to be a slave to the economic demands of others.[18] From this, we learn that the worker is entitled to
quit his or her job, even after beginning it.[19] We read too that workers,

whether laborers, professionals, or the owners of businesses, may organize and adopt trade policies that determine the prices they charge the public.[20] This "right to strike" does not include the right to inflict damages upon the employer. A worker dealing with perishable goods, for example, may not quit before completing the job.[21] We might argue on this basis that a physician, who has charge of the most perishable of "goods," may not refuse to treat a patient. This limitation, however, seems to apply only to a worker who has already begun the job. Should a doctor refuse to begin treatment in the absence of assured compensation, this law would not force him or her to provide it.

Yet surely, we might respond, the physician is not like other laborers. The physician performs a mitzvah, and one can hardly go on strike against a commandment. Moreover, the physician's mitzvah is that of *pikuach nefesh,* a duty which must be performed whenever the opportunity presents itself. As Maimonides writes, "whoever is able to save a life but does not save it violates the commandment: 'do not stand idly by the blood of your neighbor' (Lev. 19:16)."[22] Thus, once an individual seeks the services of a physician, the physician is obliged to treat that person. He or she may not turn away indigent patients on the grounds that other physicians can treat them, for perhaps the treatment offered by others will not succeed. As the rabbis remind us, it just may be the destiny of this indigent patient to be healed by this doctor.[23] Thus, we could argue, the physician does not have the same right enjoyed by other workers to withhold his or her services. The saving of life must take precedence over the physician's economic freedom.

Still, the duty to save life does not necessarily fall upon the physician as an individual. The commandment of *pikuach nefesh* is addressed to all of us, not just to a particular class of persons; the physician has no greater obligation than does anyone else to save life. This is a key element in the Jewish legal theory which permits physicians to be paid for their work:[24] when a positive commandment is incumbent upon all members of the community, no one person can be required to perform it for free.[25] Physicians are entitled to reasonable compensation because, though they render a service that only trained professionals are allowed to administer,[26] they are the agents of the community. The mitzvah they perform is our mitzvah, not just theirs. Like others who provide vital public services, they are the means by which each of us fulfills the individual responsibility to save life. Thus, if it costs money to perform the mitsvah, that expense ought to be borne by the community, by all of us together, and not by doctors alone.[27] It is arguably unfair to require that physicians treat indigent patients without adequate compensation.

Conclusion. The case before us therefore is a complex one, in moral as well as halachic terms. It involves a conflict between two traditional values-- the mitzvah of medical care and the economic freedom of the individual-- which resonate with us as liberal Jews. It follows that any proper solution will also be complex, its specific details determined by the circumstances of the community in which it is adopted. Still, our understanding of Torah and moral imperative from within the context of Reform tradition convinces us that such a solution ought to incorporate four fundamental principles.

1. Every member of the community enjoys a right to adequate medical care. As we read the tradition, this demand is paramount. Medicine is a mitzvah, the duty of *pikuach nefesh* which we owe to all whose lives are in danger. To deny medical treatment to human beings because they cannot afford to pay for it is repugnant to any decent conception of what Torah requires of us. One may debate, legitimately, both the precise definition of "adequate medical care" and the means by which it is delivered. That it must be delivered, however, cannot be doubted, as the CCAR has repeatedly made clear.[28] Our primary moral task is not to decide whether the poor shall receive treatment; it is rather to determine the fairest and most efficient way of getting it to them.

2. The ultimate responsibility for providing medical care to the indigent rests upon society as a whole.[29] Tradition teaches us that, inasmuch as each of us is commanded to save life, each of us shoulders equally the burden which this duty imposes.[30] And our Reform tradition holds that justice is a social matter. Our commitment to social justice and social action requires the conclusion that no just society can fail to meet this duty.

3. In the present case, we Jews have a special responsibility above and beyond our obligations as members of the wider community. For many years, we struggled to liberate the oppressed Jews of the former Soviet Union. We organized and lobbied to secure their right to emigrate to lands which would allow them to live as Jews in peace and freedom. We did this in fulfillment of the mitzvah of *pidyon shevuyim*, the redemption of captives, a duty which in our tradition takes precedence over all other forms of *tzedakah*.[31] Thus, although the obligation to aid the poor rests upon the entire community, we have an added measure of obligation toward these, our brothers and sisters. It would be a moral failure if, having exerted great efforts to bring them out of bondage, we were to ignore their pressing human needs once they arrive in our midst. Our ethical responsibility is not discharged until we have helped them secure housing, employment, medical care, and the other tools necessary to build lives of independence and dignity. This implies, we think, that Jewish physicians have a special and vital contribution to make.

4. Even though the provision of medical care is the responsibility of society as a whole, physicians cannot on this ground shirk the moral responsibility to render medical care to those who call upon their services. When a person seeks medical care from a physician, the physician is bound under the rubric of *pikuach nefesh* to provide it, either personally or by making arrangements for the patient to see another doctor. We are not unmindful of the just monetary demands of medical professionals. Physicians are entitled to seek compensation from the community for their services; in the event that community assistance is insufficient to meet the need, they may make other financial arrangements as they see fit. Yet we cannot help but note that physicians, even when they treat the indigent for free, still earn incomes which compare quite favorably to those of police officers, fire fighters, educators, and all others who devote their professional lives to the performance of mitzvot. We conclude that the health and lives of the poor must in principle take precedence over the economic requirements of the physicians.

We do not pretend to have the "right" solution to the intricately complex problem of health-care access in the United States. Again, we presume that the particular arrangements for providing medical care to the indigent will vary from place to place. As we see it, however, one truth is and must remain constant: under no circumstances may physicians, Jewish or otherwise, simply refuse to provide that care on the grounds that the patients lack insurance. Jewish tradition and moral decency demand no less.

NOTES

1 Exod. 15:26. See BT Sanhedrin 101a for a hint that sickness and health depend largely upon faithfulness to God's commandments and not upon medicine.

2 II Chr. 16:12.

3 This rabbinic tradition, recounted in BT Berachot 10b and BT Pesachim 56a, is derived aggadically from Isaiah 38:3. See Rashi to the *Berachot* passage, s.v. *she-ganaz sefer refu'ot.*

4 BT Berachot 60a and Rashi, s.v. *she'ein darkan shel benei ada*M. See also Rashi's explanation of the statement in the Mishnah (M. Kiddushin 4:14): "the best physician is deserving of hell." One of the reasons for this condemnation, he writes, is that the physician arrogantly regards himself, rather than God, as the healer (BT Kiddushin 82a, *s.v. tov she-barof'im*). See also notes 9 and 15, below.

5 Ramban also cites Exod. 15:26 in this regard; see at note 1.

6 BT Baba Kamma 85a, from Exod. 21:19. This, says Ramban, is not a grant of permission to the patient, who in any event ought *not* to resort to medicine. As he has chosen the "habit" of medicine, however, separating himself from "the congregation of God," the physician may treat him without incurring divine punishment.

7 R. Natan Zvi Friedman, *Otzar Ha-Rabbanim*, Tel Aviv, 1975, identifies about 80 significant rabbinic personalities as physicians.

8 BT Baba Kama 46b and Sanhedrin 17b.

9 Thus, King Asa's sin is not that he consulted physicians but rather that he placed his reliance totally upon them, forgetting that the physician is God's agent in the healing of disease. See *Bayit Hadash* to *Tur,* YD 336 and *Metsudat David* to II Chr. 16:12. Maimonides, Commentary to M. Pesachim 4:9, interprets the case of King Hezekiah so as to avoid its anti-medical implications, and he sharply rejects the suggestion that reliance upon medicine is evidence of a lack of trust in God. As for "the best physician is deserving of hell" (see note 4), R. Shmuel Edels explains that this refers to the arrogant physician who, thinking he is the best, injures or even kills his patient out of a refusal to consult other doctors (Maharsha, BT Kiddushin 82a). See also Sirach 38:1-8 on the physician and the pharmacist as the instruments of God's healing.

10 Nachmanides, *Torat Ha-Adam*, ed. H.D. Chavel, Jerusalem, 1964, pp. 41-42. Rabbis through the ages have sought to resolve this position with that of Ramban on Lev. 26:11. Their general approach is to declare that, while in an ideal past we were able to rely upon spiritual healing, we no longer merit that status. On the contrary: today we are forbidden to abandon the workings of the natural world and to rely instead upon miracles. See *Turey Zahav, Sh.A.,* YD 336, no. 1, and R. Chaim Azulao Y.D. *Birkei Yosef,* YD 336, n. 2. See also R. Yitschak Arama, *Akedat Yitzchak*, Vayishlach, who rather than resolving the contradiction rejects Ramban's position in Leviticus on the basis of Biblical evidence.

11 BT Yoma 85b, from Lev. 18:5.

12 Ramban cites M. Yoma 8:5-6. The physician's role in deciding when the laws of Shabbat and Yom Kippur must be set aside is discussed in *Sh.A.,* OC 328 and 618.

13 BT Sanhedrin 73a; Rambam, Commentary to M. Nedarim 4:4.

14 *Tur* and *Sh.A.*, YD 336:1.

15 Rashi to M. Kiddushin 4:14 (82a).

16 See R. Meir Steinberg, *Assya*, vol. 3, 1983, pp. 341-342, who forbids physicians' strikes on this basis.

17 BT Baba Kamma 116b.

18 Commenting upon Exodus 21:6, Rabban Yochanan ben Zakai condemns the Hebrew slave who chooses continued slavery over the freedom to serve his true Master; BT Kiddushin 22b.

19 *Yad, Hilchot Sechirut* 9:4; *Sh.A., CM* 333:3.

20 BT Baba Batra 8b; *Yad,* Hilchot Mechirah 14:9; *Sh.A.,* CM 231:27-28.

21 *Sh.A., CM* 333:5.

22 *Yad,* Hilchot Rotzeah 1:14, from BT Sanh. 73a.

23 *YT* Nedarim 4:2; *Sh.A., YD* 336:1.

24 Can one be paid for performing a mitzvah? Not precisely, say the rabbis; but one may be compensated for the expense incurred in doing that mitzvah as well as for the time which one might otherwise have spent in gainful employment. See *Sh.A., YD* 336:2.

24 Ramban, *Torat Ha-Adam*, p. 45; Isserles, *Sh.A., YD* 336:3.

26 *Sh.A.,* YD 336:1.

27 See R. Eliezer Waldenberg, *Resp. Tzitz Eliezer*, v. 5, *Ramat Rachel*, ch. 24, no. 6. On this reasoning, R. Shelomo Goren permits doctors to strike. So long as they provide medical treatment at a reasonable cost, the responsibility for meeting that cost rests upon the government. See *Sefer Assya*, v. 5, 1986, pp. 41-54.

28 See the resolution in support of a national health care system that would provide comprehensive medical benefits to all residents of the United States; "National Health Care," *CCAR Yearbook*, v. ci, 1991, pp. 32-34.

29 See M. Sotah 9:6 on Deut. 21:7.

30 As is the case with *tzedakah*, an "equal share" will differ depending upon an individual's financial means; see *Sh.A., YD* 248:1. The point is that we must all contribute and not leave the responsibility with the physicians alone.

31 BT Baba Batra 8a-b; *Yad,* Hilchot Matanot Aniyim 8:10. See our *teshuvah* 5753.5, "On the Redemption of Captives," above.

Testing Emergency Medical Procedures Without the Consent of the Patient
5755.11

She'elah

A physician who specializes in the research and development of cardiac resuscitation technology wants to know the ethical and halachic issues involved in testing without consent. In many cases, the consent of the patient cannot be obtained prior to his or her cardiac arrest. Obtaining surrogate consent is not always practical, since the patient may well die without immediate treatment. There is a great need to test new emergency therapies, since current survival rates under standard manual cardiopulmonary resuscitation (CPR) are dismal. On the other hand, the critical condition of a small percentage of patients might actually be worsened prior to stopping these tests, despite ongoing supervision. (Rabbi Joseph A. Edelheit, Minneapolis)

Teshuvah

Jewish tradition has much to say concerning the practice of medicine. It also addresses the issue of individual consent, whether and under what circumstances a person is entitled to refuse medical care, as well as the distinction between proven and yet-to-be proven (experimental) methods of treatment. As Reform Jews, meanwhile, we are the heirs and the creators of a stream of Jewish tradition which places great positive value upon both scientific progress and personal autonomy. Taken together, these teachings and affirmations pull us toward opposite and contradictory conclusions when we face this difficult question. Yet we shall need to consider all of them as we seek to forge a consistent and satisfying Jewish ethical message.

The Dilemma.

The practice of medicine is understood as a mitzvah, a religious requirement under Jewish law. Thus, despite the fact that the Talmud speaks of a "permit" (*reshut*) rather than a duty to heal[1] and despite various indications in the sources of a negative attitude toward medicine and physicians,[2] most authorities regard medicine as the primary means by which we fulfill the commandment to save life (*pikuach nefesh*).[3] This duty applies to one's own life as it does to the lives of others;[4] it would follow that a person is not entitled to refuse lifesaving medical treatment. The sixteenth-century authority R. David ibn Zimra drew just this conclusion when he condemned as a "pious fool" a person who refused to violate the Shabbat in order to prepare medication. "This is no act of piety but of suicide. He is therefore compelled to do what the physicians prescribe."[5] Contemporary authorities concur that the patient "must do as the doctor orders."[6] On this basis we could argue that traditional Jewish law requires a patient to accept CPR and that emergency medical personnel are entitled to administer the therapy even if the patient is incapable of expressing consent.

The difficulty with this argument is that the CPR method under discussion is experimental in nature. The doctors, that is, are not yet certain as to its therapeutic effects. And under Jewish law, a patient is under no obligation to accept medical treatment whose efficacy is doubtful or untested.[7] Moreover, as the *she'elah* indicates, the condition of "a small percentage of patients" might actually worsen under the use of this therapy rather than the more conventional methods of CPR. The doctors therefore cannot necessarily presume the patient's consent before testing this therapy upon him or her. To proceed with the test upon a person who has no moral obligation to accede to it and who, if conscious, might well refuse consent, is to invite strenuous objection on ethical grounds. By what authority do we ignore the patient's right to make an informed choice to accept--or reject--medical treatment? And what statement do we as a community make concerning our own values when we arrogate this right to ourselves? We Jews, who remember all too well the experiments conducted by Nazi "scientists" upon the inmates of concentration camps, surely recoil at the specter of a scientific establishment which turns human beings into involuntary subjects of experimentation.

On the other hand, we liberals have historically placed great faith and trust in the power of reason and science to improve the human condition. We therefore cannot ignore the critical importance of scientific experimentation to the advancement of medicine. The very institution of "modern medicine" whose achievements we praise and upon which we rely to protect our lives is largely the product of testing and experimentation, much of it upon human subjects. In many cases there is no alternative to testing upon humans. For example, the current, "accepted" methods of CPR could only have attained that status because they were tested and perfected upon human beings who were experiencing cardiac emergency. Should we place severe restraints upon physicians' ability to test new and promising emergency procedures, we may prevent them from developing the tools needed to save countless lives in the future.

The dilemma is this: the patient has no moral obligation to accept treatment that is potentially dangerous and whose lifesaving--i.e., medical--properties are doubtful. At the same time, it is precisely by testing such treatments upon human subjects, who in cases of emergency are usually unable to express their desires, that doctors learn how to save lives, to fulfill the commandment of pikuach nefesh, to do "medicine" at all. Is there an answer that strikes a proper balance between the legitimate concern for patient autonomy and the equally legitimate needs of medical science?

Halachic Considerations.

No such answer is to be found in the responsa of contemporary halachic authorities. We think, however, that one can be derived through a consideration of the Jewish law on scientific experimentation on humans. The answer consists of three parts: first, that persons are allowed to subject themselves to controlled and careful scientific experimentation; second, that there exists in some cases a general ethical duty to submit to experimentation; and third, that in certain emergency situations physicians may *within reasonable limits* administer an experimental remedy to the patient.

1. ### Scientific Experimentation Upon Human Subjects. May a person volunteer to serve as a subject in a scientific experiment? A factor which argues for a prohibitive answer is the Talmudic tradition which forbids a person from inflicting physical injury upon his or her body.[8] Maimonides cites this rule as halachah, but it is significant that he limits the prohibition to injury caused

"by way of contempt" for the body.[9] How he derived this limitation is not clear; some suggest that, since physical injury can be financially compensated and that an injured person is entitled to waive the damages, the Rambam rules that the person is similarly entitled to inflict self-injury when that act is the source of some benefit.[10] The contemporary halachic debate concerning cosmetic surgery revolves around this point. Those who permit cosmetic surgery argue that, while an individual is ordinarily forbidden to inflict self-injury, the benefits which may accrue from an improved appearance demonstrate that the procedure is not undertaken out of "contempt". That conclusion can obviously be debated; this Committee, among others, has expressed serious reservations over the supposed "benefits" of cosmetic surgery.[11] On the other hand, careful and legitimate medical experimentation holds the promise of increasing our fund of the kind of knowledge that may one day cure terrible diseases and save countless lives. Surely this constitutes an acceptable warrant for an individual to waive the prohibition against self-injury in order to submit to scientific experiment.

2. <u>The Ethical Duty to Submit to Experimentation.</u> This "right" to volunteer as a subject in a scientific experiment can also be expressed in the language of obligation. It is well-known that the tradition holds the preservation of life (*pikuach nefesh*) to supersede virtually all other commandments[12] and that we have a positive duty to rescue those whose lives are endangered when we can do so.[13] Indeed, that we are commanded (rather than merely permitted) to practice medicine is based on this recognition of an obligation to save the lives of others.[14] We would not suggest on the basis of this teaching that every person is required to volunteer as a subject in a scientific experiment, any more than we would conclude that the commandment to practice medicine obliges every person to become a physician. Rather, just as a person who does possess medical knowledge is said to have an ethical duty to use that knowledge to treat disease and to save lives, it can be argued that one who has the opportunity to participate in an experiment or study directed at the advancement of medicine has something of an obligation to do so. This may be especially true in our case, where the individual has no choice but to receive

CPR and where the experimental therapy, which must be tested upon humans, has the potential of saving numerous lives which would be lost under current procedures of resuscitation.

The difficulty with this argument is that, while Jewish law requires me to save the life of another, it does not obligate me to endanger my own life to do so. The very text which establishes the duty of *pikuach nefesh* declares that we are to perform the mitzvot so as to "live by them" and not place our lives in jeopardy. Thus, while I am commanded to save a drowning person, I am not obliged to make the attempt if in doing so I place my own life at risk.[16] The predominant halachic position extends this to instances of less-than-mortal risk: I am not required--and perhaps am forbidden--to assume potential danger (*safek sakanah*) in order to rescue a person whose life is in clear and present danger (*vadai sakanah*).[17] According to this view, there is no duty to submit to a scientific experiment, even one that could result in the discovery of life-saving information, so long as there is any significant degree of risk involved. On the other hand, this view is not unanimous: some authorities hold that the halachah does not prohibit an individual from entering into a situation of potential danger in order to rescue a person facing *vadai sakanah*.[18] It is, moreover, quite possible that the predominant view is in error and that the Talmudic and other sources upon which it is based do not forbid--and perhaps require--an individual to enter into *safek sakanah* to save another in clear and present danger.[19]

Our own conception of individual moral responsibility leads us to favor the latter, more stringent position. Most of us, we think, would prefer to live in a community whose members, rather than insisting rigidly upon their personal safety at all costs, are prepared to assume a limited degree of risk to save the lives of their neighbors. This is not, we stress, a call for an ethic of self-sacrifice; we do not believe that all people must live according to the terms of *midat chasidut*, a saintly standard of behavior. On the contrary: we would argue that the proposed standard is an eminently reasonable one that lies well within the reach of normal human beings. It represents the minimal level of care and concern for the lives and welfare of others below which an ethical community is scarcely imaginable. This standard, if not the dominant view among halachists, is thus both arguably the more accurate interpretation of the sources and certainly the more exalted expression of Jewish thought. Under its terms, an individual would be permitted to volunteer as a subject in an experiment aimed at discovering life-saving information so long as whatever risk he or she assumes by participating is less than *vadai sakanah*. Indeed, in some cases, where the potential for saving life is both real and vital, participation in such an experiment could well take on the status of a moral duty.

3. <u>Emergency Experimental Treatment Without the Patient's Consent.</u> The case at hand, however, is no ordinary experiment. By foregoing the accepted methods of cardiopulmonary resuscitation in order to test new ones, medical professionals may well be withholding life-sustaining care from a patient in critical condition. Remember, too, that the survival chances of a small percentage of patients will worsen under these experimental procedures. Their use might therefore place a patient in a situation of *vadai sakanah*, and while self-sacrifice may be admirable, Jewish tradition does not suggest that an individual must undertake mortal danger in order to save the life of another.[20] Is there an ethical rationale which would ever permit the testing of new methods of CPR in the absence of a patient's consent?

It might be useful to compare our question to the employment of randomized clinical trials (RCTs) in medical experimentation. In these trials, subjects/patients are randomly assigned to different therapies or placebos in an effort to keep variables other than the differing treatments from distorting the results of the study. While this method offers great scientific value, it poses serious ethical problems. The physician's primary responsibility, after all, is to the health of the patient; is this responsibility not violated when the patient is given a placebo instead of the treatment that the other subjects receive? The answer clearly is "yes" if we know that by including the patient in the experiment we lessen his or her chances for recovery. On the other hand, those who favor RCTs respond that these methods *are* ethical, provided they are utilized only when there is genuine doubt as to the efficacy of existing therapies, whether standard or experimental, so that "no patient...will receive a treatment known to be less effective or more dangerous than another available alternative."[21]

Conclusion.

Let us translate this discussion into the Jewish vernacular. It is a mitzvah to heal, to practice medicine. Under the terms of this requirement, physicians are obligated to provide the accepted and recognized medical therapies to patients who come to them, and patients, in turn, are obliged to accept them. A placebo is not therapeutic; it does not qualify as *refu'ah*, medical treatment. We are, of course, aware that belief in the efficacy of the placebo may, in some cases, contribute to the patient's healing. In our case, however, the experimental method of CPR is by no means a placebo. It is in fact a new technique which offers great promise in the saving of life. Nor is it obvious that the experimental method is less therapeutic to the patient than the standard methods. As the *she'elah* points out, though the condition of some patients might deteriorate under the use of the experimental method, the survival rates under current methods are in any event "dismal". Given the unsatisfactory nature of current therapies, there would seem to be no reason to conclude that the new method is, in general, less therapeutic or medically efficacious than the standard one.

Our conclusion, then, is that emergency lifesaving therapies such as the one under discussion may *in certain cases* be tested upon patients without their express consent. This is because in those cases the experimental therapies qualify as legitimate medicine (*refu'ah*) which an individual is obligated to accept in fulfillment of the mitzvah of *pikuach nefesh*, the saving of life. These therapies are legitimate medicine under the following conditions:

1. The physicians are reasonably certain that the experimental therapy is neither significantly more dangerous nor less efficacious than the standard therapies. This "reasonable certainty"[22] applies to the individual patient as well as to the population as a whole: if there is reason to suspect that this individual will fare worse under the experimental therapy, he or she must receive the standard treatment.

2. The medical personnel on the scene immediately discontinue the test once it becomes evident that the experimental method is not achieving the desired result. The strictest supervision must be maintained, for the life of *this* patient takes pri-

ority at all times over the potential lifesaving knowledge that can be gleaned by the test.

We add a final caveat. As we stated above, society ignores at its moral peril the requirement that patients be informed of their medical treatment and that they consent to it. While in some situations, such as this one, informed consent is difficult or impossible to obtain in advance, medical professionals must undertake every effort to educate the community as to the state of technology in various medical fields, the need for further research, and the therapeutic options available to physicians in specific situations. For we know that a medical establishment that does not meet the duty of disclosure to the public will soon lose the confidence of the public and, necessarily, its ability to function as an instrument of healing.

NOTES

1 BT Bava Kama 85a, from Exod. 21:19.

2 See II Chronicles 16:12 and Isaiah 38:3, and BT Berachot 10b and Pesachim 56a on the latter; BT Berachot 60a and Rashi, s.v. *she'ein darkan shel benei adam;* BT Kiddushin 82a (M. Kid. 4:14) and Rashi, s.v. *tov shebarof'im.* For a general statement of this position, see Ramban on Lev. 26:11.

3 Ramban, *Torat Ha'Adam,* Chavel ed. (Jerusalem, 1964), pp. 41-42. He notes that the prohibitions against work on Shabbat and Yom Kippur are set aside in cases when life is in danger and that we customarily rely upon a physician's diagnosis to determine when danger exists. His words are embodied in the *Tur* and the *Sh.A.,* YD 336. Maimonides, by contrast, learns the mitzvah of medical practice from Deut. 22:2 and the Talmudic discussion in BT Sanh. 73a (Rambam, Commentary on M. Nedarim 4:4). See our responsum 5754.14, "Treatment of the Terminally Ill," above.

4 Lev. 18:5 and BT Sanh. 74a: a person may violate almost any commandment in order to save his own life. The Rambam adds that, should he in such a case choose instead to follow the commandment and thereby lose his life, he is guilty of suicide (*Yad,* Yesodey HaTorah 5:1).

5 *Resp. Radbaz,* v. 1, no. 1139.

6 R. Eliezer Yehudah Waldenberg, *Resp. Tzitz Eliezer,* v. 5, *Ramat Rachel,* ch. 20; R. Ovadyah Yosef, Resp. *Yechaveh Da'at,* v. 1, no. 61.

7 R. Ya'akov Emden, *Mor uKetzi'ah* 328; R. Moshe Raziel in *Techumin 2* (1981), 335-336.

8 M. Bava Kama 8:6 (90b); BT Bava Kama 91a-b. The Talmud cites here the familiar midrash (on Num. 6:11) concerning the nazir, who is regarded as a "sinner" because he denies himself the legitimate pleasures of wine: "if such a person is a 'sinner', then *kal va-chomer* is one who inflicts physical pain upon himself a 'sinner'".

9 *Yad,* Hilchot Chovel uMazik 5:1.

10 Thus, in pietistic communities where physical means of atonement are practiced a person may hire another to administer the beatings; *Sh.A.* of R. Shneur Zalman of Liady, *Sh.A.,* CM, *Hilkot Nizkey HaGuf,* no. 4. See R. Simchah Hakohen Kook in *Sefer Asya,* v. 3 (1983), 292.

11 See our responsum 5752.7, "On the Permissibility of Cosmetic Surgery", above, and the literature cited therein.

12 Lev. 18:5; BT Yoma 85b and Sanhedrin 74a; *Yad,* Hilchot Yesodey HaTorah 5:1; *Sh.A.,* YD 157:1.

13 Lev. 19:16; BT Sanhedrin 73a; *Yad,* Hilchot Rotseach 1:14; *Sh.A.,* CM 426:1.

14 The authorities are divided as to the source of the commandment to heal. Nachmanides locates it in Ex. 21:19 and Lev. 18:5 (*Torat Ha'Adam,* Chavel ed., 41-42), while Maimonides relies upon Deut. 22:2 and BT Sanhedrin 73a (*Commentary to* M. *Nedarim* 4:4).

15 Lev. 18:5; BT Yoma 85b and Rashi s.v. *deShmuel.*

16 *Minchat Chinuch, mitzvah* 237, no. 2. We might also cite the famous passage concerning the two wanderers in the desert (BT Bava Metsi`a 62a). The law is generally thought to follow R. Akiva, who rules that the traveller holding the container of water is not obliged to share the water with his fellow, since "your life takes precedence over his."

17 See, in general, Aaron Kirschenbaum, "The 'Good Samaritan' and Jewish Law," *Dine Israel* 7 (1976), 46 and 51, and the essay by Avraham Avidan in Torah shebe`al Peh 16 (1974), 129-134. Sources include *Bayit Chadash, Tur* CM 426; *Sefer Me'irat Eynayim,* CM 426, n. 2; *Shulchan Aruch of R. Shneur Zalman of Liady,* Hilchot Nizkey HaGuf, part 5; R. Naftali Zvi Yehudah Berlin, *Ha`amek HaShe'elah, she'ilta* 147, end; and R. Eliezer Yehudah Waldenberg, *Resp. Tzitz Eliezer* 9, no. 17, ch. 5.

18 *Aruch HaShulchan,* CM 426, no. 4; *Torah Temimah* to Lev. 19:16, no. 10. See also R. Yosef Karo, *Beit Yosef,* CM 426 and *Kesef Mishneh,* Hilchot Rotzeach 1:14.

19 For a detailed version of this argument see *Journal of Reform Judaism* 36 (Winter 1989), 53-65.

20 This statement needs some qualification. Some authorities, for example, do not apply this rule to a situation of wartime, when soldiers are indeed required to endanger themselves for the good of their comrades and of the nation; see Avidan (above, no. 17), 131ff. Then there is the position of R. Avraham Yitzchak HaKohen Kuk, who holds that in cases of communal emergency the individual Jew must be prepared to sacrifice his life on behalf of his people; *Resp. Mishpat Kohen,* no. 142-144.

21 Tom L. Beauchamp and James F. Childress, *Principles of Biomedical Ethics* (New York, 1989), 351.

22 It is not our province to define "reasonable certainty" with statistical precision. Any measure we adopt (say, a less-than-five-percent chance that the experimental treatment will prove less effective or more dangerous than the standard one) would be in some sense an arbitrary one. As is the case with all general legal standards, the parameters of "reasonable certainty" are set through a process of reasoned evaluation by those charged with making the decision. In this case, a medical judgment must be rendered by medical experts. If, in their informed opinion, the standard of "reasonable certainty" is met, then our answer applies. On the function of "expert medical opinion" in halachic judgment, see *Sh.A.,* OC 618 and *Mishnah Berurah ad loc.*

COLLECTED REFORM RESPONSA

Chatinover, Steven Ross, A Topical Index of Reform Responsa, CCAR, 1992

Freehof, Solomon B., Reform Responsa, HUC Press, 1960
— Recent Reform Respons, HUC Press, 1963
— Current Reform Responsa, HUC Press, 1969
— Modern Reform Responsa, HUC Press, 1971
— Contemporary Reform Responsa, HUC Press, 1974
— Reform Responsa for Our Time, HUC Press, 1977
— New Reform Responsa, HUC Press, 1980
— Today's Reform Responsa, HUC Press, 1990

Jacob, Walter, Contemporary American Reform Responsa, CCAR, 1987
— Questions and Reform Jewish Answers, CCAR, 1992
— ed., American Reform Responsa, CCAR, 1983

Schwartz, Jacob D. Responsa of the CCAR, UAHC 1954.

INDEX

A

B

C